# WELCOME TO FUNDAMENTALS OF STRATEGY

**Strategy is a crucial subject**. It's about the overall direction of all kinds of organisations, from multinationals to entrepreneurial start-ups, from charities to government agencies, and many more. Strategy raises the big questions about these organisations – how they grow, how they innovate and how they change. As a manager of today or of tomorrow, you will be involved in shaping, implementing or communicating these strategies.

Our aim in writing *Fundamentals of Strategy* is to give you a clear understanding of the fundamental issues and techniques of strategy, and to help you get a great final result in your course. Here's how you might make the most of the text:

- Focus your time and attention on the fundamental areas of strategy in just **10 carefully selected chapters**.
- Read the **illustrations** and the **case examples** to clarify your understanding of how the concepts of strategy translate into an easily recognisable, real-world context.
- Follow up on the **recommended key readings** at the end of each chapter. They're specially selected as accessible and valuable sources that will enhance your learning and give you an extra edge in your course work.

*Fundamentals of Strategy* is available with **MyStrategyLab**, and you can register at **www.mystrategylab.com**\* to find essential student learning material including:

- A **personalised study plan** based on feedback that identifies your strengths and weaknesses, then recommends a tailored set of resources that will help to develop your understanding of strategy.
- **Video resources**, including author videos on key concepts and case studies that put a spotlight on strategy in practice.

Also available is:

- **The Strategy Experience Simulation**, which gives you practical hands-on experience of strategic decision-making in organisations. As a Director of the Board, you must deal with opportunities as they arise, and your decisions will affect the company's performance. Choose wisely!

We want *Fundamentals of Strategy* to give you what you need: a clear and concise view of the subject, an ambition to put that into practice, and – of course – success in your studies. We hope that you'll be just as intrigued by the key issues of strategy as we are!

So, read on and good luck!

*Gerry Johnson*
*Richard Whittington*
*Kevan Scholes*
*Duncan Angwin*
*Patrick Regnér*

\*P.S. In order to log in to the website, you'll need to register with the access code included in the access card, or you can purchase access online at **www.mystrategylab.com**.

**Gerry Johnson, BA, PhD,** is Emeritus Professor of Strategic Management at Lancaster University School of Management. He has also taught at Strathclyde Business School, Cranfield School of Management, Manchester Business School and Aston University. He is the author of numerous books and his research has been published in many of the world's foremost management journals. He is also a partner in the consultancy partnership Strategy Explorers (see **www.strategyexplorers.com**), where he works on issues of strategy development and strategic change.

**Richard Whittington, MA, MBA, PhD,** is Professor of Strategic Management at the Saïd Business School, University of Oxford. He is author or co-author of nine books and is Associate Editor of the *Strategic Management Journal*. He has had full or visiting positions at the Harvard Business School, HEC Paris, Imperial College London, the University of Toulouse and the University of Warwick. He is a partner in Strategy Explorers and active in executive education and consulting. His current research focuses on strategy practice.

**Kevan Scholes, MA, PhD, DMS, CIMgt, FRSA,** is Principal Partner of Scholes Associates, specialising in strategic management. He is also Emeritus Professor of Strategic Management and formerly Director of the Sheffield Business School. He has extensive experience of teaching strategy internationally as well as working in the private and public sector. He is a Companion of The Chartered Management Institute.

**Duncan Angwin, MA, MPhil, MBA, PhD,** is Professor of Strategy at Oxford Brookes University. He is author of six books and over 40 journal articles and serves on several editorial boards. He sits on the advisory board of the M&A research centre, Cass Business School, London and on the Academic Council of ENPC Paris. He is active internationally in executive education and consulting, His current research focuses on mergers and acquisitions, strategy practice and international management.

**Patrick Regnér, BSc, MSc, PhD,** is Professor of Strategic Management at Stockholm School of Economics. He has published numerous articles in leading academic journals in the US and Europe and he serves on several editorial boards. He has extensive experience of teaching strategy internationally on all academic levels. He is a Senior Advisor at a strategy advisory firm and conducts executive training and consulting with leading organisations worldwide. His research interests are in strategy creation and change and international management.

Follow the authors' latest comments on the strategy issues of this book at **https://twitter.com/ExploreStrategy**.

# FUNDAMENTALS OF STRATEGY

## THIRD EDITION

**GERRY JOHNSON**
Lancaster University Management School

**RICHARD WHITTINGTON**
Saïd Business School, University of Oxford

**KEVAN SCHOLES**
Sheffield Business School

**DUNCAN ANGWIN**
Oxford Brookes University

**PATRICK REGNÉR**
Stockholm School of Economics

Harlow, England • London • New York • Boston • San Francisco • Toronto • Sydney • Auckland • Singapore • Hong Kong
Tokyo • Seoul • Taipei • New Delhi • Cape Town • São Paulo • Mexico City • Madrid • Amsterdam • Munich • Paris • Milan

**Pearson Education Limited**
Edinburgh Gate
Harlow CM20 2JE
United Kingdom
Tel: +44 (0)1279 623623
Web: www.pearson.com/uk

First published 2009 (print)
Second edition published 2012 (print and electronic)
**Third edition published** 2015 (print and electronic)

ISBN: 978-1-292-01721-1 (print)
       978-1-292-01725-9 (PDF)
       978-1-292-01722-8 (eText)

**British Library Cataloguing-in-Publication Data**
A catalogue record for the print edition is available from the British Library

**Library of Congress Cataloguing-in-Publication Data**
Johnson, Gerry.
   Fundamentals of strategy / Gerry Johnson, Lancaster University Management School Richard Whittington,
Saïd Business School, University of Oxford, Kevan Scholes, Sheffield Business School, Duncan Angwin,
Oxford Brookes University, Patrick Regnar, Stockholm School of Economics. -- Third Edition.
      pages cm
   ISBN 978-1-292-01721-1 (Print) -- ISBN 978-1-292-01725-9 (PDF) -- ISBN 978-1-292-01722-8 (eText)
   1. Business planning.  2. Strategic planning.  3. Business planning--Case studies.  4. Strategic planning--
Case studies.  I. Whittington, Richard, 1958-  II. Scholes, Kevan.  III. Title.
   HD30.28.J6495 2015
   658.4'012--dc23
                                                                                    2014029518

10 9 8 7 6 5 4 3 2
18 17 16 15

Print edition typeset in Minion Pro 10/12.5pt by 35
Print edition printed and bound in Slovakia by Neografia

NOTE THAT ANY PAGE CROSS REFERENCES REFER TO THE PRINT EDITION

# FUNDAMENTALS OF STRATEGY ONLINE

A wide range of supporting resources are available at:

## MyStrategyLab

Register to create your own personal account using the access code supplied with your copy of the book,* and access the following teaching and learning resources:

### Resources for students

- **A dynamic eText** of the book that you can search, bookmark, annotate and highlight as you please
- **Self-assessment questions** that identify your strengths before recommending a personalised study plan that points you to the resources which can help you achieve a better grade
- **Author videos** explaining key concepts in the book
- **Video cases** that show managers talking about strategic issues in their own organisations
- **Revision flashcards** to help you prepare for your exams
- **A multi-lingual online glossary** to help explain key concepts
- Guidance on **how to analyse a case study**
- **Links** to relevant sites on the web so you can explore more about the organisations featured in the case studies
- **Classic cases** – over 30 case studies from previous editions of the book

### Resources for instructors

- **Instructor's manual**, including extensive teaching notes for cases and suggested teaching plans
- **PowerPoint slides**, containing key information and figures from the book
- **Secure testbank**, containing over 600 questions

For more information, please contact your local Pearson Education sales representative or visit **www.mystrategylab.com**

*If you don't have an access code, you can still access the resources by purchasing access online. Visit **www.mystrategylab.com** for details. A sample selection of these resources is also available at **www.pearsoned.co.uk/fos2**

# CONTENTS

# 3  STRATEGIC CAPABILITIES                                              48

# 4  STRATEGIC PURPOSE                                                   77

## APPENDIX: EVALUATING STRATEGIES

# ABOUT *FUNDAMENTALS* OF STRATEGY

Based on the tenth edition of the market-leading *Exploring Strategy*, this book concentrates on the fundamental issues and techniques of strategy. The book will particularly suit those on short courses in strategy focused on strategy analysis, or studying strategy as part of a wider degree, perhaps in the sciences or engineering. Students can be sure that they have the essential materials in this book, while knowing that they can easily go deeper into particular topics by referring to the complete *Exploring Strategy*. There they will find extended treatments of the issues covered here, as well as greater attention to issues of strategy development and change and the role of the strategist. *Exploring Strategy* also offers more cases and deeper exploration of issues through 'key debates', 'strategy lenses' and 'commentaries'. (A brief contents of *Exploring Strategy* can be found on pp. xiv and xv.'

Teachers familiar with *Exploring Strategy* will find that the definitions, concepts and the content of *Fundamentals of Strategy* are entirely consistent, making it easy to teach courses using the different books in parallel.

*Fundamentals of Strategy* has ten chapters, with the emphasis on what *Exploring Strategy* terms the 'strategic position' and 'strategic choices' facing organisations. Under 'strategic position', *Fundamentals* introduces environmental analysis, strategic capability and strategic purpose (which includes a discussion of culture and strategy). Under 'strategic choices', the book addresses business-level strategy, corporate-level strategy, international strategy, strategy innovation and mergers and acquisitions. The final tenth chapter, 'Strategy in action', raises implementation issues such as organisational structure, management processes and strategic change. There is also an appendix providing the bases of strategy evaluation.

We believe that *Fundamentals of Strategy* brings the proven benefits of *Exploring Strategy* to the growing number of students on shorter courses. We hope that you will enjoy using it too.

A guide to getting the most from all the features and learning materials of *Fundamentals of Strategy* follows this preface.

*Gerry Johnson*
*Richard Whittington*
*Kevan Scholes*
*Duncan Angwin*
*Patrick Regnér*
*April 2014*

# GETTING THE MOST FROM
# *FUNDAMENTALS OF STRATEGY*

*Fundamentals of Strategy* builds on the established strengths of *Exploring Strategy,* proven over ten best-selling editions. A range of in-text features and supplementary resources have been developed to enable you and your students to gain maximum added value to the teaching and learning of strategy.

- **Outstanding pedagogical features**. Each chapter has clear learning outcomes, definitions of key concepts in the margins, practical questions associated with real-life Illustrations, and concise end-of-chapter case examples through which students can easily apply what they have learnt.

- **Up-to-date materials**. *Fundamentals of Strategy* is based on the latest 10th edition of *Exploring Strategy*. Our references are up to date, so that you can easily access the latest research. Cases and examples are fresh and engage with student interests and day-to-day experience.

- **Range of examples**. This edition maintains the wide range of examples used in the text, Illustrations and cases. We draw from all over the world, with no bias to North America, and use examples from the public and voluntary sectors as well as the private.

  *Fundamentals of Strategy* does not include any longer cases. If you wish to supplement the book with any of the case studies included in *Exploring Strategy*, please consult your local Pearson Education representative to find out what their Custom Publishing programme can do for you.

- **Attractive text layout and design**. We make careful use of colour and photography to improve clarity and ease of 'navigation' through the text. Reading the text should be an enjoyable and straightforward process.

- **Teaching and learning support**. If you are using *MyStrategyLab* you and your students can access a wealth of resources at **www.mystrategylab.com**, including the following:

### Resources for students

- A dynamics eText
- Self-assessment questions
- Author video discussions
- Video cases and author videos
- Revision flashcards
- A multi-lingual glossary
- Links to relevant websites
- Classic cases

### Resources for lecturers

- Instructor's manual
- PowerPoint slides
- A testbank of assessment questions

This book is available with an access card for **MyStrategyLab**, but if your book did not come with an access card you can purchase access online at www.mystrategylab.com. There is also a companion website available at www.pearsoned.co.uk/fos2 which contains a sample selection of these materials.

- **Video resources** are available on line. These have been specially created for in-class use and contains briefings on key concepts by the authors, and material to support video assignments identified at the end of each chapter of *Fundamentals of Strategy*.

  1 Author videos include:
    Introducing Strategy, The Environment, Strategic Capabilities, Organization Culture, Competitive Strategy, Corporate Strategy, International Strategy, Innovation Strategy, Mergers, Acquisitions and Alliances, Strategic Change, Integration and Case Studies.
  2 Video case studies include:
    British Heart Foundation, Nationwide and Pearson, CISCO, South Western Ambulance Trust and Love Da Pop.

You can order and find out more about these resources from your local Pearson Education representative (**www.pearsoned.co.uk/replocator**).

- **Teachers' workshop**. We run an annual workshop to facilitate discussion of key challenges and solutions in the teaching of strategic management. Details of forthcoming workshops can be found at **www.pearsoned.co.uk/strategyworkshop**.

- **Complementary textbooks**. *Exploring Strategy* provides deeper and more extensive coverage of the theory and practice of strategy. A brief table of contents from the tenth edition is listed below:

  1 Introducing strategy

  **Part I** THE STRATEGIC POSITION

  2 The environment
  3 Strategic capabilities
  4 Strategic purpose
  5 Culture and strategy
    Commentary The strategy lenses

  **Part II** STRATEGIC CHOICES

  6 Business strategy
  7 Corporate strategy and diversification
  8 International strategy
  9 Innovation and entrepreneurship
  10 Mergers, acquisitions and alliances
    Commentary on Part II Strategic choices

# GUIDED TOUR

## Setting the scene

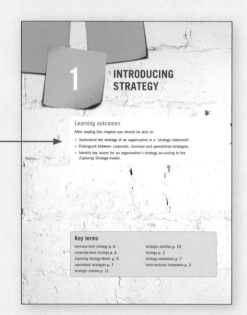

Learning outcomes enable you to check that you have understood all the major areas by the end of the chapter.

## 'Strategy in the real world

The **case example** at the end of each chapter allows exploration of topics covered in the chapter.

**Illustrations** showcase the application of specific strategic issues in the real world so that you can identify and relate theory to practice.

# 'Checking your understanding

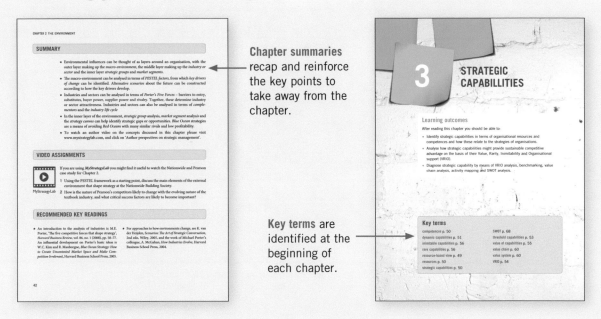

**Chapter summaries** recap and reinforce the key points to take away from the chapter.

**Key terms** are identified at the beginning of each chapter.

**Video cases** enable you to engage with and learn from the experience of senior managers responsible for determining and implementing strategy.

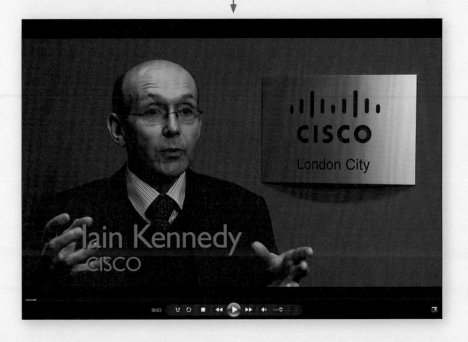

# 1

# INTRODUCING STRATEGY

## Learning outcomes

After reading this chapter you should be able to:

- Summarise the strategy of an organisation in a '*strategy statement*'.
- Distinguish between *corporate*, *business* and *operational* strategies.
- Identify key issues for an organisation's strategy according to the *Exploring Strategy* model.

## Key terms

business-level strategy p. 6

corporate-level strategy p. 6

*Exploring Strategy* Model p. 9

operational strategies p. 7

strategic choices p. 11

strategic position p. 10

strategy p. 2

strategy statements p. 7

three-horizons framework p. 3

## 1.1 INTRODUCTION

Strategy is about key issues for the future of organisations. For example, how should Apple, primarily a devices company, compete in the computer and tablet market with Google, primarily a search company? Should universities concentrate their resources on research excellence or teaching quality or try to combine both? How should a small video games producer relate to dominant console providers such as Microsoft and Sony? What should an arts group do to secure revenues in the face of declining government subsidies?

All these are strategy questions, vital to the future survival of the organisations involved. Naturally such questions concern entrepreneurs and senior managers at the top of their organisations. But these questions matter much more widely. Middle managers have to understand the strategic direction of their organisations, both to know how to get top management support for their initiatives and to explain organisational strategy to their staff. Anybody looking for a management-track job needs to be ready to discuss strategy with their potential employer. Indeed, anybody taking a job should first be confident that their new employer's strategy is actually viable. There are even specialist career opportunities in strategy, for example as a strategy consultant or as an in-house strategic planner, often key roles for fast-track young managers. Investors too need to understand strategy if they are to evaluate the viability of the businesses they invest in. Bankers need to understand the strategies of the businesses they lend to.

This book addresses the fundamental strategic issues important to managers, employees, consultants, investors and bankers. It takes a broad approach to strategy, looking at both the economics of strategy and the people side of managing strategy in practice. *Fundamentals of Strategy* is relevant to any kind of organisation responsible for its own direction into the future. Thus the book refers to large private-sector multinationals and small entrepreneurial start-ups; to public-sector organisations such as schools and hospitals; and to not-for-profits such as charities or sports clubs. Strategy matters to almost all organisations, and to everybody working in them.

## 1.2 WHAT IS STRATEGY?[1]

In this book, **strategy is the long-term direction of an organisation.** Thus the long-term direction of Amazon is from book retailing to internet services in general. The long-term direction of Disney is from cartoons to diversified entertainment. This section examines the practical implication of this definition of strategy; distinguishes between different levels of strategy; and explains how to summarise an organisation's strategy in a 'strategy statement'.

### 1.2.1 Defining strategy

Defining strategy as the long-term direction of an organisation implies a more comprehensive view than some influential definitions. Figure 1.1 shows the strategy definitions of three leading strategy theorists: Alfred Chandler and Michael Porter, both from the Harvard Business 'the determination of the long-run goals and objectives of an enterprise and the adoption of courses of action and the allocation of resource necessary for carrying out these goals'

**Alfred D. Chandler**

'Competitive strategy is about being different. It means deliberately choosing a different set of activities to deliver a unique mix of value'

**Michael Porter**

'a pattern in a stream of decisions'

**Henry Mintzberg**

'the long-term direction of an organisation'

*Exploring Strategy*

**Figure 1.1** Definitions of strategy

*Sources*: A.D. Chandler, *Strategy and Structure: Chapters in the History of American Enterprise*, MIT Press, 1963, p. 13; M.E. Porter, What is Strategy?, *Harvard Business Review*, 1996, November–December, p. 60; H. Mintzberg, *Tracking Strategies: Towards a General Theory*, Oxford University Press, 2007, p. 3.

School, and Henry Mintzberg, from McGill University, Canada. Each points to important but distinct elements of strategy. Chandler emphasises a logical flow from the determination of goals and objectives to the allocation of resources. Porter focuses on deliberate choices, difference and competition. On the other hand, Mintzberg uses the word 'pattern' to allow for the fact that strategies do not always follow a deliberately chosen and logical plan, but can emerge in more ad hoc ways. Sometimes strategies reflect a series of incremental decisions that only cohere into a recognisable pattern – or 'strategy' – after some time.

All of these strategy definitions incorporate important elements of strategy. However, this book's definition of strategy as 'the long-term direction of an organisation' has two advantages. First, the long-term direction of an organisation can include both deliberate, logical strategy and more incremental, emergent patterns of strategy. Second, long-term direction can include both strategies that emphasise difference and competition, and strategies that recognise the roles of cooperation and even imitation.

The three elements of this strategy definition – the long term, direction and organisation – can each be explored further. The strategy of Vice Media illustrates important points (see Illustration 1.1):

● *The long term.* Strategies are typically measured over years, for some organisations a decade or more. The importance of a long-term perspective on strategy is emphasised by the 'three-horizons' framework in Figure 1.2 (below). **The three-horizons framework suggests organisations should think of themselves as comprising three types of business or activity, defined by their 'horizons' in terms of years.** *Horizon 1* businesses are basically

## ILLUSTRATION 1.1    Vice pays

**Beginning in 1994 as a government subsidised free 'zine' in Montreal, Vice Media now pursues an ambitious strategy of diversification and globalisation.**

Vice Media is a global business, with a declared ambition to be the largest online media company in the world. But at its heart is still the original print magazine, *Vice*, specialising in fashion, music, lifestyle and current affairs. With a good deal of nudity, satire and violence, the magazine is regarded as edgy by some, puerile by others. An early spin-off book, *The Vice Guide to Sex, Drugs and Rock and Roll*, gives an idea of its market position. *Vice* magazine is paid for by advertising and distributed free via style-conscious clothing retailers.

However, since the late 1990s, the company has steadily diversified into a number of businesses, including clothing retail, web video, a record label, book publishing, live events, an advertising agency, television and film production, and even a London pub. By 2012, Vice Media was operating in 34 countries around the world. Revenues were approaching $200 m, with an estimated company value of around $1 bn (€750 m; £600 m).

The magazine had been started as a government work-creation scheme by three friends with no publishing experience, Suroosh Alvi, Gavin McInnes and Shane Smith. The magazine had originally been *The Voice of Montreal*, a newspaper for the local community. It soon drifted from its mission, and the three founders each borrowed $5,000 Canadian (€4,000; £3,000) to buy it out. It was said that the magazine got its title 'Vice' because the *Village Voice* magazine of New York threatened to sue them over its name. True or not, *Vice* was a very good fit with the magazine's provocative content and style.

Outside investors were soon attracted to the magazine's strong connection with its youth audience. The first investor was the Normal Network, which in 1998 bought one quarter of the group for $1 m (US), implying a total value of $4 m. This injection of capital allowed *Vice* to move its base to New York and helped its diversification into clothing retail. When Normal Network went bust in 2000, another investor, Barrontech, stumped up more capital. In 2007, the media giant

Viacom helped *Vice* into video. This partnership was said to have provoked the departure of co-founder Gavin McInness, distrustful of corporate constraints on creative freedom. In 2011, a consortium of external investors that included the world's largest advertising agency, WPP, injected a sum rumoured at between $50 and $100 m. These new funds helped launch *Vice* in China and India. New ventures were also envisaged in gaming and sports.

Co-founder Suroosh Alvi explained to the *Financial Times* the advantages to advertising partners of Vice Media's wide range of businesses and territories: 'Diversification of our media and pushing quality content through it on a global level has played massively for us. It's created a deep engagement with our audience and made a compelling story for brand partners as well, who are signing up platform-wide and doing international buy-ins. It's a bit better than publishing a magazine in a single territory.'

*Vice*'s approach is informal, however. Another co-founder, Shane Smith, recalled the early days: 'We didn't have a business plan or any idea of what we were doing. We just loved magazines and loved making the magazine. And we didn't have anything else to do, so we kept doing it.' As for *Vice* today: 'It's a totally insane working environment. It's like an incestuous family. It's a weird culture and we love it. Keeping that culture is one of our big challenges going forward.'

*Sources: National Post*, 19 July 2000; *Financial Times*, 19 November 2009; *Forbes*, 1 January 2012.

### Questions

1 How does Vice Media's strategy fit with the various strategy definitions of Alfred Chandler, Michael Porter and Henry Mintzberg (see Figure 1.1)?

2 What seems to account for Vice Media's success and is it sustainable?

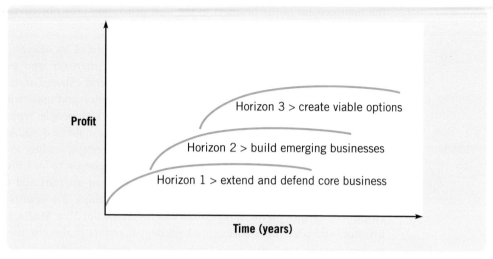

**Figure 1.2** Three horizons for strategy

*Note*: 'profit' on the vertical axis can be replaced by non-profit objectives; 'business' can refer to any set of activities; 'time' can refer to a varying number of years.

*Source*: M. Baghai, S. Coley and D. White, *The Alchemy of Growth*, Texere Publishers, 2000. Figure 1.1, p. 5.

the current core activities. In the case of Vice Media, Horizon 1 includes the original *Vice* magazine. *Horizon 1* businesses need defending and extending but the expectation is that in the long term they will likely be flat or declining in terms of profits (or whatever else the organisation values). *Horizon 2* businesses are emerging activities that should provide new sources of profit. For Vice, that might include the new China business. Finally, there are *Horizon 3* possibilities, for which nothing is sure. These are typically risky research and development projects, start-up ventures, test-market pilots or similar: at Vice Media, these might be the gaming and sports initiatives. For a fast-moving organisation like Vice Media, *Horizon 3* might generate profits only a couple of years from the present time. In a pharmaceutical company, where the R&D and regulatory processes for a new drug take many years, *Horizon 3* might be a decade ahead. While timescales might differ, the basic point about the 'three-horizons' framework is that managers need to avoid focusing on the short-term issues of their existing activities. Strategy involves pushing out Horizon 1 as far as possible, at the same time as looking to Horizons 2 and 3.

- *Strategic direction*. Over the years, strategies follow some kind of long-term direction or trajectory. The strategic direction of Vice Media is from the original print magazine to diversified youth media services. Sometimes a strategic direction only emerges as a coherent pattern over time. Typically, however, managers and entrepreneurs try to set the direction of their strategy according to long-term *objectives*. In private-sector businesses, the objective guiding strategic direction is usually maximising profits for shareholders. However, profits do not always set strategic direction. First, public-sector and charity organisations may set their strategic direction according to other objectives: for example, a sports club's objective may be to move up from one league to a higher one. Second, even in the private sector profit is not always the sole criterion for strategy. Thus family businesses may sometimes sacrifice the maximisation of profits for family objectives, for example passing down the management of the business to the next generation. The objectives behind strategic direction always need close scrutiny.

- *Organisation*. In this book, organisations are not treated as discrete, unified entities. Organisations involve complex relationships, both internally and externally. This is because organisations typically have many internal and external *stakeholders*, in other words people and groups that depend on the organisation and upon which the organisation itself depends. Internally, organisations are filled with people, typically with diverse, competing and more or less reasonable views of what should be done. At Vice Media, the three co-founders had clashed over corporate partnerships, leading to the departure of Gavin McInness. In strategy, therefore, it is always important to look *inside* organisations and to consider the people involved and their different interests and views. Externally, organisations are surrounded by important relationships, for example with suppliers, customers, alliance partners, regulators and investors. For Vice Media, relationships with investors and advertisers were crucial. Strategy therefore is also crucially concerned with an organisation's external *boundaries*: in other words, questions about what to include within the organisation and how to manage important relationships with what is kept outside.

Because strategy typically involves managing people, relationships and resources, the subject is sometimes called 'strategic management'. This book takes the view that managing is always important in strategy. Good strategy is about the practicalities of managing as well as the analysis of strategising.

## 1.2.2 Levels of strategy

Inside an organisation, strategies can exist at three main levels. Again they can be illustrated by reference to Vice Media (Illustration 1.1):

- **Corporate-level strategy is concerned with the overall scope of an organisation and how value is added to the constituent businesses of the organisational whole.** Corporate-level strategy issues include geographical scope, diversity of products or services, acquisitions of new businesses, and how resources are allocated between the different elements of the organisation. For Vice Media, diversifying from the original magazine into retail, publishing and video are corporate-level strategies. Being clear about corporate-level strategy is important: determining the range of businesses to include is the basis of other strategic decisions, such as acquisitions and alliances.

- **Business-level strategy is about how the individual businesses should compete in their particular markets** (for this reason, business-level strategy is often called 'competitive strategy'). These individual businesses might be standalone businesses, for instance entrepreneurial start-ups, or 'business units' within a larger corporation (as the magazine is within Vice Media). Business-level strategy typically concerns issues such as innovation, appropriate scale and response to competitors' moves. In the public sector, the equivalent of business-level strategy is decisions about how units (such as individual hospitals or schools) should provide best-value services. Where the businesses are units within a larger organisation, business-level strategies should clearly fit with corporate-level strategy.

- **Operational strategies are concerned with how the components of an organisation deliver effectively the corporate- and business-level strategies in terms of resources, processes and people.** For example, Vice Media had to keep raising external finance to fund its rapid growth: its operational strategy is partly geared to meeting investment needs. In most businesses, successful business strategies depend to a large extent on decisions that are taken, or activities that occur, at the operational level. Operational decisions need therefore to be closely linked to business-level strategy. They are vital to successful strategy implementation.

This need to link the corporate, business and operational levels underlines the importance of *integration* in strategy. Each level needs to be aligned with the others. The demands of integrating levels define an important characteristic of strategy: strategy is typically *complex*, requiring careful and sensitive management. Strategy is rarely simple.

### 1.2.3 Strategy statements

David Collis and Michael Rukstad[2] at the Harvard Business School argue that all entrepreneurs and managers should be able to summarise their organisation's strategy with a 'strategy statement'. **Strategy statements should have three main themes: the fundamental *goals* (mission, vision or objectives) that the organisation seeks; the *scope* or domain of the organisation's activities; and the particular *advantages* or capabilities it has to deliver all of these.** Goals are discussed further in Chapter 4, but meanwhile these three strategy statement themes are explained as follows, with examples in Illustration 1.2:

- *Mission.* This relates to goals, and refers to the overriding purpose of the organisation. It is sometimes described in terms of the apparently simple but challenging question: '*what business are we in?*'. The mission statement helps keep managers focused on what is central to their strategy.

- *Vision.* This too relates to goals, and refers to the desired future state of the organisation. It is an aspiration which can help mobilise the energy and passion of organisational members. The vision statement, therefore, should answer the question: '*what do we want to achieve?*'

- *Objectives.* These are more precise and ideally quantifiable statements of the organisation's goals over some period of time. Objectives might refer to profitability or market share targets for a private company, or to examination results in a school. Objectives introduce discipline to strategy. The question here is: '*what do we have to achieve in the coming period?*'

- *Scope.* An organisation's scope or domain refers to three dimensions: customers or clients; geographical location; and extent of internal activities ('vertical integration'). For a university, scope questions are twofold: first, which academic departments to have (a business school, an engineering department and so on); second, which activities to do internally themselves (vertically integrate) and which to externalise to subcontractors (e.g. whether to manage campus restaurants in-house or to subcontract them).

- *Advantage.* This part of a strategy statement describes how the organisation will achieve the objectives it has set for itself in its chosen domain. In competitive environments, this refers to the *competitive* advantage: for example, how a particular company or sports club will achieve goals in the face of competition from other companies or clubs. In order to

## ILLUSTRATION 1.2    Strategy statements

**Both Samsung Electronics, the Korean telecommunications, computing and TV giant, and the University of Utrecht, a leading Dutch university, publish a good deal about their strategies.**

### Samsung Electronics

At Samsung, we follow a simple business philosophy: to devote our talent and technology to creating superior products and services that contribute to a better global society.

Every day, our people bring this philosophy to life. Our leaders search for the brightest talent from around the world, and give them the resources they need to be the best at what they do. The result is that all of our products – from memory chips that help businesses store vital knowledge to mobile phones that connect people across continents – have the power to enrich lives. And that's what making a better global society is all about.

As stated in its new motto, Samsung Electronics' vision is: 'Inspire the World, Create the Future'. This new vision reflects Samsung Electronics' commitment to inspiring its communities by leveraging Samsung's three key strengths: 'New Technology', 'Innovative Products', and 'Creative Solutions'. As part of this vision, Samsung has mapped out a specific plan of reaching $400 bn in revenue and becoming one of the world's top five brands by 2020. To this end, Samsung has also established three strategic approaches in its management: 'Creativity', 'Partnership' and 'Talent'.

As we build on our previous accomplishments, we look forward to exploring new territories, including health, medicine and biotechnology. Samsung is committed to being a creative leader in new markets and becoming a truly No. 1 business going forward.

### Utrecht University, Strategic Plan 2012–16

The University's core mission is to: educate young people; train new generations of researchers; produce academics who have both specialist knowledge and professional skills; conduct groundbreaking research; and address social issues and work towards solving them.

#### Education targets

- Utrecht University will manage to retain third place in the top six of [Dutch] general research universities with the highest number of Bachelor's programmes rated good/excellent.
- The percentage of (permanent) lecturers with a basic teaching qualification will grow from 20 per cent in 1999 via 60 per cent in 2010 to a projected total of 80 per cent in 2016.
- By 2016, the number of scheduled contact hours and other structural education-related hours in . . . full-time Bachelor's programmes will total 12–18 hours per week.
- The percentage of students enrolled in entrepreneurship courses will increase from 1 per cent in 2006, via 3 per cent in 2010 to a projected total of 5 per cent in 2016.

#### Strengths

- A university-wide education model and a broadly supported educational culture.
- Innovative educational developments that are adopted by institutions around the country.
- A broad range of instruments for the professionalisation and assessment of teaching staff.
- The largest Summer School in Europe, serving as a centre for internationalisation.

*Sources*: Edited extracts from www.samsung.com and the University of Utrecht Strategic Plan, 2012–16, www.uu.nl.

> ### Questions
>
> 1 Construct short strategy statements covering the goals, scope and advantage of Samsung and the University of Utrecht. How much do the different private- and public-sector contexts matter?
>
> 2 Construct a strategy statement for your own organisation (university, sports club or employer). What implications might this statement have for your particular course or department?

achieve a particular goal, the organisation needs to be better than others seeking the same goal. In the public sector, advantage might refer simply to the organisation's capability in general. But even public-sector organisations frequently need to show that their capabilities are not only adequate, but superior to other rival departments or perhaps to private-sector contractors.

Collis and Rukstad suggest that strategy statements covering goals, scope and advantage should be no more than 35 words long. Brevity keeps such statements focused on the essentials and makes them easy to remember and communicate. Thus for Vice Media, a strategy statement might be: 'to build the world's largest online media group, focused on youth and with competitive advantages in terms of the diversity and international range of our businesses and the strength of our relationships with key partners'. The strategy statement of American financial advisory firm Edward Jones is more specific: 'to grow to 17,000 financial advisers by 2012 by offering trusted and convenient face-to-face financial advice to conservative individual investors through a national network of one-financial adviser offices'. Of course, such strategy statements are not always fulfilled. Circumstances may change in unexpected ways. In the meantime, however, they can provide a useful guide both to managers in their decision making and to employees and others who need to understand the direction in which the organisation is going. The ability to give a clear strategy statement is a good test of managerial competence in an organisation.

As such, strategy statements are relevant to a wide range of organisations. For example, a small entrepreneurial start-up can use a strategy statement to persuade investors and lenders of its viability. Public-sector organisations need strategy statements not only for themselves, but also to reassure clients, funders and regulators that their priorities are the right ones. Voluntary organisations need persuasive strategy statements in order to inspire volunteers and donors. Thus, organisations of all kinds frequently publish materials relevant to such strategy statements on their websites or annual reports. Illustration 1.2 provides published materials on the strategies of two very different organisations: the technology giant Samsung from the private sector and the Dutch University of Utrecht from the public sector.

## 1.3 THE *EXPLORING STRATEGY* MODEL

This book draws on a three-part model of strategy that emphasises the interconnected nature of strategic issues. The **Exploring Strategy Model** includes understanding *the strategic position* of an organisation; assessing *strategic choices* for the future; and managing *strategy in action*. Figure 1.3 shows these elements and defines the broad coverage of this book. However, this book concentrates on the fundamental strategic issues involved in strategic position and strategic choices, treating strategy in action more briefly (our related book *Exploring Strategy* explores this third set of issues in detail). The following sections of this chapter introduce the strategic issues that arise under each of these elements of the *Exploring Strategy* Model.

Figure 1.3 could show the model's three elements in a linear sequence – first understanding the strategic position, then making strategic choices and finally turning strategy into action. Indeed, this logical sequence is implicit in the definition of strategy given by Alfred Chandler (Figure 1.1) and many other textbooks on strategy. However, as Henry Mintzberg recognises,

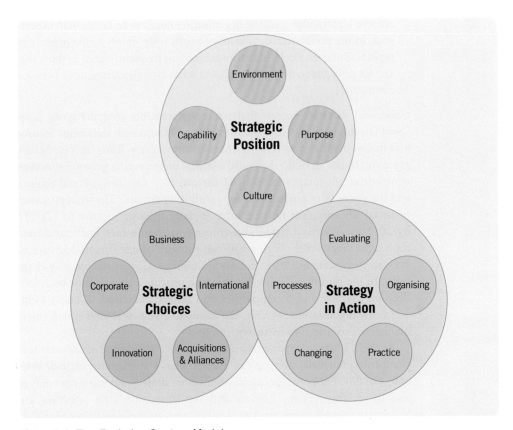

**Figure 1.3** The *Exploring Strategy* Model

in practice the elements of strategy do not always follow this linear sequence. Choices often have to be made before the position is fully understood. Sometimes, too, a proper understanding of the strategic position can only be built from the experience of trying a strategy out in action. The real-world feedback that comes from launching a new product is often far better at uncovering the true strategic position than remote analysis carried out in a strategic planning department at head office. The interconnected circles of Figure 1.3 are designed to emphasise this potentially non-linear nature of strategy. Position, choices and action should be seen as closely related, and in practice none has priority over another.

The *Exploring Strategy* Model thus provides a comprehensive and integrated framework for analysing an organisation's position, considering the choices it has and putting strategies into action. Each of the chapters can be seen as asking fundamental strategy questions and providing the essential concepts and techniques to help answer them. Working systematically through questions and answers provides the basis for persuasive strategy recommendations.

### 1.3.1 Strategic position

The strategic position is concerned with the impact on strategy of the external environment, the organisation's strategic capability (resources and competences), the organisation's

**purpose and the organisation's culture**. Understanding these four factors is central for evaluating future strategy. These issues, and the fundamental questions associated with them, are covered in the first four chapters of this book:

- *Environment.* Organisations operate in a complex political, economic, social and technological world. These environments vary widely in terms of their dynamism and attractiveness. The fundamental question here relates to the *opportunities and threats* available to the organisation in this complex and changing environment. Chapter 2 provides key frameworks to help in focusing on priority issues in the face of environmental complexity and dynamism.

- *Strategic capability.* Each organisation has its own strategic capabilities, made up of its *resources* (e.g. machines and buildings) and *competences* (e.g. technical and managerial skills). The fundamental question on capability regards the organisation's strengths and weaknesses (e.g. where is it at a competitive advantage or disadvantage?). Are the organisation's capabilities adequate to the challenges of its environment and the demands of its goals? Chapter 3 provides tools and concepts for analysing such capabilities.

- *Strategic purpose.* Most organisations claim for themselves a particular purpose, as encapsulated in their *vision*, *mission* and *objectives*. But often this purpose is unclear, contested or unrealistic. The third fundamental question therefore is: what is the organisation's strategic purpose; what does it seek to achieve? Here the issue of *corporate governance* is important: how to ensure that managers stick to the agreed purpose. Questions of purpose and accountability raise issues of *corporate social responsibility and ethics*: is the purpose an appropriate one and are managers sticking to it? Purpose and ethics will in turn be closely associated with *organisational culture*, implying the importance of cultural fit with the desired strategy. Chapter 4 provides concepts for addressing these issues of purpose.

The *Exploring Strategy* Model points to the following positioning issues for Vice Media (Illustration 1.1). What is the future of *Vice* magazine given the environmental shift from print to internet media? Are its distinctive capabilities in youth media sustainable, given the ageing profiles of its two remaining founders? Is Vice Media's dedication to rapid growth funded by corporate partners consistent with the kind of creativity defended by departing co-founder Gavin McInness? Is the original 'weird' culture, as championed by Shane Smith, still a source of advantage, or is it now a constraint on what is fast becoming a diversified, global media conglomerate?

## 1.3.2 Strategic choices

**Strategic choices** involve the options for strategy in terms of both the *directions* in which strategy might move and the *methods* by which strategy might be pursued. For instance, an organisation might have a range of strategic directions open to it: the organisation could diversify into new products; it could enter new international markets; or it could transform its existing products and markets through radical innovation. These various directions could be pursued by different methods: the organisation could acquire a business already active in the product or market area; it could form alliances with relevant organisations that might help its new strategy; or it could try to pursue its strategies on its own. Typical strategic choices, and the related fundamental questions, are covered in Chapters 5–9 of this book, as follows:

- *Business strategy.* There are strategic choices in terms of how the organisation seeks to compete at the individual business level. For example, a business unit could choose to be the lowest cost competitor in a market, or the highest quality. The fundamental question here, then, is how should the business unit compete? Key dilemmas for business-level strategy, and ways of resolving them, are discussed in Chapter 5.

- *Corporate strategy and diversification.* The highest level of an organisation is typically concerned with issues of corporate scope; in other words, which businesses to include in the portfolio. This relates to the appropriate degree of *diversification*, with regard to products offered and markets served. Corporate-level strategy is also concerned with internal relationships, both between business units and with the corporate head office. Chapter 6 provides tools for assessing diversification strategies and the appropriate relationships within the corporate portfolio.

- *International strategy.* Internationalisation is a form of diversification, but into new geographical markets. Here the fundamental question is: where internationally should the organisation compete? Chapter 7 examines how to prioritise various international options and key strategies for pursuing them.

- *Innovation strategy.* Most existing organisations have to innovate constantly simply to survive. Fundamental strategy questions therefore are whether the organisation is innovating appropriately and how it should respond to the innovations of competitors. Chapter 8 considers key choices about innovation and helps in selecting between them.

- *Acquisitions and alliances.* Organisations have to make choices about methods for pursuing their strategies. Many organisations prefer to build new businesses with their own resources. Other organisations develop by acquiring other businesses or forming alliances with complementary partners. The fundamental question in Chapter 9, therefore, is whether to buy another company, ally or to go it alone.

Again, issues of strategic choice are live in the case of Vice Media (Illustration 1.1). The *Exploring Strategy* Model asks the following kinds of questions here. Should Vice Media compete predominantly with cheap web video or move up market with film and TV? How far should it widen the scope of its businesses: does the London pub really belong in the portfolio? How should Vice Media manage its partnerships with the various corporate giants, already the cause of disputes over creativity? And should Vice Media be allowed to continue to innovate in its 'insane' free-wheeling style?

## 1.3.3 Strategy in action

Strategy in action is concerned with how chosen strategies are actually put into practice. Chapter 10 covers three key issues for strategy in action:

- *Structuring* an organisation to support successful performance. A key question here is how centralised or structured should the organisational structure be. Structure matters for who is in charge and who is accountable.

- *Systems* are required to control the way in which *strategy is implemented*. Planning and performance systems are important to getting things done. The issue here is how to ensure that strategies are implemented according to plan.

- Leading *strategic change* is typically an important part of putting strategy into action. How should change be led? Here key questions include the speed and comprehensiveness of change.

With regard to strategy in action, the *Exploring Strategy* Model raises the following kinds of questions for Vice Media. What kind of structure does Vice Media need in order to organise its wide range of activities and country operations? Given its growing scale, is the 'insane' environment of Vice Media still adequate, or does the company need to invest in more managerial systems? How should the surviving co-founders lead any changes that may be necessary as Vice Media grows? All these issues, and related ones to do with strategic planning and practice, are dealt with more extensively in the authors' *Exploring Strategy*, 10th edition.

## 1.4 STRATEGY DEVELOPMENT PROCESSES

The previous section introduced strategic position, strategic choices and strategy in action. However, strategies do not always develop in a logical sequence of analysis, choice and action. There are two broad accounts of strategy development:

- The *rational-analytic view* of strategy development is the conventional account. Here strategies are developed through rational and analytical processes, led typically by top managers. These processes result in a strategic plan, typically containing the kind of elements outlined in Table 1.1. There is a linear sequence. The typical plan begins with statements of the overall strategy and mission, vision and objectives. Then there are environmental and capability analyses. Next a range of strategic options will be evaluated, with one proposed ahead of the others. The final elements of a strategic plan are putting the resources in place and addressing the key change processes. Each of these elements is covered in chapters in this book. The basis assumption in this rational-analytic view is that strategies are typically *intended*, in other words the product of deliberate choices. This rational-analytical view is associated with theorists such as Alfred Chandler and Michael Porter, in Figure 1.1.

**Table 1.1** Key Elements in a Strategic Plan[3]

| |
|---|
| The Strategy Statement (Chapter 1) |
| Mission, vision and objectives (Chapter 4) |
| Environmental analysis (Chapter 2) |
| Capability analysis (Chapter 3) |
| Strategic Options and Proposed Strategies (Chapters 5–9; Appendix) |
| Resources (Appendix) |
| Key Changes (Chapter 10) |

- The *emergent strategy view* is the alternative broad explanation of how strategies develop. In this view, strategies often do not simply develop as intended or planned, but tend to emerge in organisations over time as a result of ad hoc, incremental or even accidental actions. Good ideas and opportunities often come from practical experience at the bottom of the organisation, not just from management at the top. Even the best laid plans may need to be abandoned as new opportunities arise or the organisation learns from the marketplace. Learning from experience can be as valuable as planning in advance. This emergent view is particularly associated with Henry Mintzberg, referenced in Figure 1.1. The non-linear nature of the *Exploring Strategy* Model (Figure 1.3) reflects the possible role of emergent strategy.

The rational-analytic and emergent views of strategy development are not mutually exclusive. Intended strategies can often succeed, especially in stable markets where there are few surprises. Moreover, an organisation's key stakeholders – employees, owners, customers, regulators and so on – will typically want to see evidence of deliberate strategy-making: it is rarely acceptable to say that everything is simply emergent. The tools and concepts throughout the book are particularly helpful in this deliberate strategy-making. But still it is wise to be open as well to the possibilities of emergence. Inflexible plans can hinder learning and prevent the seizing of opportunities. Moreover, strategic choices do not always come about as a result of simple rational analysis: cultural and political processes in organisations can also drive changes in strategy, as will become apparent in the discussions in Chapter 4.

This book allows for both the rational-analytical view and the emergent view. It is generally sensible for managers to start with a rational-analytical approach, and this is what many of the tools and concepts in this book are designed to help with. However, it is also sensible to allow for emergence and learning in action, and the roles of culture and politics in organisations should not be overlooked. Emergence is likely to have played a big role in Vice Media, for example (Illustration 1.1).

## SUMMARY

- Strategy is the *long-term direction* of an organisation. A *strategy statement* should cover the *goals* of an organisation, the *scope* of the organisation's activities and the *advantages* or *capabilities* the organisation brings to these goals and activities.

- *Corporate-level strategy* is concerned with an organisation's overall scope; *business-level strategy* is concerned with how to compete; and *operational strategy* is concerned with how corporate- and business-level strategies are actually delivered.

- The *Exploring Strategy* Model has three major elements: understanding the *strategic position*, making *strategic choices* for the future and managing *strategy in action*.

- Strategy develops both through *rational-analytic* processes and through *emergence*.

- To watch an author video on the concepts discussed in this chapter please visit www.mystrategylab.com, and click on 'Author perspectives on strategic management'.

## VIDEO ASSIGNMENTS

MyStrategyLab

If you are using *MyStrategyLab* you might find it useful to watch the British Heart Foundation case study for Chapter 1.

1 Refer to section 1.2.3 and Illustration 1.2 as a guide and use the video to help you write a strategy statement for the British Heart Foundation. Why is such a statement useful to the BHF?

2 Show how the *Exploring Strategy* Model (Figure 1.3) can be used to map key strategic management issues for the BHF. Identify the key challenges facing the BHF.

## RECOMMENDED KEY READINGS

It is always useful to read around a topic. As well as the specific references below, we particularly highlight:

- Two stimulating overviews of strategic thinking in general, aimed particularly at practising managers, are C. Montgomery, *The Strategist: Be the Leader your Business Needs*, Harper Business, 2012; and R. Rumelt, *Good Strategy/Bad Strategy: the Difference and Why it Matters*, Crown Business, 2011.
- Two accessible articles on what strategy is, and might not be, are M. Porter, 'What is strategy?', *Harvard Business Review*, November–December 1996, pp. 61–78;

and F. Fréry, 'The fundamental dimensions of strategy', *MIT Sloan Management Review*, vol. 48, no. 1 (2006), pp. 71–5.
- For contemporary developments in strategy practice, business newspapers such as the *Financial Times*, *Les Echos* and the *Wall Street Journal* and business magazines such as *Business Week*, *The Economist*, *L'Expansion* and *Manager-Magazin*. Several of these have well-informed Asian editions. See also the websites of the leading strategy consulting firms: www.mckinsey.com; www.bcg.com; www.bain.com.

## REFERENCES

1. The question 'What is strategy?' is discussed in R. Whittington, *What Is Strategy – and Does it Matter?*, 2000; and M.E. Porter, 'What is strategy?', *Harvard Business Review*, November–December 1996, pp. 61–78.
2. D. Collis and M. Rukstad, 'Can you say what your strategy is?', *Harvard Business Review*, April 2008, pp. 63–73.
3. A practical introduction to strategic planning is V. Evans, *FT Essential Guide to Developing a Business Strategy: How to Use Strategic Planning to Start Up or Grow Your Business*, FT Publishing International, 2013.

# Glastonbury: from hippy weekend to international festival

Steve Henderson, Leeds Metropolitan University

Following on from Woodstock in 1969, many have been inspired to create their own music festival. While some of these events have come and gone, the longevity and location of Fuji Rock Festival in Japan, Roskilde in Denmark, Coachella in the USA, Rock al Parque in Colombia illustrate the established international nature of this market (see Table 1). One of the longest established is Glastonbury Festival where, in 2013, the Rolling Stones were added to the long list of acts (from Paul McCartney to Oasis) that have appeared there. It started in 1970 when 1,500 hippy revellers paid £1 (€1.2; $1.5) for their ticket and gathered on a farm near Glastonbury Tor to be plied with free milk and entertainment from a makeshift stage. Now, Glastonbury is a major international festival that attracts over 150,000 attendees. Without any information about the performers, the 2013 festival tickets – priced at over £200 – sold out within a few hours.

In those early days, the vision was developed by local farmer, Michael Eavis, whose passion for music and social principles led to a weekend of music as a means of raising funds for good causes. It was a social mission rooted in the hippy counter-culture of the 1960s and events such as the Woodstock Festival. Today, the Glastonbury Festival attendee finds that those early days of hippy idealism are a long way off. The scale of the organisation demands

Source: Mat Cardy/Stringer/Getty Images.

strong management to support the achievement of the festival's social aims.

At first, the statutory requirements for an event held on private land were minimal. Jovial policemen looked over hedges while recreational drugs were sold from tables near the festival entrance as if this was just a slightly unusual village fête. Needless to say, the festival began to attract the attention of a number of different groups, especially

**Table 1** International music festivals

| Festival | Country | Started | Estimated capacity[1] | 2013 pricing |
|---|---|---|---|---|
| Woodstock | USA | 1969 | 400,000 | Price/free |
| Glastonbury | UK | 1970 | 130,000 | £205 (weekend) |
| Reading/Leeds Festival | UK | 1971[2]/1999 | 162,000 | £197.50 (weekend) |
| Roskilde | Denmark | 1971 | 103,000 | £195 (three days) |
| Rock am Ring/Rock im Park | Germany | 1985/1993 | 150,000 | £150 (weekend) |
| Rock al Parque | Colombia | 1995 | 88,000 | Free |
| Benicassim | Spain | 1995 | 55,000 | £150 (four days) |
| V Festival – Weston Park/Hylands Park | UK | 1996 | 160,000 | £185 (weekend) |
| Fuji Rock | Japan | 1997 | More than 100,000 | £305 (three days) |
| Coachella | USA | 1999 | 75,000 | £220 (three days) |
| Peace & Love | Sweden | 1999 | 2,000 | £170 (five days) |

[1] Based on daily capacity
[2] Existed from 1961 as a Jazz Festival

as legislation around the running of events tightened. Eavis struggled with local residents who hated the invasion of their privacy; with hippy activist groups whose contribution in helping at the festival gave them a sense of ownership; with drug dealers carrying on their activities on the fringes of the festival; and with fans climbing over the fences to get free access.

The continued expansion has resulted in a festival with over ten stages covering jazz, dance, classical, world music and other genres. Added to this, there is comedy, poetry, circus, theatre and children's entertainment alongside more esoteric street theatre performances. Much of this is organised into specific grassy field areas where, for example, the DanceVillage uses a number of tents dedicated to different types of dance music. Indeed, such is the range of entertainment on offer that some attendees spend the whole weekend at the festival without seeing a single live music act. Though the Eavis family remain involved with the main programme, much of the other entertainment is now managed by others. Reflecting this shift towards more diverse entertainment, the name of the festival was changed from Glastonbury Fayre (reflecting the ancient cultural heritage of the area) to the Glastonbury Festival for Contemporary Performing Arts.

In some years, like 2012, the festival is forced to take a year off to allow the farmland to recover from the trampling of thousands of pairs of feet. Not only is this wise for agricultural reasons but it also gives the local residents a rest from the annual invasion of festival goers. Despite this, the festival has met with a number of controversies such as when a large number of gatecrashers spoilt the fun in 2000. This caused the festival to be fined due to exceeding the licensed attendance and excessive noise. Furthermore, health and safety laws now impose on event management a 'duty of care' to everyone on the festival site. To address these health and safety concerns, support was sought from Melvin Benn who ran festivals for the Mean Fiddler events organiser. With a steel fence erected around the perimeter, Melvin Benn helped re-establish the festival in 2002 after a year off.

In 2006, Mean Fiddler was taken over and renamed Festival Republic by major music promoters, Live Nation and MCD Productions. In a worrying move, Live Nation announced that it would entice a number of major artists to appear on the weekend normally used by Glastonbury at a new festival called Wireless. Based in London, this seemed set to offer a city-based alternative to Glastonbury. Later, in 2010, Live Nation acquired Ticketmaster in a controversial move that extended its control over the ticketing of its own and other events.

This shift among the major music promoters indicated not only their interest in the ownership of key events but their desire to control income streams and the customer interface.

Elsewhere in the world of live entertainment, the success of Glastonbury had not gone unnoticed and the music festival market showed considerable growth. Some of the other festivals tried to capitalise on features that Glastonbury could not offer. For example, Glastonbury was famous for its wet weather with pictures of damp revellers and collapsed tents being commonplace. Live Nation's city-based Wireless Festival offered the opportunity to sleep under a roof at home or hotel, as opposed to risking the weather outdoors. Alternatively, Benicassim in southern Spain offered a festival with an excellent chance of sunshine and top acts for the price of a low-cost airline ticket. Other festivals noted that Glastonbury attendees enjoyed the wider entertainment at the event. In doing this, they realised that many festival goers were attracted by the whole social experience. So, sidestepping major acts and their related high fees, smaller festivals were created for just a few thousand attendees. These offered entertainment in various formats, often in a family-friendly atmosphere. Freddie Fellowes, organiser of the Secret Garden Party, describes this 'boutique' type of festival as a chance 'to be playful, to break down barriers between people and create an environment where you have perfect freedom and perfect nourishment, intellectually and visually'. Festival Republic, the rebranded Mean Fiddler, created a boutique festival on a larger scale with its Latitude Festival. Similarly, Rob da Bank, a BBC DJ, put together Bestival on The Isle of Wight where the attendees are encouraged to join in the fun by appearing in fancy dress. Quite clearly, audiences are now being presented with a wide range of festivals to consider for their leisure-time entertainment.

Many of these festivals attract sponsors with some becoming prominent by acquiring naming rights on the festival, e.g. the Virgin brand's support of V Festival. Others have low-profile arrangements involving so-called 'contra' deals as opposed to sponsorship payments. For example, Glastonbury has official cider suppliers who typically boost their brand by giving the festival a preferential deal on their products in exchange for publicity. Though these commercial relationships are sometimes spurned by the smaller festivals that see the branding as an intrusion on their social environment, larger festivals often need such relationships to survive. In order to attract sponsors, large festivals are turning to radio and television broadcasters as a means to expand the audience and offer wider exposure for the sponsor. Indeed, in

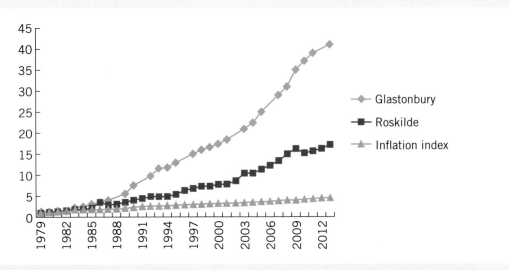

**Figure 1** Glastonbury ticket price trend, 1979–2013, relative to Roskilde festival prices and inflation (all rebased to 1979) [as in ES 10]

2011, the BBC sent around 250 staff members down to Glastonbury for broadcasting aimed at satisfying the interest of the armchair viewer/listener.

With such huge demand for their talents, artists can have a lucrative summer moving between festivals. Similarly, audiences can make lengthy treks to their favourite festivals. For some, this has caused environmental concerns with Glastonbury's rural location, poor transport links and large audience being cited as a specific problem. On the other hand, artists are finding not only that the festivals offer a good source of income but also that private parties and corporate entertainment have emerged as alternative, often greater, income opportunities. One newspaper claimed that George Michael pocketed more than £1.5 m to entertain revellers at the British billionaire-retailer Sir Philip Green's 55th birthday party in the Maldives. Hence, for major artists, the summer has become a case of 'cherry picking' their favourite festivals or seeking out the most lucrative opportunities.

Over time, the shift from small, homespun event to corporate-controlled festival has provided awkward situations for Michael Eavis – from the difficulties with establishment politicians who felt the event was out of control to the demands of counter-cultural groups such as the travelling hippies. However, along the way, the festival has maintained its aim of supporting charities like CND and, later, Greenpeace, Oxfam and a number of local charities. In the mind of the audience, this helps position the festival as a fun event with a social conscience.

In recent years, Glastonbury has sold all its tickets and is relatively highly priced to many competitors (Figure 1). Indeed, since 1979, Glastonbury has been moving its prices up significantly faster than both inflation and the comparable Danish Roskilde Festival.

At the same time, it continues to make donations to favoured causes, confirming the financial viability of the current business model. Indeed, the festival's iconic status has helped it to become a rite of passage for many young music fans. Yet, in 2008, Eavis publicly registered concern over the ageing nature of the Glastonbury audience and announced that Jay-Z, an American rap artist, was to headline in order to help attract younger people. Reflecting on the 2008 festival, Michael Eavis displayed concerns over the future, saying: 'Last year I thought that maybe we'd got to the end and we'd have to bite the bullet and fold it all up. A lot of the bands were saying Glastonbury had become too big, too muddy and too horrible.'

Audiences and artists are the two key factors that underpin financial success at these events, as successful festival promoters are well aware. Despite the fact that Michael's daughter, Emily Eavis, and her husband were taking on more of the workload and Michael himself has become more of a figurehead for this event, these comments from the festival's founder highlight worries in key strategic areas that would be troubling for management. Others pointed to the strong relationships Live Nation were developing with artists via 360 degree deals that meant both parties would profit not only from live performances but also from some combination of merchandise, publishing and recordings too. Both Jay-Z in 2008 and U2 who headlined in 2011 had such relationships and encouraged some observers to accuse the festival of adopting corporate elements that took them away from their core social image.

In 2012, the year of the London Olympics when Glastonbury took a break, Melvin Benn and Festival Republic amicably parted company with the festival. Citing the demands of expanding international festival responsibilities on Benn, the separation of the two seems aimed at re-establishing independence and removing some of the more recent corporate aspects to the festival. Thanking Melvin Benn for his efforts, the Eavis family find themselves firmly back in control and planning the way forward for this iconic festival in a market that is facing difficult recessionary times.

*Sources*: The history of Glastonbury is charted on the website, www.glastonburyfestivals.co.uk/history, while details of ownership and finances are available through Companies House; most of the background to the festival and related market has been drawn from online news resources such as the BBC, *Times Online*, *the Independent* and *the Guardian*, or industry magazines such as *Music Week*. See also: *Watchmojo: The History of the Glastonbury Festival*: https://www. youtube.com/watch?v=b2bXzuB7sZw.

## Questions

1 Sticking to the 35-word limit suggested by Collis and Rukstad in section 1.2.3, what strategy statement would you propose for the Glastonbury Festival?

2 Carry out a 'three-horizons' analysis (section 1.2.1) of the Glastonbury Festival, in terms of both existing activities and possible future ones. How might this analysis affect its future strategic direction?

3 Using the headings of environment, strategic capability, strategic purpose and culture seen in section 1.3.1, identify key positioning issues for the Glastonbury Festival and consider their relative importance.

4 Following on from the previous questions and making use of section 1.3.2, what alternative strategies do you see for the Glastonbury Festival?

5 Converting good strategic thinking into action can be a challenge: examine how the Glastonbury Festival has achieved this by considering the elements seen in section 1.3.3.

# 2  THE ENVIRONMENT

## Learning outcomes

After reading this chapter, you should be able to:

- Analyse the broad macro-environment of organisations in terms of political, economic, social, technological, ecological and legal factors *(PESTEL).*

- Construct alternative *scenarios* to address possible environmental changes.

- Analyse the attractiveness of industries and markets using *Porter's Five Forces* and *industry life cycles.*

- Analyse strategic and competitor positions in terms of *complementors, strategic groups, market segments* and '*Blue Oceans*'.

- Use these various concepts and techniques to recognise environmental *threats* and *opportunities.*

## Key terms

barriers to entry p. 31

Blue Oceans p. 41

buyers p. 32

complementor p. 33

critical success factors p. 40

industry p. 27

key drivers for change p. 25

market p. 28

market segment p. 39

PESTEL framework p. 22

Porter's Five Forces Framework p. 28

rivals p. 28

strategic groups p. 37

strategy canvas p. 39

substitutes p. 32

suppliers p. 33

value curves p. 40

value innovation p. 40

## 2.1 INTRODUCTION

The environment is what gives organisations their means of survival. It creates opportunities and it presents threats. For example, the rise of the Chinese economy has created opportunities for Western mobile phone manufacturers, at the same time as producing threats in terms of new competitors such as ZTE and Huawei. Although the future can never be predicted perfectly, it is clearly important that entrepreneurs and managers try to analyse their environments as carefully as they can in order to anticipate and – if possible – influence environmental change.

This chapter therefore provides frameworks for analysing changing and complex environments. These frameworks are organised in a series of 'layers' briefly introduced here and summarised in Figure 2.1.

- *The macro-environment* is the highest-level layer. This consists of broad environmental factors that impact to a greater or lesser extent on almost all organisations. Here, the PESTEL framework can be used to identify how future issues in the *political, economic, social, technological, ecological and legal* environments might affect organisations. This PESTEL analysis provides the broad 'data' from which to identify *key drivers of change*. These key drivers can be used to construct *scenarios* of alternative possible futures.

- *Industry*, or *sector*, forms the next layer within this broad general environment. This is made up of organisations producing the same sorts of products or services. Here the

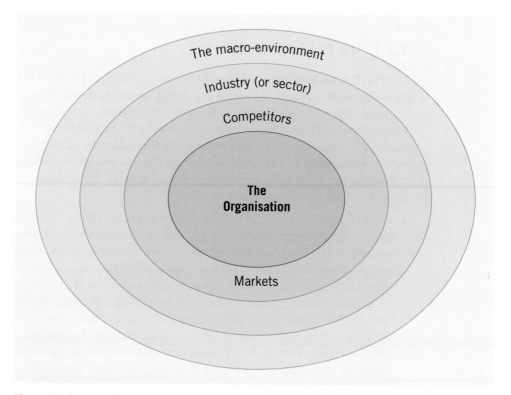

**Figure 2.1** Layers of the business environment

*Five Forces* framework is particularly useful in understanding the attractiveness of particular industries or sectors and potential threats from outside the present set of competitors. *Complementors* identify opportunities for cooperation within and across industries.

- *Competitors and markets* are the most immediate layer surrounding organisations. Here the concept of *strategic groups* can help identify different kinds of competitors. Similarly, in the marketplace, customers' expectations are not all the same, which can be understood through the concept of *market segments*. Finally, competitors' relative positions can be analysed using the *strategy canvas*, helping also to identify '*Blue Ocean*' opportunities in the marketplace.

This chapter works through these three layers in turn, starting with the macro-environment.

## 2.2 THE MACRO-ENVIRONMENT

This section introduces two interrelated tools – PESTEL and scenarios – for analysing the broad macro-environment of an organisation. PESTEL provides a wide overview and scenarios build on this in order to consider how the macro-environment might change. Both PESTEL and scenarios, however, can be overwhelming in the amount of issues that they uncover. So throughout this section we shall emphasise techniques and concepts that help focus the analysis on what is likely to matter most, particularly the *key drivers for change*.

### 2.2.1 The PESTEL framework

The **PESTEL framework** categorises environmental factors into key types.[1] PESTEL highlights six environmental factors in particular: political, economic, social, technological, ecological and legal. This range of factors underlines that the environment is not just about economic forces: there is an important *non-market* environment. Organisations needs to consider both market and non-market aspects of strategy (see Illustration 2.1 on BP).[2]

In practice, political, economic, social, technological, ecological and legal factors are often interconnected. Nevertheless, going through each of the six PESTEL factors helps raise a wide range of potentially relevant issues, as follows:

- *Politics* highlights the role of the state and other political forces. The state is often important as a direct economic actor, for instance as potential customer, supplier or owner of businesses. But there are also influences from various political movements, campaign groups or concerned media. Figure 2.2 is a matrix that helps identify both the relative importance of the state as direct economic actor and exposure to other political influences. Thus the state is often both the owner and key customer for defence companies, which are also exposed to political campaigning against the arms trade. Food companies are mostly privately owned and operate in private-sector markets, but are still exposed to great political pressures from campaigners for fair trade, labour rights and healthy eating. Canals are often state-owned but nowadays are not usually politically sensitive. Industries can rapidly change positions: thus after the financial crisis of 2008, banks moved towards both greater state ownership and increased political criticism.

# ILLUSTRATION 2.1    Oil's troubled waters

## In 2013, the controversial oil giant BP faced a complex environment.

BP is one of the world's largest oil and gas companies. It operates right across exploration, production, refining, distribution and marketing. It has about 21,000 service stations worldwide, half in the United States, 40 per cent in Europe. The largest sources of its oil production are Russia (about 45 per cent) and the USA (20 per cent); the USA accounts for about a quarter of its natural gas production and Russia about 10 per cent. Since 2005, BP has had a small alternative energy business, active in biofuels and windpower. In 2010, BP's Deepwater Horizon oil rig exploded, causing 11 deaths and an oil slick in the Gulf of Mexico covering 180,000 km². In 2012, the US government fined BP more than $4 bn (about £2.5 bn; €3 bn) for the disaster, and many court cases are still pending.

Some headline features of BP's environment include:

- *Political*: More than 80 per cent of the world's oil reserves are owned by state-controlled enterprises, the largest being Saudi Aramco and the Iranian National Oil Company. In 2013, BP's oil business in Russia was transferred from a controversial alliance with a group of leading Russian businessmen to a partnership with Rosneft, the state-controlled Russian oil company, in which BP would hold 18 per cent of the shares.
- *Economic*: *Forbes* magazine reports predictions of economic growth between 2012 and 2020 of 7 per cent per annum for China, about 2 per cent for the United States and 1 per cent for Europe. Oil prices peaked at about $120 a barrel in 2008, before dropping to around $30 as recession took hold in 2009, and recovering to around $100 in 2012. New extractive technologies led natural gas prices in the USA to fall 30 per cent between 2011 and 2013.
- *Social*: Car usage is falling in many European economies. After having doubled in the preceding 30 years, miles travelled in the United Kingdom by motor vehicles have fallen by about 1 per cent between 2008 and 2012; miles travelled by train reached a record in 2012, having increased by 50 per cent since the mid-1990s. From 2008 to 2012, the number of driving tests taken in the United Kingdom fell by about 17 per cent.
- *Technology*: New technologies include the exploitation of 'fire ice' (gas hydrates under the sea) and 'fracking', the extraction of gas by fracturing underground rock to produce 'shale gas'. Fire ice might eventually equal 4,000 times all the natural gas consumed in the US in 2010; fracking offers the prospect of doubling the world's available natural gas supply by 2020.
- *Ecological*: Fracking is liable to pollute local water supplies and even trigger small earthquakes. According to Cornell University, about 8 per cent of the gas extracted by fracking is released direct into the atmosphere, potentially a major contribution to global warming. In the USA, natural gas costs about $50 per megawatt hour to produce; wave $500; tidal $450; biomass $130; on-shore wind $80.
- *Legal*: The Deepwater Horizon disaster has led to new safety regulations for deepwater drilling. The European Union, where 90 per cent of oil extraction is from the sea, has imposed stricter exploration licensing procedures, risk assessment and financial guarantees against the costs of accidents. New regulations in the USA are estimated to increase costs by $1.5 m per oil well. In 2012, the USA banned BP from tendering for all government contracts.

*Sources*: BP Annual Report, 2012; *Business Week*, 7 March 2013; *Forbes*, 26 March 2012.

### Questions

1 Which of the above PESTEL factors offer the most important opportunities to BP, and which the most important threats?

2 Which of the above factors spill over from one PESTEL category to another? Does this matter?

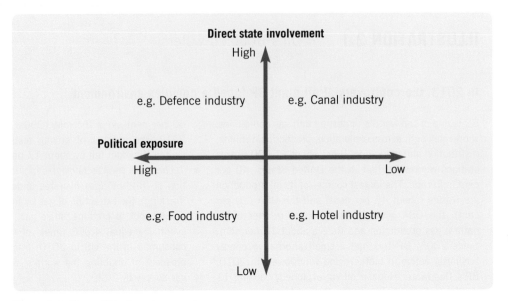

**Figure 2.2** The political environment

- *Economics* refers to macro-economic factors such as exchange rates, business cycles and differential economic growth rates around the world. It is important for a business to understand how its markets are affected by the prosperity of the economy as a whole. Managers should avoid over-confidence at the top of the business cycle, and excessive caution at the bottom. They should have a view on how changing exchange rates may affect viability in export markets and vulnerability to imports.

- *Social* influences include changing cultures and demographics. Thus, for example, the ageing populations in many Western societies create opportunities and threats for both private and public sectors. Changing cultural attitudes can also raise strategic challenges: for example, new ethical attitudes are challenging previously taken-for-granted strategies in the financial services industry.

- *Technological* influences refer to influences such as the internet, nano technology or the rise of new composite materials. As in the case of the internet in retailing, new technologies open up opportunities for some (e.g. Amazon), while challenging others (traditional stores).

- *Ecological* stands specifically for 'green' environmental issues, such as pollution, waste and climate change. Environmental regulations can impose additional costs, for example with pollution controls, but they can also be a source of opportunity, for example the new businesses that emerged around mobile phone recycling.

- *Legal* embraces legislative and regulatory constraints or changes. For example, legal changes might include restrictions on company mergers and acquisitions or new tax treatments of profits earned overseas. On the other hand, legal changes can provide opportunities, as for example the liberalisation of foreign investment in India.

As can be imagined, analysing these factors and their interrelationships can produce long and complex lists. Rather than getting overwhelmed by a multitude of details, it is necessary to step back eventually to identify the *key drivers for change*. **Key drivers for change are the environmental factors likely to have a high impact on the future success or failure of strategy**. Typical key drivers will vary by industry or sector. Thus a retailer may be primarily concerned with social changes driving customer tastes and behaviour, for example forces encouraging town centre shopping, and economic changes, for example rates of economic growth and employment. Public-sector managers are likely to be especially concerned with social change (e.g. rising youth unemployment), political change (e.g. changing government priorities) and legislative change (new training requirements). Identifying key drivers for change helps managers to focus on the PESTEL factors that are most important and which must be addressed most urgently. Without a clear sense of the key drivers for change, managers will not be able to take the decisions that allow for effective action.

## 2.2.2 Building scenarios

When the business environment has high levels of uncertainty arising from either complexity or rapid change (or both), it is impossible to develop a single view of how environmental influences might affect an organisation's strategies – indeed it would be dangerous to do so. Scenario analyses are carried out to allow for different possibilities and help prevent managers from closing their minds to alternatives. Thus scenarios offer plausible alternative views of how the business environment might develop in the future.[3] Scenarios typically build on PESTEL analyses and key drivers for change, but do not offer a single forecast of how the environment will change. The point is not to predict, but to encourage managers to be alert to a range of possible futures: for this reason, analyses typically produce three or four distinct scenarios. Effective scenario-building can help build strategies that are robust in the face of environmental change.

Illustration 2.2 shows an example of scenario planning for the global fashion industry to 2025. Rather than incorporating a multitude of factors, the authors focus on two key drivers which (i) have high potential impact; (ii) are uncertain; (iii) are largely independent from each other. These two drivers are the extent to which the world becomes more interconnected and the speed with which society, and fashion, changes. Both of these drivers may produce very different futures, which can be combined to create four internally consistent scenarios for the next decade and a half. The authors do not predict that one will prevail over the others, nor do they allocate relative probabilities. Prediction would close managers' minds to alternatives, while probabilities would imply a spurious kind of accuracy.

While there are many ways to carry out scenario analyses, five basic steps are often followed:[4]

- *Defining scenario scope* is an important first step. Scope refers to the subject of the scenario analysis and the time span. For example, scenario analyses can be carried out for a whole industry globally, or for particular geographical regions and markets. While businesses typically produce scenarios for industries or markets, governments often conduct scenario analyses for countries, regions or sectors (such as the future of healthcare or higher education). Scenario time spans can range from a decade or so (as in Illustration 2.2) or for just three to five years ahead. The appropriate time span is determined partly by the expected life of investments. In the energy business, where oil fields, for example, might have a life span of several decades, scenarios often cover 20 years or more.

# ILLUSTRATION 2.2    Scenarios for the global fashion industry, 2025

## Levi's uses students to investigate alternative futures.

During 2009–10, the clothing company Levi Strauss & Co., known worldwide for its jeans, worked with Masters students at the London College of Fashion to produce four scenarios for the global fashion industry in the coming 15 years. Levi Strauss knew that fashion was facing massive changes in fabric technologies, manufacturing locations, retailing and much more. It wanted to understand what kinds of futures it might have to deal with.

The students identified many important drivers that could simply be taken for granted: for instance, an ageing population and increasing natural resource constraints. However, they highlighted two key drivers that involved high uncertainty and that were largely independent of each other, and so could create divergent scenarios: interconnectivity and speed of change. The first driver offers two extreme points: on the one hand, a highly connected world with low trade barriers, integrated communications internationally and a homogenisation of cultures; on the other hand, a fragmented world with falling long-distance trade and strengthening regional identities. The second driver offers a range between fast change and slow change: a fast world would be one in which media and communications are increasingly instant, capital moves easily and people live hectic lives; a slow world would imply less emphasis on consumption and more conservatism in cultures.

The divergent directions of the two key drivers define four scenarios for 2025. The first is 'Slow is beautiful', based on a slow world with high interconnectivity. In this scenario, durability and sustainability would be highly important, but interconnectivity would allow people to swap and refurbish old clothes very easily: 'vBay' (like eBay) would emerge as a hugely popular website dedicated to vintage clothing. The second scenario, 'Community couture', would also be slow because of growing resource constraints, climate change and poverty, while political barriers would reduce interconnectivity in the form of international

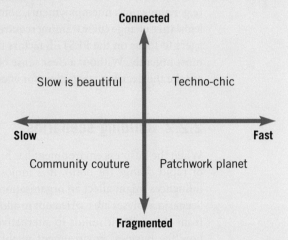

trade: new, fashionable clothes would only be for the privileged. 'Techno-chic' on the other hand would be the product of a fast-paced interconnected world: clothes would be 'smart', changing colour, carrying embedded media and even controlling bodily health. Pharmaceutical companies could be in the clothing business. Finally, the 'Patchwork planet' scenario imagines low interconnectivity but rapid change. In a 'Patchwork planet', fast-growing emerging economies would be culturally confident, so that national rather than global fashions would prevail: Western clothes might even be banned in some countries.

*Source*: http://www.forumforthefuture.org/project/fashion-futures-2025/overview.

---

### Questions

1 Which scenario would Levi Strauss most desire and which would it most fear?

2 What are the implications of these fashion industry scenarios for other industries, for example hotels or retail?

- *Identifying the key drivers for change* comes next. Here PESTEL analysis can be used to uncover issues likely to have a major *impact* upon the future of the industry, region or market. In the fashion industry, key drivers range from demographics to technology. However, two additional criteria are relevant: *uncertainty*, so that it is worthwhile considering different possible scenarios; and *mutual independence*, so that the drivers are capable of producing significantly divergent or opposing outcomes. In the oil industry, for example, political stability in the oil-producing regions is one major uncertainty; another is the capacity to develop major new oil fields, thanks to new extraction technologies. These could be selected as key drivers for scenario analysis because both are uncertain and regional stability is not closely correlated with technological advance.

- *Developing scenario 'stories'*: as in films, scenarios are basically stories. Having selected opposing key drivers for change, it is necessary to knit together plausible stories that incorporate both key drivers and other factors into a coherent whole. Thus in Illustration 2.2, the 'Techno-chic' scenario brings together in a consistent way a more global and integrated culture with a rapid rate of social, technological and economic change. But completing the story of 'Techno-chic' would also involve incorporating other consistent factors: for example, rapid development in China and India where low cost becomes supplanted by technological sophistication as source of advantage; free markets to allow rapid growth and international trade; and the creation of an under-employed working class whose cheap labour and outdated technological skills are no longer needed.

- *Identifying impacts* of alternative scenarios on organisations is the next key stage of scenario building. 'Techno-chic' might have a very negative impact for many traditional fashion labels and retailers who could not keep up with hi-tech clothing and distribution. On the other hand, 'Community couture' could see the strengthening of local craft producers. It is important for an organisation to carry out *robustness checks* in the face of each plausible scenario and to develop *contingency plans* in case they happen.

- *Establishing early warning systems*: once the various scenarios are drawn up, organisations should identify indicators that might give early warning about the final direction of environmental change, and at the same time set up systems to monitor these. Effective monitoring of well-chosen indicators should facilitate prompt and appropriate responses. In Illustration 2.2, indicators of a 'Slow is beautiful' trend might be low wage growth and rises in religious observance.

## 2.3 INDUSTRIES AND SECTORS

The previous section looked at how forces in the macro-environment might influence the success or failure of an organisation's strategies. But the impact of these general factors tends to surface in the more immediate environment through changes in the competitive forces surrounding organisations. An important aspect of this for most organisations will be competition within their industry, sector or market. **An industry is a group of firms producing products and services that are essentially the same.**[5] Examples are the automobile industry and the airline industry. Industries are also often described as 'sectors', especially in public services (e.g. the health sector or the education sector). Industries and sectors are often made up of several specific markets. **A market is a group of customers for specific products or services that are essentially the same (e.g. a particular geographical market).** Thus the automobile industry has markets in North America, Europe and Asia, for example.

This section concentrates on industry analysis, starting with Michael Porter's *Five Forces Framework* and then introduces two additional concepts, *complementors* and *industry life cycles*. While the following section will address markets in more detail, this section will refer to markets and most of the concepts apply similarly to markets and industries.

## 2.3.1 Competitive forces – the Five Forces Framework

Industries vary widely in terms of their attractiveness, as measured by how easy it is for participating firms to earn high profits. One key determinant of profitability is the extent of competition, actual or potential. Where competition is low, and there is little threat of new competitors, participating firms should normally expect good profits.

**Porter's Five Forces Framework[6] helps identify the attractiveness of an industry in terms of five competitive forces: (i) threat of entry, (ii) threat of substitutes, (iii) power of buyers, (iv) power of suppliers and (v) extent of rivalry between competitors.** These five forces together constitute an industry's 'structure' (see Figure 2.3), which is typically fairly stable. For Porter, an attractive industry structure is one that offers good profit potential. His essential message is that where the five forces are high, industries are not attractive to compete in. Excessive competitive rivalry, powerful buyers and suppliers and the threat of substitutes or new entrants will all combine to squeeze profitability.

Although initially developed with businesses in mind, the Five Forces framework is relevant to most organisations. It can provide a useful starting point for strategic analysis even where profit criteria may not apply. In the public sector, it is important to understand how powerful suppliers can push up costs; among charities, it is important to avoid excessive rivalry within the same market. Moreover, once the degree of industry attractiveness has been understood, the five forces can help set an agenda for action on the various critical issues that they identify: for example, what can competitors do to control excessive rivalry in a particular industry? The rest of this section introduces each of the five forces in more detail. Illustration 2.3 on the evolving steel industry provides examples.

### Competitive rivalry

At the centre of Five Forces analysis is the rivalry between the existing players – 'incumbents' in an industry. The more competitive rivalry there is, the worse it is for incumbents. **Competitive rivals are organisations with similar products and services aimed at the same customer group (i.e. not substitutes).** In the European airline industry, Air France and British Airways are rivals; high-speed trains are a 'substitute' (see below). Five factors tend to define the extent of rivalry in an industry or market:

- *Competitor balance.* Where competitors are of roughly equal size there is the danger of intensely rivalrous behaviour as one competitor attempts to gain dominance over others, through aggressive price cuts for example. Conversely, less rivalrous industries tend to have one or two dominant organisations, with the smaller players reluctant to challenge

**ILLUSTRATION 2.3**    The consolidating steel industry

**Five Forces analysis helps understand the attractiveness of an industry.**

For a long time, the steel industry was seen as a static and unprofitable one. Producers were nationally based, often state-owned and frequently unprofitable – the early 2000s saw 50 independent steel producers going into bankruptcy in the USA alone. But there then followed a surge in confidence. During 2006, Mittal Steel paid $35 bn (€24.5 bn) to buy European steel giant Arcelor, creating the world's largest steel company. The following year, Indian conglomerate Tata bought Anglo-Dutch steel company Corus for $13 bn. But these acquisitions were made just before the onset of the Great Recession in 2008 and further turmoil in the world steel industry.

### New entrants

In the last two decades, China has become a major force in the world steel industry. Between the early 1990s and 2011, Chinese producers increased their capacity seven times. Although the Chinese share of world production reached over 45 per cent by 2011, most of this was directed at the domestic market. None the less, China was the world's largest steel exporter in 2011, and there were fears that any slowdown in domestic demand would lead to a surge into international markets. The Chinese companies Herbei and Baosteel are ranked number two and number three in the world.

### Substitutes

Steel is a nineteenth-century technology, increasingly substituted for by other materials such as aluminium in cars, plastics and aluminium in packaging and ceramics and composites in many high-tech applications. Steel's own technological advances sometimes work to reduce need: thus steel cans have become about one-third thinner over the last few decades.

### Buyer power

The major buyers of steel are the global car manufacturers. Car manufacturers are sophisticated users, often leading in the technological development of their materials. In North America at least, the decline of the once dominant 'Big Three' – General Motors, Ford and Chrysler – has meant many new domestic buyers, with companies such as Toyota, Nissan, Honda and BMW establishing local production plants. Another important user of steel is the metal packaging industry. Leading can producers such as Crown Holdings, which makes one-third of all food cans produced in North America and Europe, buy in large volumes, coordinating purchases around the world.

### Supplier power

The key raw material for steel producers is iron ore. The big three ore producers – Vale, Rio Tinto and BHP Billiton – control about 70 per cent of the market for internationally traded ore. Iron ore prices had multiplied four times between 2005 and 2008, and, despite the recession, were still twice 2005's level in 2012.

### Competitive rivalry

World steel production increased by about 50 per cent between 2000 and 2008, dropped about 10 per cent in 2009, before recovering to reach a record in 2012. Despite acquisitions by companies such as Mittal and Tata, the industry is fragmented. The top five producers still accounted for only 17 per cent of world production in 2012, up only 3 per cent since 2000. The world's largest company, ArcelorMittal, accounted for just 7 per cent of production. Over-capacity in the European steel industry was estimated at 25 per cent in 2012, but when ArcelorMittal tried to close down its Florange plant, the French government threatened to nationalise it. After a cyclical peak in 2008, the world steel price was down 40 per cent by 2012, basically the same as in 2005.

---

### Questions

1 How attractive is the world steel industry? What accounts for this?

2 In the future, what might change to make the steel industry less attractive or more attractive?

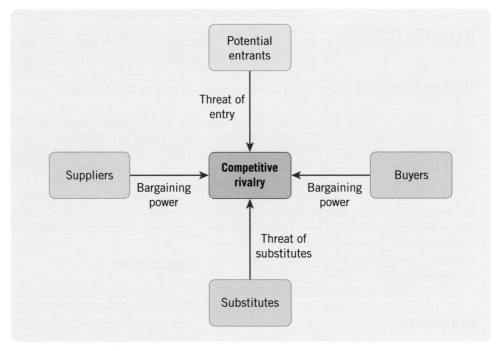

**Figure 2.3** The Five Forces Framework

*Source*: Adapted from *Competitive Strategy: Techniques for Analysing Industries and Competitors* The Free Press
(by Michael E. Porter 1998) with the permission of Simon & Schuster Publishing Group from the Free Press edition.
Copyright © 1980, 1998 by The Free Press. All rights reserved.

the larger ones directly (e.g. by focusing on niches to avoid the 'attention' of the dominant
companies).

- *Industry growth rate*. In situations of strong growth, an organisation can grow with the
  market, but in situations of low growth or decline, any growth is likely to be at the expense
  of a rival, and meet with fierce resistance. Low-growth markets are therefore often associated with price competition and low profitability. The *industry life cycle* influences growth
  rates, and hence competitive conditions: see section 2.3.2.

- *High fixed costs*. Industries with high fixed costs, perhaps because they require large investments in capital equipment or initial research, tend to be highly rivalrous. Companies will
  seek to spread their costs (i.e. reduce unit costs) by increasing their volumes: to do so, they
  typically cut their prices, prompting competitors to do the same and thereby triggering
  price wars in which everyone in the industry suffers. Similarly, if extra capacity can only
  be added in large increments (as in many manufacturing sectors, for example a chemical
  or glass factory), the competitor making such an addition is likely to create short-term
  over-capacity in the industry, leading to increased competition to maximise capacity usage.

- *High exit barriers*. The existence of high barriers to industry exit – in other words, closure or
  disinvestment – tends to increase rivalry, especially in declining industries. Excess capacity
  persists and consequently incumbents fight to maintain market share. Exit barriers might
  be high for a variety of reasons: for example, high redundancy costs or high investment in
  specific assets such as plant and equipment which others would not buy.

- *Low differentiation.* In a commodity market, where products or services are poorly differentiated, rivalry is increased because there is little to stop customers switching between competitors and the only way to compete is on price.

### The threat of entry

How easy it is to enter the industry influences the degree of competition. The greater the threat of entry, the worse it is for incumbents in an industry. An attractive industry has high barriers to entry in order to reduce the threat of new competitors. **Barriers to entry are the factors that need to be overcome by new entrants if they are to compete in an industry.** Five important entry barriers are:

- *Scale and experience.* In some industries, *economies of scale* are extremely important: for example, in the production of automobiles or the advertising of fast-moving consumer goods. Once incumbents have reached large-scale production, it will be very expensive for new entrants to match them and until they reach a similar volume they will have higher unit costs. This scale effect is increased where there are high *investment requirements* for entry, for example research costs in pharmaceuticals or capital equipment costs in automobiles. Barriers to entry also come from *experience curve* effects that give incumbents a cost advantage because they have learnt how to do things more efficiently than an inexperienced new entrant could possibly do (see section 5.2.1). Until the new entrant has built up equivalent experience over time, it will tend to produce at higher cost.

- *Access to supply or distribution channels.* In many industries manufacturers have had control over supply and/or distribution channels. Sometimes this has been through direct ownership (vertical integration), sometimes just through customer or supplier loyalty. In some industries this barrier has been overcome by new entrants who have bypassed retail distributors and sold directly to consumers through e-commerce (e.g. Dell Computers and Amazon).

- *Expected retaliation.* If an organisation considering entering an industry believes that the retaliation of an existing firm will be so great as to prevent entry, or mean that entry would be too costly, this is also a barrier. Retaliation could take the form of a price war or a marketing blitz. Just the knowledge that incumbents are prepared to retaliate is often sufficiently discouraging to act as a barrier.

- *Legislation or government action.* Legal restraints on new entry vary from patent protection (e.g. pharmaceuticals), to regulation of markets (e.g. pension selling), through to direct government action (e.g. tariffs). Of course, organisations are vulnerable to new entrants if governments remove such protection, as has happened with deregulation of the airline industry.

- *Differentiation.* Differentiation means providing a product or service with higher perceived value than the competition; its importance will be discussed more fully in section 5.2. Cars are differentiated, for example, by quality and branding. Steel, by contrast, is by and large a commodity, undifferentiated and therefore sold by the tonne. Steel buyers will simply buy the cheapest. Differentiation reduces the threat of entry because of increasing customer loyalty.

## The threat of substitutes

**Substitutes are products or services that offer a similar benefit to an industry's products or services, but have a different nature**. For example, aluminium is a substitute for steel; a tablet computer is a substitute for a laptop; charities can be substitutes for public services. Managers often focus on their competitors in their own industry, and neglect the threat posed by substitutes. Substitutes can reduce demand for a particular type of product as customers switch to alternatives – even to the extent that this type of product or service becomes obsolete. However, there does not have to be much actual switching for the substitute threat to have an effect. The simple risk of substitution puts a cap on the prices that can be charged in an industry. Thus, although Eurostar trains have no direct competitors in terms of rail services from Paris to London, the prices it can charge are ultimately limited by the cost of flights between the two cities.

There are two important points to bear in mind about substitutes:

- *The price/performance ratio* is critical to substitution threats. A substitute is still an effective threat even if more expensive, so long as it offers performance advantages that customers value. Thus aluminium is more expensive than steel, but its relative lightness and its resistance to corrosion gives it an advantage in some automobile manufacturing applications. It is the ratio of price to performance that matters, rather than simple price.

- *Extra-industry effects* are the core of the substitution concept. Substitutes come from outside the incumbents' industry and should not be confused with competitors' threats from within the industry. The value of the substitution concept is to force managers to look outside their own industry to consider more distant threats and constraints. The higher the threat of substitution, the less attractive the industry is likely to be.

## The power of buyers

**Buyers are the organisation's immediate customers, not necessarily the ultimate consumers** (for example, the 'buyers' for Unilever's shampoo products are typically supermarkets, not ordinary consumers). If buyers are powerful, then they can demand cheap prices or product or service improvements liable to reduce profits.

*Buyer power* is likely to be high when some of the following three conditions prevail:

- *Concentrated buyers.* Where a few large customers account for the majority of sales, buyer power is increased. This is the case on items such as milk in the grocery sector in many European countries, where just a few retailers dominate the market. If a product or service accounts for a high percentage of the buyers' total purchases, their power is also likely to increase as they are more likely to 'shop around' to get the best price and therefore 'squeeze' suppliers more than they would for more trivial purchases.

- *Low switching costs.* Where buyers can easily switch between one supplier and another, they have a strong negotiating position and can squeeze suppliers who are desperate for their business. Switching costs are typically low for weakly differentiated commodities such as steel.

- *Buyer competition threat.* If the buyer has the capability to supply itself, or if it has the possibility of acquiring such a capability, it tends to be powerful. In negotiation with its suppliers, it can raise the threat of doing the suppliers' job themselves. This is called *backward vertical integration* (see section 6.4), moving back to sources of supply, and might occur if satisfactory prices or quality from suppliers cannot be obtained. For example, some steel companies have gained power over their iron ore suppliers as they have acquired iron ore mines for themselves.

### The power of suppliers

**Suppliers are those who supply the organisation with what it needs to produce the product or service**. As well as fuel, raw materials and equipment, this can include labour and sources of finance. The factors increasing supplier power are the converse to those for buyer power. Thus *supplier power* is likely to be high where there are:

- *Concentrated suppliers*. Where just a few producers dominate supply, suppliers have more power over buyers. The iron ore industry is now concentrated in the hands of three main producers, leaving the steel companies, still relatively fragmented, in a weak negotiating position for this essential raw material.

- *High switching costs*. If it is expensive or disruptive to move from one supplier to another, then the buyer becomes relatively dependent and correspondingly weak. Microsoft is a powerful supplier because of the high switching costs of moving from one operating system to another. Buyers are prepared to pay a premium to avoid the trouble, and Microsoft knows it.

- *Supplier competition threat*. Suppliers have increased power where they are able to cut out buyers who are acting as intermediaries. Thus airlines have been able to negotiate tough contracts with travel agencies as the rise of online booking has allowed them to create a direct route to customers. This is called *forward vertical integration*, moving up closer to the ultimate customer.

## 2.3.2 Complementors and industry life cycles

Five Forces analysis can be supplemented by analysis of complementors and industry life cycles.

### Complementors

Some analysts argue that industry analyses need to include a 'sixth force': organisations that are complementors rather than simple competitors. **An organisation is your complementor if it enhances your business attractiveness to customers or suppliers.**[7] Thus for the Microsoft software business, McAfee computer security is a complement because its Windows software is more attractive to customers when securely protected. Even competing airline companies can be complementary to each other because for a supplier like Boeing it is more attractive to invest in particular improvements for two customers rather than one. Complementarity implies a significant shift in perspective. While Porter's Five Forces sees organisations as battling against each other for share of industry value, complementors may *cooperate* to increase the total value available. If Microsoft and McAfee keep each other in touch with their product developments, they increase the value of both their products. Opportunities for cooperation

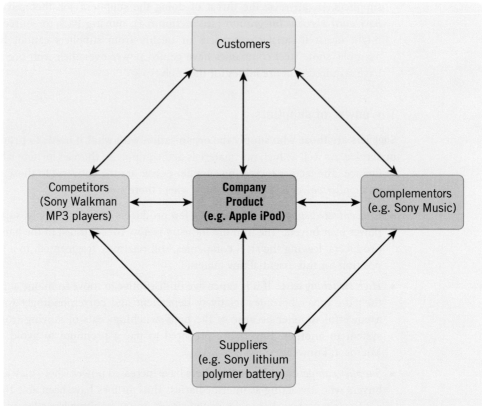

* An organisation is your complementor if:
  (i) customers value your product more when they have the other organisation's product than when they have the product alone (e.g. sausage and mustard);
  (ii) it's more attractive for suppliers to provide resources to you when it's also supplying the other organisation than when it's supplying you alone (airlines and Boeing).

*Note*: Organisations can play more than one role. Thus Sony Music (publisher of AC/DC, Sade etc) is a complementor to Apple's iPod; Sony is also a supplier of batteries to the iPod; Sony also competes with its own MP3 players.

**Figure 2.4** The value net

*Source*: Adapted from 'The Right Game', *Harvard Business Review*, July–August, pp. 57–64 ( Brandenburger, A. and Nalebuff, B. 1996), reprinted by permission of Harvard Business Review. Copyright © 1996 by the Harvard Business School Publishing Corporation. All rights reserved.

can be seen through a *value net*: a map of organisations in a business environment demonstrating opportunities for value-creating cooperation as well as competition. In Figure 2.4's value net analysis of the audio MP3 industry, Sony is a complementor, supplier and competitor to Apple's iPod. Sony and Apple have an interest in cooperating as well as competing.

## The industry life cycle

The power of the Five Forces typically varies with the stages of the industry life cycle. The industry life-cycle concept proposes that industries typically have four stages, similar to the life cycle of a human being. Although it is important to recognise that industries do not always follow standard life cycles, the model does raise valuable questions with regard to change in the Five Forces.[8]

The initial *development stage* of an industry is an experimental one, typically with few players, little direct rivalry and highly differentiated products. The Five Forces are likely to be weak, therefore, though profits may actually be scarce because of high investment requirements. The next stage is one of *high growth*, with rivalry low as there is plenty of market opportunity for everybody. Low rivalry and keen buyers of the new product favour profits at this stage, but these are not certain. Barriers to entry may still be low in the growth stage, as existing competitors have not built up much scale, experience or customer loyalty. Suppliers can be powerful too if there is a shortage of components or materials that fast-growing businesses need for expansion. The *shake-out stage* begins as the market becomes increasingly saturated and cluttered with competitors. Profits are variable, as increased rivalry forces the weakest competitors out of the business. In the *maturity stage*, barriers to entry tend to increase, as control over distribution is established and economies of scale and experience curve benefits come into play. Products or services tend to standardise, with relative price becoming key. Buyers may become more powerful as they become less avid for the industry's products and more confident in switching between suppliers. Profitability at the maturity stage relies on high market share, providing leverage against buyers and competitive advantage in terms of cost. Finally, the *decline stage* can be a period of extreme rivalry, especially where there are high exit barriers, as falling sales force remaining competitors into dog-eat-dog competition. However, survivors in the decline stage may still be profitable if competitor exit leaves them in a monopolistic position. Figure 2.5 summarises some of the conditions that can be expected at different stages in the life cycle.

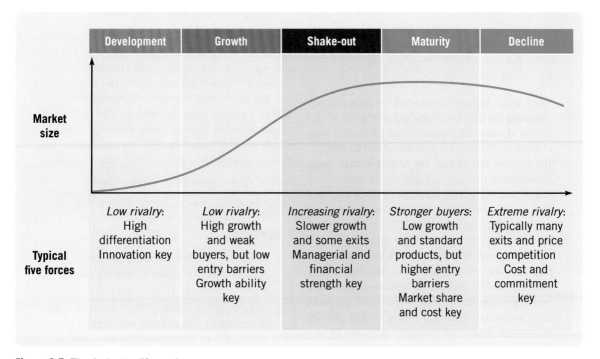

**Figure 2.5** The industry life cycle

# ILLUSTRATION 2.4 — Chugging and the structure of the charity sector

## Industry structure contributes to inefficiency and aggression in the United Kingdom's charity sector.

The charity sector has become controversial in the United Kingdom. The aggressive fund-raising of some charities is epitomised by workers soliciting donations from shoppers on a commission basis. Such is their perceived aggression that these charity workers are known as 'chuggers', compared with the violent street-crime of 'muggers'.

In 2008, there were 189,000 charities registered in England and Wales, 95 per cent having annual incomes of less than £500,000. However, about 80 per cent of all charity income is raised by the largest 20 charities, headed by Cancer Research UK (2008 income, £355 m (~€390 m; ~$532 m)). According to *Charity Market Monitor*, in 2008, the top 300 charities averaged a 0.9 per cent increase in income, but the largest 10 managed income growth of 2.3 per cent (excluding impact of mergers).

The United Kingdom government introduced the 2006 Charities Act with the specific intention of assisting mergers between independent charities. This had followed a report of the Charity Commission, the regulator for charities in England and Wales, which had commented on the charity sector thus:

'Some people believe that there are too many charities competing for too few funds and that a significant amount of charitable resource could be saved if more charities pooled their resources and worked together . . . The majority of charities are relatively small, local organisations that rely entirely on the unpaid help of their trustees and other volunteers. They may have similar purposes to many other charities but they are all serving different communities. The nature of these charities suggests that there are less likely to be significant areas of overlap . . . It is the much larger, professionally run, charities which, because of their size, tend to face charges of duplication, waste and over-aggressive fund-raising. While there are some clear advantages to be had from a healthy plurality of charities, which are constantly refreshed by new charities pursuing new activities, there are also big benefits of public confidence and support to be had from showing collaborative, as opposed to over-competitive, instincts.'

Local authorities in particular were frustrated by duplication and waste, as they increasingly commission local charities to deliver services. With respect to small charities, local authority budgets are relatively large. One charity sector chief executive, Caroline Shaw, told *Charity Times* as she pursued more cooperation between local charities:

'Without a doubt there is increased competition when it comes to [local authority] commissioning . . . Our driving force has really been to try to create a more effective service for front line organisations; to offer more projects, more diverse services, more effective services. There's a huge amount [of charities] all fighting for funding. I really think that people should be looking at working more closely together.'

During 2008, more than 230 charity mergers were registered with the Charity Commission. As the recession began to put pressure on charitable donations throughout the sector, early 2009 saw the merger of two well-established charities helping the elderly in the United Kingdom, Help the Aged and Age Concern. The new charity, Age UK, has a combined income of around £160 million, including £47 million a year raised through fund-raising, and over 520 charity shops.

*Sources*: 'RS 4a – Collaborative working and mergers: Summary', http://www.charity-commission.gov.uk/publications/rs4a.asp; *Charity Times*, 'Strength in Numbers', August 2007; *Charity Market Monitor*, 2009.

### Questions

1 Which of Porter's Five Forces are creating problems for the United Kingdom's charity sector?

2 In terms of the industry life cycle, what stage is the charity industry and what type of structure does that imply?

# 2.4 COMPETITORS AND MARKETS

An industry or sector may be too high a level to provide for a detailed understanding of competition. The Five Forces can impact differently on different kinds of players. For example, Hyundai and Porsche may be in the same broad industry (automobiles), but they are positioned differently: they are protected by different barriers to entry, and competitive moves by one are unlikely to affect the other. It is often useful to disaggregate. Many industries contain a range of companies, each of which has different capabilities and competes on different bases. Some of these competitor differences are captured by the concept of *strategic groups*. Customers too can differ significantly and these can be captured by distinguishing between different *market segments*. Thinking in terms of different strategic groups and market segments provides opportunities for organisations to develop highly distinctive positionings within broader industries. Competitor differences, both actual and potential, can also be analysed using the strategy canvas and '*Blue Ocean*' thinking, the last topic in this section.

## 2.4.1 Strategic groups[9]

**Strategic groups are organisations within an industry or sector with similar strategic characteristics, following similar strategies or competing on similar bases.** These characteristics are different from those in other strategic groups in the same industry or sector. For example, in the grocery retailing industry, supermarkets, convenience stores and corner shops each form different strategic groups. There are many different characteristics that distinguish between strategic groups but these can be grouped into two major categories. First, the *scope* of an organisation's activities (such as product range, geographical coverage and range of distribution channels used). Second, the *resource commitment* (such as brands, marketing spend and extent of vertical integration). Which characteristics are relevant differs from industry to industry, but typically important are those characteristics that separate high performers from low performers.

Strategic groups can be mapped onto two-dimensional charts – for example, one axis might be the extent of product range and the other axis the extent of vertical integration (i.e. how much companies rely on in-house operations). One method for choosing key dimensions by which to map strategic groups is to identify top performers (by growth or profitability) in an industry and to compare them with low performers. Characteristics that are shared by top performers, but not by low performers, are likely to be particularly relevant for mapping strategic groups. For example, the most profitable firms in an industry might all be narrow in terms of product range, and highly vertically-integrated, while the less profitable firms might be more widely spread in terms of products and less vertically-integrated, relying on external subcontractors for instance. Here the two dimensions for mapping would be product range and vertical integration. A potential recommendation for the less profitable firms would be to cut back their product range and increase their vertical integration.

Figure 2.6 shows strategic groups among Indian pharmaceutical companies, with research and development intensity (R&D spend as a percentage of sales) and overseas focus (exports and patents registered overseas) defining the axes of the map. These two axes do explain a good deal of the variation in profitability between groups. The most profitable group is the

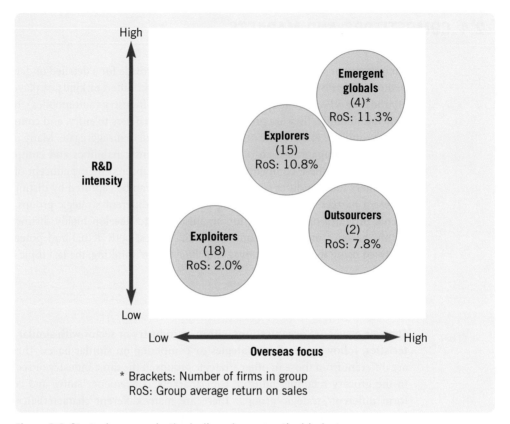

**Figure 2.6** Strategic groups in the Indian pharmaceutical industry

*Source:* Developed from R. Chittoor and S. Ray, 'Internationalisation paths of Indian pharmaceutical firms: a strategic group analysis', *Journal of International Management*, vol. 13 (2009), pp. 338–55.

Emergent globals (11.3 per cent average return on sales), those with high R&D intensity and high overseas focus. On the other hand, the Exploiter group spends little on R&D and is focused on domestic markets, and only enjoys 2.0 per cent average return on sales.

This strategic group concept is useful in at least three ways:

- *Understanding competition.* Managers can focus on their direct competitors within their particular strategic group, rather than the whole industry. They can also establish the dimensions that distinguish them most from other groups, and which might be the basis for relative success or failure. These dimensions can then become the focus of their action.

- *Analysis of strategic opportunities.* Strategic group maps can identify the most attractive 'strategic spaces' within an industry. Some spaces on the map may be 'white spaces', relatively under-occupied. In the Indian pharmaceutical industry, the white space is high R&D investment combined with focus on domestic markets. Such white spaces might be unexploited opportunities. On the other hand, they could turn out to be 'black holes', impossible to exploit and likely to damage any entrant. A strategic group map is only the first stage of the analysis. Strategic spaces need to tested carefully.

- *Analysis of mobility barriers.* Of course, moving across the map to take advantage of opportunities is not costless. Often it will require difficult decisions and rare resources. Strategic groups are therefore characterised by 'mobility barriers', obstacles to movement from one strategic group to another. These are similar to barriers to entry in Five Forces analysis. It would take a lot of investment and managerial skill to move from the Exploiter group of Indian pharmaceutical companies to the Emergent global group, however attractive that might seem. As with barriers to entry, it is good to be in a successful strategic group protected by strong mobility barriers, to impede imitation.

## 2.4.2 Market segments

The concept of strategic groups discussed above helps with understanding the similarities and differences in terms of competitor characteristics. The concept of market segment focuses on differences in *customer* needs. A **market segment**[10] **is a group of customers who have similar needs that are different from customer needs in other parts of the market.** Where these customer groups are relatively small, such market segments are often called 'niches'. Dominance of a market segment or niche can be very valuable, for the same reasons that dominance of an industry can be valuable following Five Forces reasoning.

For long-term success, strategies based on market segments must keep customer needs firmly in mind. Two issues are particularly important in market segment analysis, therefore:

- *Variation in customer needs.* Focusing on customer needs that are highly distinctive from those typical in the market is one means of building a long-term segment strategy. Steel producers might segment by industry, with automobile and domestic appliance customers having very different needs for the quality of sheet steel used in their products. Airlines segment by consumer type, business versus tourist for example. Being able to serve a highly distinctive segment that other organisations find difficult to serve is often the basis for a secure long-term strategy.

- *Specialisation* within a market segment can also be an important basis for a successful segmentation strategy. This is sometimes called a 'niche strategy'. Organisations that have built up most experience in servicing a particular market segment should not only have lower costs in so doing, but also have built relationships which may be difficult for others to break down. Experience and relationships are likely to protect a dominant position in a particular segment.

## 2.4.3 Competitor analysis and 'Blue Oceans'

Any environmental analysis should also include an analysis of position relative to competitors. As Michael Porter's Five Forces Framework underlines, reducing industry rivalry involves competitors finding differentiated positions in the marketplace. W. Chan Kim and Renée Mauborgne at INSEAD propose two concepts that help think about the relative positioning of competitors in the environment: the strategy canvas and 'Blue Oceans'.

**A strategy canvas compares competitors according to their performance on key success factors in order to establish the extent of differentiation.** Figure 2.7 shows a strategy canvas for three electrical components companies. The canvas highlights the following three features:

- **Critical success factors (*CSFs*) are those factors that either are particularly valued by customers (i.e. strategic customers) or provide a significant advantage in terms of cost.** Critical success factors are therefore likely to be an important source of competitive advantage or disadvantage. Figure 2.7 identifies five established critical success factors in this electrical components market (cost, after-sales service, delivery reliability, technical quality and testing facilities). Note there is also a new sixth critical success factor, design advisory services, which will be discussed under the third subhead, value innovation.

- **Value curves are a graphic depiction of how customers perceive competitors' relative performance across the critical success factors.** In Figure 2.7, companies A and B perform well on cost, service, reliability and quality, but less well on testing. They do not offer any design advice. They are poorly differentiated and occupy a space in the market where profits may be hard to get because of excessive rivalry between the two. Company C, on the other hand, has a radically different value curve, characteristic of a 'value innovator'.

- **Value innovation is the creation of new market space by excelling on established critical success factors on which competitors are performing badly and/or by creating new critical success factors representing previously unrecognised customer wants.** Thus in Figure 2.7, company C is a value innovator in both senses. First, it excels on the established customer need of offering testing facilities for customers' products using its components. Second, it offers a new and valued design service advising customers on how to integrate their components in order for them to create better products.

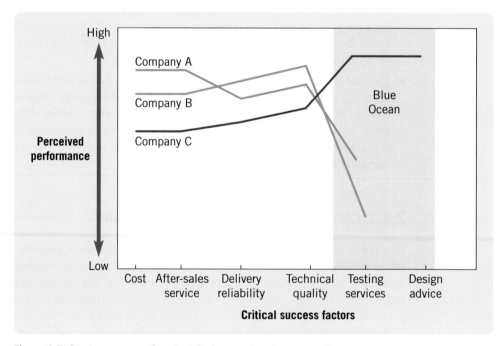

**Figure 2.7** Strategy canvas for electrical components companies

*Note*: cost is used rather than price for consistency of value curves.

*Source*: Developed from W.C. Kim and R. Mauborgne, *Blue Ocean Strategy*, Harvard Business School Press, 2005.

A value innovator is a company that competes in 'Blue Oceans'. **Blue Oceans are new market spaces where competition is minimised.**[11] Blue Oceans contrast with 'Red Oceans', where industries are already well defined and rivalry is intense. Blue Oceans evoke wide empty seas. Red Oceans are associated with bloody competition and 'red ink', in other words financial losses. The Blue Ocean concept is thus useful for identifying potential spaces in the environment with little competition. These Blue Oceans are *strategic gaps* in the marketplace.

In Figure 2.7, company C's strategy exemplifies two critical principles of Blue Ocean thinking: *focus* and *divergence*. First, company C focuses its efforts on just two factors, testing and design services, while maintaining only adequate performance on the other critical success factors where its competitors are already high performers. Second, it has created a value curve that significantly diverges from its competitors' value curves, creating a substantial *strategic gap*, or Blue Ocean, in the areas of testing and design services. This is shrewd. For company C, beating companies A and B in the areas where they are performing well anyway would require major investment and likely provide little advantage, given that customers are already highly satisfied. Challenging A and B on cost, after-sales service, delivery or quality would be a Red Ocean strategy, increasing industry rivalry. Far better is to concentrate on where a large gap can be created between competitors. Company C faces little competition for those customers who really value testing and design services, and consequently can charge good prices for them. The task for companies A and B now is to find strategic gaps of their own.

## 2.5 OPPORTUNITIES AND THREATS

The concepts and frameworks discussed above should be helpful in understanding the factors in the macro-, industry and competitor/market environments of an organisation. However, the critical issue is the *implications* that are drawn from this understanding in guiding strategic decisions and choices. The crucial next stage, therefore, is to draw from the environmental analysis specific strategic opportunities and threats for the organisation. Identifying these opportunities and threats is extremely valuable when thinking about strategic choices for the future (the subject of Chapters 5 to 9). Opportunities and threats form one half of the Strengths, Weaknesses, Opportunities and Threats (SWOT) analyses that shape many companies' strategy formulation (see section 3.4.3). In responding strategically to the environment, the goal is to reduce identified threats and take advantage of the best opportunities.

The techniques and concepts in this chapter should help in identifying environmental threats and opportunities, for instance:

- *PESTEL analysis* of the macro-environment might reveal threats and opportunities presented by technological change, or shifts in market demographics or such like factors.

- Identification of *key drivers for change* can help generate different scenarios for managerial discussion, some more threatening, others more favourable.

- *Porter's Five Forces analysis* might, for example, identify a rise or fall in barriers to entry, or opportunities to reduce industry rivalry, perhaps by acquisition of competitors.

- *Blue Ocean* thinking might reveal where companies can create new market spaces; alternatively it could help identify success factors which new entrants might attack in order to turn 'Blue Oceans' into 'Red Oceans'.

## SUMMARY

- Environmental influences can be thought of as layers around an organisation, with the outer layer making up the *macro-environment*, the middle layer making up the *industry or sector* and the inner layer *strategic groups* and *market segments*.

- The macro-environment can be analysed in terms of *PESTEL factors*, from which *key drivers of change* can be identified. Alternative *scenarios* about the future can be constructed according to how the key drivers develop.

- Industries and sectors can be analysed in terms of *Porter's Five Forces* – barriers to entry, substitutes, buyer power, supplier power and rivalry. Together, these determine industry or sector attractiveness. Industries and sectors can also be analysed in terms of *complementors* and the *industry life cycle*

- In the inner layer of the environment, *strategic group* analysis, *market segment* analysis and the *strategy canvas* can help identify strategic gaps or opportunities. *Blue Ocean* strategies are a means of avoiding *Red Oceans* with many similar rivals and low profitability.

- To watch an author video on the concepts discussed in this chapter please visit www.mystrategylab.com, and click on 'Author perspectives on strategic management'.

## VIDEO ASSIGNMENTS

MyStrategyLab

If you are using *MyStrategyLab* you might find it useful to watch the Nationwide and Pearson case study for Chapter 2.

1 Using the PESTEL framework as a starting point, discuss the main elements of the external environment that shape strategy at the Nationwide Building Society.

2 How is the nature of Pearson's competitors likely to change with the evolving nature of the textbook industry, and what critical success factors are likely to become important?

## RECOMMENDED KEY READINGS

- An introduction to the analysis of industries is M.E. Porter, 'The five competitive forces that shape strategy', *Harvard Business Review*, vol. 86, no. 1 (2008), pp. 58–77. An influential development on Porter's basic ideas is W.C. Kim and R. Mauborgne, *Blue Ocean Strategy: How to Create Uncontested Market Space and Make Competition Irrelevant*, Harvard Business School Press, 2005.

- For approaches to how environments change, see K. van der Heijden, *Scenarios: The Art of Strategic Conversation*, 2nd edn, Wiley, 2005, and the work of Michael Porter's colleague, A. McGahan, *How Industries Evolve*, Harvard Business School Press, 2004.

# REFERENCES

1. PESTEL is an extension of PEST (Politics, Economics, Social and Technology) analysis, taking more account of ecological and legal issues. For an application of PEST analysis to the world of business schools, see H. Thomas, 'An analysis of the environment and competitive dynamics of management education', *Journal of Management Development*, vol. 26, no. 1 (2007), pp. 9–21.

2. J. Doh, T. Lawton and T. Rajwani, 'Advancing non-market strategy research: institutional perspectives in a changing world', *Academy of Management Perspectives*, August (2012), pp. 22–38.

3. For a discussion of scenario planning in practice, see R. Ramirez, R. Osterman and D. Gronquist, 'Scenarios and early warnings as dynamic capabilities to frame managerial attention', *Technological Forecasting and Strategic Change*, vol. 80 (2013), pp. 825–38. For how scenario planning fits with other forms of environmental analysis such as PESTEL, see G. Burt, G. Wright, R. Bradfield and K. van der Heijden, 'The role of scenario planning in exploring the environment in view of the limitations of PEST and its derivatives', *International Studies of Management and Organization*, vol. 36, no. 3 (2006), pp. 50–76.

4. Based on P. Schoemaker, 'Scenario planning: a tool for strategic thinking'. *Sloan Management Review*, vol. 36 (1995), pp. 25–34.

5. See M.E. Porter, *Competitive Strategy: Techniques for Analyzing Industries and Competitors*, Free Press, 1980, p. 5.

6. An updated discussion of the classic framework is M. Porter, 'The five competitive forces that shape strategy', *Harvard Business Review*, vol. 86, no. 1 (2008), pp. 58–77.

7. A. Brandenburger and B. Nalebuff, 'The right game', *Harvard Business Review*, July–August 1995, pp. 57–64.

8. See A. McGahan, 'How industries evolve', *Business Strategy Review*, vol. 11, no. 3 (2000), pp. 1–16.

9. For examples of strategic group analysis, see G. Leask and D. Parker, 'Strategic groups, competitive groups and performance in the UK pharmaceutical industry', *Strategic Management Journal*, vol. 28, no. 7 (2007), pp. 723–45; and W. Desarbo, R. Grewal and R. Wang, 'Dynamic strategic groups: deriving spatial evolutionary paths', *Strategic Management Journal*, vol. 30, no. 8 (2009), pp. 1420–39.

10. A useful discussion of segmentation in relation to competitive strategy is provided in M.E. Porter, *Competitive Advantage*, Free Press, 1985, Chapter 7.

11. W.C. Kim and R. Mauborgne, 'How strategy shapes structure', *Harvard Business Review*, September 2009, pp. 73–80.

# Global forces and the advertising industry

Peter Cardwell

*This case is centred on the global advertising industry which faces significant strategic dilemmas driven by the rise of consumer spending in developing economies, technological convergence and pressures from major advertisers for results-based compensation. Strategy in this industry is further explored in* **The Strategy Experience** *simulation (http://www.mystrategylab.com/strategy-experience).*

In the second decade of the new millennium, advertising agencies faced a number of unanticipated challenges. Traditional markets and industry operating methods, developed largely in North America and Western Europe following the rise of consumer spending power in the twentieth century, were being radically reappraised.

The industry was subject to game-changing forces from the so-called 'digital revolution' with the entry of search companies like Google and Yahoo as rivals for advertising budgets. Changing patterns in global consumer markets have impacted on both industry dynamics and structure. Budgets being spent through traditional advertising agencies were being squeezed as industry rivalry intensified.

## Overview of the advertising industry

Traditionally, the business objective of advertising agencies is to target a specific audience on behalf of clients with a message that encourages them to try a product or service and ultimately purchase it. This is done largely through the concept of a brand being communicated via media channels. Brands allow consumers to differentiate between products and services and it is the job of the advertising agency to position the brand so that it is associated with functions and attributes which are valued by target consumers. These brands may be consumer brands (e.g. Coca-Cola, Nike and Mercedes Benz) or business-to-business (B2B) brands (e.g. IBM, Airbus Industrie and KPMG). Some brands target both consumers and businesses (e.g. Microsoft and Apple).

As well as private-sector brand companies, governments spend heavily to advertise public-sector services such as healthcare and education or to influence individual

**In July 2013 Maurice Levy (left), chief executive officer of Publicis Groupe SA, and John Wren, chief executive officer of Omnicom Group Inc., shake hands after signing the merger during a news conference held on the rooftop of the Publicis headquarters in Paris. In May 2014 the two companies abandoned their plan to create the world's largest advertising company, saying they couldn't overcome obstacles that had slowed progress toward the deal's completion.**

*Source*: Balint Porneczi/Bloomberg via Getty Images.

behaviour (such as 'Don't drink and drive'). For example, the UK government had an advertising budget of £285 m (€325) in 2012. Charities, political groups, religious groups and other not-for-profit organisations also use the advertising industry to attract funds into their organisation or to raise awareness of issues. Together these account for approximately 3 per cent of advertising spend.

Advertisements are usually placed in selected media (TV, press, radio, internet, etc.) by an advertising agency acting on behalf of the client brand company: thus they are acting as 'agents'. The client company employs the advertising agency to use its knowledge, skills, creativity and experience to create advertising and marketing to drive consumption of the client's brands. Clients traditionally have been charged according to the time spent on creating the advertisements plus a commission based on the media and services bought on behalf of clients. However, in recent years, larger advertisers such as Coca-Cola and Procter & Gamble have been moving away from this compensation model to a 'value' or results-based model based on a number of metrics, including growth in sales and market share.

## Growth in the advertising industry

Money spent on advertising has increased dramatically over the past two decades and is estimated in 2012 at over $165 bn (€127 bn, £102 bn) in the USA and $483 bn worldwide. While there might be a decline in recessionary years, it is predicted that spending on advertising will exceed $560 billion globally by 2015. Over 2011–12, the Dow Jones stock price index for the American media agencies sector (of which the leading advertising agencies are the largest members) rose about 15 per cent ahead of the New York Stock Exchange average (sources: bigcharts.com and dowjones.com).

The industry is shifting its focus as emerging markets drive revenues from geographic sectors that would not have been significant five to ten years ago, such as the BRIC countries and Middle East and North Africa. This shift has seen the emergence of agencies specialising in Islamic marketing, characterised by a strong ethical responsibility to consumers. Future trends indicate the strong emergence of consumer brands in areas of the world where sophisticated consumers with brand awareness are currently in the minority. (See Table 1.)

In terms of industry sectors, seven of the top 20 global advertisers are car manufacturers. However, the two major fmcg (fast-moving consumer goods) producers Procter & Gamble and Nestlé hold the two top spots for global advertising spend. Healthcare and beauty, telecommunications companies, food and beverage manufacturers, retailers and the entertainment industry are all featured in the top 20 global advertisers. The top 100 advertisers account for nearly 50 per cent of the measured global advertising economy.

## Competition in the advertising industry

Agencies come in all sizes and include everything from one- or two-person 'boutique' operations (which rely mostly on freelance outsourced talent to perform most functions), small to medium-sized agencies, large independents to multinational, multi-agency conglomerates employing over 150,000 people. The industry has gone through a period of increasing concentration through acquisition thereby creating multi-agency conglomerates such as those listed in Table 2. While these conglomerates are mainly head-quartered in London, New York and Paris, they operate globally.

**Table 1** Advertising expenditure by region. Major media (newspapers, magazines, television, radio, cinema, outdoor, internet) (US$ million, currency conversion at 2009 average rates)

| | 2009 | 2010 | 2011 | 2012 | 2013 |
|---|---|---|---|---|---|
| N America | 156,556 | 160,386 | 164,516 | 169,277 | 175,024 |
| W Europe | 100,143 | 104,225 | 107,520 | 111,300 | 114,712 |
| Asia Pacific | 99,746 | 106,021 | 113,345 | 122,000 | 130,711 |
| C & E Europe | 25,402 | 27,095 | 29,243 | 32,284 | 35,514 |
| Latin America | 25,711 | 29,315 | 31,673 | 34,082 | 36,836 |
| Africa/ME/ROW | 21,220 | 22,654 | 24,150 | 25,941 | 28,044 |
| **World** | **428,778** | **449,696** | **470,447** | **494,884** | **520,841** |

*Source*: ZenithOptimedia, September 2012.

**Table 2** Top five multi-agency conglomerates: 2011, by revenue, profit before interest and tax, number of employees and agency brands

| Group name | Revenue | PBIT | Employees | Advertising agency brands |
|---|---|---|---|---|
| WPP (UK) | £10.2 bn | £1.429 bn | 158,000 | JWT, Grey, Ogilvy, Y&R |
| Omnicom (US) | $13.9 bn | $952 m | 70,600 | BBDO, DDB, TBWA |
| Publicis Groupe (France) | €5.8 bn | €600 m | 53,807 | Leo Burnett, Saatchi & Saatchi, Publicis, BBH |
| IPG (US) | $7.0 bn | $520 m | 43,500 | McCann Erickson, FCB, Lowe & Partners |
| Havas Worldwide (France) | €1.65 bn | €220 m | 15,186 | Havas Conseil |

*Source*: Ad Age, Omnicom, WPP, Publicis Groupe, IPG, Havas.

Large multi-agency conglomerates compete on the basis of the quality of their creative teams (as indicated by industry awards), the ability to buy media more cost-effectively, market knowledge, global reach and breadth and range of services. Some agency groups have integrated vertically into higher-margin marketing services. Omnicom, through its Diversified Agency Services, has acquired printing services and telemarketing/customer care companies. Other agency groups have vertically integrated to lesser or greater degrees.

Mid-sized and smaller boutique advertising agencies compete by delivering value-added services through in-depth knowledge of specific market sectors, specialised services such as digital and by building a reputation for innovative and ground-breaking creative advertising/marketing campaigns. However, they might be more reliant on outsourced creative suppliers than larger agencies.

Many small specialist agencies are founded by former employees of large agencies, such as the breakaway from Young & Rubicam to form the agency Adam + Eve. In turn, smaller specialist agencies are often acquired by the large multi-agency conglomerates in order to acquire specific capabilities to target new sectors or markets or provide additional services to existing clients, like WPP's acquisition of a majority stake in the smaller ideas and innovation agency AKQA for $540 m 'to prepare for a more digital future'.

Recent years have seen new competition in this industry as search companies such as Google, Yahoo and Microsoft Bing begin to exploit their ability to interact with and gain information about millions of potential consumers of branded products.

Sir Martin Sorrell, CEO of WPP, the world's largest advertising and marketing services group, has pointed out that Google will rival his agency's relationships with the biggest traditional media corporations such as TV, newspaper and magazine and possibly even become a rival for the relationships with WPP's clients. WPP group spent more than $2 bn with Google in 2012 (over double the $850 m the group spent on the internet company just four years previously) and $400 m with Facebook. Sorrell calls Google a 'frenemy' – the combination of 'friend' and 'enemy'. Google is a 'friend' where it allows WPP to place targeted advertising based on Google analytics and an 'enemy' where it does not share these analytics with the agency and becomes a potential competitor for the customer insight and advertising traditionally created by WPP.

With the development of the internet and online search advertising, a new breed of interactive digital media agencies, of which AKQA is an example, established themselves in the digital space before traditional advertising agencies fully embraced the internet. These agencies differentiate themselves by offering a mix of web design/development, search engine marketing, internet advertising/marketing, or e-business/e-commerce consulting. They are classified as 'agencies' because they create digital media campaigns and implement media purchases of ads on behalf of clients on social networking and community sites such as MySpace, Facebook, YouTube and other digital media.

Online advertising budgets are increasing faster than other traditional advertising media as search companies like Google generate revenues from paid search as advertisers discover that targeted ads online are highly effective (see Table 3). By mid-2011 Google had a 40 per cent market share of the $31 bn spent on online advertising in the USA, with Facebook also increasing its share.

The disruptive change in the advertising industry at the beginning of the twenty-first century started with the internet. Many industry experts believe that convergence of internet, TV, smart phones, tablets and laptop computers

**Table 3** Advertising expenditure by medium (US$ million, currency conversion at 2009 average rates)

|  | 2009 | 2010 | 2011 | 2012 | 2013 |
|---|---|---|---|---|---|
| Newspapers | 97,237 | 94,199 | 93,019 | 92,300 | 91,908 |
| Magazines | 43,844 | 43,184 | 42,644 | 42,372 | 42,300 |
| Television | 165,260 | 180,280 | 191,198 | 202,380 | 213,878 |
| Radio | 31,855 | 31,979 | 32,580 | 33,815 | 35,054 |
| Cinema | 2,104 | 2,258 | 2,393 | 2,538 | 2,681 |
| Outdoor | 28,120 | 29,319 | 30,945 | 32,821 | 34,554 |
| Internet | 54,209 | 61,884 | 70,518 | 80,672 | 91,516 |
| **Total** | **422,629** | **443,103** | **463,297** | **486,898** | **511,891** |

*Note*: The totals in Table 3 are lower than in Table 1, since that table includes advertising expenditure for a few countries where it is not itemised by medium.

*Source*: ZenithOptimedia, September 2012.

is inevitable, which in turn will have a further major impact on the advertising industry. Advertising on mobile devices, such as smart phones and tablets, is still in its infancy but accounted for 8 per cent of all search advertising in the last quarter of 2011 and is forecast to reach 15 per cent by 2016, which has attracted Google to make acquisitions in this sector.

Factors that have driven competitive advantage to date may not be relevant to competitive advantage in the future. Traditionally this industry has embodied the idea of creativity as the vital differentiator between the best and the mediocre. Individuals have often been at the heart of this creativity. With the emergence of Google, Yahoo, Facebook and Bing, influencing and changing the media by which advertising messages are being delivered, a key question is whether creativity will be more or less important in the future, in relation to breadth of services and global reach.

*Sources and references: ZenithOptimedia,* September 2012; *Advertising Age;* Omnicom Group http://www.omnicomgroup.com; WPP Group http://www.wpp.com; Publicis http://www.publicisgroupe.com; Interpublic Group of Companies http://www.interpublic.com; Havas Conseils http://www.havas.com/havas-dyn/en/; http://www.financialcontent.com. *See also* The Strategy Experience: the Strategy Simulation designed for *Exploring Strategy:* http://www.mystrategylab.com/strategy-experience.

## Questions

1 Carry out a PESTEL analysis of the advertising industry in 2012, with particular attention to megatrends, inflexion points and weak signals.

2 Carry out a Five Forces analysis of the advertising industry in 2012. Which forces are becoming more negative or positive for the major advertising agencies?

# 3 STRATEGIC CAPABILLITIES

## Learning outcomes

After reading this chapter you should be able to:

- Identify strategic capabilities in terms of organisational resources and competences and how these relate to the strategies of organisations.

- Analyse how strategic capabilities might provide sustainable competitive advantage on the basis of their Value, Rarity, Inimitability and Organisational support (VRIO).

- Diagnose strategic capability by means of VRIO analysis, benchmarking, value chain analysis, activity mapping and SWOT analysis.

## Key terms

competences p. 50

dynamic capabilities p. 51

inimitable capabilities p. 56

rare capabilities p. 56

resource-based view p. 49

resources p. 50

strategic capabilities p. 50

SWOT p. 68

threshold capabilities p. 53

value of capabilities p. 55

value chain p. 60

value system p. 60

VRIO p. 54

## 3.1 INTRODUCTION

Chapter 2 emphasised the importance of the external environment of an organisation and how it can create both strategic opportunities and threats. However, it is not only the external environment that matters for strategy; there are also differences between organisations that need to be taken into account. For example, manufacturers of saloon cars compete within the same industry and within the same technological environment, but with markedly different success. BMW has been relatively successful consistently; Ford and Chrysler have found it more difficult to maintain their competitive position. And others, such as Rover in the UK and SAAB in Sweden, have gone out of business (even though the brands as such have been acquired by others). It is not so much the characteristics of the environment which explain these differences in performance, but the differences in their company-specific strategic capabilities in terms of the resources and competences they have. This puts the focus on variations between companies within the same environment and industry and how they vary in their strategic capabilities and arrangements. It is the strategic importance of such capabilities that is the focus of this chapter.

The key issues posed by the chapter are summarised in Figure 3.1. Underlying these are two key concepts. The first is that organisations are not identical, but have different capabilities; they are 'heterogeneous' in this respect. The second is that it can be difficult for one organisation to obtain or copy the capabilities of another. The implication for managers is that they need to understand how their organisations are different from their rivals in ways that may be the basis of achieving competitive advantage and superior performance. These concepts underlie what has become known as the **resource-based view** (RBV) of strategy[1] (sometimes labelled the 'capabilities view') pioneered by Jay Barney at University of Utah: **that the competitive advantage and superior performance of an organisation are explained by the distinctiveness of its capabilities.** Resource – or capabilities – views have become very influential, but it should be borne in mind that while the terminology and concepts employed here align with these views, readers will find different terminology used elsewhere.

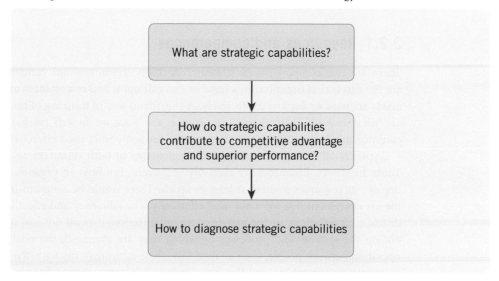

**Figure 3.1** Strategic capabilities: the key issues

The chapter has three further sections:

- Section 3.2 discusses the foundations of *strategic capability*; in particular what is meant by *resources, competences* and the related concept of *dynamic capabilities*. It also draws a distinction between *threshold capabilities* required to be able to compete in a market and *distinctive capabilities* that may be a basis for achieving competitive advantage and superior performance.

- Section 3.3 explains the ways in which distinctive capabilities can contribute to the *developing and sustaining of competitive advantage* (in a public-sector context the equivalent concern might be how some organisations sustain relative superior performance over time). In particular, the importance of the *Value, Rarity, Inimitability and Organisational support* (VRIO) of capabilities is explained.

- Section 3.4 moves on to consider different ways strategic capability might be analysed. These include *value chain analysis, VRIO analysis* and *activity system mapping*. The section concludes by explaining the use of *SWOT* analysis as a basis for pulling together the insights from the analyses of the environment (explained in Chapter 2) and of strategic capabilities in this chapter.

## 3.2 FOUNDATIONS OF STRATEGIC CAPABILITY

Given that different writers, managers and consultants use different terms and concepts, it is important to understand how concepts relating to strategic capabilities are used in this book. Here **strategic capabilities** are **the capabilities of an organisation that contribute to its long-term survival or competitive advantage.** However, to understand and to manage strategic capability it is necessary to explain its components and the characteristics of those components.[2]

### 3.2.1 Resources and competences

There are two components of strategic capability: resources and competences. **Resources are the assets that organisations have or can call upon and competences are the ways those assets are used or deployed effectively.** A shorthand way of thinking of this is that resources are 'what we *have*' (nouns) and competences are 'what we *do well*' (verbs). Other terms are common and 'capabilities' and 'competences' are sometimes used interchangeably.

Typically all strategic capabilities have elements of both resources and competences as Table 3.1 shows. Resources are certainly important, but how an organisation employs and deploys its resources matters at least as much. There would be no point in having state-of-the-art equipment if it were not used effectively. The efficiency and effectiveness of physical or financial resources, or the people in an organisation, depend not just on their existence, but on the systems and processes by which they are managed, the relationships and co-operation between people, their adaptability, their innovative capacity, the relationship with customers and suppliers, and the experience and learning about what works well and what does not.

**Table 3.1** Components of strategic capabilities

| Strategic capability | | |
|---|---|---|
| **Resources: what we have (nouns), e.g.** | | **Competences: what we do well (verbs), e.g.** |
| Machines, buildings, raw materials, products, patents, databases, computer systems | Physical | Ways of achieving utilisation of plant, efficiency, productivity, flexibility, marketing |
| Balance sheet, cash flow, suppliers of funds | Financial | Ability to raise funds and manage cash flows, debtors, creditors, etc. |
| Managers, employees, partners, suppliers, customers | Human | How people gain and use experience, skills, knowledge, build relationships, motivate others and innovate |

**Long-term survival and competitive advantage**

## 3.2.2 Dynamic capabilities[3]

If they are to provide a basis for long-term success, strategic capabilities cannot be static; they need to change. University of Berkeley economist David Teece has introduced the concept of **dynamic capabilities**, by which he means **an organisation's ability to renew and recreate its strategic capabilities to meet the needs of changing environments.** He argues that the capabilities that are necessary for efficient operations, like owning certain tangible assets, controlling costs, maintaining quality, optimising inventories, etc., are unlikely to be sufficient for sustaining superior performance.[4] These 'ordinary capabilities' allow companies to be successful and earn a living now by producing and selling a similar product or service to similar customers over time, but are not likely to provide for long-term survival and competitive advantage in the future.[5]

In other words Teece acknowledges the danger that capabilities that were the basis of competitive success can over time be imitated by competitors, become common practice in an industry or become redundant as its environment changes. So, the important lesson is that if capabilities are to be effective over time they need to change; they cannot be static. Dynamic capabilities are thus directed towards that strategic change. They are dynamic in the sense that they can create, extend or modify an organisation's existing operational capabilities. Teece suggests the following three generic types of dynamic capabilities:

- *Sensing.* Sensing implies that organisations must constantly scan, search and explore opportunities across various markets and technologies. Research and development and investigating customer needs are typical sensing activities. For example, companies in the PC operating systems industry, like Microsoft, have clearly sensed the opportunities in and threats from tablets and smart phones.

- *Seizing.* Once an opportunity is sensed it must be seized and addressed through new products or services, processes, activities, etc. Microsoft, for example, has started to seize opportunities by developing its own tablet device and software and by acquiring the mobile company Nokia.

- *Reconfiguring.* To seize an opportunity may require renewal and reconfiguration of organisational capabilities and investments in technologies, manufacturing, markets, etc. For example, Microsoft's inroad into tablets and smart phones requires major changes in its current strategic capabilities. The company must discard some of its old capabilities, acquire and build new ones and recombine them.

New product development is a typical example of a dynamic capability and strategic planning is another. They both involve activities that can sense and seize opportunities and that are intended to reconfigure capabilities.[6] Illustration 3.1 provides an example of dynamic capabilities in the context of mobile telephones.

---

## ILLUSTRATION 3.1     Dynamic capabilities in mobile telephone companies

**Dynamic capabilities can help firms sense and seize opportunities and reconfigure operational capabilities in changing environments.**

Companies in the mobile telephone industry have built on their dynamic capabilities in their effort to adapt to environmental changes and dominate the market. They have identified and evaluated new opportunities (sensing); addressed these opportunities with new products (seizing) and renewed and redeployed their capabilities accordingly (reconfiguring). This is illustrated in the table.

The pioneers in mobile telephony, Ericsson and Motorola, managed to sense and explore an entirely new mobile telephony market. They satisfied and captured value in that market by recombining and redeploying telecommunication and radio capabilities. However, they got stuck in these early mobile telephone capabilities and were followed by Nokia. Nokia sensed new opportunities as it realised that mobile phones' awkward design and functionality was not suited to what had become a mass consumer and fashion market. The company seized and addressed these new opportunities, offering improved design and functionality, building on design and consumer behaviour capabilities. Finally, Apple, with a

long legacy in consumer products, explored even further opportunities. Apple realised that most phones, even the new smart phones, still maintained a complex and unintuitive interface with limited multimedia functionalities. Apple addressed this by introducing an upgraded multimedia platform smart phone with an intuitive and simple interface combined with complementary services like the App Store and iTunes Music Store. Apple built on a recombination of its prior design, interface and consumer behaviour capabilities and new (for them) mobile phone capabilities.

While the dynamic capabilities of the mobile phone companies helped them adapt, they are no guarantee for keeping ahead permanently as the operating capabilities they developed risk becoming rigidities as markets and technologies change even further. If dynamic capabilities do not manage to detect and alleviate rigidities, competitors may emerge over time with more appropriate dynamic capabilities for the constantly changing environment.

### Questions

1 What type of dynamic capabilities could help companies avoid becoming stuck in their old capabilities?

2 a What are the possible future opportunities in mobile telephones?

  b How could they be sensed and seized?

  c What type of ordinary capabilities could possibly address them?

### 3.2.3 Threshold and distinctive capabilities

A distinction also needs to be made between strategic capabilities that are at a threshold level and those that might help the organisation achieve competitive advantage and superior performance. **Threshold capabilities are those needed for an organisation to meet the necessary requirements to compete in a given market and achieve parity with competitors in that market.** Without such capabilities the organisation could not survive over time. Indeed many start-up businesses find this to be the case. They simply do not have or cannot obtain the

| Companies | Approximate time period | Product | Sensing | Seizing | Reconfiguring |
|---|---|---|---|---|---|
| **Ericsson** (primarily Europe) **Motorola** (primarily the US) | Mid-1980s–late 1990s | Mobile phones | Need for mobile telephones: Fixed telephony did not offer mobility | Creating the first mobile telephone systems and telephones | Creating a new mobile telephone market Acquiring and building mobile telephone capabilities |
| Nokia | Late 1990s–early 2000s | Mobile phones with improved design and functionality | Need for well-designed and fashionable mobile phones: Existing mobile phones were close to their car-phone origins and maintained their awkward design and functionality | Upgrading the mobile phone to provide a richer experience in design, fashion and functionality | Entering the mobile telephone market Acquiring and building mobile telephony capabilities Building design and marketing capabilities |
| **Apple** | Late 2000s– | Mobile phones with perfected design, functionality and interface | Need for smart phones with multimedia functionality: Existing smart phones maintained a complex and unintuitive interface with limited functionalities | Upgrading the mobile phone to include an intuitive interface and multimedia functionalities containing the App store and iTunes | Entering the mobile telephone market Acquiring mobile telephony capabilities and recombining them with existing design, interface capabilities and brand Cooperating with the music and telephone app industries |

resources or competences needed to compete with established competitors. Identifying threshold requirements is, however, also important for established businesses. There could be changing *threshold resources* required to meet minimum customer requirements: for example, the increasing demands by modern multiple retailers of their suppliers mean that those suppliers have to possess a quite sophisticated IT infrastructure simply to stand a chance of meeting retailer requirements. Or they could be the *threshold competences* required to deploy resources so as to meet customers' requirements and support particular strategies. Retailers do not simply expect suppliers to have the required IT infrastructure, but to be able to use it effectively so as to guarantee the required level of service.

Identifying and managing threshold capabilities raises a significant challenge because threshold levels of capability will change as critical success factors change (see section 2.4.3) or through the activities of competitors and new entrants. To continue the example above, suppliers to major retailers did not require the same level of IT and logistics support a decade ago. But the retailers' drive to reduce costs, improve efficiency and ensure availability of merchandise to their customers means that their expectations of their suppliers have increased markedly in that time and continue to do so. So there is a need for those suppliers continuously to review and improve their logistics resource and competence base just to stay in business.

While threshold capabilities are important, they do not of themselves create competitive advantage or the basis of superior performance. **Distinctive capabilities are required to achieve competitive advantage.** These are dependent on an organisation having distinctive or unique capabilities that of value to customers and which competitors find difficult to imitate. This could be because the organisation has *distinctive resources* that critically underpin competitive advantage and that others cannot imitate or obtain – a long-established brand, for example. Or it could be that an organisation achieves competitive advantage because it has *distinctive competences* – ways of doing things that are unique to that organisation and effectively utilised so as to be valuable to customers and difficult for competitors to obtain or imitate. The emphasis is thus on the linked set of skills, activities and resources.

Bringing these concepts together, a supplier that achieves competitive advantage in a retail market might have done so on the basis of a distinctive resource such as a powerful brand, but also by distinctive competences such as the building of excellent relations with retailers. The distinctive competences that are likely to be most difficult for competitors to match and form the basis of competitive advantage will be the multiple and linked ways of providing products, high levels of service and building relationships. Section 3.3 that follows discusses in more depth the role played by distinctive resources and competences in contributing to long-term, sustainable competitive advantage and the importance of linkages between activities.

## 3.3 'VRIO' STRATEGIC CAPABILITIES AS A BASIS OF COMPETITIVE ADVANTAGE

As explained above, distinctive capabilities are necessary for sustainable competitive advantage and superior economic performance. **This section considers four key criteria by which capabilities can be assessed in terms of their providing a basis for achieving such competitive advantage: value, rarity, inimitability and organisational support – or VRIO.**[7] Figure 3.2 illustrates these four fundamental criteria and the questions they address.

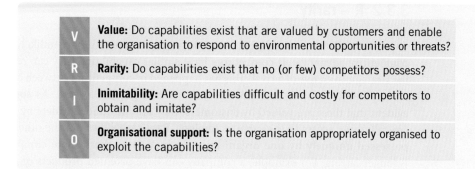

**Figure 3.2** VRIO

## 3.3.1 V – value of strategic capabilities

**Strategic capabilities are valuable when they create a product or a service that is of value to customers and if, and only if, they generate higher revenues or lower costs or both.** There are three components here:

- *Taking advantage of opportunities and neutralising threats*: the most fundamental issue is that to be valuable capabilities need to provide the potential to address the opportunities and threats that arise in the organisation's environment, which points to an important complementarity with the external environment of an organisation (Chapter 2). Capabilities are valuable if they address opportunities and/or threats and generate higher revenues or lower costs or both compared to if the organisation did not have those capabilities. For example, IKEA's cost-conscious culture, size and its intricate configuration of interlinked activities lower its costs compared to competitors and addresses opportunities of low-priced furniture that competitors do not attend to.

- *Value to customers*: it may seem an obvious point to make that capabilities need to be of value to customers, but in practice it is often ignored or poorly understood. For example, managers may seek to build on capabilities that *they* may see as valuable but which do not meet customers' critical success factors (see section 2.4.3). Or they may see a distinctive capability as of value simply because it is distinctive, although it may not be valued by customers. Having capabilities that are different from other organisations' is not, of itself, a basis of competitive advantage.

- *Cost*: the product or service needs to be provided at a cost that still allows the organisation to make the returns expected of it. The danger is that the cost of developing or acquiring the capabilities to deliver what customers especially value is such that products or services are not profitable.

Managers should therefore consider carefully which of their organisation's activities are especially important in providing such value and which are of less value. Value chain analysis and activity mapping explained in sections 3.4.1 and 3.4.2 can help here.

### 3.3.2 R – rarity

Capabilities that are valuable, but common among competitors, are unlikely to be a source of competitive advantage. If competitors have similar capabilities, they can respond quickly to the strategic initiative of a rival. This has happened in competition between car manufacturers as they have sought to add more accessories and gadgets to cars. As soon as it becomes evident that these are valued by customers, they are introduced widely by competitors who typically have access to the same technology. **Rare capabilities**, on the other hand, **are those possessed uniquely by one organisation or by a few others**. Here competitive advantage is longer-lasting. For example, a company can have patented products or services that give it advantage. Service organisations may have rare resources in the form of intellectual capital – perhaps particularly talented individuals. Some libraries have unique collections of books unavailable elsewhere; a company can have a powerful brand; or retail stores can have prime locations. In terms of competences, organisations can have unique skills developed over time or have built special relationships with customers or suppliers not widely possessed by competitors.

### 3.3.3 I – inimitability

It should be clear by now that the search for strategic capability that provides sustainable competitive advantage is not straightforward. Having capabilities that are valuable to customers and relatively rare is important, but this may not be enough. Sustainable competitive advantage also involves identifying **inimitable capabilities** – **those that competitors find difficult and costly to imitate or obtain or substitute**. If an organisation has a competitive advantage because of its particular marketing and sales skills, it can only sustain this if competitors cannot imitate, obtain or substitute for them or if the costs to do so would eliminate any gains made. Often the barriers to imitation lie deeply in the organisation in linkages between activities, skills and people.

At the risk of over-generalisation, it is unusual for competitive advantage to be explainable by differences in the tangible resources of organisations, since over time these can usually be acquired or imitated (key geographic locations, certain raw material resources, brands, etc., can, however, be exceptions). Advantage is more likely to be determined by the way in which resources are deployed and managed in terms of an organisation's activities; in other words on the basis of competences.[8] For example, as indicated above, it is unlikely that an IT system will improve an organisation's competitive standing in itself, not least because competitors can probably buy something very similar on the open market. On the other hand the competences to manage, develop and deploy such a system to the benefit of customers may be much more difficult and costly to imitate. Compared to physical assets and patents, competences, then, tend to involve more intangible imitation barriers. In particular, they often include *linkages* that integrate activities, skills, knowledge and people both inside and outside the organisation in distinct and mutually compatible ways. These linkages can make capabilities particularly difficult for competitors to imitate and three primary reasons why this may be so are discussed below.

## Complexity

The capabilities of an organisation can be difficult to imitate because they are complex and involve interlinkages. This may be for two main reasons:

- *Internal linkages.* There may be linked activities and processes that, together, deliver customer value. The discussion of activity systems in section 3.4.2 below explains this in more detail and shows how such linked sets of activities might be mapped so that they can be better understood. However, even if a competitor possessed such a map, it is unlikely that it would be able to replicate the sort of complexity it represents because of the numerous interactions between tightly knit activities and decisions.[9] This is not only because of the complexity itself but also because, very likely, it has developed on the basis of custom and practice built up over years and is specific to the organisation concerned. For example, companies like IKEA and Ryanair still enjoy competitive advantages despite the availability of countless case studies, articles and reports on their successes.

- *External interconnectedness.* Organisations can make it difficult for others to imitate or obtain their bases of competitive advantage by developing activities together with customers or partners such that they become dependent on them. This is sometimes referred to as *co-specialisation.* For example, an industrial lubricants business moved away from just selling its products to customers by coming to an agreement with them to manage the applications of lubricants within the customers' sites against agreed targets on cost savings. The more efficient the use of lubricants, the more both parties benefited.

## Causal ambiguity[10]

Another reason why capabilities might be difficult to imitate is that competitors find it difficult to discern the causes and effects underpinning an organisation's advantage. This is called *causal ambiguity.* This might be for at least two reasons. First because the capability itself is difficult to discern or comprehend, perhaps because it is based on tacit knowledge based on people's experience. For example, the know-how of the buyers in a successful fashion retailer may be evident in the sales achieved for the ranges they buy, but it may be very difficult for a competitor to see just what that know-how is. Second because competitors may not be able to discern which activities and processes are dependent on which others to form linkages that create distinctive competences. The expertise of the fashion buyers is unlikely to be lodged in the one individual or even one function. It is likely that there will be a network of suppliers, intelligence networks to understand the market and links with designers.

## Culture and history

Competences that involve complex social interactions and interpersonal relations within an organisation can be difficult and costly for competitors to imitate systematically and manage. For example, competences can become embedded in an organisation's culture. Coordination between various activities occurs 'naturally' because people know their part in the wider picture or it is simply 'taken for granted' that activities are done in particular ways. We see this in high-performing sports teams, in groups of people that work together to combine specialist skills as in operating theatres; but also, for example, in how some firms integrate

## ILLUSTRATION 3.2  Groupon and the sincerest form of flattery

**When a firm identifies a new market niche it must also make sure its strategic capabilities are valuable, rare, inimitable and supported by the organisation.**

Chicago-based Groupon was launched in 2008 by Andrew Mason with the idea to email subscribers daily deals of heavily discounted coupons for local restaurants, theatres, spas, etc. Groupon sells a coupon for a product and takes up to half of the proceeds, which represent a big discount on the product's usual price. In return, Groupon aggregates demand from the customers who receive its emails and this provides exposure to and increased business for the local merchants. The venture rapidly became the fastest-growing Internet business ever and grew into a daily deal industry giant. In 2010 Groupon rejected a $6 bn (€4.5 bn) takeover bid by Google and instead went public at $10 bn in November of 2011.

While Groupon's daily deals were valued by customers – the company quickly spread to over 40 countries – they also attracted first hundreds and later thousands of copycats worldwide. Investors started to question Groupon's business model and to what extent it had rare and inimitable strategic capabilities. In 2012 the CEO Andrew Mason denied in *Wall Street Journal* (*WSJ*) that the model was too easy to replicate:

'**There's proof. There are over 2000 direct clones of the Groupon business model. However, there's an equal amount of proof that the barriers to success are enormous. In spite of all those competitors, only a handful are remotely relevant.**'

This, however, did not calm investors and the online coupon seller's shares promptly fell by 80 per cent to its all-time low. The question thus remained – to what extent were Groupon's capabilities rare and inimitable? One significant asset Groupon had that is rare and possibly difficult to imitate is its impressive customer base of more than 50 million customers. The more customers, the better deals and this would make customers come to Groupon rather than the competitors and the cost for competitors to acquire customers would go up. Critics argued, however, that other companies such as Facebook, Google and Amazon had even broader user bases and could possibly become competitors. Further defending Groupon's competitiveness the CEO emphasised in *WSJ*

that it is not as simple as providing daily deals via email, but that a whole series of things have to work together and to imitate Groupon competitors would have to replicate everything in its 'operational complexity':

'**People overlook the operational complexity. We have 10,000 employees across 46 countries. We have thousands of salespeople talking to tens of thousands of merchants every single day. It's not an easy thing to build.**'

Another resource that Andrew Mason stressed was Groupon's advanced technology platform that allowed the company to 'provide better targeting to customers and give them deals that are more relevant to them'. Part of this platform, however, was got via acquisitions – a route competitors possibly could take as well.

If imitation is the highest form of flattery Groupon has been highly complimented. Hundreds of copycats have, however, left the business and Groupon has also beaten back more serious competitors, but the company continues to be under considerable pressure. In February 2013 founder and CEO Andrew Mason was forced to step down, which was a sign that many changes would come at Groupon.

*Sources*: All Things Digital, 2 November 2012, *Wall Street Journal*: http://allthingsd.com/20121102/groupon-shares-dive-to-new-low-a-year-after-the-ipo/; *Financial Times*, 14 May 2012; *Financial Times*, 2 March 2013; *Wall Street Journal*, 31 January 2012.

### Questions

1 Andrew Mason admits that Groupon has thousands of copycats, yet his assessment is that imitating Groupon is difficult. Do you agree?

2 Assess the bases of Groupon's strategic capabilities using the VRIO criteria (Figure 3.2 and Table 3.2).

3 Which is the most important strategic capability that provides, or could provide, Groupon with sustainable competitive advantage?

different activities in their business to deliver excellent customer service. Linked to this cultural embeddedness is the likelihood that such competences have developed over time and in a particular way. This history is specific to the organisation and cannot be imitated.

### 3.3.4  0 – organisational support

Providing value to customers and possessing capabilities that are rare and difficult to imitate provides a potential for competitive advantage. However, **the organisation must also be suitably organised to support these capabilities** including appropriate organisational processes and systems. This implies that to fully take advantage of the capabilities an organisation's structure and formal and informal management control systems need to support and facilitate their exploitation. The question of organisational support works as an adjustment factor. Some of the potential competitive advantage can be lost if the organisation is not organised in a way that it can fully take advantage of valuable and/or rare and/or inimitable capabilities.

In summary and from a resource-based view of organisations, managers need to consider whether their organisation has strategic capabilities to achieve and sustain competitive advantage. To do so they need to consider how and to what extent it has capabilities which are (i) valuable, (ii) rare, (iii) inimitable and (iv) supported by the organisation. Table 3.2 summarises the VRIO framework of capabilities and shows that there is an additive effect. Strategic capabilities provide sustainable bases of competitive advantage the more they meet all four criteria. Illustration 3.2 gives an example of the challenges in meeting these criteria in the context of an internet-based company.

## 3.4 DIAGNOSING STRATEGIC CAPABILITIES

So far this chapter has been concerned with explaining concepts associated with the strategic significance of organisations' resources and capabilities. This section now provides some ways in which strategic capabilities can be understood and diagnosed.

**Table 3.2** The VRIO framework

| Is the capability . . . | | | | |
|---|---|---|---|---|
| valuable? | rare? | inimitable? | supported by the organisation? | Competitive implications |
| No | – | – | No | Competitive disadvantage |
| Yes | No | – | ↑ | Competitive parity |
| Yes | Yes | No | ↓ | Temporary competitive advantage |
| Yes | Yes | Yes | Yes | Sustained competitive advantage |

*Source*: Adapted with the permission of J.B. Barney and W.S. Hesterly, *Strategic Management and Competitive Advantage*, Pearson, 2012.

### 3.4.1 The value chain and value system

**The value chain describes the categories of activities within an organisation which, together, create a product or service.** Most organisations are also part of a wider **value system, the set of inter-organisational links and relationships that are necessary to create a product or service.** Both are useful in understanding the strategic position of an organisation and where valuable strategic capabilities reside.

#### The value chain

If organisations are to achieve competitive advantage by delivering value to customers, managers need to understand which activities their organisation undertakes that are especially important in creating that value and which are not. This can then be used to model the value generation of an organisation. The important point is that the concept of the value chain invites the strategist to think of an organisation in terms of sets of activities. There are different frameworks for considering these categories: Figure 3.3 is a representation of a value chain as developed by Michael Porter.[11]

*Primary activities* are directly concerned with the creation or delivery of a product or service. For example, for a manufacturing business:

- *Inbound logistics* are activities concerned with receiving, storing and distributing inputs to the product or service including materials handling, stock control, transport, etc.

- *Operations* transform these inputs into the final product or service: machining, packaging, assembly, testing, etc.

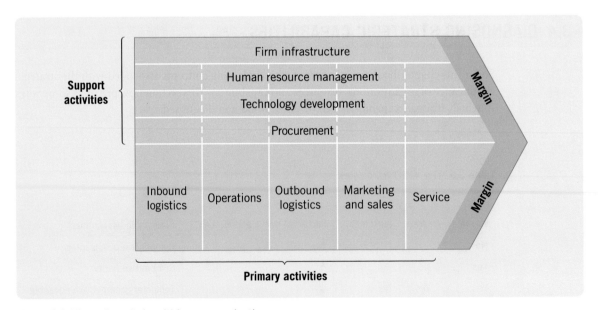

**Figure 3.3** The value chain within an organisation

*Source*: Adapted from *Competitive Advantage: Creating and Sustaining Superior Performance*, The Free Press (Porter, Michael E. 1998) with the permission of Simon & Schuster Publishing Group from the Free Press edition. Copyright © 1985, 1998 by Michael E. Porter. All rights reserved.

- *Outbound logistics* collect, store and distribute the product or service to customers; for example, warehousing, materials handling, distribution, etc.
- *Marketing and sales* provide the means whereby consumers or users are made aware of the product or service and are able to purchase it. This includes sales administration, advertising and selling.
- *Service* includes those activities that enhance or maintain the value of a product or service, such as installation, repair, training and spares.

Each of these groups of primary activities is linked to *support activities* which help to improve the effectiveness or efficiency of primary activities:

- *Procurement.* Processes that occur in many parts of the organisation for acquiring the various resource inputs to the primary activities. These can be vitally important in achieving scale advantages. So, for example, many large consumer goods companies with multiple businesses none the less procure advertising centrally.
- *Technology development.* All value activities have a 'technology', even if it is just know-how. Technologies may be concerned directly with a product (e.g. R&D, product design) or with processes (e.g. process development) or with a particular resource (e.g. raw materials improvements).
- *Human resource management.* This transcends all primary activities and is concerned with recruiting, managing, training, developing and rewarding people within the organisation.
- *Infrastructure.* The formal systems of planning, finance, quality control, information management and the structure of an organisation.

The value chain can be used to understand the strategic position of an organisation and analyse strategic capabilities in three ways:

- As a *generic description of activities* it can help managers understand if there is a cluster of activities providing benefit to customers located within particular areas of the value chain. Perhaps a business is especially good at outbound logistics linked to its marketing and sales operation and supported by its technology development. It might be less good in terms of its operations and its inbound logistics.
- In analysing the competitive position of the organisation using the *VRIO criteria* as follows:

  **V** Which *value*-creating activities are especially significant for an organisation in meeting customer needs and could they be usefully developed further?

  **R** To what extent and how does an organisation have bases of value creation that are *rare*? Or conversely are all elements of its value chain common to its competitors?

  **I** What aspects of value creation are difficult for others to *imitate*, perhaps because they are *embedded* in the activity systems of the organisation (see section 3.4.2 below)?

  **O** What parts of the value chain support and facilitate value creation activities in other sections of the value chain? For example, firm infrastructure support activities including particular formal and informal management control systems can be necessary to fully exploit value creation in the primary activities.

- To *analyse the cost and value of activities*[12] of an organisation. This could involve the following steps:

- *Identifying sets of value activities.* Figure 3.3 might be appropriate as a general framework here, or a value chain more specific to an organisation can be developed. The important thing is to ask (i) which separate categories of activities best describe the operations of the organisation and (ii) which of these are most significant in delivering the strategy and achieving advantage over competitors? For example, it is likely that in a branded pharmaceutical company research and development and marketing activities will be crucially important.

- *Relative importance of activity costs internally.* Which activities are most significant in terms of the costs of operations? Does the significance of costs align with the significance of activities? Which activities add most value to the final product or service (and in turn to the customer) and which do not? It can also be important to establish which sets of activities are linked to or are dependent on others and which, in effect, are self-standing. For example, organisations that have undertaken such analyses often find that central services have grown to the extent that they are a disproportionate cost to internal sets of activities and to the customer.

---

## ILLUSTRATION 3.3    A value system for Ugandan chilled fish fillet exports

**Even small enterprises can be part of an international value system. Analysing it can provide strategic benefits.**

A fish factory in Uganda barely made any profit. Fish were caught from small motorboats owned by poor fishermen from local villages. Just before they set out they would collect ice and plastic fish boxes from the agents who bought the catch on their return. The boxes were imported, along with tackle and boat parts. All supplies had to be paid for in cash in advance by the agents. Sometimes ice and supplies were not available in time. Fish landed with insufficient ice achieved half of the price of iced fish, and sometimes could not be sold to the agents at all. The fish factory had always processed the fillets in the same way – disposing of the waste back into the lake. Once a week, some foreign traders would come and buy the better fillets; they didn't say who they sold them to, and sometimes they didn't buy very much.

By mapping the value chain it was clear that there were opportunities for capturing more value along the chain and reducing losses. Together with outside specialists, the fish factory and the fishing community

developed a strategy to improve their capabilities, as indicated in the figure, until they became a flourishing international business, the Lake Victoria Fish Company, with regular air-freight exports around the world.

You can see more of their current operations at http://www.ufpea.co.ug/.

(The approximate costs and prices given represent the situation before improvements were implemented.)

### Questions

1 Draw up a value chain or value system for another business in terms of the activities within its component parts.

2 Estimate the relative costs and/or assets associated with these activities.

3 What are the strategic implications of your analysis?

- *Relative importance of activities externally.* How does value and the cost of a set of activities compare with the similar activities of competitors? For example, although they are both global oil businesses, BP and Shell are different in terms of the significance of their value chain activities. BP has historically outperformed Shell in terms of exploration, but the reverse is the case with regard to refining and marketing.

- *Where and how can costs be reduced?* Given the picture that emerges from such an analysis it should be possible to ask some important questions about the cost structure of the organisation in terms of the strategy being followed (or that needs to be followed in the future). For example, is the balance of cost in line with the strategic significance of the elements of the value chain? Can costs be reduced in some areas without affecting the value created for customers? Can some activities be outsourced (see section 6.5.), for example those that are relatively free-standing and do not add value significantly? Can cost savings be made by increasing economies of scale or scope; for example, through central procurement or consolidating currently fragmented activities (e.g. manufacturing units)?

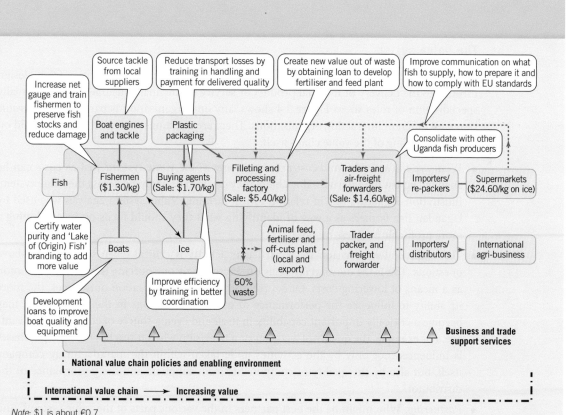

*Note*: $1 is about €0.7.

*Source*: Ian Sayers, Senior Adviser for the Private Sector, Division of Trade Support Services, International Trade Centre, Geneva. Email: sayers@intracen.org.

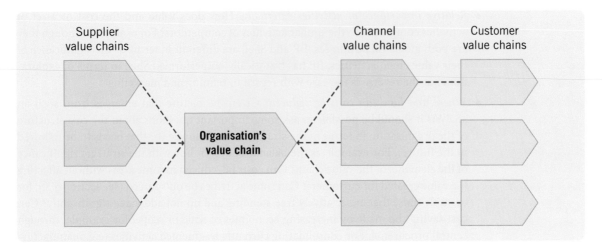

**Figure 3.4** The value system

## The value system

A single organisation rarely undertakes in-house all of the value activities from design through to the delivery of the final product or service to the final consumer. There is usually specialisation of roles so, as Figure 3.4 shows, any one organisation is part of a wider *value system* of different interacting organisations. There are questions that arise here that build on an understanding of the value chain itself:

- *What are the activities and cost/price structures of the value system?* Just as costs can be analysed across the internal value chain, they can also be analysed across the value system: Illustration 3.3 shows this in relation to fish farming. Value system analysis was used by Ugandan fish farmers as a way of identifying what they should focus on in developing a more profitable business model.

- *The 'make or buy'* decision for a particular activity is critical given some of the above questions. This is the *outsourcing* decision. Increasingly outsourcing is becoming common as a means of lowering costs. Of course, the more an organisation outsources, the more its ability to influence the performance of other organisations in the value system may become a critically important capability in itself and even a source of competitive advantage. For example, the quality of a cooker or a television when it reaches the final purchaser is influenced not only by the activities undertaken within the manufacturing company itself, but also by the quality of components from suppliers and the performance of the distributors.

- *Partnering.* Who might be the best partners in the various parts of the value system? And what kinds of relationships are important to develop with each partner? For example, should they be regarded as suppliers or should they be regarded as alliance partners (see section 9.4)?

### 3.4.2 Activity systems

The discussion so far highlights the fact that all organisations comprise sets of capabilities, but that these are likely to be configured differently across organisations. It is this variable configuration of capabilities that makes an organisation and its strategy more or less unique. So for the strategist, understanding this matters a good deal.

Value chain analysis can help with this, but so too can understanding the activity systems of an organisation. So it is important to identify what these activities are, why they are valuable to customers, how the various activities fit together and how they are different from competitors'.

A number of writers,[13] including Michael Porter, have written about the importance of mapping activity systems and shown how this might be done. The starting point is to identify what Porter refers to as 'higher order strategic themes'. In effect these are the ways in which the organisation meets the critical success factors determining them in the industry. The next step is to identify the clusters of activities that underpin each of these themes and how these do or do not fit together. The result is a picture of the organisation represented in terms of activity systems such as that shown in Illustration 3.4. This shows an activity systems map for the Scandinavian strategic communications consultancy, Geelmuyden.Kiese.[14] The core higher-order theme at the heart of its success is its knowledge, built over the years, of how effective communications can influence 'the power dynamics of decision-making processes'. However, as Illustration 3.4 shows, this central theme is related to other higher-order strategic themes, each of which is underpinned by clusters of supporting activities. Three points need to be emphasised here:

- *The importance of linkages and fit.* An activity systems map emphasises the importance of different activities that create value to customers pulling in the same direction and supporting rather than opposing each other. So the need is to understand (i) the fit between the various activities and how these reinforce each other and (ii) the fit externally with the needs of clients.

- *Relationship to VRIO.* It is these linkages and this fit that can be the bases of sustainable competitive advantage. In combination they may be *valuable* to clients, truly distinctive and therefore *rare*. Moreover, while individual components of an activity system might be relatively easy to imitate, in combination they may well constitute the complexity and causal ambiguity rooted in culture and history that makes them *inimitable*.

- *Superfluous activities.* Just as in value chain analysis, but at a more detailed level, the question can be asked: are there activities that are not required in order to pursue a particular strategy? Or how do activities contribute to value creation? If activities do not do this, why are they being pursued by the organisation? Whether Ryanair used activity mapping or not, it has systematically identified and done away with many activities that other airlines commonly have.

### 3.4.3 SWOT[15]

It can be helpful to summarise the key issues arising from an analysis of strategic capabilities discussed in this chapter and the analysis of the business environment discussed in Chapter 2

## ILLUSTRATION 3.4   Activity systems at Geelmuyden.Kiese

**The strategic capabilities of an organisation can be understood and analysed in terms of linked activities (an activity system).**

Geelmuyden.Kiese is the largest Scandinavian strategic communications consultancy – an extension of what has traditionally been known as public relations services (PR). Its clients include organisations in the financial, oil, energy, pharmaceuticals and healthcare sectors. These clients typically approach Geelmuyden.Kiese when they have a problem, the solution of which critically depends on effective external or internal communication. In this context, its services include facilitation of contacts with public agencies, officials and government, investor relations, media relations, communication campaigns for new product launches, crisis management and in-company communication on key strategic issues.

At the heart of the company's success is the knowledge it has built up since its founding in 1989 of the dynamics of decision-making processes, often within influential bodies such as government and, linked to this, 'how effective communication may move power within those decision-making processes'. This knowledge is underpinned by some key aspects in the way in which it does business.

- The company seeks to *work at a strategic level* with its clients, prioritising those clients where such work is especially valued. Here it employs its own in-house methodology, developed on the basis of years of experience, and systematically reviews the assignments it undertakes both internally and on the basis of client surveys.

- The company takes a clear stance on *integrity of communication*. It always advises openness of communication rather than suppression of information and only deals with clients that will accept such principles. It often takes a stance on this approach in controversial and high-profile issues in the public domain.
- Staff are given high degrees of *freedom* but with some absolute criteria of *responsibility*. In this regard there are strict rules for handling clients' confidential information and strict sanctions if such rules are broken.
- *Recruitment* is based on ensuring that such responsibility can be achieved. It is largely on the basis of values of openness and integrity but also humour. The emphasis tends to be on recruiting junior personnel and developing them. Geelmuyden.Kiese has learnt that this is a better way of delivering its services than recruiting established 'high-profile' consultants. Combined with its mentoring system for competence development of junior staff, it therefore believes that it offers the *best learning opportunities* in Scandinavia for young communications consultants.
- Geelmuyden.Kiese also offers *strong financial incentives* for top performance within the firm. Such performance includes rewards for the development of junior personnel but is also based on the internal evaluation of leadership qualities and performance.

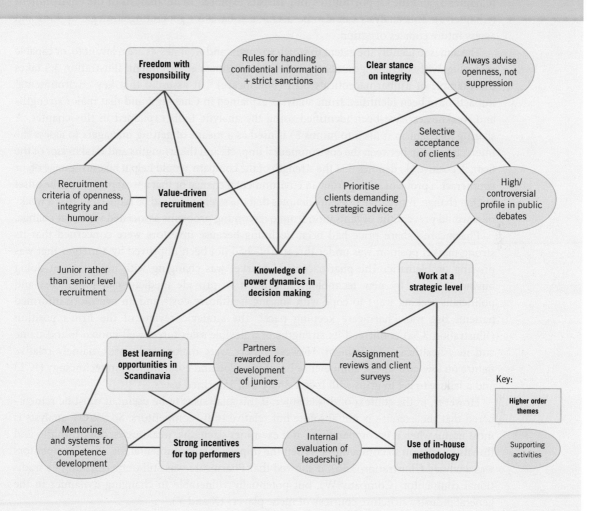

## Questions

1 Assuming Geelmuyden.Kiese managers are correct that they have capabilities that provide competitive advantage:

  a What would competitors find difficult to imitate and why?

  b Are there any activities that could be done away with without threatening that advantage?

2 If disaggregation (see section 3.4.3) is important, suggest what even more specific activities underpinning those in the activity map might be important.

to gain an overall picture of an organisation's strategic position. **SWOT provides a general summary of the Strengths and Weaknesses explored in an analysis of strategic capabilities** (Chapter 3) **and the Opportunities and Threats explored in an analysis of the environment** (Chapter 2). This analysis can also be useful as a basis for generating strategic options and assess future courses of action.

The aim is to identify the extent to which strengths and weaknesses are relevant to, or capable of dealing with, the changes taking place in the business environment. Illustration 3.5 takes the example of a pharmaceuticals firm (Pharmcare).[16] It assumes that key environmental impacts have been identified from analyses explained in Chapter 2 and that major strengths and weaknesses have been identified using the analytic tools explained in this chapter. A scoring mechanism (plus 5 to minus 5) is used as a means of getting managers to assess the interrelationship between the environmental impacts and the strengths and weaknesses of the firm. A positive (+) denotes that the strength of the company would help it take advantage of, or counteract, a problem arising from an environmental change or that a weakness would be offset by that change. A negative (−) score denotes that the strength would be reduced or that a weakness would prevent the organisation from overcoming problems associated with that change.

Pharmcare's share price had been declining because investors were concerned that its strong market position was under threat. This had not been improved by a merger that was proving problematic. The pharmaceutical market was changing with new ways of doing business, driven by new technology, the quest to provide medicines at lower cost and politicians seeking ways to cope with soaring healthcare costs and an evermore informed patient. But was Pharmcare keeping pace? The strategic review of the firm's position (Illustration 3.5a) confirmed its strengths of a flexible sales force, well-known brand name and new healthcare department. However, there were major weaknesses, namely relative failure on low-cost drugs, competence in information and communication technology (ICT) and a failure to get to grips with increasingly well-informed users.

However, in the context of this chapter, if this analysis is to be useful, it must be remembered that the exercise is not absolute but relative to its competitors. So SWOT analysis is most useful when it is comparative – if it examines strengths, weaknesses, opportunities and threats in relation to competitors. When the impact of environmental forces on competitors was analysed (Illustration 3.5b), it showed that Pharmcare was still outperforming its traditional competitor (Company W), but potentially vulnerable to changing dynamics in the general industry structure courtesy of niche players (X and Y).

There are two main dangers in a SWOT exercise:

- *Listing.* A SWOT exercise can generate very long lists of apparent strengths, weaknesses, opportunities and threats, whereas what matters is to be clear about what is really important and what is less important. So prioritisation of issues matters. Three brief rules can be helpful here. First, as indicated above, focus on strengths and weaknesses that differ in *relative* terms compared to competitors and leave out areas where the organisation is at par with competitors. Second, focus on opportunities and threats that are directly *relevant* for the specific organisation and industry and leave out general and broad factors. Third, summarise the *result* and draw concrete conclusions.

- *A summary, not a substitute.* SWOT analysis is an engaging and fairly simple tool. It is also useful in summarising and consolidating other analysis that has been explained in Chapters 2 and 3. It is not, however, a substitute for that analysis.

## ILLUSTRATION 3.5  SWOT analysis of Pharmcare

**A SWOT analysis explores the relationship between the environmental influences and the strategic capabilities of an organisation compared with its competitors.**

### (a) SWOT analysis for Pharmcare

| | Environmental change (opportunities and threats) | | | | | |
| --- | --- | --- | --- | --- | --- | --- |
| | Healthcare rationing | Complex and changing buying structures | Increased integration of healthcare | Informed patients | + | − |
| **Strengths** | | | | | | |
| Flexible sales force | +3 | +5 | +2 | +2 | 12 | 0 |
| Economies of scale | 0 | 0 | +3 | +3 | +6 | 0 |
| Strong brand name | +2 | +1 | 0 | −1 | 3 | −1 |
| Healthcare education department | +4 | +3 | +4 | +5 | 16 | 0 |
| **Weaknesses** | | | | | | |
| Limited competences in biotechnology and genetics | 0 | 0 | −4 | −3 | 0 | −7 |
| Ever lower R&D productivity | −3 | −2 | −1 | −2 | 0 | −8 |
| Weak ICT competences | −2 | −2 | −5 | −5 | 0 | −14 |
| Over-reliance on leading product | −1 | −1 | −3 | −1 | 0 | −6 |
| Environmental impact scores | +9 | +9 | +9 | +10 | | |
| | −6 | −5 | −13 | −12 | | |

### (b) Competitor SWOT analyses

| | Environmental change (opportunities and threats) | | | | |
| --- | --- | --- | --- | --- | --- |
| | Healthcare rationing | Complex and changing buying structures | Increased integration of healthcare | Informed and passionate patients | Overall impact |
| **Pharmcare** Big global player suffering fall in share price, low research productivity and post-mega-merger bureaucracy | **−3** Struggling to prove cost-effectiveness of new drugs to new regulators of healthcare rationing | **+6** Well-known brand, a flexible sales force combined with a new healthcare education department creates positive synergy | **−3** Weak ICT and lack of integration following mergers means sales, research and admin. are all underperforming | **−2** Have yet to get into the groove of patient power fuelled by the internet | **−2** Declining performance over time worsened after merger |
| **Company W** Big pharma with patchy response to change, losing ground in new areas of competition | **−4** Focus is on old-style promotional selling rather than helping doctors control costs through drugs | **−4** Traditional sales force not helped by marketing which can be unaccommodating of national differences | **+0** Alliances with equipment manufacturers but little work done across alliance to show dual use of drugs and new surgical techniques | **+4** New recruits in the ICT department have worked cross-functionally to involve patients like never before | **−4** Needs to modernise across the whole company |
| **Organisation X** Partnership between a charity managed by people with venture capital experience and top hospital geneticists | **+3** Potentially able to deliver rapid advances in genetics-based illnesses | **+2** Able possibly to bypass these with innovative cost-effective drug(s) | **+2** Innovative drugs can help integrate healthcare through enabling patients to stay at home | **+3** Patients will fight for advances in treatment areas where little recent progress has been made | **+10** Could be the basis of a new business model for drug discovery – but all to prove as yet |
| **Company Y** Only develops drugs for less common diseases | **+3** Partnering with big pharma allows the development of drugs discovered by big pharma but not economical for them to develop | **0** Focus on small market segments so not as vulnerable to overall market structure, but innovative approach might be risky | **+2** Innovative use of web to show why products still worthwhile developing even for less common illnesses | **+1** Freephone call centres for sufferers of less common illnesses Company, like patients, is passionate about its mission | **+6** Novel approach can be considered either risky or a winner, or both! |

Prepared by Jill Shepherd, Segal Graduate School of Business, Simon Fraser University, Vancouver, Canada.

### Questions

1  What does the SWOT analysis tell us about the competitive position of Pharmcare with the industry as a whole?

2  How readily do you think executives of Pharmcare identify the strengths and weaknesses of competitors?

3  Identify the benefits and dangers (other than those identified in the text) of a SWOT analysis such as that in the illustration.

| | | Internal factors | |
|---|---|---|---|
| | | **Strengths (S)** | **Weaknesses (W)** |
| **External factors** | **Opportunities (O)** | **SO Strategic options** Generate options here that use strengths to take advantage of opportunities | **WO Strategic options** Generate options here that take advantage of opportunities by overcoming weaknesses |
| | **Threats (T)** | **ST Strategic options** Generate options here that use strengths to avoid threats | **WT Strategic options** Generate options here that minimise weaknesses and avoid threats |

**Figure 3.5** The TOWS matrix

SWOT can also help focus discussion on future choices and the extent to which an organisation is capable of supporting these strategies. A useful way of doing this is to use a TOWS matrix[17] as shown in Figure 3.5. This builds directly on the information in a SWOT exercise. Each box of the TOWS matrix can be used to identify options that address a different combination of the internal factors (strengths and weaknesses) and the external factors (opportunities and threats). For example, the top left-hand box prompts a consideration of options that use the strengths of the organisation to take advantage of opportunities in the business environment. An example for Pharmcare might be the re-training of the sales force to deal with changes in pharmaceuticals buying. The bottom right-hand box prompts options that minimise weaknesses and also avoid threats; for Pharmcare this might include the need to develop its ICT systems to better service more informed patients. Quite likely this would also help take advantage of opportunities arising from changes in the buying structure of the industry (top right). The bottom left box suggests the need to use strengths to avoid threats, perhaps by building on the success of the healthcare education department to also better service informed patients.

## SUMMARY

- *The competitive advantage* of an organisation is likely to be based on the strategic *capabilities* it has that are valuable to customers and that its rivals do not have or have difficulty in obtaining. Strategic capabilities comprise both *resources and competences*.

- The concept of *dynamic capabilities* highlights that strategic capabilities need to change as the market and environmental context of an organisation changes.

- Sustainability of competitive advantage is likely to depend on an organisation's capabilities being of at least *threshold value* in a market, but also being *valuable*, relatively *rare*, *inimitable* and *supported by the organisation* and consequently fulfilling the *VRIO* criteria.

- Ways of diagnosing organisational capabilities include:
  - *VRIO analysis* of strategic capabilities as a tool to evaluate whether they contribute to competitive advantage.
  - Analysing an organisation's *value chain* and *value system* as a basis for understanding how value to a customer is created and can be developed.
  - *Activity mapping* as a means of identifying more detailed activities which underpin strategic capabilities.
  - *SWOT analysis* as a way of drawing together an understanding of the strengths, weaknesses, opportunities and threats an organisation faces.
- To watch an author video on the concepts discussed in this chapter please visit www.mystrategylab.com, and click on 'Author perspectives on strategic management'.

## VIDEO ASSIGNMENTS

MyStrategyLab

If you are using *MyStrategyLab* you might find it useful to watch the CISCO case study for Chapter 3.

1 Using the video, identify the distinctive strengths and capabilities that give CISCO a competitive advantage.

2 Using Figure 3.2 and Table 3.2 from the text and referring to the VRIO criteria, explain how CISCO may be able to sustain its competitive advantage over time.

## RECOMMENDED KEY READINGS

- For an understanding of the resource-based view of the firm, an early and much cited paper is by Jay Barney: 'Firm resources and sustained competitive advantage', *Journal of Management*, vol. 17 (1991), pp. 99–120. An overview of RBV research is written by Jay B. Barney, David J. Ketchen Jr and Mike Wright; 'The future of resource-based theory: revitalization or decline?', *Journal of Management*, vol. 37, no. 5 (2011), pp. 1299–315.
- For a critical discussion of the use and misuse of SWOT analysis see T. Hill and R. Westbrook, 'SWOT analysis: it's time for a product recall', *Long Range Planning*, vol. 30, no. 1 (1997), pp. 46–52.

## REFERENCES

1. The concept of resource-based strategies was introduced by B. Wernerfelt, 'A resource-based view of the firm', *Strategic Management Journal*, vol. 5, no. 2 (1984), pp. 171–80. The seminal and most cited paper is by Jay Barney, 'Firm resources and sustained competitive advantage', *Journal of Management*, vol. 17, no. 1 (1991), pp. 99–120.

2. The literature most commonly differentiates between 'resources' and 'capabilities'. See, for example, an early article by Raphael Amit and Paul Schoemaker: R. Amit, and P.J.H Schoemaker, 'Strategic assets and organizational rent', *Strategic Management Journal*, vol. 14 (1993), pp. 33–46; and Jay Barney's book: J.B. Barney, *Gaining and sustaining competitive advantage*, Addison-Wesley,

1997. The term 'core competences' was promoted by Gary Hamel and C.K. Prahalad in the early 1990s: G. Hamel and C.K. Prahalad, 'The core competence of the corporation', *Harvard Business Review*, vol. 68, no. 3 (1990), pp. 79–91. 'Capabilities' is, however, a more common term today, but it is sometimes used interchangeably with 'competences' in the literature. Later 'capabilities' has been distinguished into 'operational capabilities' and 'dynamic capabilities'. David Teece and his co-authors were first to introduce 'dynamic capabilities': D.J. Teece, G. Pisano and A. Shuen, 'Dynamic Capabilities and strategic management', *Strategic Management Journal*, vol. 18, no. 7 (1997), pp. 509–533. Sid Winter later explained the differences between 'ordinary' and 'dynamic capabilities': S.G. Winter, 'Understanding dynamic capabilities', *Strategic Management Journal*, vol. 24 (2003), no. 10, pp. 991–5.

3. For summary papers on dynamic capabilities see I. Barreto, 'Dynamic capabilities: a review of past research and an agenda for the future', *Journal of Management*, vol. 36, no. 1 (2010), pp. 256–80. The most comprehensive book on dynamic capabilities is written by C. Helfat, S. Finkelstein, W. Mitchell, M. Peteraf, H. Singh, D. Teece and S. Winter, *Dynamic Capabilities: Understanding Strategic Change in Organizations*, Blackwell Publishing, 2007.

4. David Teece has written about dynamic capabilities originally in D.J. Teece, G. Pisano and A. Shuen: 'Dynamic capabilities and strategic management', *Strategic Management Journal*, vol. 18, no. 7 (1997), pp. 509–34. More recently he has expanded his explanation in D.J. Teece, 'Explicating dynamic capabilities: the nature and microfoundations of (sustainable) enterprise performance', *Strategic Management Journal*, vol. 28, vol. 1 (2007), pp. 1319–50.

5. Sid Winter has explained the differences between ordinary and dynamic capabilities in S.G. Winter, 'Understanding dynamic capabilities', *Strategic Management Journal*, vol. 24, no. 10 (2003), pp. 991–5.

6. For a list of examples of dynamic capabilities see K.M. Eisenhardt and J.A. Martin, 'Dynamic capabilities: what are they?', *Strategic Management Journal*, vol. 21, no. 10/11 (2000), pp. 1105–21.

7. The VRIO criteria were introduced by Jay Barney in J.B. Barney, *Gaining and sustaining competitive advantage*, Addison-Wesley, 1997. Originally the acronym *VRIN* was used to also emphasise Non-substitutability and how competitors must not be able to substitute a valuable, rare and inimitable capability for another, but this is now encompassed in the inimitability criterion (see 1 above; Barney, 1991).

8. This is borne out in a meta-study of research on RBV by S.L. Newbert, 'Empirical research on the Resource Based View of the firm: an assessment and suggestions for future research', *Strategic Management Journal*, vol. 28 (2007), pp. 121–46.

9. For an explanation of how complex capabilities and strategies contribute to inimitability see J.W. Rivkin, 'Imitation of complex strategies', *Management Science*, vol. 46, no. 6 (2000), pp. 824–44.

10. The seminal paper on causal ambiguity is S. Lippman and R. Rumelt, 'Uncertain imitability: an analysis of interfirm differences in efficiency under competition', *Bell Journal of Economics*, vol. 13 (1982), pp. 418–38. For a summary and review of research on causal ambiguity see A.W. King, 'Disentangling interfirm and intrafirm causal ambiguity: a conceptual model of causal ambiguity and sustainable competitive advantage', *Academy of Management Review*, vol. 32, no. 1 (2007), pp. 156–78.

11. An extensive discussion of the value chain concept and its application can be found in M.E. Porter, *Competitive Advantage*, Free Press, 1985.

12. For an extended example of value chain analysis see 'Understanding and using value chain analysis' by Andrew Shepherd in *Exploring Techniques of Analysis and Evaluation in Strategic Management*, edited by Veronique Ambrosini, Prentice Hall, 1998.

13. See M. Porter, 'What is strategy?', *Harvard Business Review*, Nov.–Dec. (1996), pp. 61–78; and N. Siggelkow, 'Evolution towards fit', *Administrative Science Quarterly*, vol. 47, no. 1 (2002), pp. 125–59.

14. We are grateful for this example based on the doctoral dissertation of Bjorn Haugstad, *Strategy as the Intentional Structuration of Practice: Translation of Formal Strategies into Strategies in Practice*, submitted to the Saïd Business School, University of Oxford, 2009.

15. The idea of SWOT as a common-sense checklist has been used for many years: for example, S. Tilles, 'Making strategy explicit', in I. Ansoff (ed.), *Business Strategy*, Penguin, 1968. See also T. Jacobs, J. Shepherd and G. Johnson's chapter on SWOT analysis in V. Ambrosini (ed.), *Exploring Techniques of Strategy Analysis and Evaluation*, Prentice Hall, 1998. For a critical discussion of the (mis)use of SWOT, see T. Hill and R. Westbrook, 'SWOT analysis: it's time for a product recall', *Long Range Planning*, vol. 30, no. 1 (1997), pp. 46–52.

16. For background reading on the pharmaceutical industry see, for example, 'From vision to decision Pharma 2020', PWC, www.pwc.com/pharma, 2012; 'The pharmaceutical industry', Scherer, F.M., *Handbook of health economics*, vol. 1 (2000), part B, pp. 1297–336; 'A wake-up call for Big Pharma', *McKinsey Quarterly*, December 2011; and Gary Pisano, *Science Business*, Harvard Business School Press, 2006.

17. See H. Weihrich, 'The TOWS matrix – a tool for situational analysis', *Long Range Planning* (April 1982), pp. 54–66.

## Rocket Internet – will the copycat be imitated?

### Introduction

Rocket Internet is a very successful Berlin-based start-up incubator and venture capital firm. It starts, develops and funds e-commerce and other online consumer businesses. It has 25 offices around the world with over 700 employees and an additional 15,000 in its portfolio companies. It has helped create and launch over 100 start-ups and is currently active in more than 50 portfolio companies across more than 40 countries.

The company was founded by the Samwer brothers, Alexander, Oliver and Marc. After going to Silicon Valley in the late 1990s they became inspired by the Californian entrepreneurial culture and especially eBay. The brothers offered eBay to create a German version of the online auction house, but they received no reply from eBay. Instead they launched their own eBay clone, Alando, and adapted it to German conditions. A month later they were acquired by eBay for $50 m. This was to be their first great online success, but far from the last.

Next the brothers created Jamba, a mobile phone content platform. It was sold to VeriSign, a network infrastructure company, for $273 m in 2004. Since then they have become experts in spotting promising business models, especially in the USA, and imitating and scaling them internationally quicker than the originals. This model is the basis of Rocket Internet, which was founded in 2007. Several of their ventures have been acquired by the company with the original idea (see table). Two of their most high-profile ventures after Alando were CityDeal, which was sold off to American Groupon, and eDarling sold to American eHarmony.

**The Samwer brothers**

*Source*: Dieter Mayr Photography.

The company's model has frequently been criticised for simply being a copycat machine without any original ideas and some have even claimed it is a scam that rips off the originals. However, the question remains: if Rocket Internet has been so incredibly successful and what it does is simply copying, why has no one successfully imitated Rocket Internet yet? The brothers, through Oliver Samwer, defend their model in *Wired*:

'**But look at the reality. How many car manufacturers are out there? How many washing-machine manufacturers are there? How many Best Buys? Did someone write that Dixons copied Best Buy, or did anyone ever write that Best Buy copied Dixons, or that [German electronics retailer] Media Markt copied Dixons? No, they talk about Media Markt. They talk about Dixons. They talk about Best Buy. What is the difference? Isn't it all the same thing?'**

*Source*: http://www.economist.com/node/21525394#

| Company | Founded | Business | Buyer | Founded | Price, $m | Transaction date |
|---|---|---|---|---|---|---|
| Alando | 1999 | Online marketplace | eBay | 1995 | 50 | 1999 |
| cember.net | 2005 | Online business network | Xing | 2003 | 6.4 | 2008 |
| eDarling | 2009 | Online dating | eHarmony | 1998 | 30% stake* | 2010 |
| GratisPay | 2009 | Virtual currency for online games | SponsorPay | 2009 | *na*[†] | 2010 |
| CityDeal | 2009 | Discount deals for consumers | Groupon | 2008 | 126[†] | 2010 |
| Viversum | 2003 | Online astrology | Questico | 2000 | na | 2010 |

*With option to buy more [†] Including a stake in Groupon

*Source*: Gründerszene.de.

## Finance and expert teams

Rocket Internet has strong financial backup from its main investor globally, Kinnevik, a Swedish investment company. Kinnevik also contributes with its long-time experience from investing in new businesses and its global network of contacts. Many other investors invest directly in the start-ups and in the later growth stages, among them the American investment bank J.P. Morgan. To work with the investors and structure the financial solutions Rocket Internet has a team of about 35 experts in finance at the Berlin headquarters.

While Rocket Internet has the financial skills needed for an incubator and venture capital firm, it also develops the concepts of new ventures, provides the technology platforms and combines various skills necessary for setting up new ventures. It has about 250 specialists working at the Berlin head office. These specialists are part of diverse expert teams. Engineering including IT software, programming and web design skills are of course essential for product development. At head office there are around 200 engineers who have access to state-of-the art technologies and tools.

There are several other expert teams as well, not least in marketing, including experts in customer management, customer relationship marketing and online marketing. Other teams include Operations, Business Intelligence and HR. Apart from this expertise Rocket Internet has a Global Venture Development programme that includes a global mobile task force of entrepreneurial talents that can bring further know-how to all international markets. This task force includes venture developers with functional skills in product development, supply management, operations and online marketing. They rotate every 4–6 months to a new venture in another part of the world.

## Human resource management and culture

The HR team recruit not only regular staff support for Rocket Internet, but also specialists for the expert teams and Global Venture Development programme and, not least, the founders of the ventures. Based on their Silicon Valley entrepreneurial spirit they emphasise personal drive rather than good school grades. Head of HR, Vera Termuhlen, explains to VentureVillage.com:

> 'All in all, it doesn't matter if an applicant is from an elite university. For the area of global venture development, we look for applicants that are hands-on, first-class, have analytical skills, describe themselves as entrepreneurs, have a passion for the online start-up scene along and a

> willingness to work internationally, often in exotic locations like the Philippines or Nigeria.'

The co-founders and managing directors of the individual ventures establish all operations, build the team around a venture, and develop the business. They act as entrepreneurs and hold personal stakes in a venture's equity. Recruiting them is central and Rocket Internet normally recruits extraordinary, ambitious MBA-level graduates with high analytic skills from within the local regions where the venture is set up. As Alexander Kudlich, Managing Director of Rocket Internet, says:

> 'We are looking for those who from an analytical point of view understand the beauty of the business model, understand the rationale and understand what a huge opportunity is. Sometimes we say we are looking for analytical entrepreneurs rather than accidental billionaires.'

The company emphasises not only strong expertise, but 'a close cultural connection to Rocket Internet'. Rocket Internet has an intense entrepreneurial working culture that is highly performance driven including high pressure, long working hours, often from 09.00 to 23.00, and little job security. While this is attractive to some, the culture has also been criticised for being too tough and aggressive. Rocket Internet's Managing Director Alexander Kudlich comments on the culture:

> 'I would describe our culture as very focused, we have young teams – the average age is below 30. There is no place where you get more freedom and where you can take as much responsibility as you want. The only thing we want back is accountability.'

## Identification of business models and execution

While some of Rocket Internet's skills are common among other Berlin incubators and indeed incubators throughout Europe, the company is more of an international venture builder compared to most. Expertise is shared throughout the portfolio of ventures globally and its best practice can be applied across the diverse business models (ranging from online fashion to payments to deals to social networking). Compared to many other incubators, the function of the headquarters is central. While entrepreneurs are hired to oversee individual ventures, overall strategy for Rocket Internet is largely shaped at the head office. In particular, this is the case in the identification of new ideas, concepts and business models. The four managing directors at head office lead the scanning for and identification of novel and proven online and mobile transaction-based business models that are internationally scalable. Former Managing Director Florian Heinemann explains in *Wired*: 'We take a pretty systematic look at business models that are already out there and we basically try to define whether a model suits our competence and is large enough that it's worth it for us to go in there.'

Another significant aspect of Rocket Internet's centralised model is the speed at which it can launch novel business models internationally. This is different compared to many US counterparts, but also European ones. Rocket Internet has an international infrastructure and distribution network that build ventures on an international scale in just a few months. The capacity for multiplying business models has been demonstrated repeatedly for diverse types of online business models. As Managing Director Kudlich explains in *Wall Street Journal*:

**'When we identify a business model we can, within a few weeks, build a platform out of our central teams. In the meantime the local Rocket offices will have hired or allocated the people who will execute on the ground . . . That gives us the speed. The combination of access to the best talent in each country combined with highly standardised or modular approach in terms of platform and systems which are rolled out by our headquarters.'**

In brief, Rocket Internet specialises in execution rather than innovation. This is also how the management defend their model when they are blamed for simply being a clone machine. Oliver Samwer says that they are 'execution entrepreneurs' rather than 'pioneering entrepreneurs'. Managing Director Kudlich explains to *Inc. Magazine*: 'Which is harder: to have the idea of selling shoes online or to build a supply chain and warehouse in Indonesia? Ideas are important. But other things are more important.'

Paradoxically, even though Rocket Internet often builds on others' ideas it prefers to keep its own ideas for itself as explained by Marc Samwer in the *New York Times*: 'We really don't like to speak about our investments since our track record encourages people to set up competing sites . . . Ideas travel much faster these days.'

## The future

Rocket Internet's success has continued. Zalando, which initially mimicked the online shoe retailing business in the USA by Zappos, now part of Amazon, has expanded into clothing and jewellery. Sales are rising rapidly; annual revenues for 2011 were $650 m and Rocket Internet claim $130 m in revenue per month. Recently it has also launched

an Amazon clone, Lazada in South East Asia and a mobile payments company, Payleven, inspired by American Square.

Rocket Internet has, however, started to attract imitators of its own. One of the operations is Wimdu, a copy of the American Airbnb, which allows individual home and apartment owners to list their properties as holiday accommodation. However, Airbnb quickly formed a partnership with another Berlin incubator, Springstar, and they have since been rolling out Airbnb globally. Similarly, the original company responded swiftly when Rocket Internet imitated Fab.com, a designer deal site, with its Bamarang. Fab acquired Casacanda, a parallel European site, and quickly relaunched it as a Fab internationally and Rocket Internet had to close down Bamarang. Rocket Internet is even facing imitators from within. Two of its managing directors have together with other former employees left to set up the Berlin incubator 'Project A Ventures'. There are thus signs that Rocket Internet may eventually be imitated itself.

*Sources and references:* Joel Kaczmarek, 'An inside look at Rocket Internet', *VentureVillage.com*, 18 November 2012; Max Chafkin, 'Lessons from the world's most ruthless competitor', *Inc. Magazine*, 29 May 2012; Ben Rooney, 'Rocket Internet leads the clone war', *The Wall Street Journal*, 14 May 2012; Gerrit Wiesmann, 'Zalando to set foot in seven new countries', *Financial Times*, 26 March 2012; Tim Bradshaw, 'Facebook backers to take stake in Zalando', *Financial Times*, 2 February 2012; Matt Cowan, 'Inside the clone factory', *Wired UK*, 2 March 2012; Robert Levine, 'The kopy kat kids', *Cnnmoney.com*, 2 October 2007; *New York Times*, 3 December 2006; *The Economist*, 'Attack of the clones', 6 August 2011.

---

## Questions

1 Based on the data from the case (and any other sources available) use the frameworks from the chapter and analyse the strategic capabilities of Rocket Internet:

  **a** What are its resources and competences?

  **b** What are its threshold, distinctive and dynamic capabilities?

2 Based on your initial analysis and answers to question 1, carry out a VRIO analysis for Rocket Internet. What do you conclude? To what extent does Rocket Internet have strategic capabilities with sustained competitive advantage?

3 What is the importance of the Samwer brothers? What would happen if they left or sold the company?

# 4 STRATEGIC PURPOSE

## Learning outcomes

After reading this chapter you should be able to:

- Consider appropriate ways to express the *strategic purpose* of an organisation in terms of statements of *values*, *vision*, *mission* or *objectives*.
- Identify the influences of different *ownership structures* on strategic purpose.
- Understand the *governance issues* of an organisation.
- Undertake *stakeholder analysis* as a means of identifying the influence of different stakeholder groups in terms of their power and interest.
- Identify differences in the *corporate responsibility* stances taken by organisations.
- Understand how *organisational culture* can influence purpose and strategy.

## Key terms

corporate governance p. 84

corporate social responsibility p. 92

cultural web p. 96

governance chain p. 84

mission statement p. 79

objectives p. 80

organisational culture p. 94

paradigm p. 95

shareholder model p. 85

stakeholder mapping p. 89

stakeholders p. 78

statements of corporate values p. 80

vision statement p. 80

## 4.1 INTRODUCTION

Euan Sutherland had been recruited in 2013 as Chief Executive to tackle major problems the UK Co-Operative Group faced, not least in its banking business. Established in 1844 as a mutual society with close links to the UK Labour Party, the 'Co-Op' espoused social as well as economic aims and was run by a board elected by its members. But it had run into problems. The Co-Op Bank had pulled out of a major expansion programme to acquire 630 retail premises from a competitor. Major losses had led to the need to raise funds from institutional investors. And at the end of 2013 the Group's previous chairman, who had been appointed despite a lack of banking experience, had been arrested for buying illegal drugs. By early 2014 the Group was facing a £1.2 billion debt. Sutherland argued that the Co-Op needed a greater focus on financial objectives and was seeking to change the board to a more conventional PLC structure. On this he faced major opposition from those wanting to preserve the elected board structure they saw as fundamental to the Co-Op's social mission and political heritage. It was this opposition that led to Sutherland's resignation in March 2014, claiming that the business was 'ungovernable'.

The previous two chapters have looked at the influence of the environment and capabilities on an organisation's strategic position. The example of the Co-Operative Society also shows the importance of other influences on strategy development: being clear about what purposes drive strategy; and who and what influences such purpose, not least the cultural heritage of the organisation. These are the concerns of this chapter. An important concept here is that of **stakeholders, those individuals or groups that depend on an organisation to fulfil their own goals and on whom, in turn, the organisation depends**. An underlying question is whether the strategic purpose of the organisation should be determined in response to the expectations of a particular stakeholder, for example shareholders, or incorporate broader stakeholder interests – such as employees, customers, the local community or, more broadly, the good of society: a question that was central in The Co-Op. Figure 4.1 summarises the different influences on strategic purpose discussed in the chapter:

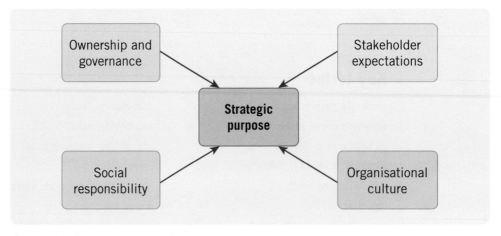

**Figure 4.1** Influences on strategic purpose

- Section 4.2 develops the discussion in Chapter 1 about ways in which organisations express *strategic purpose*, including statements of *mission, vision, values* and *objectives.*

- Section 4.3 considers the *ownership* structures and the *corporate governance* framework within which organisations operate. The concern, then, is both with the way in which owners influence strategic purpose, but also with how formally constituted bodies such as investors or boards of directors do so. In turn this raises issues of *accountability*: who are strategists accountable to?

- It is important to understand how different *stakeholders* may be involved in determining purpose and strategy. Section 4.4 addresses the different power and interest of various stakeholders through *stakeholder analysis.*

- Section 4.5 is concerned with issues of *social responsibility*. Here the question is which purposes an organisation *should* fulfil and how managers should respond to the expectations society has of their organisations.

- Finally section 4.6 considers how *organisational culture* can influence the purpose and the strategy of an organisation. It also provides a framework – *the cultural web* – by which the culture of an organisation can be understood.

## 4.2 MISSION, VISION, VALUES AND OBJECTIVES

Harvard University's Cynthia Montgomery[1] argues that defining and expressing a clear and motivating purpose for the organisation is at the core of a strategist's job. In the absence of such clarity, those who work within the organisation and those who observe it from the outside have to interpret for themselves why the organisation is doing what it is doing. Further, if the stakeholders of an organisation can relate to such a purpose it can be highly motivating.

Montgomery's view is that the stated purpose of the organisation should address two related questions: *how* does the organisation make a difference; and *for whom*? She suggests that executives need to find ways of expressing this in ways that are easy to grasp and that people can relate to. There are four ways in which executives typically attempt to do this:

- A **mission statement** aims **to provide employees and stakeholders with clarity about what the organisation is fundamentally there to do.** This is often referred to in terms of the apparently simple but challenging question: 'What business are we in?' Two linked questions that can clarify this are: 'What would be lost if the organisation did not exist?' and 'How do we make a difference?' Though they do not use the term 'mission statement', Jim Collins and Jerry Porras[2] suggest this can be addressed by starting with a descriptive statement of what the organisation does, then delving deeper into the purpose of what the organisation is there for by asking 'why do we do this?' They use the example of managers in a gravel and asphalt company arriving at the conclusion that its mission is to make people's lives better by improving the quality of built structures. At the University of Utrecht (see Illustration 1.2), the mission includes educating students, training the next generation of researchers and addressing social issues. In the example at the beginning of the chapter a core difference between Euan Sutherland and many members of the Co-Operative Society was the priority to be given to the social mission of the organisation.

- A **vision statement is concerned with the future the organisation seeks to create**. It is an aspiration that will enthuse, gain commitment and stretch performance. So here the question is: 'What do we want to achieve?' Porras and Collins suggest managers can identify this by asking: 'If we were sitting here in twenty years what do we want to have created or achieved?' They cite the example of Henry Ford's original vision that the ownership of a car should be within the reach of everyone.

- **Statements of corporate values communicate the underlying and enduring core 'principles' that guide an organisation's strategy and define the way that the organisation should operate.**[3] So a question to ask is: 'Would these values change with circumstances?' And if the answer is 'yes' then they are not 'core' and not 'enduring'. An example is the importance of leading-edge research in some universities. Whatever the constraints on funding, such universities hold to the enduring centrality of this.

- **Objectives are statements of specific outcomes that are to be achieved.** These are often expressed in financial terms, for example a desired level of sales, profit or share valuation levels. Organisations may also have quantified market-based objectives such as market share, levels of customer service, repeat business and so on. Sometimes objectives focus on the basis of competitive advantage: for example, low-cost airlines such as Ryanair set objectives on turnaround time for their aircraft because this is at the core of their distinctive low-cost advantage. Increasingly organisations are also setting objectives referred to as 'the triple bottom line', by which is meant not only economic objectives such as those above, but also environmental and social objectives (see section 4.5 below).

Not all organisations develop formalised statements of vision, mission and values, or necessarily use those terms. Illustration 4.1 provides an example of how one organisation seeks to clarify its purpose using rather different language.

Vision, mission and values statements can be bland and too wide-ranging. Objectives can seem attractively precise by contrast. However, while objectives are useful for guiding and monitoring performance in the short term, visions, missions and values can offer a longer-term view and more enduring sources of direction and motivation. It does, however, remain crucial to make vision, mission and values statements meaningful. Three principles can help achieve this:

- *Focus*: statements should focus attention and help guide decisions. For example Apple's founder Steve Jobs regarded as crucial the ability to say 'no' to non-core activities. And Google's value of 'fast' can guide choices between strategic options with different levels of complexity: Google's product development managers will cut product features which slow down essential search and advertising functions, even if they might be nice to have.

- *Motivational*: statements should motivate employees to do their best. They should not be so bland as to be applicable to nearly all organisations, but rather be distinctive and authentic to the organisation in question. They should also stretch organisational performance to higher levels. Thus Apple's vision of making computers available to everybody inspired Steve Jobs' employees in the early years of the company.

- *Clear*: in order to motivate employees in their day-to-day work, visions, missions and values should be easy to communicate, understand and remember. Thus founder Mark Zuckerberg identified three of Facebook's values as 'move fast', 'be bold' and 'be open': these are clear, memorable and actionable.

**ILLUSTRATION 4.1**    Mozilla's mission: beyond Firefox

## Can the Mozilla Foundation's mission and principles guide and motivate it into a new generation of products beyond its Firefox browser?

The Mozilla Foundation is a non-profit organisation that originated in the late 1990s from the old web-browser company Netscape. Mozilla's best known product is the Firefox open source web-browser, produced largely for free by a community of volunteer software developers. In 2012, Firefox had about 25 per cent share of the world's browser market, recently overtaken by Google's Chrome. About 85 per cent of Mozilla's revenue is a contract with Google, renewed for three years in 2011, which pays the Foundation in return for using Google as Firefox's default search engine.

Mozilla says the following about itself:

**'Mozilla's mission is to promote openness, innovation and opportunity on the web.**

**What we do**
**We do this by creating great software, like the Firefox browser, and building movements, like Drumbeat [the community of software developers], that give people tools to take control of their online lives.**

**What we strive for**
**As a non-profit organisation, we define success in terms of building communities and enriching people's lives instead of benefiting shareholders. We believe in the power and potential of the Internet and want to see it thrive for everyone, everywhere.'**

Mozilla also publishes what it calls a 'Manifesto', containing a set of principles intended 'to make Mozilla contributors proud of what we're doing and motivate us to continue'. Principles of the Manifesto include:

- The internet is a global public resource that must remain open and accessible.
- The internet should enrich the lives of individual human beings.
- Individuals' security on the internet is fundamental and cannot be treated as optional.

- Individuals must have the ability to shape their own experiences on the internet.
- Free and open-source software promotes the development of the internet as a public resource.

In 2012, Mozilla was developing a range of new initiatives. The most notable was 'Pancake', a cloud-based framework that allows users to carry and manage their personal data wherever they go. One objective of Pancake is to counter the way mobile apps are fragmenting the internet. Mozilla's President, Mitchell Baker, explained to the BBC: 'The internet was meant to be connected – not siloed. We really do want to encourage developers to develop across devices, using the same kind of power and explosive innovation and freedoms that the web has given us over the last 15 years.'

For Mitchell Baker, 'the reason for [these] initiatives is not driven by revenue. It is driven because we cannot fulfil the Mozilla mission unless we have a presence in these other spaces.' She continued, referring particularly to Mozilla's users and developers: 'Our stakeholders – we don't have shareholders – are not looking for a financial return on investment. The return on their time and energy and goodwill that they're looking for is the product that they like, and an internet that has a layer of user sovereignty in it.'

*Sources*: Mozilla website, 2012; and www.bbc.co.uk, 'Life after Firefox', 10 April 2012.

### Questions

1 Mozilla does not produce a formal vision statement. Based on the materials here, what do you think Mozilla's vision would be?

2 How do Mozilla's mission and principles influence its approach to new initiatives? Is there any danger in its apparent priorities?

Whatever statements of mission, vision, values are employed, or whatever the objectives that are set, it is important to understand who and what influences what they are. The rest of the chapter examines this.

## 4.3 OWNERS AND MANAGERS

Purpose is likely to be established by an organisation's owners and/or managers. Owners and managers are not always the same and their interests can diverge. This section explains different kinds of ownership models and the issues involved in reconciling owners' and managers' interests.

### 4.3.1 Ownership models

There are four basic ownership models, each with different implications for strategic purpose. Figure 4.2 shows these. The horizontal axis of the figure concerns the dominant modes of management, ranging from wholly *professional* (with managers employed for their professional expertise) to wholly *personal* (with management determined by personal connections to ownership as is often the case in family firms). The vertical axis describes the extent to which purpose is focused on profit exclusively or as one of a mix of motives. The four ownership

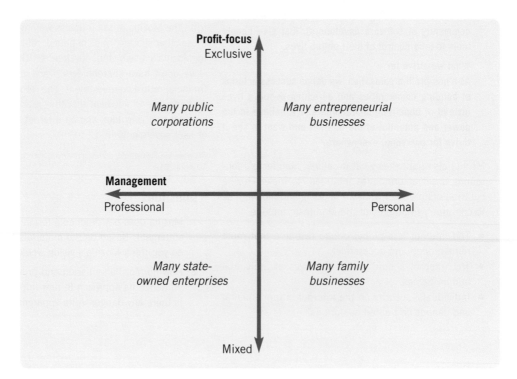

**Figure 4.2** Ownership, management and purpose

models in the figure help provide an understanding of the relationship between ownership, management and purpose.

- *Public companies* (often called publicly traded companies or public limited companies) are common in the USA, northern Europe, Japan and many others countries. These companies sell their shares to the public, with ownership typically in the hands of individual investors or institutions such as pension funds, banks or insurance companies. Usually owners do not manage public companies themselves, but delegate that function to professional managers. In principle, these managers work to make a financial return for their owners. If shareholders are not satisfied financially, they can either sell the shares or seek the removal of the managers. In terms of Figure 4.2 therefore, most public companies focus on profit. The extent to which this is so will vary, however, not least as a result of the extent to which owners and managers prioritise the single-minded pursuit of profit or the pursuit of wider social goals (see section 4.5 below).

- *State-owned enterprises* are wholly or majority owned by governments. About 80 per cent of stock market value is accounted for by state-owned companies in China, 60 per cent in Russia and 40 per cent in Brazil. Privatisation has reduced the role of state-owned enterprises in many developed economies, but quasi-privatised agencies such as hospital trusts in the United Kingdom operate in a similar way. In state-owned enterprises, politicians typically delegate day-to-day control to professional managers, though they may intervene on major strategic issues. State-owned enterprises usually have to earn a profit or surplus in order to fund investment and build financial reserves, but they are also likely to pursue a range of other objectives in keeping with government policy. For Chinese state-owned enterprises, for example, securing access to overseas resources such as minerals and energy is an important objective.

- *Entrepreneurial businesses* are businesses substantially owned and controlled by their founders. For example Lakshmi Mittal remains chairman and chief executive of his creation, Arcelor Mittal, the largest steel company in the world. Nonetheless, as they grow, entrepreneurial businesses are likely both to rely more on professional managers to cope with increasing complexity and to draw in external investors to fund new opportunities. Typically entrepreneurial companies need to focus on profit in order to survive and grow, though the personal missions of the founder may well influence purpose. For example, Richard Branson's view that the oligopolistic nature of some industries needs to be challenged has influenced the purpose of Virgin, the company he founded in the 1970s (see the case example in Chapter 6).

- *Family businesses* are where ownership by the founding entrepreneur has passed on to his or her family. Typically they are small to medium-sized enterprises, but can be very big: Ford, Fiat, Samsung and Walmart are all under family ownership, with significant family involvement in top management roles. Often the family retains a majority of voting shares, while releasing the remainder to the public on the stock market. Half of stock market-listed companies in the 10 largest Asian markets are effectively family-controlled.[4] Management may be partly professionalised, whilst top management remains ultimately under family control: thus the Chief Executive of Ford is a non-family member, but the Executive Chairman is William Ford Jr. For family businesses, retaining control over the company, passing on management to the next generation and ensuring the company's long-term survival are often very important objectives, and these might rule out profit-maximising strategies that involve high risk or require external finance.

As well as these four basic types of ownership, there are other variants. *Not-for-profit* organisations, such as Mozilla (Illustration 4.1), are typically owned by a charitable foundation: they may need to make a surplus to fund investment and protect against hard times, but fundamentally exist to pursue social missions. The *partnership* model, in which the organisation is owned and controlled by senior employees (its partners), is important in many professional services such as law and accounting. There are also *employee-owned* firms, which spread ownership among employees such as the major retailer John Lewis in the United Kingdom. *Mutual firms* – such as the Co-Operative Society for most of its existence – are owned by their customers or members. Typically not-for-profits, partnerships and employee-owned firms are restricted in their ability to raise external finance, making them more conservative in their strategies.

Clearly it is important for managers to understand how the ownership of their organisation relates to its strategic purpose. It is, however, also important for them to understand the ownership of other organisations with which they engage, for example competitors and partners. Without this understanding it is easy to be surprised by competitors or partners with different priorities to theirs. For example, Western public mining companies have often found themselves outbid for overseas mining opportunities by Chinese state-owned companies keen to secure supplies almost regardless of immediate profit.

## 4.3.2 Corporate governance

The varying roles of owners and professional managers raise issues of **corporate governance.**[5] **Corporate governance is concerned with the structures and systems of control by which managers are held accountable to those who have a legitimate stake in an organisation.**[6] Those with such a stake are typically the owners, but may include other groups such as employee representatives. Connecting their interests with management action is a vital part of developing strategy. Failures in corporate governance have contributed to calamitous strategic choices in many leading companies, even resulting in the complete destruction of global companies such as the energy giant Enron in 2001 and the leading investment bank Lehman Brothers in 2008. With the survival of whole organisations at stake, governance is increasingly recognised as a key strategic issue. Euan Sutherland was arguing that the governance structure he inherited at the Co-Operative Society contributed to the problems the group faced.

Managers and stakeholders are linked together in a **governance chain** which **shows the roles and relationships of different groups involved in the governance of an organisation.** In a small family business, the governance chain is simple: there are family shareholders, a board with some family members and there are managers, some of whom may be family too. Here there are just three layers in the chain. In large businesses, however, influence on governance can be complex. Figure 4.3 shows a governance chain for a typical large, public corporation. Here the size of the organisation means there are extra layers of management internally, while being publicly quoted introduces more investor layers too. Individual investors (the ultimate beneficiaries) often invest in public companies through investment funds, such as unit trusts or pension funds, which invest in a range of companies on their behalf. Such funds are typically controlled by trustees, with day-to-day investment activity undertaken by investment managers. So the ultimate beneficiaries may not even know in which companies they have a financial stake and have little power to influence the companies' boards directly.

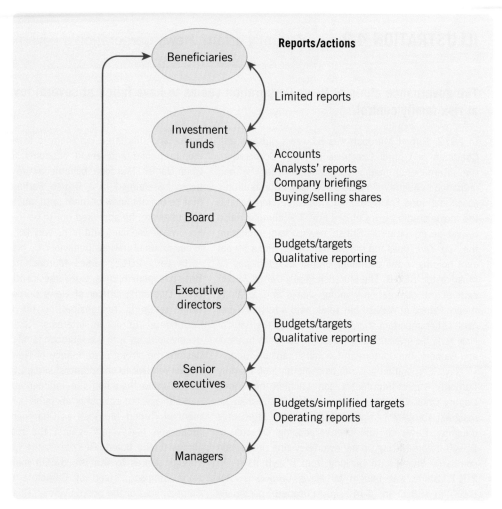

**Figure 4.3** The chain of corporate governance: typical reporting structures
*Source*: Adapted from David Pitt-Watson, Hermes Fund Management

## 4.3.3 Different governance models

The governing body of an organisation is normally a board of directors, the primary responsibility of which is typically to ensure that an organisation fulfils the wishes and purposes of those whom it represents. However, who the board represents varies. In the private sector in some parts of the world it is primarily shareholders, but in other parts of the world it is a broader or different stakeholder base. In the public sector, the governing body is accountable to the political arm of government – possibly through some intermediary such as a funding body.

At the most general level there are two governance models, though there are variants on each:[7]

**The shareholder model prioritises shareholder interests and is dominant in public companies, especially in the USA and UK.** It is this model that Sutherland wished to introduce at the UK

## ILLUSTRATION 4.2     A family affair? News Corporation's governance crisis

**The governance chain at News Corporation seems to have failed at several levels, putting at risk family control.**

In 2012, Rupert Murdoch was 81 years old and still Chairman and Chief Executive of News Corporation, the international media conglomerate that he had launched in Australia in the 1950s. News Corporation's assets included Fox News, the *Wall Street Journal* and the movie studio 20th Century Fox. The company also owned several leading British newspapers, including the *Sun*, *The Times* and the *Sunday Times*, and a 39 per cent holding in the dominant United Kingdom pay-TV broadcaster, BSkyB. The Murdoch family owned 39 per cent of the corporation's voting shares and a family friend, Prince Al Waleed bin Talal, held a further 7 per cent. Other important shareholders included the Bank of New York, the investment management company Invesco, and Calpers, the Californian teachers' pension fund.

News Corporation was run as something of a family fiefdom. Rupert Murdoch's son Lachlan had been Deputy Chief Operating Officer until 2005, when he resigned abruptly for unexplained reasons. Murdoch's daughter Elisabeth had been Managing Director of BSkyB before setting up her own television production company, Shine, with backing from BSkyB itself. In 2011, Shine was bought by News Corporation for £290 m (€350 m; $440 m): Elisabeth personally received more than half this sum, at the same time as retaining her role as Shine's Chairman and Chief Executive and joining the News Corporation main board. Some News Corporation shareholders accused the company of paying too much for Shine. Another of Rupert's sons was James, who was News Corporation's Deputy Chief Operating Officer. At the start of 2012, James was also Chairman of BSkyB and Chairman and Chief Executive of News Corporation Europe and Asia, overseeing a range of international assets including the group's British newspapers.

This last position placed James Murdoch in the front line of the telephone hacking scandal that engulfed News Corporation's British newspapers during 2011–12. In a fiercely competitive market, News Corporation's tabloid newspaper editors had encouraged journalists to get the most sensational stories they could, and this often led them to break into people's mobile phone and email accounts. It was unclear when James Murdoch became aware of these practices: he claimed in a British Parliamentary inquiry that he did not know of them until much later. If James was unaware, he appeared not to be in close control of his own newspapers and to be very lax in investigating accusations of lawless behaviour by his employees.

In early 2012, James Murdoch resigned all his British responsibilities. But James continued as Deputy Chief Operating Officer of News Corporation globally, while retaining responsibilities for the company's Continental European interests. Shareholders were deeply unhappy with the Murdoch family's management, despite the strong performance of News Corporation's shares relative to competitors' since 2009. In October 2011, more than half the independent shareholders had either voted against or abstained on the reappointment of Rupert Murdoch as Chairman and a similar proportion had voted against the reappointment of James to the board. Of course, the family controlled enough shares to win the overall majority. However, Anne Simpson, Head of Corporate Governance for Calpers, said of the hostile votes: 'This sends a strong signal to the News Corp board that investors are looking for robust independence. It's a vote in favour of board rejuvenation.'

*Main sources: Financial Times, 25 October 2011 and 3 April 2012.*

### Questions

1 With reference to Figure 4.3, at what levels did the governance chain at News Corporation seem to fail?

2 Given that News Corporation's share price was outperforming competitors', why would shareholders vote against the Murdochs' management at News Corporation? What else could they do?

Co-Operative Society. Shareholders have priority in regard to the wealth generated by the company, as opposed to employees for example. There is a separation of ownership and management, arguably meaning that strategic decision making by managers is more objective in the face of potentially conflicting expectations of different stakeholders. The shareholder interest in a company is assumed to be largely financial. Shareholders can vote for the board of directors according to the number of their shares and, in the pure model at least, there are many shareholders so that no single shareholder dominates. Shareholders can also exert control indirectly through the trading of shares. Dissatisfied shareholders may sell their shares, leading to a drop in the company's share price and an increased threat to directors of takeover by other firms.

There are, however, potential disadvantages of the shareholder model:

- *Diluted monitoring.* Where there are many shareholders, each with small stakes and often with many other investments, any single shareholder may not think it worthwhile monitoring performance closely. This may allow managers to sacrifice shareholder value to pursue their own agendas.

- *Vulnerable minority shareholders.* Where corporate governance regulation is weak, the shareholder model can be abused to allow the emergence of dominant shareholders who may exploit their voting power to the disadvantage of minority shareholders.

- *Short-termism.* The need to make profits for shareholders may encourage managers to focus on short-term gains at the expense of long-term projects, such as research and development.

The **stakeholder model recognises the wider set of interests that have a stake in an organisation's success such as employees, local communities, local governments, major suppliers and customers and banks.** The Co-Operative Society had long been governed by people elected by members (usually customers) or associated community or political interest groups. Shareholders are also stakeholders, of course, but in the stakeholder model they are likely to take larger stakes in companies than in the pure shareholder model and to hold these stakes longer term, thus reducing pressure on management for short-term results. Some of these stakeholders, for example banks and employees, may be formally represented on boards.

There are also argued disadvantages to the stakeholder model:

- *Weaker decision making.* Close monitoring by powerful stakeholders could lead to interference, slowing down of decision processes and the loss of management objectivity on critical decisions.

- *Uneconomic investments.* Due to lack of financial pressure from shareholders, long-term investments may be made in projects where the returns may be below market expectations.

- *Reduced innovation and entrepreneurship.* Because investors fear conflicts with the interests of other stakeholders, and because selling shares may be harder, they are less likely to provide capital for risky new opportunities.

# 4.4 STAKEHOLDER EXPECTATIONS

It should be clear by now that managers' decisions about the purpose and strategy of their organisation are influenced by the expectations of various stakeholders. Even in a shareholder

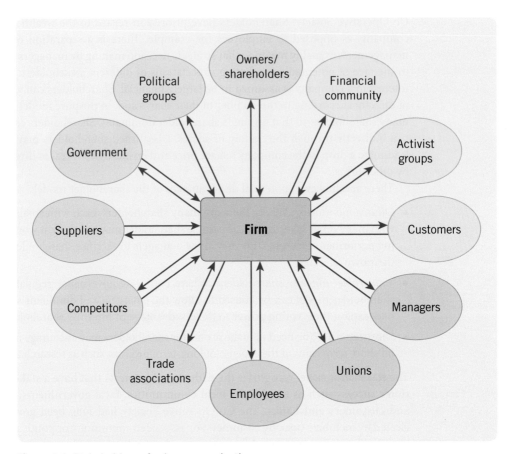

**Figure 4.4** Stakeholders of a large organisation

*Source*: Adapted from R.E. Freeman, *Strategic Management: A Stakeholder Approach*, Pitman, 1984. Copyright 1984 by R. Edward Freeman.

model managers cannot ignore stakeholders such as employees, local communities and government. This poses a challenge because there may be many stakeholders, especially for a large organisation (see Figure 4.4), with different, perhaps conflicting, expectations. This means that managers need to take a view on (i) which stakeholders will have the greatest influence, (ii) which expectations they need to pay most attention to and (iii) to what extent the expectations and influence of different stakeholders vary.

## 4.4.1 Stakeholder groups

External stakeholders can be divided into four types in terms of the nature of their relationship with the organisation and how they might affect the success or failure of a strategy:

- *Economic stakeholders*, including suppliers, competitors, customers, distributors, banks and shareholders.

- *Social/political stakeholders*, such as policy makers, regulators and government agencies that may directly influence the organisation or the context in which it operates.

- *Technological stakeholders*, such as key adopters, standards agencies and suppliers of complementary products or services (e.g. applications for particular mobile phones).
- *Community stakeholders*, who are affected by what an organisation does; for example, those who live close to a factory or, indeed, wider society. These stakeholders have no formal relationship with the organisation but may take action (e.g. through lobbying or activism) to influence the organisation.

The influence of these different types of stakeholders is likely to vary in different situations. For example, the 'technological group' will be crucial for strategies of new product introduction whilst the 'social/political' group may be particularly influential in the public-sector or for companies operating in different countries with different political and legal systems.

Since the expectations of stakeholder groups will differ, it is not unusual for conflict to exist regarding the importance or desirability of aspects of strategy (see Illustration 4.3 on EADS for an example of conflict among stakeholders). In most situations, a compromise will need to be reached or it may be possible to look for compatible stakeholder expectations. For example, managers of the English conservation tourist attraction, the Eden Project, looked for 'synergies around purpose' amongst different stakeholders to obtain support and funding for the project. Both the European Union and the local economic development agency were interested in developing the economy of Cornwall where the Eden Project is based and the Millennium Commission, a government-sponsored funding body, was interested in developing local iconic architecture.

## 4.4.2 Stakeholder mapping

Stakeholder mapping can be used to gain an understanding of stakeholder influence. **Stakeholder mapping identifies stakeholder interest and power and helps in understanding political priorities.** These two dimensions form the basis of the matrix shown as Figure 4.5. The matrix classifies stakeholders in relation to the *power* they hold and the extent to which they are likely to show *interest* in supporting or opposing a particular strategy. The positions of different stakeholders on the matrix are likely to vary according to each issue, especially with regard to the amount of interest they have. Stakeholder groups are also likely to vary in their power according to the governance structures under which they operate (see section 4.3). For example, in some countries banks may take a 'semi-detached' view of strategy, but be part of the governance structures in others.

In order to show the way in which the matrix may be used, take the example of a business where managers are seeking to ensure the compliance of stakeholders with their own assessment of strategic imperatives. In this context the matrix indicates the type of relationship that managers might typically establish with stakeholder groups in the different quadrants. Clearly, the acceptability of strategies to *key players* (segment D) is of major importance. These might be major investors or individuals or agencies with a lot of power – for example, a major shareholder in a family firm or a government funding agency in a public-sector organisation. Often the most difficult issues relate to stakeholders in segment C. Although these might normally be relatively passive, a disastrous situation can arise when their level of interest is underrated and they reposition to segment D and frustrate the adoption of a new strategy. Institutional shareholders such as pension funds or insurance firms can fall

## ILLUSTRATION 4.3 — Conflict at the European Aeronautic Defence and Space Company

**Strains emerged between stakeholders in this complex consortium, with political repercussions.**

The European Aeronautic Defence and Space Company (EADS) was established in 2000 as a means to group some of Europe's most important aeronautics and related activities. In particular, EADS brought together Aérospatiale-Matra of France, DaimlerChrysler Aerospace AG (DASA) of Germany, and Construcciones Aeronáuticas SA (CASA) of Spain. By 2013, EADS included Airbus, the world's leading manufacturer of commercial aircraft; Airbus Military covering tanker, transport and mission aircraft; Eurocopter, the world's largest helicopter supplier; Astrium, the European leader in space programmes such as Ariane and Galileo; and Cassidian, a major provider of defence and security systems for missiles and fighter jets. With revenues of €50 bn (about £40 bn or $65 bn) and 120,000 employees, EADS was one of Europe's largest manufacturers, exporters and investors in R&D, besides spending €31 bn annually with suppliers, mostly in Europe.

The ownership of EADS is complex, with 50.66 per cent owned by a three-way international partnership. The partners are SOGEADE (22.36 per cent), two-thirds owned by the French state and one-third owned by the French media company Lagardère; the German car manufacturer Daimler AG (22.36 per cent), representing the German government and some major German banks as well; and SEPI (5.44 per cent), a Spanish state holding company. The remainder of the stock is traded publicly, though the French state owns a further 0.06 per cent of this stock. EADS had made substantial losses in 2009, but returned to profitability in the following two years.

During 2011–12, the chief executive, Frenchman Louis Gallois, was promoting a strategy of greater internationalisation. This internationalisation, he argued, required a reduction in French and German state ownership. State ownership restricted EADS's ability to make major acquisitions in the US and emerging markets. Overseas acquisitions could access valuable technologies and manufacturing bases, and help win orders in markets where a local presence was seen as critical. Gallois also believed that the ownership structure gave the 'controlling shareholders a feeling of being trapped and always creating the risk of inequalities between different categories of shareholders'.

Early 2012 saw furious arguments between German and French partners. The immediate cause was the decision to move EADS's overall headquarters from Munich to Toulouse, the location of the subsidiary Airbus headquarters and with more than 16,000 staff already. Although there were only 300 staff involved in the EADS headquarters move, the German deputy economics minister wrote a letter to EADS alleging an 'unacceptable' bias towards French management and production in France. He particularly complained that €500 m aid supplied by the German government for the development of the A350 aircraft had not led to the promised strengthening of Airbus's north German sites in Hamburg (with 13,000 employees) and Bremen (with more than 3,000 employees). He demanded that the company put more Germans in top posts at Airbus or risk losing German development aid and export-credit guarantees. German anxiety was increased by the fact that two-thirds of EADS's revenues came from civil Airbus sales, while Germany was home to the Cassidian military division, whose revenues were falling because of government spending cuts. CEO Gallois responded that the German minister's letter was not in 'accordance with the governance of a listed company. We will choose the best industrial set-up in the company's interests – without external interference.'

*Main sources: Financial Times, 19 June 2011, 2 March 2012, 8 March 2012.*

### Questions

1 With reference to the power/interest matrix (Figure 4.5), how would powerful stakeholders' level of interest vary with regard to the location of the EADS headquarters and internationalisation?

2 Given the ownership structure, is CEO Gallois right to assert the primacy of company interests and reject German ministerial 'interference'?

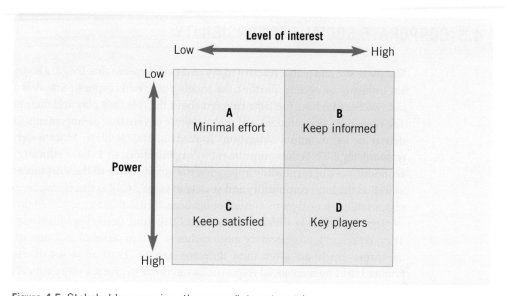

**Figure 4.5** Stakeholder mapping: the power/interest matrix

*Source*: Adapted from A. Mendelow, *Proceedings of the Second International Conference on Information Systems,* Cambridge, MA, 1986

into this category. They may show little interest unless share prices start to dip, but may then demand to be heard by senior management. Managers might choose to address the expectations of stakeholders in segment B, for example community groups, through information provision. It may be important not to alienate such stakeholders because they can be crucially important 'allies' in influencing the attitudes of more powerful stakeholders: for example, through lobbying.

Stakeholder mapping can also help in understanding three other issues:

- Who the key *blockers* and *facilitators* of a strategy are likely to be and the appropriate response.

- Whether *repositioning* of certain stakeholders is desirable and/or feasible: for example, to lessen the influence of a key player or to ensure that there are more key players who will champion the strategy (this is often critical in the public-sector context).

- *Maintaining* the level of interest or power of some key stakeholders: for example, public 'endorsement' by powerful suppliers or customers may be critical to the success of a strategy. It may also be necessary to discourage some stakeholders from repositioning themselves. This is what is meant by *keep satisfied* in relation to stakeholders in segment C, and to a lesser extent *keep informed* for those in segment B.

All this can raise difficult ethical issues for managers in deciding the role they should play in the political activity surrounding stakeholder management. For example, should managers be simple, honest brokers balancing the conflicting expectations of all stakeholder groups? Or should they be answerable to one stakeholder – such as shareholders – and hence is their role to ensure the acceptability of their strategies to other stakeholders? Or are they, as many authors suggest, the real power themselves, constructing strategies to suit their own purposes and managing stakeholder expectations to ensure acceptance of these strategies?

## 4.5 CORPORATE SOCIAL RESPONSIBILITY

The sheer size and global reach of many companies means that they are bound to have significant influence on society. Further, the widely publicised corporate scandals and failures of the last two decades have fuelled a concern about the role they play and their purpose in society. The regulatory environment and the corporate governance arrangements for an organisation determine its minimum obligations towards its stakeholders. More widely, **corporate social responsibility (CSR) is the commitment by organisations to 'behave ethically and contribute to economic development while improving the quality of life of the workforce and their families as well as the local community and society at large'.**[8] CSR is therefore concerned with how an organisation exceeds its minimum obligations to stakeholders specified through regulation.

Organisations take different stances on CSR. Four stereotypes illustrate these differences. They, represent a progressively more inclusive 'list' of stakeholder interests and explain how companies might act given these different stances.[9] Illustration 4.4 discusses how clothing retailer H&M pursues social responsibility in order to give it a more ethical profile than some of its rivals and pre-empt protests against the clothing industry's traditionally wasteful and exploitative practices.

- *The laissez-faire view* (literally 'let do' in French) represents an extreme stance: that the only responsibility of business is to make a profit and provide for the interests of shareholders.[10] It is for government to protect society through legislation and regulation: organisations need to do no more than meet these minimum obligations. Expecting companies to go beyond this confuses decision making and undermines the accountability of managers to their shareholders.

- *Enlightened self-interest* is guided by the recognition of the long-term financial benefit to the shareholder of well-managed relationships with other stakeholders. It is argued that this makes good business sense and is important for long-term financial success. Working constructively with suppliers or local communities can increase the 'value' available for all stakeholders to share: for example, helping improve the quality of marginal suppliers in the developing world can create a stronger overall supply chain; supporting education in the local workforce will increase the availability of skilled labour.

- A *forum for stakeholder interaction* explicitly incorporates multiple stakeholder interests and expectations rather than just shareholders as influences on organisational purposes and strategies. Here the argument is that the performance of an organisation should be measured in a more ways than just through the financial bottom line. Rather, social responsibility can be measured in terms of *the triple bottom line* – social and environmental benefits as well as profits. Companies might retain uneconomic units to preserve jobs, avoid manufacturing or selling 'anti-social' products and be prepared to bear reductions in profitability for the social good.

- *Shapers of society* regard financial considerations as of secondary importance or a constraint. These are visionary organisations, seeking to change society and social norms. Many stakeholders involved with the Co-Operative Society would see this as central to that organisation. Charities are also typically committed to this kind of stance as are some public-sector organisations. There are also *social entrepreneurs* who found new organisations that earn revenues but pursue a specific social purpose.

## ILLUSTRATION 4.4     H&M's sustainability strategy

**Swedish clothing retailer H&M claims to be pursuing a strategy that delivers profits, environmental gains and worker benefits.**

H&M is the world's second-largest clothing retailer, just behind Inditex, owner of Zara. It has 2,500 stores worldwide, operating in 44 countries. It sells about 550 million items of clothing per year. As such, it has traditionally been a leader in so-called 'fast-fashion', the retailing of cheap fashion items which are designed to be worn only a few times before disposal.

Fast-fashion is a voracious industry. There are now 30–50 trend-driven fashion seasons a year. Eighty billion garments are made annually worldwide, from virgin resources. There are 40 million garment workers in the world, predominantly making fast-fashion. A garment worker in Bangladesh, a major supplier, earns an average monthly wage of $40. A pair of underpants costs about one pence (or roughly a Euro cent) to make in a Third World sweatshop. Fast-fashion is a target of international campaign groups such as the 'Clean Clothes Campaign'.

During 2012, the Clean Clothes Campaign organised mass 'faint-ins' in prominent stores such as Gap, Zara and H&M across Europe, drawing attention to how under-nourished women workers frequently faint at work in Third World garment factories. A Clean Clothes spokesperson says: 'The human cost of brands like H&M or Zara paying poverty wages is seen when hundreds of workers pass out due to exhaustion and malnutrition... For decades, global fashion brands have made excuses about why they shouldn't pay a living wage. It's not a choice, it's a pressing necessity. Hiding behind... company codes of conduct is no longer acceptable.'

In 2012, H&M launched its new 'Conscious' range of clothing, making use of a large proportion of recycled materials and more environmentally-friendly virgin materials such as hemp. The company's website explained the motivation: 'Our vision is that all business operations shall be run in a way that is economically, socially and environmentally sustainable.' This was accompanied by a Sustainability Report with some impressive statistics: for example, 2.5 million shoes were made during 2011 using lower-impact water-based solvents and H&M was the biggest user of organic cotton in the world.

*Guardian* journalist Lucy Singh asked H&M's Head of Sustainability, Helena Helmersson, whether she could offer guarantees for the sustainability of the company's products across its ranges. Helmersson responded:

**'I don't think guarantee is the right word. A lot of people ask for guarantees: "Can you guarantee labour conditions? Can you guarantee zero chemicals?" Of course we cannot when we're such a huge company operating in very challenging conditions. What I can say is that we do the very best we can with a lot of resources and a clear direction of what we're supposed to do. We're working really hard... Remember that H&M does not own any factories itself. We are to some extent dependent on the suppliers – it is impossible to be in full control.'**

Between 2006 and 2012, H&M's share price has increased by more than a third, well ahead of the local Stockholm market index. Sales too have increased by a third and total operating profit after tax in this period has been nearly SEK98 billion (€11 billion). H&M's return on capital employed for year-end 2011 is 47.1 per cent.

*Main sources: Guardian, 7 April 2012; Ecouterre, 21 September 2012; www.hm.com; H&M Concsious Actions and Sustainability Report, 2011.*

---

### Questions

1 Where would you place H&M in terms of the four stances on social responsibility?

2 What are the kinds of triple-bottom-line measures that would be appropriate for a sustainable strategy in clothing retail?

## 4.6 CULTURAL INFLUENCES

Returning to the story of Euan Sutherland's resignation at the Co-Operative Society, some argued that the problems arose not least because of a clash of cultures; that Sutherland's back-gound was from a corporate culture alien to that of the Co-Op. **Organisational culture is the taken-for-granted assumptions and behaviours that make sense of people's organisational context** and therefore contributes to how groups of people respond to and behave in relation to issues they face. It can have important influences on the development and change of organisational strategy. For example, the purpose of an organisation may not always be stated explicitly; nonetheless there may be a 'taken for granted' purpose embedded in the history and culture of the organisation. Or it could be that, despite an explicit statement of purpose and of the strategy, the organisation's strategic direction continues to be driven by its culture. Understanding the underlying cultural influences on an organisation is therefore important.

Different cultural contexts are likely to influence people in an organisation. The sections that follow explain geographically based cultures and organisational culture and then show how culture can be analysed and characterised as a means of understanding its influences on organisational purposes and strategies.

### 4.6.1 Geographically based cultures

Many writers, perhaps the most well known of whom is Geert Hofstede,[11] have shown how attitudes to work, authority, equality and other factors differ from one country to another. Organisations that operate internationally need to understand and cope with such differences, which can manifest themselves in terms of different standards, values and expectations in the various countries in which they operate. For example, Wal-Mart failed to develop its retail presence in Germany and China because it failed to understand how local shopping behaviour differed from that in the USA.

### 4.6.2 Organisational culture

Edgar Schein[12] suggests that culture can be conceived as consisting of four different layers:

- *Values* as formally stated by an organisation may be easy to identify since they are explicit, perhaps written down (see section 4.2). The values driving a strategy may, however, be different from those in formal statements. For example, in the last decade, many banks espoused values of shareholder value creation, careful risk management and high levels of customer service. But they indulged in highly risky lending, resulting in the need for huge government financial support. It is therefore important to delve beneath espoused values to uncover underlying, perhaps taken-for-granted, values that can help explain the strategy actually being pursued by an organisation.

- *Beliefs* are more specific. They can typically be discerned in how people talk about issues the organisation faces: for example, a belief that the company should not trade with particular countries or a belief in the importance of high levels of customer service.

- *Behaviours* are the day-to-day ways in which an organisation operates and can be seen by people both inside and often outside the organisation. This includes the work routines, how the organisation is structured and controlled and 'softer' issues around symbolic behaviours (see section 4.6.5). These behaviours may become the taken-for-granted 'ways we do things around here' that are potentially the bases for inimitable strategic capabilities (see section 3.3.3) but also significant barriers to achieving strategic change if that becomes necessary (see Chapter 10).

- *Taken-for-granted assumptions* are the core of an organisation's culture which in this book we refer to as the 'organisational paradigm'. The **paradigm is the set of assumptions held in common and taken for granted in an organisation** which guide people about how to view and respond to different circumstances that organisation faces. The paradigm can underpin successful strategies by providing a basis of common understanding in an organisation, but can also be a problem, for example when major strategic change is needed (see Chapter 10), or when organisations try to merge and find that the paradigms of the merged organisations are incompatible. The importance of the paradigm is discussed further in section 4.6.5.

### 4.6.3 Organisational subcultures

There may be aspects of culture that pervade the whole organisation. However, there may also be important *organisational subcultures*. These could relate to the structure of the organisation: for example, the differences between geographical divisions in a multinational company, or between functional groups such as finance, marketing and operations. Such differences between business functions can relate to the different nature of work in different functions. For example, in a major oil company differences are likely between those functions engaged in 'upstream' exploration, where time horizons may be in decades, and those concerned with 'downstream' retailing, with much shorter market-driven time horizons.

### 4.6.4 Culture's influence on strategy

The taken-for-granted nature of culture is what makes it centrally important in relation to strategy and the management of strategy. There are at least two potential benefits:

- *Cultural 'glue'.* If there is coherence around that which is taken for granted and that is in line with the strategy it can mean that the organisation is easier to manage. For example Josephine Rydberg-Dumont, president of IKEA, argues that, because all IKEA employees cohere around the founding principles and values of the firm, it reduces the need for constant supervision. Moreover, since one such value is the benefit of constantly questioning the status quo, it 'fuels' IKEA's innovation.

- *A basis of competitive advantage:* It may be possible for competitors to imitate products or technologies. It is much more difficult for them to imitate that which is taken for granted which may, then, provide a basis sustaining competitive advantage over rivals (see section 3.3.3).

There are, however, potential problems:

- *Captured by culture.* Managers, faced with a changing business environment, are more likely to attempt to deal with the situation by searching for what they can understand and cope with in terms of the existing culture. For example, managers may seek to extend the market for their business, but assume that it will be similar to their existing market, and therefore set about managing the new venture in much the same way as they have been used to. Culture is, in effect, an unintended driver of strategy.

- *Cultural barriers to change.* Significant strategic change may be problematic because the culture is difficult to change. People may accept, in principle, the need for such change but they do not readily stop conforming to established rules, routines and reporting relationships or change long-standing assumptions about the organisation.

- *Managing culture.* Because it is difficult to observe, identify and control that which is taken for granted, it is also difficult to manage. This is why having a way to analyse culture so as to make it more evident is important – the subject of the next section.

## 4.6.5 Analysing culture: the cultural web

In order to understand the existing culture and its effects it is important to be able to analyse a culture. If this is to be done, it is important to emphasise the need to surface that which is taken for granted. For example there is a danger in seeing public statements of an organisation's values, beliefs and purposes – for example, in annual reports, mission or values statements and business plans – as useful descriptions of the organisational culture. This is not to suggest that there is any organised deception. It is simply that the statements of values and beliefs are often carefully considered and carefully crafted statements of the aspirations of a particular stakeholder (such as the CEO) rather than descriptions of the actual culture.

The **cultural web**[13] is a means of analysing culture. The **cultural web shows the behavioural, physical and symbolic manifestations of a culture** that inform and are informed by the taken-for-granted assumptions, or paradigm. The cultural web can be used to understand culture in any of the frames of reference discussed above but is most often used at the organisational and/or functional levels. It is shown in Figure 4.6 which also includes questions that can be used in an analysis of culture. The elements of the cultural web are as follows:

- The *paradigm* is at the core of the web. As previously defined it is the set of assumptions held in common and taken for granted in an organisation: in effect it is the *collective experience* applied to a situation to make sense of it and inform a likely course of action. The assumptions of the paradigm are, quite likely, very basic and may or may not align with the logic of a strategy. For example, a common problem in technology and engineering firms is the propensity of people to focus on the technical excellence of products rather than customers' perceived needs. Even if the rational view is to build a strategy around the engineering business's customer needs, people in those organisations may still interpret issues and behave in line with its paradigm. So understanding what the paradigm is and how it informs debate on strategy matters. The problem is that, since it is unlikely to be talked about, or even be something that people are conscious of, trying to identify it can be difficult. One way of gaining insight into a paradigm is to focus initially on other aspects of the cultural web

**Stories**
- What core beliefs do stories reflect?
- What stories are commonly told, e.g. to newcomers?
- How do these reflect core assumptions and beliefs?
- What norms do the mavericks deviate from?

**Symbols**
- What objects, events or people do people in the organisation particularly identify with?
- What are these related to in the history of the organisation?
- What aspects of strategy are highlighted in publicity?

**Routines and rituals**
- Which routines are emphasised?
- Which are embedded in history?
- What behaviour do routines encourage?
- What are the key rituals?
- What assumptions and core beliefs do they reflect?
- What do training programmes emphasise?
- How easy are rituals/routines to change?

**Power structures**
- Where does power reside? Indicators include:
  (a) status
  (b) claim on resources
  (c) symbols of power
- Who 'makes things happen'?
- Who stops things happening?

**Control systems**
- What is most closely monitored/controlled?
- Is emphasis on reward or punishment?
- Are controls rooted in history or current strategies?
- Are there many/few controls?

**Organisational structures**
- What are the formal *and* informal structures?
- How rigid are the structures?
- Do structures encourage collaboration or competition?
- What types of power structure do they support?

> **Overall**
> - What do the answers to these questions suggest are the (few) fundamental assumptions that are the paradigm?
> - How would you characterise the dominant culture?
> - How easy is this to change?
> - How and to what extent do aspects of the web interrelate and re-enforce each other?

**Figure 4.6** The cultural web: some useful questions

because these are to do with more visible manifestations of culture. Moreover these other aspects are likely to act to reinforce the assumptions within that paradigm.

- *Routines* are 'the way we do things around here' on a day-to-day basis. They lubricate the working of the organisation, and may provide a basis for distinctive organisational capabilities. They can also represent a taken-for-grantedness about how things should happen which, again, can guide how people respond to issues but be difficult to change. For example, managers trying to achieve greater customer focus in engineering firms often report that customer-facing sales engineers routinely tend to tell customers what they need rather than listening to their needs.

- The *rituals* of organisational life are activities or special events that emphasise, highlight or reinforce what is important in the culture. Examples include training programmes, interview panels, promotion and assessment procedures, sales conferences and so on. An extreme example, of course, is the ritualistic training of military recruits to prepare them for the discipline required in conflict.

- The *stories* told by members of an organisation to each other, to outsiders, to new recruits and so on, may act to embed the present in its organisational history and also flag up important events and personalities. They typically have to do with successes, disasters, heroes, villains and mavericks (who deviate from the norm). They can also be a way of letting people know what is conventionally important in an organisation.

- *Symbols* are objects, events, acts or people that convey, maintain or create meaning over and above their functional purpose. For example, offices and office layout, cars and job titles have a functional purpose, but are also typically signals about status and hierarchy. The form of language used in an organisation can also be revealing. For example, in a major teaching hospital in the UK, consultants described patients as 'clinical material'. Whilst this might be amusing, it reveals an underlying assumption about patients that might play a significant role in influencing the strategy of an organisation. Although symbols are shown separately in the cultural web, it should be remembered that many elements of the web are symbolic. So, routines, control and reward systems and structures are not only functional but also symbolic.

- *Power* is the ability of individuals or groups to persuade, induce or coerce others into following certain courses of action. So *power structures* are distributions of power to groups of people in an organisation. The most powerful individuals or groups are likely to be closely associated with the paradigm. For example it is not unusual to find powerful executives who have long association with long-established ways of doing things.

- *Organisational structures* are the roles, responsibilities and reporting relationships in organisations. These are likely to reflect power structures, and how they manifest themselves emphasises which roles and relationships really matter in an organisation. Formal hierarchical, mechanistic structures may emphasise that strategy is the province of top managers and everyone else is 'working to orders'. Structures with less emphasis on formal reporting relationships might indicate more participative strategy making.

- *Control systems* are the formal and informal ways of monitoring and supporting people within and around an organisation and tend to emphasise what is seen to be important in the organisation. They include measurements and reward systems. For example, public-service organisations have often been accused of being concerned more with stewardship of funds than with quality of service. This is reflected in their control systems, which are more about accounting for spending rather than with quality of service.

As the banking crisis of 2009 onwards developed, many familiar with the banking industry blamed the problems on 'the banking culture', which needed to change. Illustration 4.5 shows a cultural web drawn up on the basis of interviews with past and current employees of the retail side of Barclays Bank. Before the deregulation of the banks by the UK government in the 1990s, Barclays, in common with other retail banks, had a paternalistic culture in terms of both assumptions about customers and the way in which staff were treated. There was also an emphasis on avoiding risk. The branches themselves were where bank staff 'looked after'

# ILLUSTRATION 4.5 The cultural web of Barclays Retail in the 2000s

**The cultural web can be used to identify the taken-for-granted behaviours and assumptions of an organisation.**

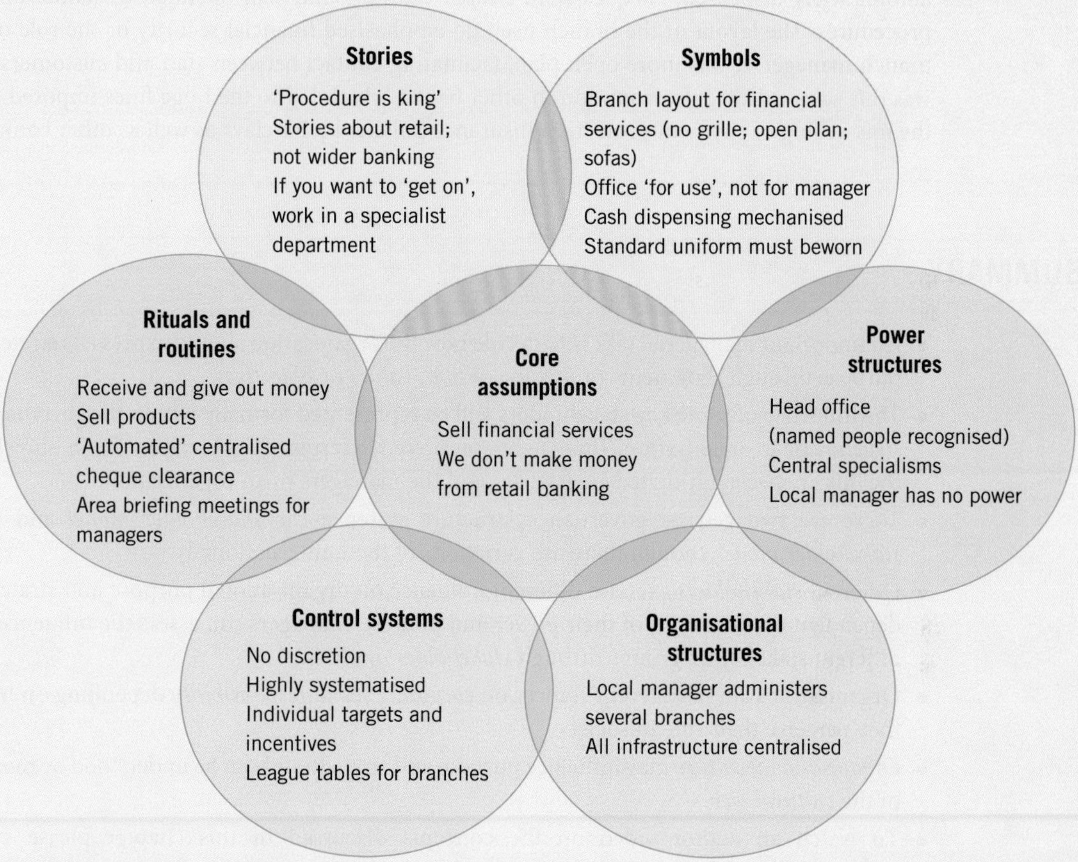

**Stories**

'Procedure is king'
Stories about retail;
not wider banking
If you want to 'get on',
work in a specialist
department

**Symbols**

Branch layout for financial
services (no grille; open plan;
sofas)
Office 'for use', not for manager
Cash dispensing mechanised
Standard uniform must be worn

**Rituals and routines**

Receive and give out money
Sell products
'Automated' centralised
cheque clearance
Area briefing meetings for
managers

**Core assumptions**

Sell financial services
We don't make money
from retail banking

**Power structures**

Head office
(named people recognised)
Central specialisms
Local manager has no power

**Control systems**

No discretion
Highly systematised
Individual targets and
incentives
League tables for branches

**Organisational structures**

Local manager administers
several branches
All infrastructure centralised

## Questions

1  How might the web help those seeking to address the problems of 'the banking culture'?
2  How do the various elements of the web interrelate?
3  Draw up a cultural web for an organisation of your choice.

customers, processed their cash and cheques. It was also where the branch manager, often a 'pillar of the community,' interviewed important customers and made decisions about their loans and credit limits. This culture changed with the growing importance of investment banking on the profits of Barclays (together with other banks) and the centralisation of bank services and operations. Retail banking became secondary to investment banking. The branches became vehicles for selling financial services; staff were incentivised to do so; the local branch manager was no more and local discretion was removed. Cash was increasingly automatically dispensed, cheques were cleared centrally and staff operated to standardised procedures. The layout of the branch itself de-emphasised financial security or the role of a branch manager; it was more open plan, facilitating contact between staff and customers. It was this sales culture, also common in other banks, which led to the huge fines imposed for the mis-selling of payment protection insurance policies by Barclays as well as other banks.

## SUMMARY

- An important managerial task is to decide how the organisation should express its strategic purpose through statements of *mission, vision, values* or *objectives*.
- The influence of some key stakeholders will be represented formally within the *governance structure* of an organisation. This can be considered in terms of a *governance chain*, showing the links between ultimate beneficiaries and the managers of an organisation.
- There are two generic governance structure systems: the *shareholder model* and the *stakeholder model*, though there are variations of these internationally.
- Different *stakeholders* exercise different influence on organisational purpose and strategy, dependent on the extent of their power and interest. Managers can assess the influence of different stakeholder groups through *stakeholder analysis*.
- Organisations adopt different stances on *corporate social responsibility* depending on how they perceive their role in society.
- *Organisational culture* may influence purpose and strategy and can be understood by means of the *cultural web*.
- To watch an author video on the concepts discussed in this chapter please visit www.mystrategylab.com, and click on 'Author perspectives on strategic management'.

## VIDEO ASSIGNMENTS

MyStrategyLab

If you are using *MyStrategyLab* you might find it useful to watch the case study for Chapter 4 (which features various companies).

1 Using the video interviews and section 4.5 of the text, discuss the importance of corporate social responsibility to the companies featured in the video.

2 How does corporate social responsibility relate to stakeholder expectations and governance in determining the purpose of an organisation? Use the companies featured in the video as examples.

## RECOMMENDED KEY READINGS

- The case for the importance of clarity of strategic values and vision is especially strongly made by J. Collins and J. Porras, *Built to Last: Successful Habits of Visionary Companies*, Harper Business, 2002 (in particular see Chapter 11).
- A good review of important ideas in both corporate governance and corporate social responsibility is S. Benn and D. Bolton, *Key Concepts in Corporate Responsibility*, Sage, 2011. Specifically on corporate governance, a leading guide is B. Tricker, *Corporate Governance: Principles, Policies and Practices*, 2nd edn, Oxford University Press, 2012.
- For a comprehensive and critical explanation of organisational culture see Mats Alvesson, *Understanding Organisational Culture*, Sage, 2002.

## REFERENCES

1. Cynthia A. Montgomery, 'Putting leadership back into strategy', *Harvard Business Review*, Jan 2008, pp. 54–60.
2. J. Collins and J. Porras, 'Building your company's vision', *Harvard Business Review*, Sept–Oct, 1996, pp. 65–77.
3. P. Lencioni, 'Make your values mean something', *Harvard Business Review*, vol. 80, no. 7 (2002), pp. 113–17.
4. Credit Suisse, *Asian Family Businesses Report 2011: Key Trends, Economic Contribution and Performance*, Singapore, 2011.
5. Useful general references on corporate governance are: R. Monks and N. Minow (eds), *Corporate Governance*, 4th edn, Blackwell, 2008. Also see Ruth Aguilera and Gregory Jackson, 'The cross-national diversity of corporate governance: dimensions and determinants', *Academy of Management Review*, vol. 28, no. 3 (2003), pp. 447–65.
6. This definition is based on, but adapted from, that in S. Jacoby, 'Corporate governance and society', *Challenge*, vol. 48, no. 4 (2005), pp. 69–87.
7. S. Letza, X. Sun and J. Kirkbride, 'Shareholding versus stakeholding: a critical review of corporate governance', *Corporate Governance*, vol. 12 no. 3 (2005), pp. 242–62. Within this broad classification, there are other models: see, for example, A. Murphy and K. Topyan, 'Corporate governance: a critical survey of key concepts, issues, and recent reforms in the US', *Employee Responsibility and Rights Journal*, vol. 17, no. 2 (2005), pp. 75–89.
8. This definition is based on that by the World Business Council for Sustainable Development.
9. Based on research undertaken at the Center for Corporate Citizenship at the Boston College, reported in P. Mirvis and B. Googins, 'Stages of corporate citizenship', *California Management Review*, vol. 48, no. 2 (2006), pp. 104–26.
10. Often quoted as a summary of Milton Friedman's argument is M. Friedman: 'The social responsibility of business is to increase its profits', *New York Times Magazine*, 13 September 1970.
11. See G. Hofstede, *Culture's Consequences*, Sage, 2nd edn, 2001.
12. This definition of culture is taken from E. Schein, *Organisational Culture and Leadership*, 2nd edition, Jossey-Bass, 1997, p. 6.
13. A fuller explanation of the cultural web can be found in G. Johnson, *Strategic Change and the Management Process*, 1987, and G. Johnson, 'Managing strategic change: strategy, culture and action', *Long Range Planning*, vol. 25, Blackwell, no. 1 (1992), pp. 28–36.

## Bonuses and 'gaming' at Barclays Bank

In 2012 Bob Diamond, the CEO of Barclays Bank, resigned in the wake of government, shareholder and media criticism of the bank's manipulation of the inter-bank lending rate, Libor. That criticism was often linked to a condemnation of the culture at Barclays, in particular the investment arm of the bank, which the UK Financial Services Authority called 'a culture of gaming' and BBC's *Panorama* programme dubbed a 'bonus culture'.

### Quaker origins

What was so widely condemned as malpractice at Barclays seemed alien to a bank with its origins. The founding families were from the Quaker religious movement, with their emphasis on sobriety, pacifism and high ethical standards, and their descendants were still in important executive positions in the mid-twentieth century. As the *Financial Times* observed:

> 'In many ways the bank resembled a club and, as so often with British clubs, the thing worked surprisingly well despite its flaws . . . It was, in fact, the most innovative of the British clearing banks in the post-war period. In 1967 it installed the world's first automated cash teller machine . . . Barclays also came up with the first plastic payment device, Barclaycard, still outstandingly successful.'

The success did not continue: 1986 brought 'Big Bang', the deregulation of financial markets in the UK. One effect was the entry of US investment banks, so increasing competition and doing away with the 'clubby' culture of the past. Barclays responded by attempting a rapid growth strategy with disastrous results; by the early 1990s it needed to raise additional funds through two rights issues.

### The development of investment banking

Barclays began in 1809 and, as Overend, Gurney & Co., built a reputation for accepting bills from other banks to reinvest in businesses – an early form of investment banking. However, poor investments led to bankruptcy in the 1890s contributing to the merger of several Quaker banks in

**Bob Diamond**
*Source*: Rex Features.

1896 to form Barclays. Barclays therefore inherited investment banking, as well as risk aversion and a conservative approach to growth, which lasted until the late 1980s.

The interest in investment banking received a huge impetus after Big Bang. Barclays embarked on acquisitions including a stock broker. The outcome was the formation of an investment bank – Barclays de Zoete Wedd (BZW). In common with other investment banks who got involved in equities trading, however, Barclays had great difficulty combining conventional and investment banking in a coherent model. As the *Financial Times* put it:

> 'The chief problem was culture. As Michael Lewis, author of *Liar's Poker*, a commentary on Wall Street in the 1980s, memorably put it, a commercial banker was someone who had a wife, a station wagon, 2.2 children and a dog that brought him his slippers when he returned home from work at 6 pm. An investment banker, by contrast, was a breed apart, a member of a master race of dealmakers. He possessed vast, almost unimaginable talent and ambition.

**If he had a dog it snarled. He had two little red sports cars yet wanted four. To get them, he was, for a man in a suit, surprisingly willing to cause trouble.'**

Investment banking was notorious for its hard work and 'hard play'. It was common for investment bankers to work through the night or to be seen to be doing so – stories had it that they would own two suit jackets so they could leave one on the back of the chair to pretend they were still in the office working. It was also a 'can-do' mentality which legitimated, for example, a day trip to Australia for a one-hour meeting. No expense was spared on flights, entertainment or accommodation provided a big deal was signed. There was also much visible excess with traders spending thousands of pounds a night at champagne bars.

## The development of investment banking

In 1994 Martin Taylor, a former *Financial Times* journalist who had been chairman of Courtaulds Textiles, was appointed as chief executive of Barclays. His initial assessment was that BZW was underperforming in a highly competitive and overcrowded market. He decided to bring in new personnel and this included Bob Diamond, who had established a reputation as a trader in investment banking at CS First Boston in New York.

Martin Taylor's concerns continued. In 1997 he presented a paper to the board arguing that the various activities of BZW lacked scale in an increasingly global market and that Barclays should exit investment banking. The board did not accept the argument, believing that Barclays needed to further develop its investment banking. They did, however, succumb to investor pressure on the relatively low returns being generated from BZW and decided to dispose of its corporate finance business, leaving an emphasis on trading, Bob Diamond's area of expertise. Martin Taylor resigned in 1998.

Throughout the first decade of the new century, Bob Diamond's influence grew. A past employee of Barclays investment arm, interviewed in a BBC *Panorama* programme, claimed that Bob Diamond 'installed Wall Street values into Barclays; it was every man for himself . . . It was all about doing ever bigger deals' and being willing to take 'extreme risks' to make 'super profits' and generate huge bonuses for the traders involved. Diamond also grew the much criticised Structured Capital Markets 'tax planning' business, which many saw as Barclays 'tax avoidance' business. Employing only a hundred people by 2010 this business was generating £1 (€1.2; $1.5) billion a year in profits. This was where the highest bonuses were paid.

Bob Diamond succeeded in growing the trading arm of the bank into a major profit contributor accounting for 58 per cent of Barclays' overall pre-tax earnings by 2011. He also succeeded in achieving a powerful position on Wall Street for Barclays with what the *Financial Times* described as the 'opportunistic grab for Lehman Brothers' US business after its collapse in 2008'. His reward was to become chief executive of the whole bank early in 2011. Yet, there were already signs of future problems. There were investigations into the mis-selling of payment protection insurance by the retail banks and for the manipulation of the inter-bank lending rate, Libor, to generate unfair profits, in both of which Barclays was heavily involved. Traders at Barclays were under investigation for allegedly manipulating Californian electricity prices. There was widespread criticism of the bank's tax avoidance activities and public criticism of Bob Diamond's huge remuneration package, estimated by the BBC *Panorama* programme to be around £120 million between 2007 and 2012. While Barclays publicity still made reference to its Quaker heritage, its reputation was 'in tatters'. Bob Diamond resigned in 2012.

## Bonuses and tribal bonding

Many attributed Barclays' problems to the 'bonus culture' so evident in the investment bank. The *Financial Times* quoted Philip Augar, who ran NatWest's global equities business between 1992 and 1995:

> **'The battleground between conventional bankers and investment bankers usually concerned pay and resources . . . the bonus round in an investment bank is the most important time of year. Get it wrong and the business unravels; pay too much and profitability is shot to ribbons. In a universal institution, the retail and commercial bankers often, maybe always, feel that too many of the investment profits are being paid to staff and inevitably resent the fact that investment bankers' bonuses are bigger than their own. For their part, the investment bankers always fear that the management wants to build the investment side on the cheap.'**

Barclays was criticised for continuing to pay high bonuses to staff even after the financial crisis of 2008–9. BBC's *Panorama* calculated that in 2010–11 payments to shareholders had amounted to £1.4 billion while payment of bonuses for staff amounted to £6 billion. Martin Taylor, interviewed on the *Panorama* programme, argued that, in effect, shareholders were subsidising the payment of bonuses and that the bonus levels were unjustified.

However the *Guardian* newspaper argued that the roots of the problem were not just a matter of remuneration. It asked why people inside Barclays who knew what was happening with regard to Libor did nothing and suggested it was because of a culture 'of fierce tribal bonding':

'. . . it is clear that at least some people in finance are not primarily driven by money. But they are afraid, powerless, or both. Indeed, if you had to design a working environment that encouraged short-termist conformism and discouraged whistle blowing, then the finance sector would be your blueprint.

Take job security. In most big banks you can receive notice and find yourself being marched out of the building by security five minutes later. Some banks have annual "cullings", but even those who have avoided this have been going through redundancy rounds because of the harsh economic climate . . . If this creates a climate of fear, consider the average career pattern. Most people try to switch banks or roles every few years. Imagine when you know there is a huge problem in your bank – you also know it's time to move on to the next job.

Add to this the fact that people in finance are generally overpaid, so if they move to another industry they have to take a cut – which affects their ability to pay school fees and mortgages. That is assuming they can find a job – because (in 2012) the economy isn't exactly booming and skills that are highly valued in finance are next to worthless elsewhere.

Finally, there's the psychological dynamic, perhaps the strongest of all. Most high-flyers in investment banks describe their job not as work, but as a life . . . Bankers work in teams, and the ethic there is: you are with us or you're against us. Speaking out makes you vulnerable. If you have a guilty secret hidden somewhere, they'll find it and expose you . . . If you go public about something in the bank you believe to be wrong, in one stroke you place yourself outside of that world. It's not just your job – it's your identity.'

## The future

By 2012 and following the similarly questionable behaviour of UK banks such as RBS and Lloyds, as well as other European banks such as UBS and US banks such as J.P. Morgan, the whole business model of UK banks was being questioned. The Vickers Commission, established by the UK government to review the future of banking, was considering the separation of retail from investment banking. Early in 2013 there was a European Union directive stating that bankers' bonuses could be no more than one year's salary unless approved by shareholders. The new Barclays CEO Antony Jenkins also undertook a strategic review of the firm, examining the performance and reputation of 75 business units. In February 2013 this concluded that 39 business units were in good shape, 15 needed some attention, 17 needed serious attention to avoid closure or sale and four would definitely be sold or closed, one of which was its Structured Capital Markets business unit. Investment banking would remain with only modest proposed changes.

An internal memo from Jenkins to all Barclays staff also stated:

'Over a period of almost 20 years, banking became too aggressive, too focused on the short term, too disconnected from the needs of our customers and clients, and wider society. We were not immune at Barclays from these mistakes . . . Performance assessment will be based not just on what we deliver but on how we deliver it. We must never again be in a position of rewarding people for making the bank money in a way which is unethical or inconsistent with our values.'

Going forwards, Barclays staff would receive training on the central importance of five core values: respect, integrity, service, excellence and stewardship.

*Sources*: John Plender, 'How traders trumped Quakers', *Financial Times*, 6 July 2012.
*Panorama*: 'Inside Barclays: Banking on Bonuses', 11 February 2013. http://www.youtube.com/watch?v=FejXTeLAQOY.
Joris Luyendijk, 'Barclays emails reveal a climate of fear and fierce tribal bonding among traders', *Guardian*, 28 June 2012.
P. Jenkins, D. Schäfer and J. Thompson, 'Evangelism belies change at Barclays', *Financial Times*, 12 February 2013.

### Questions

1 How might issues of corporate governance explain the problems that arose at Barclays?

2 Who were the major stakeholders influencing the strategy of Barclays' investment banking? In your view, who should they have been?

3 Undertake a cultural web analysis of Barclays Bank's investment arm.

# 5 BUSINESS STRATEGY

## Learning outcomes

After reading this chapter you should be able to:

- Identify *strategic business units* (SBUs) in organisations.
- Assess business strategy in terms of the generic strategies of *cost leadership*, *differentiation* and *focus*.
- Identify business strategies suited to *hypercompetitive* conditions.
- Assess the benefits of *cooperation* in business strategy.

## Key terms

competitive advantage p. 107

competitive strategy p. 107

cost-leadership strategy p. 108

differentiation p. 112

focus strategy p. 113

strategic business unit p. 106

## 5.1 INTRODUCTION

This chapter is about strategic choices at the level of strategic business units. A **strategic business unit (SBU) supplies goods or services for a distinct domain of activity.** A small business focused on a single market, such as a restaurant or specialist retailer, would count as strategic business unit. Often, though, SBUs refer to businesses within a large diversified corporation. For example, a large consumer products company such as Unilever has a range of strategic business units, for example its ice cream business or its hair products business. Each of these business units must decide how it should operate in its own particular market. For example, Unilever's ice-cream business has to decide how it will compete against Nestlé's ice-cream business on a range of dimensions including product features, pricing, branding and distribution channels. These kinds of *business* strategy issues are distinct from the question as to whether Unilever should own an ice-cream business in the first place: this is a matter of *corporate* strategy, the subject of Chapter 6.

Figure 5.1 shows the main themes that provide the structure for the rest of the chapter. The chapter has two main themes:

- *Generic competitive strategies*, including *cost leadership, differentiation, focus* and *hybrid* strategies.
- *Interactive strategies*, building on the notion of generic strategies to consider interaction with competitors, especially in *hypercompetitive environments*, including *cooperative strategies*.

Business strategy is not just relevant to the private business sector. Charities and public-sector organisations both cooperate and compete. Thus charities compete between each other for support from donors. Public-sector organisations also need to be 'competitive' against comparable organisations in order to satisfy their stakeholders, secure their funding and protect themselves from alternative suppliers from the private sector. Although some of the detailed implications may vary between sectors, wherever comparison is possible with other similar organisations, basic principles of business strategy are likely to be relevant. Very few organisations can afford to be demonstrably inferior to peers, and almost all have to make choices on key competitive variables such as costs, prices and quality.

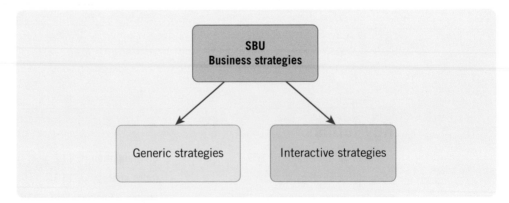

**Figure 5.1** Business strategy

## 5.2 GENERIC COMPETITIVE STRATEGIES

This section introduces the competitive element of business strategy, with cooperation addressed particularly in section 5.3. **Competitive strategy is concerned with how an SBU achieves competitive advantage in its domain of activity.** Competitive strategy therefore involves issues such as costs, product/service features and branding. In turn, **competitive advantage is about how an SBU creates value for its users both greater than the costs of supplying them and superior to that of rival SBUs.** Competitive advantages should underpin competitive strategies. There are two important features of competitive advantage. To be *competitive* at all, the SBU must ensure that customers see sufficient value that they are prepared to pay more than the costs of supply. To have an *advantage*, the SBU must be able to create greater value than competitors. In the absence of a competitive advantage, an SBU's competitive strategy is always vulnerable to competitors with better products or offering lower prices.

Michael Porter[1] argues that there are two fundamental means of achieving competitive advantage. An SBU can have structurally lower costs than its competitors. Or it can have products or services that are 'differentiated' from competitors' products in ways that are so valued by customers that it can charge higher prices. In defining competitive strategies, Porter adds a further dimension based on the scope of customers that the business chooses to serve. Businesses can choose to focus on narrow customer segments, for example a particular demographic group such as the youth market. Alternatively they can adopt a broad scope, targeting customers across a range of characteristics such as age, wealth or geography.

Porter's distinctions between cost, differentiation and scope define a set of 'generic' strategies: in other words, basic types of strategy that hold across many kinds of business situations. These three generic strategies are illustrated in Figure 5.2. In the top left-hand corner is a strategy of *cost leadership*, as exemplified in the British women's clothing market by retailers such as the leading multinational Primark. Operating in many countries across Europe, Primark is able to use economies of scale and tight cost discipline to serve a wide range of women with reasonably fashionable clothing at a good price. By contrast, the entrepreneurially-controlled Monsoon pursues a strategy of *differentiation*: it offers women of all ages the arty style ('boho chic') of its hippy founder, but at significantly higher prices. The third generic strategy is *focus*, involving a narrow competitive scope. Porter distinguishes between cost focus and differentiation focus, but for him narrow scope is such a distinctive fundamental principle that these two are merely variations on the same basic theme of narrowness. For example, in the United Kingdom the retail chain Evans pursues a *differentiation focus* strategy: supported by the 'plus-sized' singer Beth Ditto, Evans achieves a higher price by focusing specifically on women needing larger-sized clothing. On the other hand, major supermarkets tend to pursue *cost focus* strategies, targeting shoppers who are simply looking for good-value standard clothing for their families. The rest of this section discusses these three generic strategies in more detail.

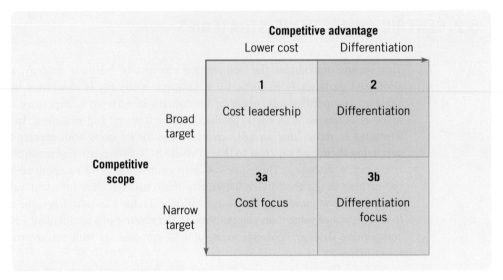

**Figure 5.2** Three generic strategies

## 5.2.1 Cost leadership

**Cost-leadership strategy involves becoming the lowest-cost organisation in a domain of activity.** There are four key *cost drivers* that can help deliver cost leadership, as follows:

- *Input costs* are often very important, for example labour or raw materials. Many companies seek competitive advantage through locating their labour-intensive operations in countries with low labour costs. Examples might be service call centres in India or manufacturing in China. Location close to raw material sources can also be advantageous, as for example the Brazilian steel producer CSN which benefits from its own local iron-ore facilities.

- *Economies of scale* refer to how increasing scale usually reduces the average costs of operation over a particular time period, perhaps a month or a year. Economies of scale are important wherever there are high fixed costs. Fixed costs are those costs necessary for a level of output: for example, a pharmaceutical manufacturer typically needs to do extensive R&D before it produces a single pill. Economies of scale come from spreading these fixed costs over high levels of output: the average cost due to an expensive R&D project halves when output increases from one million to two million units. Economies of scale in purchasing can also reduce input costs. The large airlines, for example, are able to negotiate steep discounts from aircraft manufacturers. For the cost-leader, it is important to reach the output level equivalent to the *minimum efficient scale*. Note, though, that *diseconomies of scale* are possible. Large volumes of output that require special overtime payments to workers or involve the neglect of equipment maintenance can soon become very expensive. As in Figure 5.3, therefore, the economies of scale curve is typically somewhat U-shaped, with the average cost per unit actually increasing beyond a certain point.

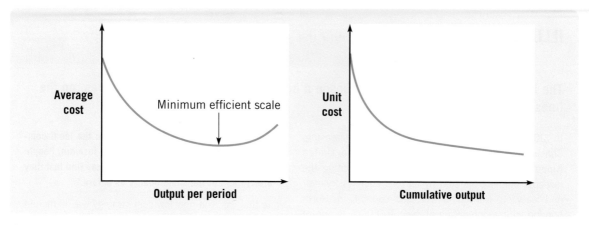

**Figure 5.3** Economies of scale and the experience curve

- *Experience*[2] can be a key source of cost efficiency. The *experience curve* implies that the cumulative experience gained by an organisation with each unit of output leads to reductions in unit costs (see Figure 5.3). For example, for many electronic components per unit costs can drop as much as 95 per cent every time the accumulated volume doubles. There is no time limit: simply the more experience an organisation has in an activity, the more efficient it gets at doing it. The efficiencies are basically of two sorts. First, there are gains in labour productivity as staff simply learn to do things more cheaply over time (this is the specific *learning curve* effect). Second, costs are saved through more efficient designs or equipment as experience shows what works best. The experience curve has three important implications for business strategy. First, entry timing into a market is important: early entrants into a market will have experience that late entrants do not yet have and so will gain a cost advantage. Second, it is important to gain and hold market share, as companies with higher market share have more 'cumulative experience' simply because of their greater volumes. Finally, although the gains from experience are typically greatest at the start, as indicated by the steep initial curve in Figure 5.3, improvements normally continue over time. Opportunities for cost reduction are theoretically endless. Figure 5.3 compares the experience curve and economies of scale in order to underline the contrast here. Unlike scale, where diseconomies appear beyond a certain point, the experience curve implies at worst a flattening of the rate of cost reduction. Cost savings due to accumulated experience are continuously available.

- *Product/process design* also influences cost. Efficiency can be 'designed in' at the outset. For example, engineers can choose to build a product from cheap standard components rather than expensive specialised components. Organisations can choose to interact with customers exclusively through cheap web-based methods, rather than via telephone or stores. Organisations can also tailor their offerings in order to meet the most important customer needs, saving money by ignoring others: this, arguably, is the strategy of Barnet, the 'easyCouncil' (Illustration 5.1). In designing a product or service, it is important to recognise *whole-life costs*: in other words, the costs to the customer not just of purchase but of subsequent use and maintenance. In the photocopier market, for example, Canon eroded Xerox's advantage (which was built on service and a support network) by designing a copier that needed far less servicing.

## ILLUSTRATION 5.1    easyCouncils: a not so easy low-cost strategy

**The London Borough of Barnet has chosen a budget airline model for its services, on the lines of easyJet.**

In 2008–9, with pressures on budgets increasing, Conservative-Party-controlled councils in the United Kingdom were looking to save costs by adopting the low-cost model pioneered by airlines such as Ryanair and easyJet. Barnet, a borough council in North London with a population of over 300,000, is one of the pioneers.

The Conservative borough council was led at the time by a former PwC management consultant, Mike Freer. In a context of falling central government subsidies, and wanting to save local taxes, the council was looking to cut costs by £15 m (~€16.5 m;~$22.5 m) a year. In 2008, the council launched a consultation process on radical reform called 'Future Shape'. In 2009, it declared its intention to adopt a budget airline model, which council officials dubbed 'easyCouncil'.

Mike Freer gave some examples. Just as budget airlines allow passengers to pay extra for priority boarding, in future householders will be able to pay extra to jump the queue in order to get faster responses on planning applications for new buildings or house extensions. Similarly, as airline passengers can choose whether to have a meal or not (and pay accordingly), users of adult social care will be allowed to choose their own options. Freer explained to the *Guardian*:

'In the past we would do things for our residents rather than letting them choose for themselves. We would tell them they need one hour help shopping, or one hour cleaning, meals-on-wheels, and they would get it, like it or not. Instead, we will assess what level of personal care they need, place a value on it and give them the budget. If they say, "Frankly, I'd like a weekend in Eastbourne [a holiday resort]", they can have it.'

Opposition Labour leader Alison Moore warned in the *Guardian*:

'There is a real danger of problems in the local community and that vulnerable people will lose out. People who are dependent on care services may find that they aren't there at the same quality as before.'

None the less, the new low-cost strategy was launched in 2009. Unfortunately, the costs of retraining staff, building an in-house delivery team, hiring consultants and closing facilities were higher than originally projected. The council estimated it spent £1.5 m on delivering the first year of the reform programme. On the other hand, savings were slower to come through than expected, with a series of strikes by council workers resisting job cuts and the transfer of many employees to private-sector subcontractors. Savings in the first year were just £1.4 m, less than half of what had been projected. Alison Moore, leader of the Opposition, commented: 'Barnet claim that easyCouncil is all about a relentless drive for efficiency, so it is absurd that in the first year, they've spent more money than they've saved.' By this time, Mike Freer had moved on to become a Member of Parliament. However, Lynne Hillan, the new council leader, said it was too soon to judge. Big savings would come soon: 'The programme took longer to establish than planned because we took the decision to develop an in-house team of officers. I've no doubt this will give us the most efficient process and the greatest long-term savings.'

*Sources*: *Guardian*, 27 August 2009; *Guardian*, 26 October 2010; *The Economist*, 22 September 2012.

### Questions

1  What are the advantages and disadvantages of this approach to low-cost council services?

2  In what sense do borough councils 'compete'?

Porter underlines two tough requirements for cost-based strategies. First of all, the principle of competitive advantage indicates that a business's cost structure needs to be *lowest* cost (i.e. lower than all competitors'). Having the second-lowest cost structure implies a competitive disadvantage against somebody. Competitors with higher costs than the cost-leader are always at risk of being undercut on price, especially in market downturns. For businesses competing on a cost basis, cost leadership is always more secure than being second or third in terms of costs.

Porter's second requirement is that low cost should not be pursued in total disregard for quality. To sell its products or services, the cost-leader has to be able to meet market standards. For example, low-cost Chinese car producers seeking to export into Western markets need to offer not only cars that are cheap, but also cars that meet acceptable norms in terms of style, service network, reliability, resale value and other important characteristics. Cost-leaders have two options here:

- *Parity* (in other words, equivalence) with competitors in product or service features valued by customers. Parity allows the cost-leader to charge the same prices as the average competitor in the marketplace, while translating its cost advantage wholly into extra profit (as in the second column of Figure 5.4). The Brazilian steel producer CSN, with its cheap iron-ore sources, is able to charge the average price for its steel, and take the cost difference in greater profit.

- *Proximity* (closeness) to competitors in terms of features. Where a competitor is sufficiently close to competitors in terms of product or service features, customers may only require small cuts in prices to compensate for the slightly lower quality. As shown in the third column in Figure 5.4, the proximate cost-leader still earns better profits than the average competitor because its lower price eats up only a part of its cost advantage. This proximate cost-leadership strategy might be the option chosen initially by Chinese car manufacturers in export markets, for example.

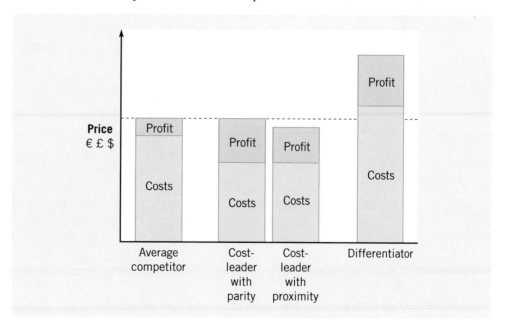

**Figure 5.4** Costs, prices and profits for generic strategies

## 5.2.2 Differentiation strategies

For Porter, the principal alternative to cost leadership is differentiation.[3] **Differentiation involves uniqueness along some dimension that is sufficiently valued by customers to allow a price premium.** Relevant points of differentiation vary between markets. Within each market too, businesses may differentiate along different dimensions. Thus in clothing retail, competitors may differentiate by store size, locations or fashion. In cars, competitors may differentiate by safety, style or fuel efficiency. Where there are many alternative dimensions that are valued by customers, it is possible to have many different types of differentiation strategy in a market. Thus, even at the same top end of the car market, BMW and Mercedes differentiate in different ways, the first typically with a sportier image, the second with more conservative values.

The strategy canvas provides one means of mapping these various kinds of differentiation (see section 2.4.3).

Managers can identify potential for differentiation by using perceptual mapping of their products or services against those of competitors. For example, Figure 5.5 maps customer perceptions of American airline companies in the 2000s along two bundles of attributes: flight performance attributes such as delays, and service attributes such as baggage problems or boarding complaints. Most of the larger airlines are quite closely bunched together. For example, US Air and Delta are not significantly differentiated from each other in terms of

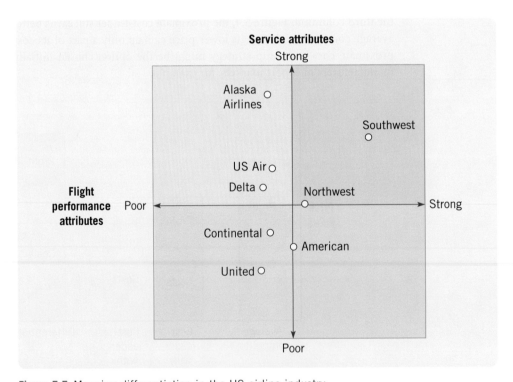

**Figure 5.5** Mapping differentiation in the US airline industry

*Source*: Simplified from Figure 1, in D. Gursoy, M. Chen and H. Kim (2005) 'The US airlines relative positioning', *Tourism Management*, 26, 5, 57–67: p. 62. Some of these airlines have since merged.

on-time flights, and they are perceived similarly in terms of service elements such as boarding, ticketing and reservations. One airline that does stand out as a differentiator is Southwest, which does well in terms of both flight delays and service. In the period studied, Southwest was also the most profitable of these airlines. It seems that Southwest was able to differentiate on attributes that were highly valued by its customers.

However, the attributes on which to differentiate need to be chosen carefully. Differentiation strategies require clarity about two key factors:

- *The strategic customer.* It is vital to identify clearly the strategic customer on whose needs the differentiation is based. This is not always straightforward. For example, for a newspaper business, the strategic customers could be readers (who pay a purchase price), advertisers (who pay for advertising), or both. Finding a distinctive means of prioritising customers can be a valuable source of differentiation.

- *Key competitors.* It is very easy for a differentiator to draw the boundaries for comparison too tightly, concentrating on a particular niche. Thus specialist Italian clothing company Benetton originally had a strong position with its specialist knitwear shops. However, it lost ground because it did not recognise early enough that general retailers such as Marks & Spencer could also compete in the same product space of colourful pullovers and similar products.

There is an important condition for a successful differentiation strategy. Differentiation allows higher prices, but usually comes at a cost. To create a point of valuable differentiation typically involves additional investments, for example in R&D, branding or staff quality. The differentiator can expect that its costs will be higher than those of the average competitor. But, as shown in the fourth column of Figure 5.4, the differentiator needs to ensure that the additional costs of differentiation do not exceed the gains in price. It is easy to pile on additional costs in ways that are not valued sufficiently by customers. The historic failures under British ownership of the luxury car companies Rolls-Royce and Bentley against top-end Mercedes cars are partly attributable to the expensive crafting of wood and leather interiors, the full cost of which even wealthy customers were not prepared to pay for. Just as cost-leaders should not neglect quality, so should differentiators attend closely to costs, especially in areas irrelevant to their sources of differentiation. As in Illustration 5.2, Volvo's differentiation strategy in the Indian bus market seems to have involved keeping an eye on costs as well.

### 5.2.3 Focus strategies

Porter distinguishes focus as the third generic strategy, based on competitive scope. A **focus strategy targets a narrow segment or domain of activity and tailors its products or services to the needs of that specific segment to the exclusion of others.** Focus strategies come in two variants, according to the underlying sources of competitive advantage, cost or differentiation. In air travel, Ryanair follows a *cost focus strategy*, targeting price-conscious holiday travellers with no need for connecting flights. In the domestic detergent market, the Belgian company Ecover follows a *differentiation focus* strategy, gaining a price premium over rivals on account of its ecological cleaning products.

The focuser achieves competitive advantage by dedicating itself to serving its target segments better than others which are trying to cover a wider range of segments. Serving a broad range of segments can bring disadvantages in terms of coordination, compromise or inflexibility. Focus strategies are able to seek out the weak spots of broad cost-leaders and differentiators:

- *Cost focusers* identify areas where broader cost-based strategies fail because of the added costs of trying to satisfy a wide range of needs. For instance, in the United Kingdom food retail market, Iceland Foods has a cost-focused strategy concentrated on frozen and chilled foods, reducing costs against generalist discount food retailers such as Aldi which have all the complexity of fresh foods and groceries as well as their own frozen and chilled food ranges.

- *Differentiation focusers* look for specific needs that broader differentiators do not serve so well. Focus on one particular need helps to build specialist knowledge and technology, increases commitment to service and can improve brand recognition and customer loyalty. For example, ARM Holdings dominates the world market for mobile phone chips, despite being only a fraction of the size of the leading microprocessor manufacturers, AMD and Intel, which also make chips for a wide range of computers.

Successful focus strategies depend on at least one of three key factors:

- *Distinct segment needs.* Focus strategies depend on the distinctiveness of segment needs. If segment distinctiveness erodes, it becomes harder to defend the segment against broader competitors. For example, when the boundaries blurred between smart phones used by general consumers and smart phones used by business people, it has become easier for Apple to attack the distinctive niche once dominated by BlackBerry's business phones.

- *Distinct segment value chains.* Focus strategies are strengthened if they have distinctive value chains that will be difficult or costly for rivals to construct. If the production pro-cesses and distribution channels are very similar, it is easy for a broad-based differentiator to push a specialised product through its own standardised value chain at a lower cost than a rival focuser. In detergents, Procter & Gamble cannot easily respond to Ecover because achieving the same ecological friendliness would involve transforming its purchasing and production processes.

- *Viable segment economics.* Segments can easily become too small to serve economically as demand or supply conditions change. For example, changing economies of scale and greater competition have eliminated from many smaller cities the traditional town-centre department stores, with their wider ranges of different kinds of goods from hardware to clothing.

## 5.2.4 'Stuck in the middle'?

Porter claims that managers face a crucial choice between the generic strategies of cost leader-ship, differentiation and focus. According to him, it is unwise to blur this choice. As earlier, the lowest-cost competitor can always undercut the second lowest-cost competitor. For a company seeking advantage through low costs, therefore, it makes no sense to add extra costs by half-hearted efforts at differentiation. For a differentiator, it is self-defeating to make economies that jeopardise the basis for differentiation. For a focuser, it is dangerous to move

## ILLUSTRATION 5.2    Volvo's different Indian buses

**Volvo has a strategy to sell buses at nearly four times the prevailing market price.**

The Indian bus market has long been dominated by two home players, subsidiaries of major Indian conglomerates: Tata Motors and Ashok Leyland. The two companies made simple coaches on a design that had hardly changed for decades. On top of a basic truck chassis, the two companies bolted a rudimentary coach body. Engines were a meagre 110–120 horse-power, and roared heartily as they hauled their loads up the steep mountain roads of India. Mounted at the front, the heat from the over-strained engines would pervade the whole bus. Air conditioning was a matter of open windows, through which the dust and noise of the Indian roads would pour. Suspension was old-fashioned, guaranteeing a shaky ride on pot-holed roads. Bags were typically slung on the top of the bus, where they were easily soiled and at high risk of theft. But at least the buses were cheap, selling to local bus companies at around Rs 1.2 m (€15,000; $21,000).

In 1997, Swedish bus company Volvo decided to enter the market, with buses priced at Rs 4 m, nearly four times as much as local products. Akash Passey, Volvo's first Indian employee, commissioned a consultancy company to evaluate prospects. The consultancy company recommended that Volvo should not even try. Passey told the *Financial Times*: 'My response was simple – I took the report and went to the nearest dustbin and threw it in.' Passey entered the market in 2001 with the high-priced luxury buses.

Passey used the time to develop a distinctive strategy. His basic product had superior features. Volvo's standard engines were 240–250 hp and mounted at the back, ensuring a faster and quieter ride. Air conditioning was standard of course. The positioning of the engine and the specific bus design of the chassis meant a more roomy interior, plus storage for bags internally. But Passey realised this would not be enough. He commented to the *Financial Times*: 'You had to do a lot of things to break the way business is done normally.'

Volvo offered post-sale maintenance services, increasing life expectancy of buses from three to ten years, and allowing bus operating companies to dispense with their own expensive maintenance workshops. Free training was given to drivers, so they drove more safely and took more care of their buses. The company advertised the benefits of the buses direct to customers in cinemas, rather than simply promoting them to the bus operators. To kick-start the market, Volvo supplied about 20 subsidised trial units to selected operators. Volvo trainees rode these buses, alerting the company immediately when something went wrong so Volvo could immediately send its engineers. Faster, smoother and more reliable travel allowed the bus operators to increase their ticket prices for the luxury Volvo buses by 35 per cent.

Business people and the middle classes were delighted with the new Volvo services. Speedier, more comfortable journeys allowed them to arrive fresh for meetings and potentially to save the costs of overnight stays. Tata and Ashok Leyland both now produce their own luxury buses, with Mercedes and Isuzu following Volvo into the market. None the less, the phrase 'taking a Volvo' has become synonymous with choosing a luxury bus service in India, rather as 'hoover' came to refer to any kind of vacuum cleaner.

In 2008, Volvo opened a new state-of-the-art bus factory in Bangalore. It is Volvo's most efficient bus factory worldwide, producing a fully built bus in 20–25 days. Annual capacity is 1,000 buses per year.

*Source*: Adapted from J. Leahy, 'Volvo takes a lead in India', *Financial Times*, 31 August 2009.

### Questions

1. Rank the elements of Passey's strategy for Volvo in order of importance. Could any have been dispensed with?

2. How sustainable is Volvo's luxury bus strategy?

outside the original specialised segment, because products or services tailored to one set of customers are likely to have inappropriate costs or features for the new target customers. This was a problem for BlackBerry as it tried to move its secure business phones into the broader consumer market, for which the availability of apps was more important than the business need of email encryption. Porter's argument is that it's generally best that managers choose which generic strategy they are pursuing and then stick rigorously to it. Otherwise there is a danger of being *stuck in the middle*, doing no strategy well.

Although there are cases of companies apparently combining the cost-leadership and differentiation strategies, Porter's warning about the danger of being stuck in the middle provides a useful discipline for managers. It is very easy for them to make incremental decisions that compromise the basic generic strategy. As profits accumulate, the successful cost-leader will be tempted to stop scrimping and saving. In hard times, a differentiator might easily cut back the R & D or advertising investments essential to its long-term differentiation advantage. Consistency with generic strategy provides a valuable check for managerial decision making.

## 5.2.5 The Strategy Clock

The Strategy Clock provides another way of approaching the generic strategies (see Figure 5.6), one which gives more scope for *hybrid* strategies.[4] The Strategy Clock has two distinctive features. First, it is focused on prices to customers rather than costs to the organisation: because prices are more visible than costs, the Strategy Clock can be easier to use in comparing competitors. Second, the circular design of the clock allows for more continuous choices than Michael Porter's sharp contrast between cost leadership and differentiation: there is a full range of incremental adjustments that can be made between the 7 o'clock position at the bottom of the low-price strategy and the 2 o'clock position at the bottom of the differentiation strategy. Organisations often travel around the clock, as they adjust their pricing and benefits over time.

The Strategy Clock identifies three zones of feasible strategies, and one zone likely to lead to ultimate failure:

- *Differentiation (zone 1)*. This zone contains a range of feasible strategies for building on high perceptions of product or service benefits among customers. Close to the 12 o'clock position is a strategy of *differentiation without price premium*. Differentiation without a price premium combines high perceived benefits and moderate prices, typically used to gain market share. If high benefits also entail relatively high costs, this moderate pricing strategy would only be sustainable in the short term. Once increased market share has been achieved, it might be logical to move to *differentiation with price premium* closer to a 1 or 2 o'clock position. Movement all the way towards the 2 o'clock position is likely to involve a focus strategy, in Michael Porter's terms. Such a *focused differentiation* strategy targets a niche where the higher prices and reduced benefits are sustainable, for instance because of a lack of competition in a particular geographical area.

- *Low-price (zone 2)*. This zone allows for different combinations of low prices and low perceived value. Close to the 9 o'clock position, a standard *low-price* strategy would gain market share, by combining low prices with reasonable value (at parity with competitors).

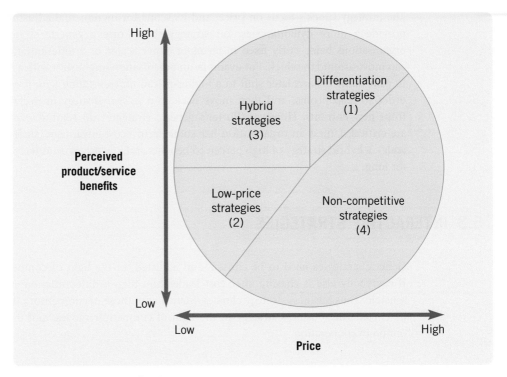

**Figure 5.6** The Strategy Clock

*Source*: Adapted from D. Faulkner and C. Bowman, *The Essence of Competitive Strategy*, Prentice Hall, 1995.

To be sustainable, this strategy needs to be underpinned by some cost advantage, such as economies of scale gained through increased market share. Without such a cost advantage, cuts in benefits or increases in prices become necessary eventually. A variation on the standard low-price strategy is the *no-frills* strategy, close to the 7 o'clock position. No-frills strategies involve both low benefits and low prices, similar to low-cost airlines such as Ryanair (which even proposed to charge for use of its on-board toilets).

- *Hybrid strategy (zone 3)*. A distinctive feature of the Strategy Clock is the space it allows between low-price and differentiation strategies.[5] Hybrid strategies involve both lower prices than differentiation strategies, and higher benefits than low-price strategies. Hybrid strategies are often used to make aggressive bids for increased market share. They can also be an effective way of entering a new market, for instance overseas. Even in the case of innovations with high benefits, it can make sense to price low initially in order to gain experience curve efficiencies or lock-in through network effects. Some companies sustain hybrid strategies over long periods of time: for example, furniture store IKEA, which uses scale advantages to combine relatively low prices with differentiated Swedish design (see Chapter case example).

- *Non-competitive strategies (zone 4)*. The final set of strategies occupies a zone of unfeasible economics, with low benefits and high prices. Unless businesses have exceptional strategic lock-in, customers will quickly reject these combinations. Typically these strategies lead to failure.

The Strategy Clock's focus on price, and its scope for incremental adjustments in strategy, provide a more dynamic view on strategy than Porter's generic strategies. Instead of organisations being fairly fixed in terms of either a cost or a differentiation strategy, they can move around the clock. For example, an organisation might start with a *low-price* strategy to gain market share, later shift to a higher-priced *differentiation with premium* strategy in order to reap profits, and then move back to a *hybrid strategy* in order to defend itself from new entrants. However, Porter's generic strategies do remind managers that costs are critical. Unless an organisation has some secure cost advantage (such as economies of scale), a hybrid strategy of high perceived benefits and low prices is unlikely to be sustainable for long.

## 5.3 INTERACTIVE STRATEGIES

Generic strategies need to be chosen, and adjusted, in the light of competitors' strategies. If everybody else is chasing after cost leadership, then a differentiation strategy might be sensible. Thus business strategy choices *interact* with those of competitors. This section starts by considering business strategy in the light of competitor moves, and then addresses the option of cooperation.

### 5.3.1 Interactive price and quality strategies

Richard D'Aveni depicts competitor interactions in terms of movements against the variables of price (the vertical axis) and perceived quality (the horizontal axis), similar to the Strategy Clock: see Figure 5.7.[6] Although D'Aveni applies his analysis to the very fast-moving environments he terms 'hypercompetitive', similar reasoning applies wherever competitors' moves are interdependent.

Figure 5.7 shows different organisations competing by emphasising either low prices or high quality or some mixture of the two. Graph (i) starts with a 'first value line', describing various trade-offs in terms of price and perceived quality that are acceptable to customers. The cost-leading firm (here L) offers relatively poor perceived quality, but customers accept this because of the lower price. While the relative positions on the graph should not be taken exactly literally, in the car market this cost-leading position might describe some of Hyundai's products. The differentiator (D) has a higher price, but much better quality. This might be Mercedes. In between, there are a range of perfectly acceptable combinations, with the mid-point firm (M) offering a combination of reasonable prices and reasonable quality. This might be Ford. M's strategy is on the first value line and therefore entirely viable at this stage. On the other hand, firm U is uncompetitive, falling behind the value line. Its price is higher than M's, and its quality is worse. U's predicament is typical of the business that is 'stuck in the middle', in Porter's terms. U no longer offers acceptable value and must quickly move back onto the value line or fail.

In any market, competitors and their moves or counter-moves can be plotted against these two axes of price and perceived value. For example, in graph (i) of Figure 5.7, the differentiator (D) makes an aggressive move by substantially improving its perceived quality while

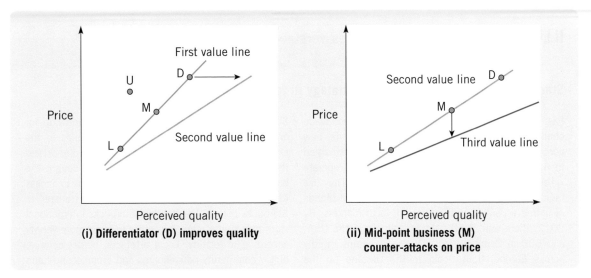

**Figure 5.7** Interactive price and quality strategies

*Note*: axes are not necessarily to linear scales.

*Source*: Adapted from *Hypercompetition: Managing the Dynamics of Strategic Manoeuvring*, The Free Press (D'Aveni, Richard with Robert Gunther 1994) with the permission of Simon & Schuster Publishing Group from the Free Press edition. Copyright © 1994 by Richard D'Aveni. All rights reserved.

holding its prices. This improvement in quality shifts customer expectations of quality right across the market. These changed expectations are reflected by the new, second value line (in green). With the second value line, even the cost-leader (L) may have to make some improvement to quality, or accept a small price cut. But the greatest threat is for the mid-point competitor, M. To catch up with the second value line, M must respond either by making a substantial improvement in quality while holding prices, or by slashing prices, or by some combination of the two.

However, mid-point competitor M also has the option of an aggressive counter-attack. Given the necessary capabilities, M might choose to push the value line still further outwards, wrong-footing differentiator D by creating a third value line that is even more demanding in terms of the price-perceived quality trade-off. The starting point in graph (ii) of Figure 5.7 is all three competitors L, M and D successfully reaching the second value line (uncompetitive U has disappeared). However, M's next move is to go beyond the second value line by making radical cuts in price while sustaining its new level of perceived quality. Again, customer expectations are changed and a third value line (in red) is established. Now it is differentiator D that is at most risk of being left behind, and it faces hard choices about how to respond in terms of price and quality.

Plotting moves and counter-moves in these terms underlines the dynamic and interactive nature of business strategy. Economically viable positions along the value line are always in danger of being superseded as competitors move either downwards in terms of price or outwards in terms of perceived quality. The generic strategies of cost leadership and differentiation should not be seen as static positions, but as dynamic trajectories along the axes of price and quality. The movement towards more 'local' Starbucks stores demonstrates the need to be continually moving along the trajectory of differentiation (see Illustration 5.3).

## ILLUSTRATION 5.3 — McCafés versus Starbucks

**Starbucks coffee chain changes its strategy in response to McDonald's challenge.**

Fast food chain McDonald's has launched a worldwide challenge to coffee giant Starbucks with its new concept, McCafés. The McCafé concept had emerged in Australia in the 1990s. McCafés typically operate within or next to regular McDonald's outlets. They use high-quality coffee machines and sell different blends of coffee according to the tastes of local markets. By 2012, there were 1,500 McCafé outlets in the USA, and 600 in Germany. McCafés are spreading rapidly across Europe, from Spain to the Ukraine (in the United Kingdom, McCafé products are still sold under the usual McDonald's brand).

Starbucks is the world's largest coffee chain, with nearly 20,000 stores across 60 countries from Canada to China. Founded in 1971, Starbucks was bought as a small Seattle coffee shop chain by Howard Schultz in 1988. The Starbucks' original concept was good coffee, brewed in an intimate atmosphere by skilled 'barristas'. Schultz expanded rapidly, with his first store outside North America opening in Tokyo in 1996. In 2001, Schultz retired as CEO and under the next two CEOs Starbucks continued its expansion. But in 2007, performance was beginning to flag. Schultz wrote a famous 'Valentine's Day memo' to the then CEO, complaining that growth had led to a 'commoditisation' of the Starbucks' concept. The introduction of automatic espresso machines to speed up service removed the distinctive coffee odour in the shops and deskilled the barristas. The next year, Schultz returned to the helm as CEO.

As he started back in his old job, Howard Schultz proclaimed:

'We are laser-focused on delivering the finest quality coffee and getting the customer experience right every time. We have. . . . been putting our feet into the shoes of our customers and are responding directly to their needs. Our customers are telling us they want value and quality and we will deliver that in a way that is meaningful to them and authentic to Starbucks.'

Schultz famously closed all the stores worldwide for an afternoon in order to retrain the barristas in the skills of brewing good coffee. Starbucks also improved its food offerings: in 2012, the company bought the bakery chain La Boulange for $100 m. So as to access its innovative, quality food products for transfer to Starbucks outlets, the standard Starbucks international store format was relaxed in order to allow more variety according to locality. Local artefacts, bolder colours, bigger community noticeboards and even second-hand furniture were used to create more individual stores. Starbucks stores offered free wi-fi to users.

McDonald's is aiming to match Starbucks' changes. Thus McDonald's too introduced free wi-fi. The quality and price of McDonald's coffees are highly competitive. Thus a McCafé frappé drink cost $3.99 for a 16 ounce drink in 2012 (against $4.20 for a Big Mac burger); Starbucks' equivalent frappuccino cost $5.45. The Canadian *Globe and Mail* reviewed the two companies' products in 2011. The comment on McCafé was: 'It tastes like a combination of damp forest and uncleaned coffee maker.' As for the Starbucks product, it was 'bitter; burnt toast. This is so bad, it's the antithesis of coffee.' Overall, the *Globe and Mail* rated McCafé as slightly superior.

*Sources*: *Financial Times*, 26 May 2009; smartmoney.com, 23 July 2012; the *Globe and Mail*, 8 November 2011.

### Questions

1 Plot the moves of McDonald's and Starbucks on the axes of price and perceived quality, as in Figure 5.7.

2 What should be done by a company with a similar original position to Starbucks, but operating in a market where McCafé has not yet arrived (e.g. Costa Coffee in the United Kingdom)?

## 5.3.2 Cooperative strategy

So far the emphasis has been on competition and competitive advantage. However, the inter-active moves and counter-moves in section 5.3.1 make it clear that sometimes competition can escalate in a way that is dangerous to all competitors. It can be in the self-interest of organisations to restrain competition. Moreover, advantage may not always be achieved just by competing. Cooperation between some organisations in a market may give them advantage over other competitors in the same market, or potential new entrants. In short, one form of interactive strategy is cooperation, not just competition.[7]

Figure 5.8 illustrates various kinds of benefits from cooperation between firms in terms of Michael Porter's five forces of buyers, suppliers, rivals, entrants and substitutes (section 2.3.1). Key benefits of cooperation are as follows:

- *Suppliers*. In Figure 5.8, cooperation between rivals A and B in an industry will increase their purchasing power against suppliers. Sometimes this increased cooperation is used simply to squeeze supplier prices. However, cooperation between rivals A and B may

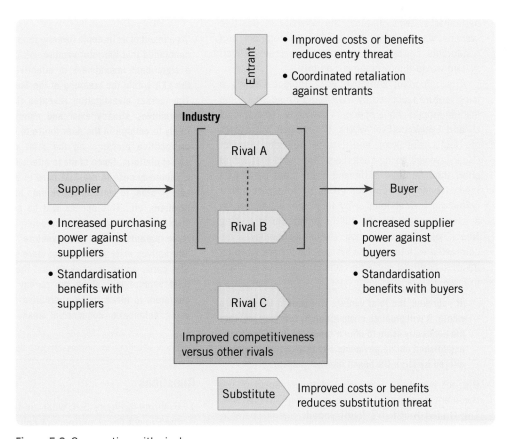

**Figure 5.8** Cooperating with rivals

*Source*: Adapted from *Competitive Strategy: Techniques for Analysing Industries and Competitors*, The Free Press (by Michael E. Porter 1998) with the permission of Simon & Schuster Publishing Group from the Free Press edition. Copyright © 1980, 1998 by The Free Press. All rights reserved.

## ILLUSTRATION 5.4    Mobile payment systems: cooperating to pay

**Cooperative agreements in mobile payment systems may leave some players out.**

The opportunities in mobile payment systems ('mobile wallets') attracted a very wide range of competitors and approaches. In 2011, the value of mobile payments worldwide was $240 bn, a sum expected to triple in the following five years. Companies which could skim even a tiny percentage of this total through offering mobile payment services could earn fortunes. Moreover, they would have access to valuable data about which consumers bought what, where and when. It was hardly surprising that companies as diverse as Google, Apple, Facebook, PayPal, Visa, Barclays and BlackBerry were crowding into the new market, each with its own particular systems. Indeed, the diversity of possible systems was creating confusion, with retailers and restaurants hesitating to adopt before seeing which system would finally come out on top.

One important initiative was 'Project Oscar', a joint venture launched by the United Kingdom's three leading mobile phone operators Vodafone, Telefónica's $O_2$ and EverythingEverywhere, the merged businesses of DeutscheTelekom and France Telecom. Project Oscar involved giving customers SIM cards that would allow them to store debit and credit card details on their phones and pay for goods or transport either online via their mobile or by tapping the handset on a special reader at the till or ticket barrier, using Near Field Communication (NFC) technology. This contrasted with the Google system, for instance, which involved getting a whole new phone. The three partners in Project Oscar declared:

'If approved, the joint venture will benefit UK plc as a whole. It will promote competition by bringing together the necessary scale to offer a credible alternative to the established online payments and advertising platforms offered by large US-based internet players.'

But not everybody was happy at the prospect of the dominant phone operators collaborating in this way. The United Kingdom's fourth mobile phone operator, Three, complained:

'The JV (Project Oscar) will control and sell access to over 90 per cent of UK mobile subscribers and their data, thus allowing Deutsche Telekom, France Telecom, Vodafone and Telefónica to foreclose the market to third-parties and neatly do away with the inconvenience of competing with each other.'

In April 2012, with the support of Google, Three successfully referred the joint venture to the European competition authorities.

The European Commission investigated, aware of a long history of illicit collusion between the various mobile phone operators in Europe. However, the Commission came down in favour of Project Oscar. It declared:

'As a result of its in-depth investigation, the Commission concluded that the joint venture will not likely lead to a significant impediment to effective competition in the EEA within the meaning of the Merger Regulation. The market investigation revealed that a number of alternatives already exist and much more are very likely to emerge in the near future to ensure adequate competitive pressure on the joint venture's mobile wallet platform. Some of these alternatives may rely on a secure access to the SIM card of the mobile handsets in order to store sensitive data like bank account numbers, etc. This access will be controlled by the mobile network operators, including in particular the three parents of the joint venture. However, other alternatives exist which do not store sensitive data on SIM cards and it is unlikely that the creation of the joint venture will allow the parent mobile network operators to block these alternative routes to market using technical or commercial means.'

*Sources: Guardian*, 7 March 2012; *Financial Times*, 8 March 2012 and 29 April 2012; *Communications World*, 5 September 2012.

### Questions

1 In terms of Figure 5.8, what are the benefits to the Project Oscar partners of collaboration?

2 What options are available now to the excluded Three?

enable them to standardise requirements, allowing suppliers to make cost reductions to all parties' benefit. For example, if two car manufacturers agreed on common component specifications, their suppliers could gain economies through production of the standardised part on a greater scale (this kind of *complementarity* is discussed in Chapter 2).

- *Buyers*. Conversely, cooperation between rivals A and B will increase their power as suppliers vis-à-vis buyers. It will be harder for buyers to shop around. Such *collusion* between rivals can help maintain or raise prices, though it may well attract penalties from competition regulators. On the other hand, buyers may benefit if their inputs are standardised, again enabling reductions in costs that all can share. For example, if food manufacturers supplying a retailer agree on common pallet sizes for deliveries, the retailer can manage its warehouses much more efficiently.

- *Rivals*. If cooperative rivals A and B are getting benefits with regard to both buyers and suppliers, other competitors without such agreements – in Figure 5.8, rival C – will be at a competitive disadvantage. Rival C will be in danger of being squeezed out of the industry. This was the predicament of mobile phone operator Three in Illustration 5.4.

- *Entrants*. Similarly, potential entrants will likely lack the advantages of the combined rivals A and B. Moreover, A and B can coordinate their retaliation strategies against any new entrant, for example by cutting prices by the same proportions in order to protect their own relative positions while undermining the competitiveness of the new entrant.

- *Substitutes*. Finally, the improved costs or efficiencies that come from cooperation between rivals A and B reduce the incentives for buyers to look to substitutes. Steel companies have cooperated on research to reduce the weight of steel used in cars, in order to discourage car manufacturers from switching to lighter substitutes such as aluminium or plastics.

Further kinds of cooperation will be considered under alliance strategy in section 9.4.

## SUMMARY

- Business strategy is concerned with seeking competitive advantage in markets at the level of *strategic business units* (SBUs) rather than *corporate* level.

- Porter's framework and the Strategy Clock define various *generic strategies*, including *cost-leadership*, *differentiation*, *focus* and *hybrid* strategies.

- *Cooperative strategies* may offer alternatives to competitive strategies or may run in parallel.

- To watch an author video on the concepts discussed in this chapter please visit www.mystrategylab.com, and click on 'Author perspectives on strategic management'.

## VIDEO ASSIGNMENTS

MyStrategyLab

If you are using *MyStrategyLab* you might find it useful to watch the CISCO case study for Chapter 6.

1 Explain the concept of generic strategy using either Porter's framework or the Strategy Clock drawing on examples from the IT sector.

2 Using section 5.4, explain how 'cooperative strategies' are used by CISCO to enhance its competitive advantage.

## RECOMMENDED KEY READINGS

- The foundations of the discussions of generic competitive strategies are to be found in the writings of Michael Porter, which include *Competitive Strategy* (1980) and *Competitive Advantage* (1985), both published by Free Press.

- Hypercompetition, and the strategies associated with it, are explained in Richard D'Aveni, *Hypercompetitive Rivalries: Competing in Highly Dynamic Environments*, Free Press, 1995.

## REFERENCES

1. This section draws heavily on M. Porter, *Competitive Advantage*, Free Press, 1985. For a more recent discussion of the generic strategies concept, see J. Parnell, 'Generic strategies after two decades: a reconceptualisation of competitive strategy', *Management Decision*, vol. 48, no. 8 (2006), pp. 1139–54.

2. See A.C. Hax and N.S. Majluf, in R.G. Dyson (ed.), *Strategic Planning: Models and Analytical Techniques*, Wiley, 1990.

3. B. Sharp and J. Dawes, 'What is differentiation and how does it work?', *Journal of Marketing Management*, vol. 17, nos 7/8 (2001), pp. 739–59, reviews the relationship between differentiation and profitability.

4. See D. Faulkner and C. Bowman, *The Essence of Competitive Strategy*, Prentice Hall, 1995.

5. For empirical support for the benefits of a hybrid strategy, see E. Pertusa-Ortega, J. Molina-Azorín and E. Claver-Cortés, 'Competitive strategies and firm performance: a comparative analysis of pure, hybrid and "stuck-in-the-middle" strategies in Spanish firms', *British Journal of Management*, vol. 20, no. 4 (2008), pp. 508–23.

6. R. D'Aveni, *Hypercompetition: Managing the Dynamics of Strategic Maneuvering*, Free Press, 1994.

7. A useful book on collaborative strategies is Y. Doz and G. Hamel, *Alliance Advantage: The Art of Creating Value through Partnering*, Harvard Business School Press, 1998.

# The IKEA approach
Kevan Scholes*

'In times when many nations and people face economic challenges our vision of creating a better everyday life for the many people is more relevant than ever. To make it possible to furnish functionally, individually and sustainably – even when the economy is tight.'

This was Mikael Ohlsson, IKEA's Chief Executive, speaking in 2012 while reporting a sales increase of 6.9 per cent (to €25.2 billion), profits of €3 billion and share gains in most markets. At the same time average prices had fallen by 2.6 per cent. IKEA had become the world's largest home furnishings company with 287 stores in 26 countries and employing 131,000 people.

## The home furnishings market

By the late 2000s home furnishings was a huge market worldwide with retail sales in excess of $US600 bn in items such as furniture, household textiles and floor coverings. More than 50 per cent of these sales were in furniture stores. Table 1 compares the geographical spread of the market and IKEA sales by region.

## IKEA's competitors

The home furnishings market was highly fragmented with competition occurring locally rather than globally. In each region that IKEA had stores it would typically face competitors of several types:

- Multinational furniture retailers (like IKEA) all of whom were considerably smaller than IKEA. These included the Danish company Jysk (turnover ~€2.5 bn).

Source: The Asahi Shimbun/Getty Images.

- Companies specialising in just part of the furniture product range and operating in several countries – such as Alno from Germany in kitchens.

- Multi-branch retail furniture outlets whose sales were mainly in one country such as DFS in the UK. The US market was dominated by such players (e.g. Bed, Bath & Beyond Inc. with revenues of some $US9 bn).

- Non-specialist companies who carried furniture as part of a wider product range. In the UK the largest operator

**Table 1** The geographical spread of the market and of IKEA sales by region

|  | Europe | Americas | Asia/Pacific |
|---|---|---|---|
| % of global market | 52 | 29 | 19 |
| % of IKEA sales | 79 | 14 | 7 |

was the Home Retail Group whose subsidiary Argos offered some 33,000 general merchandise products through its network of 340 stores and online sales. Despite this more generalist offering Argos was number one in UK furniture retailing. General DIY companies such as Kingfisher (through B&Q in the UK and Castorama in France) were attempting to capture more of the bottom end of the furniture market.

- Small and/or specialised retailers and/or manufacturers. These accounted for some 90 per cent of the market in Europe.

## IKEA's approach

IKEA had been founded by Ingvar Kamprad in 1943 in the small Swedish town of Älmhult. But it did not open its first major furniture store until 1958. The company's success had been achieved through the now legendary IKEA business model – revolutionary in the furnishing industry of its early years (see Table 2). The guiding business philosophy of Kampard was that of improving the everyday life of people by making products more affordable. This was achieved by massive (20 per cent +) reductions in sales prices vs competitors which, in turn, required aggressive reductions in IKEA's costs.

## Reasons for success

In his book *The IKEA Edge* published in 2011, Anders Dahlvig reflected on the reasons for IKEA's success before, during and after his period as CEO (1999–2009). He felt that the success of IKEA was built on a clear and detailed understanding of the furnishing market and IKEA's success criteria:

> 'IKEA's success has grown from stability and consistency regarding the big picture but with lots of action and innovation in the detail (evolution rather than revolution)' . . . (IKEA's five success criteria were): 1. Design, function, and quality at low prices; 2. Unique (Scandinavian) design; 3. Inspiration, ideas and complete solutions; 4. Everything in one place; 5. "A day out", the shopping experience . . . You may well say that they are similar to those of most companies. The difference, in my opinion, is that IKEA is much better at delivering on these customer needs than are other retailers . . . Most competitors focus on one or at most two of these customer needs. High-street shops focus on design and inspiration. Out-of-town low-cost retailers focus on price. Department stores focus on choice. The real strength of IKEA lies in the combination of all five.

## IKEA's competitive strategy

Dahlvig explained IKEA's approach to competition:

> 'You can choose to adapt your company's product range to the markets you are operating in, or you can choose to shift the market's preference towards your own range and style. IKEA has chosen the latter. By doing this, the company can maintain a unique and distinct profile.

**Table 2** IKEA's 'upside-down' business model

| Element of the business model | Traditional furniture retailer | IKEA |
|---|---|---|
| Design | Traditional | Modern (Swedish) |
| Target households | Older, established | Families with children |
| Style of shop | Small specialist shops | All furnishing items in big stores |
| Location | City centre | Out-of-town |
| Product focus | Individual items | 'Room sets' |
| Marketing | Advertising | Catalogue (free) |
| Price | High | Low |
| Product assembly | Ready assembled | Flat pack – self-assembly |
| Sourcing | Local | Global |
| Brand | Manufacturers' | IKEA |
| Financial focus | Gross margin | Sales revenue |
| Overheads | Often high | Frugal – no perks |

*This case was prepared by Kevan Scholes, Emeritus Professor of Strategic Management at Sheffield Business School. It is intended as a basis for class discussion and not as an illustration of good or bad management practice. © Kevan Scholes 2013. Not to be reproduced or quoted without permission.

This is, however, a more difficult path to follow.' '. . . A significant understanding of the customer's situation at home is the basis for IKEA's product development and the creation of the main media through which the product is presented to the public.' '. . . For most competitors, having the lowest price seems to mean being 5 to 10 per cent cheaper than the competition on comparable products. At IKEA, this means being a minimum 20 per cent cheaper and often up to 50 per cent cheaper than the competition.'

## Global expansion

By 1999 IKEA was operating 158 stores in 29 countries with a turnover the equivalent of €7.6 bn. Despite IKEA's strong global position Dahlvig felt there was much opportunity and need for improvement:

'So far growth has come from going "wide but thin". We have stores in 29 countries but with limited market share in most markets. Now we enter a new phase where the focus will be to go "deep" and concentrate on our existing markets . . . We shall focus on continued strong volume growth, 10 per cent pa for 10 years.'

He explained his reasoning:

'Why make the change? First of all, we were impelled by the changing character of the competition. For many years, the competition had been very fragmented and local in nature. However, many of the very big retail companies were shifting strategy. From being local, they were looking to a global expansion, not least in the emerging markets like China, Russia and Eastern Europe. They were also broadening their product range, moving away from food or traditional DIY products towards more home furnishing. These were big companies with much more muscle than IKEA's traditional competitors. They had both financial resources and operational retailing competence on a par with IKEA. One way to dissuade them from entering into the home furnishing arena was to aggressively reduce prices and increase the company's presence with more stores in all local markets in the countries where IKEA was operating. Market leadership in each market was the objective. Another reason for the shift in strategy was cost efficiency. Growing sales in existing stores is the most cost-efficient way to grow the company.'

## Managing the value chain

Dahlvig explained that IKEA's strategy crucially requires the 'design' and control of IKEA's wider value chain in detail:

'The secret is the control and coordination of the whole value chain from raw material, production, and range development, to distribution into stores. Most other companies working in the retail sector have control either of the retail end (stores and distribution) or the product design and production end. IKEA's vertical integration makes it a complex company compared to most, since it owns both production, range development, distribution, and stores. . . . This included backward integration by extending the activities of Swedwood (IKEA's manufacturing arm) beyond furniture factories, into control over the raw materials, saw mills, board suppliers, and component factories.'

'(The challenge) . . . is how to combine strong specialist functions within "one" company view and approach . . . differentiation through controlling the whole value chain is key to success. There are some very important factors that have helped keep the company together: a strong vision, the business idea, company values, a common store concept, a common product range, and a common distribution and buying organisation.'

'The one disappointment (in my 10 years) was that the cost level did not decrease as much as planned. We'd needed productivity gains of 10 per cent p.a. or more, and we managed only around a 4 to 6 per cent. Better than planned margins compensated for this, and thus the profit level was in line with the plan. Nevertheless, a low price company must be a low cost company.'

## China and India

IKEA first opened in China in 1998 and it had eight stores by 2012. The Chinese market was extremely challenging for a company that had built global success through standardisation. The main problems were that in developing markets IKEA products were expensive relative to local competitors and the consumer shopping expectations were centred on small, local shops and personal service. So inevitably there had to be some flexibility in approach by IKEA. For example, it presented an image as exclusive Western European interior design specialists – popular with younger, affluent, city dwellers. The shops were smaller than usual for IKEA and typically nearer city centres. Because DIY was not well developed in China IKEA offered home delivery and assembly services. Catalogues were only available *in store*. Crucially stores were allowed to source almost 50 per cent locally (against the company average of about 25 per cent) in order to keep prices competitive.

This experience would be useful when IKEA entered India. It was announced in 2012 that IKEA was to invest €1.5 bn in opening 25 stores over 15 to 20 years.

## New leaders but same formula?

Michael Ohlsson succeeded Dahlvig as CEO in 2009 – having already worked for IKEA for 30 years. The company commented: 'Mikael Ohlsson has strong implementation skills and is a great ambassador of the IKEA Culture. He is well suited to continue the change process that Anders Dahlvig has initiated.'

Indeed, despite extremely challenging economic conditions the company's success continued, exceeding €25 bn sales by 2012. In September 2012 IKEA announced that Ohlsson would retire in 2013 and be succeeded by another internal appointee – Peter Agnefjäll (18 years at IKEA). Agnefjäll told Reuters that 'under his leadership, the company will increase the number of store openings between 20 and 25 every year, from 2014 to 2015.'

So perhaps the IKEA approach still had a bright future?

*Sources and references:* 'Welcome inside 2011' from IKEA website: www.ikea.com; IKEA website 2012; the DataMonitor report on Global Home Furnishings Retail Industry Profile (reference code: 0199–2243, publication date: April 2008); Anders Dahlvig, *The Ikea Edge*, McGraw-Hill, 2011; U. Johansson and A. Thelander, 'A standardised approach to the world? IKEA in China', *International Journal of Quality and Service Sciences*, vol. 1, no. 2 (2009), pp. 199–219; Reuters, 23 June 2012; IKEA press release, 24 April 2009; Reported by www.valuewalk.com, 18 September 2012.

### Questions

1 Identify where and how IKEA has achieved cost leadership.

2 Identify how IKEA has achieved differentiation from its competitors.

3 Explain how IKEA tries to ensure that its 'Hybrid' strategy remains sustainable and does not become 'stuck-in-the-middle'.

4 What are the lessons from China about IKEA's approach?

# 6 CORPORATE STRATEGY AND DIVERSIFICATION

## Learning objectives

After reading this chapter, you should be able to:

- Identify alternative strategy options, including *market penetration*, *product development*, *market development* and *diversification*.
- Distinguish between different diversification strategies (*related* and *conglomerate* diversification) and evaluate *diversification drivers*.
- Assess the relative benefits of *vertical integration* and *outsourcing*.
- Analyse the ways in which a *corporate parent* can add or destroy value for its portfolio of business units.
- Analyse *portfolios* of business units and judge which to invest in and which to divest.

## Key terms

## 6.1 INTRODUCTION

Chapter 5 was concerned with *competitive strategy* – the ways in which a single business unit (SBU) or organisational unit can compete in a given market space, for instance through cost leadership or differentiation. However, organisations may choose to enter many new product and market areas. For instance, Tata Group, one of India's largest companies began as a trading organisation and soon moved into hotels and textiles. Since then it has diversified further into steel, motors, consultancy, technologies, tea, chemicals, power and communications. As organisations add new units and capabilities, their strategies may no longer be solely concerned with *competitive strategy* in one market space at the business-level, but with *corporate-level* choices concerning different businesses or markets. These choices, indicated in Figure 6.1, inform decisions about how broad an organisation should be. The 'scope' of an organisation is central to *corporate strategy* and the focus of this chapter.

**Scope is concerned with how far an organisation should be diversified in terms of products and markets.** One way of thinking about this is in terms of different strategies, according to the novelty of products or markets. Another way of increasing the scope of an organisation is *vertical integration*, where an organisation acts as an internal supplier or a customer to itself (as for example an oil company supplies its petrol to its own petrol stations). The organisation may also decide to *outsource* certain activities – to 'dis-integrate' by subcontracting an internal activity to an external supplier – as this may improve organisational efficiency.

Scope raises two other key themes. If an organisation has decided to operate in different areas of activity, what should be the role of the 'corporate-level' (head-office) executives, who act as 'parents' to the individual business units that make up the organisation's portfolio?

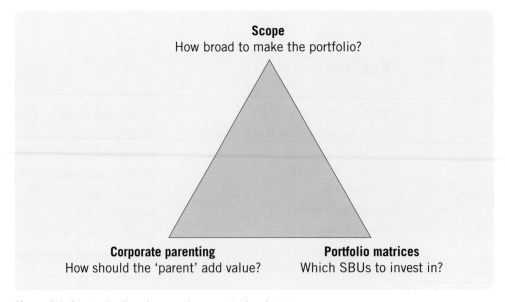

**Figure 6.1** Strategic directions and corporate-level strategy

How do corporate-level activities, decisions and resources add value to the actual businesses? The second theme is, within an overall diversification strategy, which specific business units should be included in the corporate *portfolio* and how should they be managed financially? Here, portfolio matrices are useful techniques to help structure corporate-level choices about which businesses to invest in and which to divest.

This chapter is not just about large commercial businesses. Even small businesses may consist of a number of business units. For example, a local building company may be undertaking contract work for local government, work for industrial buyers and for local homeowners. Not only are these different market segments, but the mode of operation and capabilities required for competitive success are also likely to be different. Moreover, the owner of that business has to take decisions about the extent of investment and activity in each segment. Public-sector organisations such as local government or health services also provide different services, which correspond to business units in commercial organisations.

## 6.2 STRATEGY DIRECTIONS

The Ansoff product/market growth matrix[1] is a corporate strategy framework for generating four basic directions for organisational growth: see Figure 6.2. Typically an organisation starts in the zone around point A, the top left-hand corner of Figure 6.2. According to Ansoff, the organisation may choose between *penetrating* still further within its existing sphere or increasing its diversity along the two axes of increasing novelty of markets or increasing novelty of products. This process of increasing the diversity of the range of products and/or

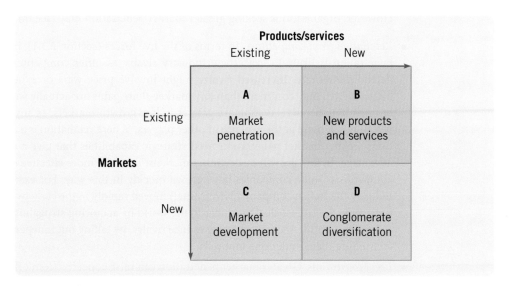

**Figure 6.2** Corporate strategy directions

*Source*: Adapted from H.I. Ansoff, *Corporate Strategy*, Penguin, 1988, Chapter 6. Ansoff originally had a matrix with four separate boxes, but in practice strategic directions involve more continuous axes. The Ansoff matrix itself was later developed – see Reference 1.

markets served by an organisation is known as **'diversification'. Diversification involves increasing the range of products or markets served by an organisation. Related diversification involves expanding into products or services with relationships to the existing business**. Thus on Ansoff's axes the organisation has two related diversification strategies available: moving to zone B, *developing new products* for its existing markets or moving to zone C by bringing its existing products into *new markets*. In each case, the further along the two axes, the more diversified is the strategy. Alternatively, the organisation can move in both directions at once, following a *conglomerate diversification* strategy with altogether new markets and new products (zone D). Thus **conglomerate (unrelated) diversification involves diversifying into products or services with no relationships to existing businesses**.

Ansoff's axes can be used effectively in brainstorming strategic options, checking that options in all four zones have been properly considered. Illustration 6.1 traces the evolution of a social enterprise raising questions about how businesses might think about Ansoff's matrix in choosing their strategic direction. The next section will consider each of Ansoff's four main directions. Section 6.4 will examine the additional option of *vertical integration*.

## 6.2.1 Market penetration

For a simple, undiversified business, the most obvious strategic option is often increased penetration of its existing market, with its existing products. **Market penetration implies increasing share of current markets with the current product range**. This strategy builds on established strategic capabilities and does not require the organisation to venture into uncharted territory. The organisation's scope is exactly the same. Moreover, greater market share implies increased power vis-à-vis buyers and suppliers (in terms of Porter's five forces), greater economies of scale and experience curve benefits.

However, organisations seeking greater market penetration may face three constraints:

- *Retaliation from competitors.* In terms of the five forces (section 2.3.1), increasing market penetration is likely to exacerbate industry rivalry as other competitors in the market defend their share. Increased rivalry might involve price wars or expensive marketing battles, which may cost more than any market-share gains are actually worth. The dangers of provoking fierce retaliation are greater in low-growth markets, as any gains in volume will be much more at the expense of other players. Where retaliation is a danger, organisations seeking market penetration need strategic capabilities that give a clear competitive advantage. In low-growth or declining markets, it can be more effective simply to acquire competitors. Some companies have grown quickly in this way. For example, in the steel industry the Indian company LNM (Mittal) moved rapidly in the early twenty-first century to become the largest steel producer in the world by acquiring struggling steel companies around the world. Acquisitions may reduce rivalry, by taking out independent players and controlling them under one umbrella.

- *Legal constraints.* Greater market penetration can raise concerns from official competition regulators concerning excessive market power. Most countries have regulators with the powers to restrain powerful companies or prevent mergers and acquisitions that would create such excessive power. For example, when the German T-Mobile and French Orange companies proposed to merge their UK mobile phone operations in 2010, the European

## ILLUSTRATION 6.1    Baking change into the community

### How Greyston's diversification transforms a depressed community

Probably best known for producing the brownies in the famous Ben and Jerry's ice creams, the Greyston Bakery is part of the Greyston Foundation – a $15 m (£9 m; €11.25 m) integrated network of for-profit and not-for-profit entities. The Foundation provides a wide array of services to benefit its local depressed community.

A Zen Buddhist meditation group started the bakery in 1982. They located in the poor neighbourhood of Yonkers, New York, where they perceived a need to create jobs for people in the community who were 'hard to employ' – the homeless, those with spotted employment histories, prison records and past substance-abuse problems. Radically they used an 'open hiring' practice that continues today, in which anybody who applies for a job has an opportunity to work, on a first-come, first-hired basis. Employees have to show up for work on time, perform the job, and have an appropriate attitude for three months and are then automatically made permanent employees. As SVP David Rome, says, 'we judge people based on their performance in the operation, not on their background'. There is high initial turnover but the average tenure is about three years. Greyston considers it a success when an employee moves on to a new job using their new skills. According to CEO Julius Walls, 'The company provides opportunities and resources to its employees so they can be successful not only in the workplace but in their personal lives. We don't hire people to bake brownies; we bake brownies to hire people.'

As the bakery expanded they realised providing jobs to the community wasn't enough. In 1991, working with governmental agencies, Greyston Family Inn was opened to provide permanent housing for homeless people. Currently there are three buildings, providing fifty housing units. A child day-care centre was also started with after-school care as one of the most pressing needs in the community for working parents to fill the gap left by public schools. In 1992 Greyston Health Services was formed, to help poor people with HIV/AIDS and in 1997 Issan House opened with 35 permanent housing units for those with HIV/AIDS, mental illness or chemical dependency. Other ventures

included Greyston Garden Project, 5 community-run gardens on neglected properties and a technology education centre. In 2011, a local retail bakery/café was opened and, in 2012, with the help of the Foundation's real-estate division, a new bakery was constructed, for $10 m in a public–private partnership project with the city, on a long dormant brownfield (contaminated) site.

The Foundation is an umbrella for all Greyston organisations: providing centralised management, fundraising, real-estate development, and planning services. It now comprises four interrelated organisations: bakery, healthcare services, child and family programmes, and real-estate development. The Foundation's social mission of supporting low-income people to forge a path to self-sufficiency and community transformation is blended with business collaboration to enable continual growth.

In 2012, Greyston Bakery celebrated its 30th anniversary, and received a fantastic present from New York State: to become a Benefit Corporation, allowing Greyston to demonstrate higher standards of corporate purpose, accountability and transparency. As Foundation CEO Steven Brown says, 'Really, we were a benefit corporation long before the term was coined. You're in business for a much larger community that has a stake in what you are doing. The extent that we can create value and opportunity is the path out of distress for many of these communities. It's not easy, but we're growing'.

*Sources*: www.greyston.org; http://www.pegasuscom.com/levpoints/greystonint.html; http://www.huffingtonpost.com/jesse-seaver/businesses-non-profit-social-enterprise; http://www.youtube.com/watch?v=2WLzV7JfVSc

### Questions

1  What were the motivation(s) for Greyston Bakery's diversifications?

2  Referring to the Ansoff matrix, how would you classify these diversifications?

Commission insisted that the merged companies should divest a quarter of their combined share of the key mobile phone 1800 MHz spectrum.[2]

- *Economic constraints.* Market penetration may also not be an option where economic constraints are severe, for instance during a market downturn or public-sector funding crisis. Here organisations will need to consider the strategic option of *retrenchment*, withdrawal from marginal activities in order to concentrate on the most valuable segments and products within their existing business. However, where growth is still sought after, the Ansoff axes suggest further directions, as follows.

## 6.2.2 Product development

**Product development is where organisations deliver modified or new products (or services) to existing markets.** This can involve varying degrees of diversification along the horizontal axis of Figure 6.2. For Apple, developing its products from the original iPod, through iPhone to iPad involved little diversification: although the technologies differed, Apple was targeting the same customers and using very similar production processes and distribution channels.

Despite the potential for benefits from relatedness, product development can be an expensive and high-risk activity for at least two reasons:

- *New strategic capabilities.* Product development strategies typically involve mastering new processes or technologies that are unfamiliar to the organisation. For example, the digital revolution is forcing universities to reconsider the way learning materials are acquired and provided to students and the nature of the student/academics interface. High-quality content available free on-line, and virtual engagement with students now raises the question of how universities should consider redeploying their resources in the future. Success is likely to depend on a willingness to acquire new technological capabilities, to engage in organisational restructuring and new marketing capabilities to manage customer perceptions. Thus product development typically involves heavy investments and can have high risk of project failures.

- *Project management risk.* Even within fairly familiar domains, product development projects are typically subject to the risk of delays and increased costs due to project complexity and changing project specifications over time. An extreme example is Boeing's Dreamliner 787 plane: making innovative use of carbon-fibre composites. The Dreamliner had a history of delays even before launch in 2010, required $2.5 bn (~€1.75 bn) write-offs due to cancelled orders.

Strategies for product development are considered further in Chapter 8.

## 6.2.3 Market development

If product development is risky and expensive, market development can be more attractive by being potentially cheaper and quicker to execute. **Market development involves offering existing products to new markets.** Again, the degree of diversification varies along

Figure 6.2's downward axis. Typically, of course, market development entails some product development as well, if only in terms of packaging or service. Nonetheless, market development remains a form of related diversification given its origins in similar products. Market development takes two basic forms:

- *New users.* Here an example would be aluminium, whose original users, packaging and cutlery manufacturers, are now supplemented by users in aerospace and automobiles.
- *New geographies.* The prime example of this is internationalisation, but the spread of a small retailer into new towns would also be a case.

In all cases, it is essential that market development strategies be based on products or services that meet the *critical success factors* of the new market (see section 2.4.3). Strategies based on simply off-loading traditional products or services in new markets are likely to fail. Moreover, market development faces similar problems to product development. In terms of strategic capabilities, market developers often lack the right marketing skills and brands to make progress in a market with unfamiliar customers. On the management side, the challenge is coordinating between different users and geographies, which might all have different needs.

### 6.2.4 Conglomerate diversification

Conglomerate (or unrelated) diversification takes the organisation beyond both its existing markets and its existing products (i.e. zone D). In this sense, it radically increases the organisation's scope. Conglomerate diversification strategies can create value as businesses may benefit from being part of a larger group. This may allow consumers to have greater confidence in the business unit's products and services than before and larger size may also reduce the costs of finance. However, conglomerate strategies are often not trusted by many observers because there are no obvious ways in which the businesses can work together to generate additional value, over and above the businesses remaining on their own. In addition, there is often an additional bureaucratic cost of the managers at headquarters who control them. For this reason, conglomerate companies' share prices can suffer from what is called the 'conglomerate discount' – in other words, a lower valuation than the combined individual constituent businesses would have on their own. In 2012, French conglomerate Vivendi, with wide interests in mobile telephony and media, had a break-up value estimated as at least twice the value of its shares. Its management stoked speculation when it said 'discussions about selling off some assets were "not taboo".'

## 6.3 DIVERSIFICATION DRIVERS

Diversification might be chosen for a variety of reasons, some more value-creating than others.[3] Growth in organisational size is rarely a good enough reason for diversification on its own: growth must be profitable. Indeed, growth can often be merely a form of 'empire building', especially in the public sector. Diversification decisions need to be approached sceptically.

Four potentially value-creating drivers for diversification are as follows.

- *Exploiting economies of scope.* **Economies of scope refer to efficiency gains through applying the organisation's existing resources or competences to new markets or services.**[4] If an organisation has under-utilised resources or competences that it cannot effectively close or sell to other potential users, it is efficient to use these resources or competences by diversification into a new activity. In other words, there are economies to be gained by extending the scope of the organisation's activities. For example, many universities have large resources in terms of halls of residence, which they must have for their students but which are under-utilised out of term-time. These halls of residence are more efficiently used if the universities expand the scope of their activities into conferencing and tourism during vacation periods. Economies of scope may apply to both *tangible* resources, such as halls of residence, and *intangible* resources and competences, such as brands or staff skills.

- *Stretching corporate management competences ('dominant logics').* This is a special case of economies of scope, and refers to the potential for applying the skills of talented corporate-level managers (referred to as 'corporate parenting skills' in section 6.5) to new businesses. The **dominant logic is the set of corporate-level managerial competences applied across the portfolio of businesses.**[5] Corporate-level managers may have competences that can be applied even to businesses not sharing resources at the operating-unit level. See the discussion of dominant logic at Berkshire Hathaway in Illustration 6.3 later.

- *Exploiting superior internal processes.* Internal processes within a diversified corporation can often be more efficient than external processes in the open market. This is especially the case where external capital and labour markets do not yet work well, as in many developing economies. In these circumstances, well-managed conglomerates can make sense, even if their constituent businesses do not have operating relationships with each other. For example, China has many conglomerates because they are able to mobilise internal investment, develop managers and exploit networks in a way that stand-alone Chinese companies, relying on imperfect markets, cannot. For example, China's largest privately owned conglomerate, the Fosun Group, owns steel mills, pharmaceutical companies and China's largest retailer, Yuyuan Tourist Mart.[6]

- *Increasing market power.*[7] Being diversified in many businesses can increase power vis-à-vis competitors in at least two ways. First, having the same wide portfolio of products as a competitor increases the potential for *mutual forbearance.* The ability to retaliate across the whole range of the portfolio acts to discourage the competitor from making any aggressive moves at all. Two similarly diversified competitors are thus likely to forbear from competing aggressively with each other. Second, having a diversified range of businesses increases the power to *cross-subsidise* one business from the profits of the others. On the one hand, the ability to cross-subsidise can support aggressive bids to drive competitors out of a particular market. On the other hand, knowing this power to cross-subsidise a particular business, competitors without equivalent power will be reluctant to attack that business.

Where diversification creates value, it is described as 'synergistic'.[8] **Synergy refers to the benefits gained where activities or assets complement each other so that their combined effect is greater than the sum of the parts** (the famous $2 + 2 = 5$ equation). Thus a film company and a music publisher would be synergistic if they were worth more together than separately – if the music publisher had the sole rights to music used in the film company productions, for instance. However, synergies are often harder to identify and more costly to extract in practice than managers like to admit.

Indeed, some drivers for diversification involve negative synergies, in other words value destruction. Three potentially value-destroying diversification drivers are:

- *Responding to market decline* is one common but doubtful driver for diversification. Rather than let the managers of a declining business invest spare funds in a new business, conventional finance theory suggests it is usually best to let shareholders find new growth investment opportunities for themselves. For example, Kodak, the US photo film corporation, spent billions of dollars on diversification acquisitions in order to compensate for market decline in its main product, but most failed and Kodak went bankrupt. Shareholders might have preferred Kodak simply to hand back the large surpluses generated for decades beforehand.

- *Spreading risk* across a range of markets is another common justification for diversification. Again, conventional finance theory is very sceptical about risk-spreading by diversification. Shareholders can easily spread their risk by taking small stakes in dozens of very different companies themselves. Diversification strategies, on the other hand, are likely to involve a limited range of fairly related markets. While managers might like the security of having more than one market, shareholders typically do not need each of the companies they invest in to be diversified as well – they would prefer managers to concentrate on managing their core business as well as they can.

- *Managerial ambition* can sometimes drive inappropriate diversification. It is argued that the managers of British banks such as Royal Bank of Scotland (at one point the fifth largest bank in the world) and HBOS (Britain's largest housing-lender) promoted strategies of excessive growth and diversification into new markets during the first decade of the twenty-first century. Such growth and diversification gave the managers short-term benefits in terms of managerial bonuses and prestige. But going beyond their areas of true expertise soon brought financial disaster, leading to the nationalisation of RBS and the takeover of HBOS by rival Lloyds bank.

## 6.4 VERTICAL INTEGRATION

As well as diversification, another direction for corporate strategy can be vertical integration. Vertical integration describes entering activities where the organisation is its own supplier or customer. Thus it involves operating at another stage of the value system (see section 3.4.2). This section considers both vertical integration and vertical dis-integration, particularly in the form of outsourcing.

### 6.4.1 Forward and backward integration

Vertical integration can go in either of two directions:

- **Backward integration** refers to development into activities concerned with the inputs into the company's current business (i.e. they are further back in the value network). For example, the acquisition by a car manufacturer of a component supplier would be a backward integration move.

- **Forward integration** refers to development into activities concerned with the outputs of a company's current business (i.e. are further forward in the value network). For a car manufacturer, forward integration would be into car retail, repairs and servicing.

Thus vertical integration is like diversification in increasing corporate scope. The difference is that it brings together activities up and down the same value network, while diversification typically involves more or less different value networks. However, because realising synergies involves bringing together different value networks, diversification (especially related diversification) is sometimes also described as *horizontal integration*. For example, a company diversified in cars, trucks and buses could find benefits in integrating aspects of the various design or component-sourcing processes. The relationship between horizontal integration and vertical integration is depicted in Figure 6.3.

Vertical integration is often favoured because it seems to 'capture' more of the profits in a value network. The car manufacturer gains the retailer's profits as well. However, it is important to be aware of two dangers. First, vertical integration involves investment. Expensive investments in activities that are less profitable than the original core business will be unattractive to shareholders because they are reducing their *average* or overall rate of return on investment. Second, even if there is a degree of relatedness through the value network, vertical integration is likely to involve quite different strategic capabilities. Thus car

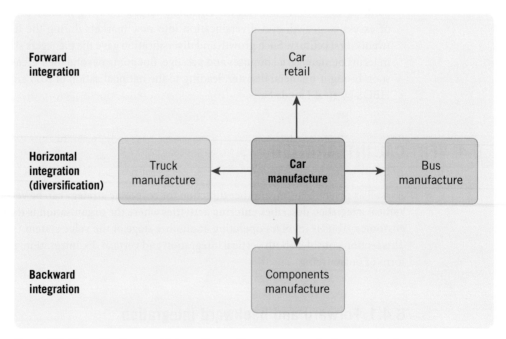

**Figure 6.3** Diversification and integration options: car manufacturer example

manufacturers who forwardly integrate into car service and repair have found that managing networks of small service outlets is very different to managing large manufacturing plants. Growing appreciation of both the risks of diluting overall returns on investment and the distinct capabilities involved at different stages of the value network has led many companies in recent years to vertically *dis*-integrate.

## 6.4.2 To integrate or to outsource?

Where a part of vertically integrated operations is not adding value to the overall business, it may be replaced through outsourcing or subcontracting. **Outsourcing is the process by which activities previously carried out internally are subcontracted to external suppliers**. Outsourcing can refer to the subcontracting of components in manufacturing, but is now particularly common for services such as information technology, customer call centres and human resource management (see Illustration 6.2). The argument for outsourcing to special-ist suppliers is often based on strategic capabilities. Specialists in a particular activity are likely to have superior capabilities than an organisation for which that particular activity is not a central part of their business. A specialist IT contractor is usually better at IT than the IT department of a steel company.

However, Nobel prize-winning economist Oliver Williamson has argued that the decision to integrate or outsource involves more than just relative capabilities.[9] In assessing whether to integrate or outsource an activity, he warns against underestimating the long-term costs of *opportunism* by external subcontractors (or indeed any other organisation in a market relationship). Subcontractors are liable over time to take advantage of their position, either to reduce their standards or to extract higher prices. Market relationships tend to fail in controlling subcontractor opportunism where:

- there are *few alternatives* to the subcontractor and it is hard to shop around;
- the product or service is *complex and changing*, and therefore impossible to specify fully in a legally binding contract;
- investments have been made in *specific assets*, which the subcontractor knows will have little value if they withhold their product or service.

Both capabilities and transaction cost reasoning have influenced the outsourcing decisions of the Royal Bank of Scotland: see Illustration 6.2.

In sum, the decision to integrate or subcontract rests on the balance between two distinct factors:

- *Relative strategic capabilities.* Does the subcontractor have the potential to do the work significantly better?
- *Risk of opportunism.* Is the subcontractor likely to take advantage of the relationship over time?

## ILLUSTRATION 6.2

### 'Out of sight – out of mind'? – Outsourcing at Royal Bank of Scotland

**In 2012, Royal Bank of Scotland (RBS) experienced a major crisis when its customers couldn't withdraw cash. Was this the consequence of outsourcing?**

In June 2012, RBS encountered severe problems when 10 million retail and business customers suddenly found they couldn't access their cash. This was highly damaging to the bank's reputation and could result in significant customer loss. The problem was faulty updating of CA-7 – critical software that controls the batch processing systems dealing with retail banking transactions. Generally regarded as 'a very common and reliable product, it processes accounts overnight via thousands of pieces of work' such as ATM transactions, bank-to-bank salary payments, and so on, and finishes by updating the account master copy with the definitive balance. Described as a huge game of Jenga [the tower game played with interlaced wood blocks], all transactions are related so everything needs to be processed in order. Thus Tuesday's batch must run before Wednesday's to avoid, for example, penalising someone who has a large sum of money leave their account on Wednesday that might put them in debt but which would be covered by money arriving on Tuesday. In updating CA-7, files were deleted or corrupted so the master copy was wrong for three nights – meaning millions of transactions were not processed. RBS branches had to extend their opening hours to reassure customers about their accounts.

Unions argued the disaster was due to 'offshoring' UK IT jobs to India: 'RBS has 40 years' experience running this system and banks as a rule don't drop the ball like this,' remarked one bank employee. However, the general banking crisis had pressured UK banks to reduce their costs. RBS, which had suffered badly from the banking crisis, let thousands of UK staff go and transferred their roles to Chennai, India. As one former employee complained, 'we were having to pass 10–20+ years worth of mainframe knowledge onto people who'd never heard of a mainframe outside of a museum . . .'

Offshore outsourcing was once heralded as the saviour of UK IT departments, cutting costs without compromising quality. Thousands of IT jobs were axed in the name of 'efficiency', many outsourced to India with much lower wages than the UK. Indeed in February 2012, RBS advertised it was urgently seeking computer graduates with several years' experience of using CA-7.

However, India's staff attrition rates in 2012 were at an all-time high with people changing jobs very quickly for just a few extra rupees, leaving insufficient time for adequate cultural awareness training. Quality at call-centres suffered. At the same time the UK was in recession with a devaluing pound greatly reducing wage disparity between India and the UK.

RBS's overseas problems were not uncommon with other banks experiencing loss of private data and in some instances criminal activity. Spanish-owned Santander UK – a bank created from Abbey National, Alliance & Leicester and Bradford & Bingley – also found that outsourced IT systems for these banks could not be trusted and so became the first of the major UK financial institutions to bring back its call centres and software from India to Britain, so that it could take care of its customer base. Ana Botin, Santander UK's chief executive, said the move was 'the most important factor in terms of satisfaction with the bank'. This 'inshoring' of strategic assets raises the question of whether strategic assets can afford to be 'out of sight and out of mind'.

*Source*: http://www.guardian.co.uk/technology/2012/jun/25/how-natwest-it-meltdown; http://www.hrzone.co.uk/topic/business-lifestyle/shoring-new-shoring-call-centres-come-back-uk/112654

### Questions

1 In terms of transaction and capability costs, why might outsourcing be attractive to companies?

2 What might be the risks of 'insourcing'?

# 6.5 VALUE CREATION AND THE CORPORATE PARENT

Sometimes corporate parents are not adding value to their constituent businesses. Where there is no added value, it is usually best to divest the relevant businesses from the corporate portfolio. Thus in 2012, Rupert Murdoch of News Corporation announced the separation of the troubled newspaper and book publishing assets from the more valuable film and TV business – the latter contributed 90 per cent of group profits. The Group could no longer add value to the former businesses, which were mired in public scandals, and these were also causing significant damage to the group's reputation as a whole. In the public sector too, units such as schools or hospitals are increasingly being given freedom from parenting authorities, because independence is seen as more effective.

## 6.5.1 Value-adding and value-destroying activities of corporate parents[10]

Any corporate parent needs to demonstrate that they create more value than they cost. This applies to both commercial and public-sector organisations. For public-sector organisations, privatisation or outsourcing is likely to be the consequence of failure to demonstrate value. Companies whose shares are traded freely on the stock markets face a further challenge. They must demonstrate they create more value than any other rival corporate parent could create. Failure to do so is likely to lead to a hostile takeover or break-up. Rival companies that think they can create more value out of the business units can bid for the company's shares, on the expectation of either running the businesses better or selling them off to other potential parents. If the rival's bid is more attractive and credible than what the current parent can promise, shareholders will back them at the expense of incumbent management.

In this sense, competition takes place between different corporate parents for the right to own and control businesses. **In this 'market for corporate control', corporate parents must show that they have parenting advantage, on the same principle that business units must demonstrate competitive advantage.** They must demonstrate that they are the best possible parent for the businesses they control. Parents therefore must have a very clear approach to how they create value. In practice, however, many of their activities can be value-destroying as well as value-creating.

### Value-adding activities[11]

There are five main types of activity by which a corporate parent can add value.

- *Envisioning*. The corporate parent can provide a clear overall vision or *strategic intent* for its business units.[12] This vision should guide and motivate the business unit managers in order to maximise corporation-wide performance through commitment to a common purpose. The vision should also provide stakeholders with a *clear external image* about what the organisation as a whole is about: this can reassure shareholders about the rationale for having a diversified strategy in the first place. Finally, a clear vision provides a *discipline* on the corporate parent to stop it wandering into inappropriate activities or taking on unnecessary costs.

- *Facilitating synergies.* The corporate parent can facilitate cooperation and sharing across the business units, so improving the *synergies* from being within the same corporate organisation. This can be achieved through incentives, rewards, and remuneration schemes.

- *Coaching.* The corporate parent can help business unit managers *develop strategic capabilities,* by coaching them to improve their skills and confidence. Corporate-wide management courses are one effective means of achieving these objectives, as bringing managers across the business to learn strategy skills also allows them to build relationships between each other and perceive opportunities for cooperation.

- *Providing central services and resources.* The centre is obviously a provider of capital for *investment.* The centre can also provide central services such as treasury, tax and human resource advice, which if centralised can have *sufficient scale* to be efficient and to build up *relevant expertise.* Centralised services often have greater *leverage:* for example, combining the purchases of separate business units increases their bargaining power for shared inputs such as energy. This leverage can be helpful in *brokering* with external bodies, such as government regulators, or other companies in negotiating alliances. Finally, the centre can have an important role in managing expertise within the corporate whole, for instance by *transferring managers* across the business units or by creating shared *knowledge management* systems via corporate intranets.

- *Intervening.* Finally, the corporate parent can also intervene within its business units in order to ensure appropriate performance. The corporate parent should be able to closely *monitor* business unit performance and *improve performance* either by replacing weak managers or by assisting them in turning around their businesses. The parent can also *challenge and develop* the strategic ambitions of business units, so that satisfactorily performing businesses are encouraged to perform even better.

## Value-destroying activities

However, there are also three broad ways in which the corporate parent can inadvertently destroy value:

- *Adding management costs.* Most simply, the staff and facilities of the corporate centre are expensive. The corporate centre typically has the best-paid managers and the most luxurious offices. It is the actual businesses that have to generate the revenues that pay for them. If their costs are greater than the value they create, then the corporate centre's managers are net value-destroying.

- *Adding bureaucratic complexity.* As well as these direct financial costs, there is the 'bureaucratic fog' created by an additional layer of management and the need to coordinate with sister businesses. These typically slow down managers' responses to issues and lead to compromises between the interests of individual businesses.

- *Obscuring financial performance.* One danger in a large diversified company is that the under-performance of weak businesses can be obscured. Weak businesses might be cross-subsidised by the stronger ones. Internally, the possibility of hiding weak performance diminishes the incentives for business unit managers to strive as hard as they can for their businesses: they have a parental safety net. Externally, shareholders and financial analysts cannot easily judge the performance of individual units within the corporate whole. Diversified companies' share prices are often marked down, because shareholders prefer the 'pure plays' of stand-alone units, where weak performance cannot be hidden.[13]

These dangers suggest clear paths for corporate parents that wish to avoid value destruction. They should keep a close eye on centre costs, both financial and bureaucratic, ensuring that they are no more than required by their corporate strategy. They should also do all they can to promote financial transparency, so that business units remain under pressure to perform and shareholders are confident that there are no hidden disasters.

Overall, there are many ways in which corporate parents can add value. It is, of course, difficult to pursue them all and some are hard to mix with others. However, corporate parenting roles tend to fall into three main types, each coherent within itself but distinct from the others.[14] These three types of corporate parenting role are summarised in Figure 6.4.

## 6.5.2 The portfolio manager

The **portfolio manager** operates as an active investor in a way that shareholders in the stock market are either too dispersed or too inexpert to be able to do. In effect, the portfolio manager is acting as an agent on behalf of financial markets and shareholders with a view to extracting more value from the various businesses than they could achieve themselves. Its role is to identify and acquire under-valued assets or businesses and improve them. The portfolio

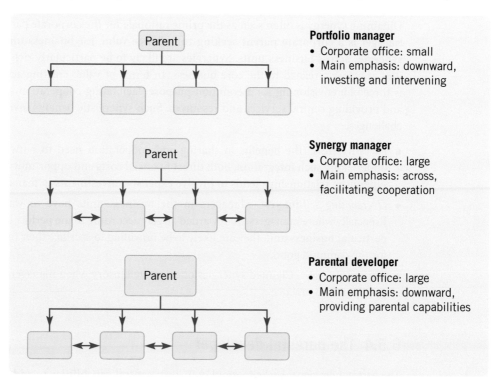

**Figure 6.4** Portfolio managers, synergy managers and parental developers
*Source:* Adapted from M. Goold, A. Campbell and M. Alexander, *Corporate Level Strategy*, Wiley, 1994.

manager might do this, for example, by acquiring another corporation, divesting low-performing businesses within it and intervening to improve the performance of those with potential. Such corporations may not be much concerned about the relatedness of the business units in their portfolio, typically adopting a conglomerate strategy. Their role is not to get closely involved in the routine management of the businesses, only to act over short periods of time to improve performance. In terms of the value-creating activities identified earlier, the portfolio manager concentrates on intervening and the provision (or withdrawal) of investment.

Portfolio managers seek to keep the cost of the centre low, for example by having a small corporate staff with few central services, leaving the business units alone so that their chief executives have a high degree of autonomy. They set clear financial targets for those chief executives, offering high rewards if they achieve them and likely loss of position if they do not. Such corporate parents can, of course, manage quite a large number of such businesses because they are not directly managing the everyday strategies of those businesses. Rather, they are acting from above, setting financial targets, making central evaluations about the well-being and future prospects of such businesses, and investing, intervening or divesting accordingly. Illustration 6.3 describes the portfolio parenting approach of Warren Buffet at Berkshire Hathaway.

### 6.5.3 The synergy manager

Obtaining synergy is often seen as the prime rationale for the corporate parent.[15] The **synergy manager is a corporate parent seeking to enhance value for business units by managing synergies across business units**. Synergies are likely to be particularly rich when new activities are closely related to the core business. In terms of value-creating activities, the focus is threefold: envisioning for a common purpose; facilitating cooperation across businesses; and providing central services and resources. Such synergistic benefits involve at least three challenges:

- *Excessive costs.* The benefits in sharing and cooperation need to outweigh the costs of undertaking such integration, both direct financial costs and opportunity costs. Managing synergistic relationships tends to involve expensive investments in management time.

- *Overcoming self-interest.* Managers in the business units have to want to cooperate. Especially where managers are rewarded largely according to the performance of their own particular business unit, they are likely to be unwilling to sacrifice their time and resources for the common good.

- *Illusory synergies.* Claimed synergies often prove illusory when managers actually have to put them into practice.

### 6.5.4 The parental developer

The **parental developer seeks to employ its own central capabilities to add value to its businesses**. This is not so much about how the parent can develop benefits *across* business units or transfer capabilities between business units, as in the case of managing synergy. Rather,

# ILLUSTRATION 6.3 — Eating its own cooking: Berkshire Hathaway's parenting

**A portfolio manager seeks to manage a highly diverse set of business units for shareholders.**

Berkshire Hathaway's plain-speaking chairman and CEO is Warren Buffett, one of the world's richest men. With annual sales of $162 bn (£97 bn; €121 bn in 2012, Buffet founded this conglomerate with a small textile business in the early 1960s. Berkshire Hathaway's businesses now are highly diverse with large insurance businesses (GEICO, General Re, NRG), manufacturers of carpets, building products, clothing and footwear, retail companies and private jet service, NetJets. The company also has significant long-term minority stakes in businesses such as Coca-Cola and General Electric. Aged 83 in 2013, Buffett remains highly active with major acquisitions in 2009 (BNSF, the second largest railway company in the United States for $34 bn), 2011 (Lubrizol, the speciality chemicals company for $9 bn cash), 2013 (Heinz, purchased with 3G Capital Management, for $23.3 bn). Since the mid-1960s, Berkshire has averaged 19.7 per cent growth in book value per year.

Berkshire Hathaway annual reports explain how Buffet and deputy chairman Charlie Munger run the business:

> 'Charlie Munger and I think of our shareholders as owner-partners, and of ourselves as managing partners. (Because of the size of our shareholdings we are also, for better or worse, controlling partners.) We do not view the company itself as the ultimate owner of our business assets but instead view the company as a conduit through which our shareholders own the assets. . . . In line with Berkshire's owner-orientation, most of our directors have a major portion of their net worth invested in the company. We eat our own cooking.'

Berkshire has a clear 'dominant logic':

> 'Charlie and I avoid businesses whose futures we can't evaluate, no matter how exciting their products may be. In the past, it required no brilliance for people to foresee the fabulous growth that awaited such industries as autos (in 1910), aircraft (in 1930) and television sets (in 1950). But the future then also included competitive dynamics that would decimate almost all of the companies entering those industries. Even the survivors tended to come away bleeding. Just because Charlie and I can clearly see dramatic growth ahead for an industry does not mean we can judge what its profit margins and returns on capital will be as a host of competitors battle for supremacy. At Berkshire we will stick with businesses whose profit picture for decades to come seems reasonably predictable. Even then, we will make plenty of mistakes.'

Buffett also explains how they manage their subsidiary businesses:

> 'We subcontract all of the heavy lifting to the managers of our subsidiaries. In fact, we delegate almost to the point of abdication: Though Berkshire has about 257,000 employees, only 21 of these are at headquarters. Charlie and I mainly attend to capital allocation and the care of our key managers. Most are happiest when they are left alone to run their businesses, and that is just how we leave them. That puts them in charge of all operating decisions and of dispatching the excess cash they generate to headquarters. By sending it to us, they don't get diverted by the various enticements that would come their way were they responsible for deploying the cash their businesses throw off. Furthermore, Charlie and I are exposed to a much wider range of possibilities for investing these funds than any of our managers could find.'

Even after Heinz and other acquisitions, Berkshire Hathaway still had a huge cash pile in 2013. The billionaire investor had his 'elephant gun loaded for a $15 bn acquisition' – a deal he was 'salivating' to do.

## Questions

1 In what ways does Berkshire Hathaway fit the archetypal portfolio manager (see section 6.5.2)?

2 With $20 bn to invest, suggest industries and businesses Warren Buffett is likely never to invest in.

parental developers focus on the resources or capabilities they have as parents which they can transfer *downwards* to enhance the potential of business units. For example, a parent could have a valuable brand or specialist skills in financial management or product development. If such parenting capabilities exist, corporate managers then need to identify a '*parenting opportunity*': a business which is not fulfilling its potential but which could be improved by applying the parenting capability, such as branding or product development. Such parenting opportunities are therefore more common in the case of related rather than unrelated diversified strategies and are likely to involve exchanges of managers and other resources across the businesses. Key value-creating activities for the parent will be the provision of central services and resources. For example, a consumer products company might offer substantial guidance on branding and distribution from the centre; a technology company might run a large central R&D laboratory.

## 6.6 THE BCG (OR GROWTH/SHARE) MATRIX

Many models exist by which managers can determine financial investment and divestment within their portfolios of businesses[16]. These models give more or less attention to:

- the *balance* of the portfolio, e.g. in relation to its markets and the needs of the corporation;

- the *attractiveness* of the business units in terms of how strong they are individually and how profitable their markets or industries are likely to be; and

- the '*fit*' that the business units have with each other in terms of potential synergies or the extent to which the corporate parent will be good at looking after them.

One of the most widely used and long-standing models for conceiving of the balance of a portfolio of businesses is the Boston Consulting Group (BCG) matrix. The **BCG matrix uses market share and market growth criteria for determining the attractiveness and balance of a business portfolio** (see Figure 6.5). High market share and high growth are, of course, attractive. However, the BCG matrix also warns that high growth demands heavy investment, for instance to expand capacity or develop brands. There needs to be a balance within the portfolio, so that there are some low-growth businesses that are making sufficient surplus to fund the investment needs of higher-growth businesses.

The growth/share axes of the BCG matrix define four sorts of business:

- A *star* is a business unit within a portfolio that has a high market share in a growing market. The business unit may be spending heavily to keep up with growth, but high market share should yield sufficient profits to make it more or less self-sufficient in terms of investment needs.

- A *question mark* (or problem child) is a business unit within a portfolio that is in a growing market, but does not yet have high market share. Developing question marks into stars, with high market share, takes heavy investment. Many question marks fail to develop, so the BCG advises corporate parents to nurture several at a time. It is important to make sure that some question marks develop into stars, as existing stars eventually become cash cows and cash cows may decline into dogs.

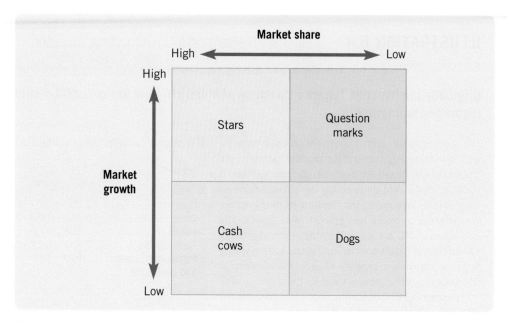

**Figure 6.5** The growth share (or BCG) matrix

- A *cash cow* is a business unit within a portfolio that has a high market share in a mature market. However, because growth is low, investments needs are less, while high market share means that the business unit should be profitable. The cash cow should then be a cash provider, helping to fund investments in question marks.

- *Dogs* are business units within a portfolio that have low share in static or declining markets and are thus the worst of all combinations. They may be a cash drain and use up a disproportionate amount of managerial time and company resources. The BCG usually recommends divestment or closure.

The BCG matrix has several advantages. It provides a good way of visualising the different needs and potential of all the diverse businesses within the corporate portfolio. It warns corporate parents of the financial demands of what might otherwise look like a desirable portfolio of high-growth businesses. It also reminds corporate parents that stars are likely eventually to wane. Finally, it provides a useful discipline to business unit managers, underlining the fact that the corporate parent ultimately owns the surplus resources they generate and can allocate them according to what is best for the corporate whole. Cash cows should not hoard their profits.

However, there are at least four potential problems with the BCG matrix:

- *Definitional vagueness.* It can be hard to decide what high and low growth or share mean in particular situations. Managers are often keen to define themselves as 'high-share' by defining their market in a particularly narrow way (for example, ignoring relevant international markets).

- *Capital market assumptions.* The notion that a corporate parent needs a balanced portfolio to finance investment from internal sources (cash cows) assumes that capital cannot be

## ILLUSTRATION 6.4    ITC's diverse portfolio: smelling sweeter

**Originally the Imperial Tobacco Company of India, ITC now has a portfolio stretching from cigarettes to fragrances.**

ITC is one of India's largest consumer goods companies, with an increasingly diversified product portfolio. Its chairman, Y.C. Deveshwar describes its strategy thus: 'It is ITC's endeavour to continuously explore opportunities for growth by synergising and blending its multiple core competences to create new epicentres of growth. The employees of ITC are inspired by the vision of growing ITC into one of India's premier institutions and are willing to go the extra mile to generate value for the economy, in the process creating growing value for the shareholders.'

Founded in 1910 as the Imperial Tobacco Company of India, with brands such as Wills, Gold Cut and John Players, ITC now holds about two-thirds of the market for cigarettes in India, with Philip Morris and BAT distant seconds with about 13 per cent each. However, cigarettes in India are highly discouraged by the Indian government, and increasingly heavily taxed.

ITC has a long diversification history. The company's original activities in the growth of leaf tobacco developed into a range of agricultural businesses, including edible oils, fruit pulp, spices and frozen foods. In the 1920s, ITC set up a packaging and printing business originally to supply its cigarette business. By 2012, this was India's largest packaging solutions provider. In 1975, ITC entered the hotel business, becoming the country's second largest operator with over 100 hotels by 2009, ranging from de luxe to economy. In 1979, the company also entered the paperboard industry, and three decades later was the country's largest producer.

The early twenty-first century saw many new diversification initiatives, especially in the booming Fast Moving Consumer Goods (FMCG) sector. Initially it started in the food business, with Kitchens-of-India ready-to-eat gourmet foods, the *Aashirvaad* wheat-flour business, Sunfeast biscuits and Bingo snacks. ITC's own agribusinesses were an important source of supply for these initiatives. By 2008 *Aashirvaad* reached over 50 per cent Indian market share, and Sunfeast and Bingo had 12 and 11 per cent respectively. At the same time, ITC took advantage of the strong brand values of its Wills cigarettes to launch Wills Lifestyle, a range of upmarket clothing stores, with its own

### ITC segmental sales and profits (Rs in Crores)

| Segment | 2011 sales | 2011 profits | 2009 sales | 2009 profits |
|---|---|---|---|---|
| Cigarettes | 22,250 | 6,907 | 15,115 | 4,184 |
| Other FMCG | 5,537 | (195) | 3,010 | (483) |
| Hotels | 996 | 279 | 1,014 | 316 |
| Agribusiness | 3,507 | 643 | 2,284 | 256 |
| Paperboard, paper and packaging | 2,579 | 936 | 1,719 | 509 |

5 Rs in Crores ~US $1,000,000, ~€700,000. Profits are before interest and tax. Figures in brackets are losses.

designs. In 2009, Wills Lifestyle was recognised as India's 'Most Admired Fashion Brand of the Year'. In 2005, ITC launched its personal care business, again using its cigarette brandnames: for example, 'Essenza Di Wills' (fragrances) and 'Fiama Di Wills' (hair and skin care).

In 2012 Australia announced that cigarette manufacturers have to sell their produce in drab green packages with graphic pictorial warnings. Market research done by the Public Health Foundation of India and Hriday, a health awareness NGO, showed more than 80 per cent people felt plain packaging would help reduce the attractiveness and appeal of tobacco products. India's Health Ministry officials warned such initiatives may be used in the future. With the cigarette industry facing systemic risk globally and manufacturer share prices being adversely affected, should ITC be concerned about its product portfolio?

*Sources*: ITC annual reports; M. Balaji, 2006, *ITC: Adding Shareholder Value through Diversifications*, IBSCDC; B. Gopal and S. Kora, 2009, *Indian Conglomerate ITC*, IBS Research Centre; *Business Standard* 6 November 2012

### Questions

1 How well does ITC's portfolio fit in terms of the BCG matrix?

2 Identify and evaluate the various synergies in ITC's business.

raised in external markets, for instance by issuing shares or raising loans. The notion of a balanced portfolio may be more relevant in countries where capital markets are under-developed or in private companies that wish to minimise dependence on external share-holders or banks.

- *Unkind to animals.* Both cash cows and dogs receive ungenerous treatment, one being milked and the second terminated or cast out of the corporate home. This treatment can cause *motivation problems*, as managers in these units see little point in working hard for the sake of other businesses. There is also the danger of the *self-fulfilling prophecy*. Cash cows will become dogs even more quickly than the model expects if they are simply milked and denied adequate investment.

- *Ignores commercial linkages.* The matrix assumes there are *no commercial ties to other business units* in the portfolio. For instance a business unit in the portfolio may depend upon keeping a dog alive. These commercial links are less important in conglomerate strategies, where divestments or closures are unlikely to have knock-on effects on other parts of the portfolio.

## SUMMARY

- Corporate strategy involves the decisions and activities above the level of business units. It is concerned with the scope of the organisation.

- Organisational *scope* is often considered in terms of *related* and *unrelated* diversification.

- Corporate parents may seek to add value by adopting different parenting roles: the *portfolio manager*, the *synergy manager* or the *parental developer*.

- The *BCG matrix* helps corporate parents manage their portfolios of businesses.

- To watch an author video on the concepts discussed in this chapter please visit www.mystrategylab.com, and click on 'Author perspectives on strategic management'.

## VIDEO ASSIGNMENTS

MyStrategyLab

If you are using *MyStrategyLab* you might find it useful to watch the *SWAST* case study.

1  Using Figure 6.2 as a starting point, explain how the South Western Ambulance Trust has developed the strategic direction of its activities.

2  What changes in corporate level strategy has SWAST had to introduce in order to combat the increasing threats in its environment? What further changes do you anticipate in the near future?

## RECOMMENDED KEY READINGS

- Capron, L. and Mitchell, W. *'Build, Borrow or Buy: solving the growth dilemma'* Harvard Business Press. 2012 provides good review of the arguments for and against different modes of growth.

- A good review of the current state of corporate portfolio management research is provided by Nippa, M., Pidua, U. and Rubner, H. 'Corporate Portfolio Management. Appraising four decades of academic research', *Academy of Management Perspectives*, November, 2011.

## REFERENCES

1. This figure is an extension of the product/market matrix: see I. Ansoff, *Corporate Strategy*, 1988, Chapter 6.

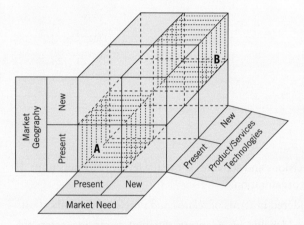

2. For the European Commission competition authority, http://ec.europa.eu/comm/competition; for the UK Competition Commission, see http://www.competition-commission.org.uk/.

3. For discussions of the challenge of sustained growth and diversification, see A. Campbell and R. Parks, *The Growth Gamble*, Nicholas Brearly (2005) and D. Laurie, Y. Doz and C. Sheer, 'Creating new growth platforms', *Harvard Business Review*, vol. 84, no. 5, (2006), 80–90.

4. On economies of scope, see D.J. Teece, 'Towards an economic theory of the multi-product firm', *Journal of Economic Behavior and Organization*, vol. 3 (1982), pp. 39–63.

5. See R. Bettis and C.K. Prahalad, 'The dominant logic: retrospective and extension', *Strategic Management Journal*, vol. 16, no. 1 (1995), pp. 5–15.

6. See C. Markides, 'Corporate strategy: the role of the centre' in A. Pettigrew, H. Thomas and R. Whittington (eds), *Handbook of Strategy and Management*, Sage, 2002.

7. These benefits are often discussed in terms of 'multimarket' or 'multipoint' competition: see J. Anand, L. Mesquita and R. Vassolo, 'The dynamics of multimarket competition in exploration and exploitation activities', *Academy of Management Journal*, vol. 52, no. 4 (2009), pp. 802–21.

8. M. Goold and A. Campbell, 'Desperately seeking synergy', *Harvard Business Review*, vol. 76, no. 2 (1998), pp. 131–45.

9. For a discussion and cases on the relative guidance of transaction cost and capabilities thinking, see R. McIvor, 'How the transaction cost and resource-based theories of the firm inform outsourcing evaluation', *Journal of Operations Management*, vol. 27, no. 1 (2009), pp. 45–63.

10. D. Collis, D. Young and M. Goold, 'The size, structure and performance of corporate headquarters', *Strategic Management Journal*, vol. 28, no. 4 (2007), pp. 383–406.

11. M. Goold, A. Campbell and M. Alexander, *Corporate Level Strategy*, Wiley, 1994, is concerned with both the value-adding and value-destroying capacity of corporate parents.

12. For a discussion of the role of clarity of mission, see A. Campbell, M. Devine and D. Young, *A Sense of Mission*, Hutchinson Business, 1990.

13. E. Zuckerman, 'Focusing the corporate product: securities analysts and de-diversification', *Administrative Science Quarterly*, vol. 45, no. 3 (2000), pp. 591–619.

14. The first two rationales discussed here are based on M. Porter, 'From competitive advantage to corporate strategy', *Harvard Business Review*, vol. 65, no. 3 (1987), pp. 43–59.

15. See A. Campbell and K. Luchs, *Strategic Synergy*, Butterworth/Heinemann, 1992.

16. A good review of the current state of corporate portfolio management research is provided by M. Nippa, U. Pidua and H. Rubner, 'Corporate Portfolio Management. Appraising four decades of academic research', *Academy of Management Perspectives*, vol. 25, no. 4, (2011) pp. 50–66.

# Strategic development at Virgin 2013

John Treciokas

## Introduction

The Virgin Group is a highly diversified organisation with one of the best-known brands in the UK. Sir Richard Branson, Virgin's charismatic founder, who is one of the UK's richest and highly regarded entrepreneurs, leads the group. However, there are signs that Richard Branson may be stepping back from Virgin's businesses to concentrate on environmental and charity activities. This is causing concern about Virgin's future, as its strategy and business model are not widely understood. Investors are now questioning the extent to which the success of Virgin is due to Branson's entrepreneurial flair rather than the group's structure and business model.

The Virgin Group has grown over the years to become one of the largest private companies in the UK. It has more than 200 branded companies worldwide, employing around 50,000 employees in 34 countries with revenues in excess of £13 billion (approx. US $21 billion) in 2011. Richard Branson has always been integral to the growth of the company from its foundation to the present day. His flamboyant style and flair for publicity generate interest and awareness, which has enabled Virgin to create a brand image that, the Group believes, adds value to any business that bears the Virgin name.

The Virgin Group is unusual in many ways, with a unique structure and distinctive image. However, questions are being raised about its sustainability. Does the parent company add value to the wide array of businesses in the group? Does the portfolio itself make strategic sense? It is also suspected the Group struggles with profitability. Will the Virgin Group survive should Richard Branson depart?

## Virgin's origins and style

The Virgin Group's beginnings can be traced to Richard Branson selling mail-order records in 1970 when he was just twenty years old. This allowed him to easily undercut high-street retailers and the business experienced rapid growth. In 1971 Richard Branson opened an Oxford Street store, which he named 'Virgin Records', to reflect his

**Richard Branson**

*Source*: Steve Bell/Rex Features.

youth and naivety in business. Further expansion followed as he moved into record publishing with an instant hit album 'Tubular Bells', by unknown musician Mike Oldfield, in 1973. Virgin Records courted controversy by signing the Sex Pistols, a 'punk rock group' whose rude and anti-establishment behaviour brought plenty of public exposure. Risk taking, optimism, irreverence and attracting publicity epitomised Branson's philosophy from the outset.

This philosophy was very visible when, in 1984, Richard Branson was inspired by an American lawyer to create a low-cost transatlantic airline – Virgin Atlantic. These routes were dominated by British Airways, and so began a long rivalry. When Virgin Atlantic managed to procure landing slots at Heathrow Airport in 1991, this rivalry intensified leading to a 'dirty tricks' campaign by British Airways against Virgin Atlantic. The ensuing court battle, which Virgin won, was bitter and fought very publicly in the media which often represented Virgin as the underdog fighting an oppressor.

Meanwhile Virgin Atlantic had huge financing needs, with initial cash for operations coming from Virgin Records and its subsequent sale to EMI for £500 m. The Group then needed an initial public offering of 35 per cent ownership of many Virgin businesses on the London and NASDAQ stock markets. This situation didn't last long however as Branson's personality was not compatible with the accountability required of a chairman of a public corporation. In 1988 he bought out the external shareholders and returned the group to private ownership.

## Virgin growth

Again a private company, the Group grew rapidly, through a mixture of acquisitions, joint ventures and new start-ups (Appendix 1 lists a selection of new businesses).

Many of the new business initiatives seem to have been pure opportunism or on the whim of Richard Branson. For instance, in explaining why Virgin Records America was established in 1987, he commented: 'We were flying there a lot so it made sense to expand there too.' Since the early 1990s when the group was primarily involved in travel/holidays and music, it expanded into a wide range of businesses. For instance, the development of digital technologies allowed Virgin to grow its retail interests into online sales of music as well as many other products including cars, financial products and wine. The beginning of cellular communications and deregulation of the telecommunications sector in the UK led to the setting up of Virgin Mobile. Deregulation of the railways in the UK provided Virgin with the opportunity to form Virgin Rail, operating a passenger rail service on the West Coast of England, and deregulation in Australia and Nigeria allowed Virgin to set up other low-cost airlines. Branson was also drawn to markets where he perceived undue conservatism, a *lack* of innovation and an under-served customer. For instance Virgin entered into health clubs (Virgin Active), biofuels (Virgin Fuels), drinks (Virgin drinks), clothing, cosmetics, comics, weddings (Virgin Bride) and, in 2012, even a

passenger service into suborbital space (Virgin Galactic). Commenting on this latest venture Richard Branson said, 'Virgin is an adventurous company because I am an adventurer as well as an entrepreneur.' In the same year Virgin Money purchased Northern Rock, a medium-sized UK mortgage provider, from the Government (who had nationalised the troubled company in the financial crisis of 2007). The move gave Virgin a much bigger stake in financial services – a growth area. The first new Virgin Money Store opened in July and by the end of the year 75 Northern Rock branches were rebranded to Virgin Money. Virgin paid £747m for Northern Rock although commentators remarked it was an excellent deal for Virgin at the taxpayers' expense.

Since 2007 Richard Branson has become increasingly interested in environmental issues, launching the 'Virgin Earth Challenge' – to remove large amounts of carbon dioxide from the atmosphere, a 'People & Planet' initiative – to ensure all Virgin companies contribute to a sustainable society, Virgin Unite, – to work with partners to improve social and environmental issues and a Virgin Green Fund to invest in companies in the renewable energy and resource efficiency sectors. It seems that Branson is turning his attention to non-profit and Corporate Social Responsibility issues.

## Corporate rationale

In 2013 Virgin had the appearance of a very untraditional multi-business organisation. The group does not provide an organisational structure chart but a discernible grouping of business has become evident within six broad categories (see Fig 1). A cursory inspection of figure 1 shows that these categories are very broad indeed, for

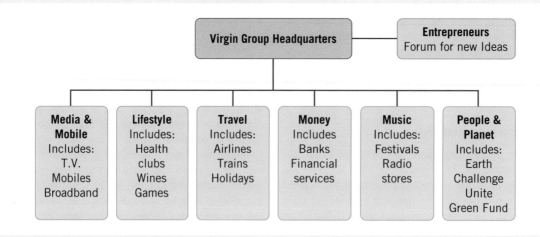

instance 'Lifestyle' includes health clubs, books, games and balloon flights!

The operating companies themselves are all separate entities, financed on a stand-alone basis. Indeed most of the companies are new start-ups and Branson's approach is for each to succeed within the first year or exit the market. The key rationale to whether Virgin backs a new venture is: 'Does an opportunity exist for restructuring a market and creating competitive advantage?' The group puts itself in the customer's shoes to see what it could make better. It also considers whether there could be beneficial interaction with other Virgin businesses.

Each business is 'ring-fenced', so that lenders to one company have no rights over the assets of another and financial results are not consolidated. Branson's view is that consolidating income and assets of the companies is misleading and irrelevant for a private company.

Virgin has a mix of privately owned and public listed companies as well as a mix of start-up small businesses and very large corporate ventures. Each may have very different strategic reasoning – some may be an attempt to keep Virgin in the public eye, some are 'anti-establishment and others about offering customers a better and more fun alternative. The businesses might also be a method of training and developing managers. The larger start-ups are serious strategic moves into new industries.

Each company has no direct lines of reporting or control in a Group with minimal management layers and no bureaucracy. This mirrors Richard Branson's disrespect for hierarchy and his preference for informality and individual responsibility from employees. Companies are linked through a complex network of parent subsidiary relations involving 'holding companies' with the ultimate Holding company being registered in the British Virgin Islands – a tax haven. The group believes that the separation of businesses enables the group to retain a spirit of entrepreneurialism, which depends on the enthusiasm and commitment of its employees. The group states on its own website that Virgin is a 'leading branded venture capital organisation' and its companies are part of a family rather than a hierarchy. 'There is a tiny board and no massive global HQ, but it works for us!'

The managers of each business are given significant autonomy once the business is up and running. This embodies Branson's ethos of shaping and building businesses around people. Managers are trusted, have high levels of responsibility and have financial incentives that could turn them into millionaires – indeed one of Branson's proudest claims is the creation of many millionaire managers.

One commonality across all the businesses is the Virgin Brand which the group says is about being the consumer's champion for value for money, good quality, brilliant customer service, innovation, anti-establishment and fun. These attributes are the way in which the group differentiates its products and services. In a number of instances observers have commented that Virgin's ventures are driven more by fun than commercial logic. For instance painting the Union Jack on Virgin Atlantic aircraft when British Airways removed theirs, or positioning an airship with the slogan 'BA can't get it up' over the London Eye, a giant Ferris wheel in central London, which BA was struggling to erect.

In addition to the brand, Richard Branson sees Virgin as adding value in three main ways. These are their public relations and marketing skills; their experience with 'greenfield' start-ups and Virgin's understanding of the opportunities presented by 'institutionalised' markets. Virgin saw an 'institutionalised' market as one dominated by a few competitors who are not giving good value to customers because they have become either inefficient, complacent or preoccupied with rivals. In addition one might add that the Group has an extensive network of contacts and partners.

There is a belief that any type of business could work if Virgin was able to leverage its distinctive capabilities to the new opportunity. There is also a shrewd sense of risk versus reward. As the company says, 'Virgin frequently creates partnerships with others and excels in combining skills, knowledge, and operational expertise from a range of industries to build exciting and successful companies'. Virgin invites entrepreneurs to submit their business ideas for consideration and possible Virgin involvement. An example of this was the Virgin Group's move into clothing and cosmetics with an initial outlay of only £1,000 whilst its partner, Victory Corporation, invested £20 million.

## Recent developments

Not all of Virgin's companies are successful and not all meet the standards of customer service that Virgin would like to see. Both Virgin Media and Virgin Rail have had many customer complaints and in the summer of 2012 Virgin Rail seemed to have lost its franchise on the West Coast railway line. Virgin managed to get this decision quashed as serious technical errors were made by the UK's Department of Transport. The company released a statement on 29 October 2012 stating the following:

'This will help ensure we deliver the best result for the passenger and taxpayer, as well as getting the best out of the private sector and the key role it plays in a successful UK rail system.'

Critics have suggested that Rail is a weakness in Virgin's portfolio and it will be interesting to see how committed Branson is to this business.

In February 2013 Liberty Global agreed to purchase Virgin Media for approximately £15 bn. Branson's own share of this was 2 per cent. Virgin will continue earning around £10 m a year for its 30-year brand-licensing agreement. To what extent Liberty will continue to use the Virgin brand and operational expertise is difficult to establish at this stage.

Much of the Virgin's brand appeal is linked to Richard Branson himself, his antics, values and personality. His appeal to the British public is his sense of fair play and irreverence. In particular he has created an image of a 'cheeky entrepreneur' who has battled the mighty 'monopoly' of British Airways. But critics suggest that this brand may now be over-extended at Virgin, have limited appeal internationally and the UK consumer may be beginning to tire of his stunts. The other lesser-known image of Richard Branson is one of a ruthless, crafty businessman always trying to get one over on his rivals.

It is difficult to discover the overall financial position of Virgin as it is made up of so many individual companies (many private and offshore) and there are no consolidated accounts. Investments in operating companies are also often transferred between group companies. Branson has argued that he pursues growth, not profits and builds companies for the long term. The group emphasises maximising return to Virgin Group equity through high financial leverage and the use of equity partners. Nonetheless, Virgin Atlantic in 2011 posted a £80.2 m loss; Virgin America has yet to post an annual profit and in its first five years of trading made a loss of approximately $500 m. Virgin Media made a profit of £93 m in 2011, but its cumulative profit and loss account stands at a negative £3,259 m. Virgin Trains in the UK made a profit of £41 m in 2011.

Richard Branson in interviews does not mention his departure but states that the Company has been carefully groomed to continue without him, and that the brand is now global and sufficiently well known such that his publicity stunts are no longer required. Richard Branson may now be allowing other people to guide the Virgin Group but observers are divided about the nature of the group's business model, with some seeing it as a private equity organisation (but many of the businesses are start-ups), or a branded venture capital organisation (but the Group incubates its own businesses). Others suggest it might be a conglomerate but the group rarely makes acquisitions. Recent appointments at the very top of Virgin are former finance experts who are not renowned for the informal collaborative and personal style epitomised by Richard Branson. If Sir Richard Branson steps aside, what will the future hold for the Virgin group – will it survive?

*References and sources*: www.virgin.com; T. Bower, Branson, Harper Perennial, 2008; www.businessweek.com, November 2007; www.reuters.com, 16 December 2009; 'Virgin rebirth', The Economist 12 September 2008; S. Goff, 'Retail Banking', Correspondent, 8 January 2010; Virgin Group's Corporate and Sustainable Development Report 2010; R. Branson, Like A Virgin. 2012; J. Treanor, http://www.guardian.co.uk/profile/jilltreanorCity editor, Guardian, 1 January 2012; http://www.ft.com/cms/s/0/a04c8138-f1f7–11e1-bba3–00144feabdc0.html#axzz2LHmLSkgB; http://www.guardian.co.uk/media/2013/feb/06/virgin-media-takeover-john-malone-liberty-global; http://www.economist.com/blogs/schumpeter/2013Ö02/libertys-takeover-virgin-media; http://www.redmayne.co.uk/research/securitydetails/financials.htm?tkr=VMED

## Questions

1 What directions of strategic development have been followed by Virgin over the period of the case (use Figure 6.2 as a guide)?

2 What is the corporate rationale for Virgin as a group of companies?

3 How does the Virgin Group as a corporate parent add value to its businesses? To what extent are these parenting skills relevant to the various businesses in the group?

4 What should the future corporate strategy be?

## Appendix 1   Strategic developments of the Virgin Group 1970–2012

| | |
|---|---|
| 1970 | Branson founds the Virgin business selling records |
| 1971 | First Virgin record shop opened |
| 1977 | Virgin record label is launched |
| 1984 | Virgin Atlantic, a long-haul airline is founded. |
| 1985 | Virgin Holidays is founded |
| 1986 | Virgin Group PLC formed |
| 1987 | Virgin Records America is launched |
| 1988–1990 | Virgin Megastores are opened in prime city locations in Europe, US and finally Japan in a joint venture with Marui. Branson takes Virgin Group PLC private for £248 m |
| 1991 | Virgin Publishing formed through merging Virgin Books and WH Allen PLC<br>Virgin Games formed |
| 1992 | Virgin Records sold for £510 m. |
| 1993 | Virgin Games floated as Virgin Interactive Entertainment PLC with Hasbro ad Blockbuster taking minority stakes<br>Virgin Radio commences broadcasting. |
| 1994 | Virgin Retail acquires Our Price chain of shops.<br>Virgin Vodka and Virgin Cola are launched as joint venture with Cott Corp.<br>Virgin City Jet service launched London to Dublin |
| 1995 | Virgin Direct launches a financial investment product in joint venture with Norwich Union. |
| 1996 | Virgin Express Airline, a low cost short haul airline starts up.<br>Virgin Net an internet service provider is launched |
| 1997 | Virgin Trains is founded to run West Coast rail franchise in the UK.<br>Virgin Cosmetics launches with four flagship stores.<br>Virgin One telephone bank account launched in collaboration with Royal Bank of Scotland.<br>Virgin Bride retail chain formed |
| 1999 | Virgin Mobile is launched in joint venture with Deutsche Telekom<br>Virgin Health starts a network of health clubs.<br>Virgin Cinemas is sold for £215 m.<br>49% of Virgin Atlantic sold to Singapore Airlines for $500 m |
| 2000 | Virgin Mobile launches US wireless phone service (JV with Sprint)<br>Virgin Mobile launches Australian wireless phone (JV with Cable and Wireless)<br>Virgin Blue launched (low cost airline – Australia)<br>Virgin Cars launched to sell on-line<br>50% of Virgin Blue sold |
| 2001 | Virgin Bikes launched |
| 2002 | Virgin Digital launched to sell online music |
| 2004 | Virgin mobile launched in Canada |
| 2005 | Virgin acquires the Holmes Place chain of health clubs |
| 2006 | Virgin Media is launched in partnership with NTL-Telewest<br>Virgin Mobile and Virgin Money launched in South Africa<br>Virgin Fuel launched<br>Virgin Cars closed |
| 2007 | Virgin Health Bank launched<br>Virgin America (airline) launched<br>Virgin Earth Challenge and World Citizen initiatives are launched |
| 2008 | Virgin Mobile launches in India in a joint venture with Tata Teleservices |
| 2009 | Virgin Green Fund launched |
| 2010 | Virgin Hotels launches<br>Virgin Racing launched (Formula 1)<br>Virgin Gaming launched<br>Virgin Produced launched (Film and TV production company)<br>Virgin Money US withdraws from the market<br>Virgin Money acquires Church House Trust to acquire UK banking licence |
| 2011 | Virgin Cosmetics and Virgin Money (USA) are closed<br>Virgin launches Virgin Oceanic, a deep sea exploration submarine<br>Virgin Active acquires Esporta for £80 m<br>Virgin Unite (charitable foundation) launches Branson's Centre for Entrepreneurship |
| 2012 | Virgin Galactic completes hot-fire rocket tests and develops a revolutionary satellite launch vehicle |

*Source*: www.virgin.com

# 7 INTERNATIONAL STRATEGY

## Learning outcomes

After reading this chapter, you should be able to:

- Assess the *internationalisation potential* of different markets.

- Identify sources of competitive advantage in international strategy, through both exploitation of *local factors* and *global sourcing*.

- Understand the difference between *global integration* and *local responsiveness* and four main types of international strategy.

- *Rank markets* for entry or expansion, taking into account attractiveness, cultural and other forms of distance and competitor retaliation threats.

- Assess the relative merits of different *market entry modes*, including joint ventures, licensing and foreign direct investment.

## Key terms

CAGE framework p. 170

global–local dilemma p. 166

global sourcing p. 164

global strategy p. 157

international strategy p. 157

Porter's Diamond p. 163

staged international expansion model p. 176

Yip's globalisation framework p. 159

## 7.1 INTRODUCTION

The last chapter introduced market development as a strategy, in relation to the Ansoff axes. This chapter focuses on a specific but important kind of market development, operating in different geographical markets. This is a challenge for many kinds of organisations nowadays. There are of course the large traditional multinationals such as Nestlé, Toyota and McDonald's. But recent years have seen the rise of emerging-country multinationals from Brazil, Russia, India and China. New small firms are also increasingly 'born global', building international relationships right from the start. Public-sector organisations too are having to make choices about collaboration, outsourcing and even competition with overseas organisations. European Union legislation requires public-service organisations to accept tenders from non-national suppliers.

Figure 7.1 identifies the five main themes of this chapter, with international strategy as the core. The themes are as follows:

- *Internationalisation drivers.* Drivers include market demand, the potential for cost advantages, government pressures and inducements and the need to respond to competitor moves. Given the risks and costs of international strategy, managers need to know that the drivers are strong to justify adopting an international strategy in the first place.

- *Geographical and firm-specific advantages.* In international competition, advantages might come from firm-specific and geographical advantages. Firm-specific advantages are the unique strategic capabilities proprietary to an organisation (as discussed in Chapter 3). Geographical advantages might come both from the geographic location of the original business and from the international configuration of their value network. Managers need to appraise these potential sources of competitive advantage carefully: if there are no competitive advantages, international strategy is liable to fail.

- *International strategy.* If drivers and advantages are sufficiently strong to merit an international strategy, then a range of strategic approaches are opened up, from the simplest export strategies to the most complex global strategies.

- *Market selection.* Having adopted the broad approach to international strategy, the question next is which country markets to prioritise and which to steer clear of. The issues here range from the economic to the cultural and political.

- *Entry mode.* Finally, once target countries are selected, managers have to determine how they should enter each particular market. Again, export is a simple place to start, but there are licensing, franchising, joint venture and wholly owned subsidiary alternatives to consider as well.

The chapter takes a cautious view on international strategy. Despite the fashionable talk of increasing 'globalisation', there are many challenges and many pressures for localisation as well.[1]

The chapter distinguishes between international strategy and global strategy. **International strategy refers to a range of options for operating outside an organisation's country of origin.** Global strategy is only one kind of international strategy. **Global strategy involves high coordination of extensive activities dispersed geographically in many countries around the world.** This chapter keeps open alternative options to full global strategy.

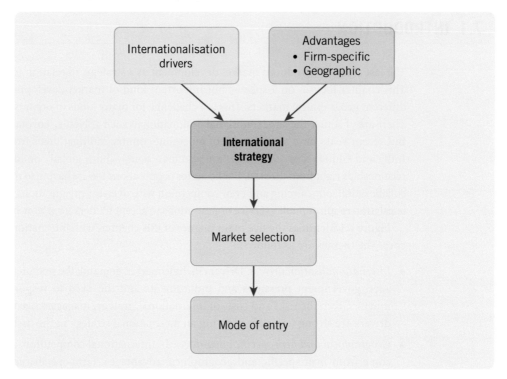

**Figure 7.1** International strategy: five main themes

## 7.2 INTERNATIONALISATION DRIVERS

There are many general pressures increasing internationalisation. Barriers to international trade, investment and migration are all now much lower than they were a couple of decades ago. Better international legal frameworks mean that it is less risky to deal with unfamiliar partners. Improvements in communications – from cheaper air travel to the internet – make movement and the spread of ideas much easier around the world. Not least, the success of new economic powerhouses such as the so-called BRICs – Brazil, Russia, India and China – is generating new opportunities and challenges for business internationally.[2]

However, not all these internationalisation trends are one-way. Nor do they hold for all industries. For example, migration is now becoming more difficult between some countries. Trade barriers still exist for some products, especially those relating to defence technologies. Many countries protect their leading companies from takeover by overseas rivals. Markets vary widely in the extent to which consumer needs are standardising – compare computer operating systems to the highly variable national tastes in chocolate. As in the Chinese retail market (Illustration 7.1), international drivers are usually a lot more complicated than that: Chinese markets not only are very different from Western ones, but also vary widely within China itself.

Given internationalisation's complexity, international strategy should be underpinned by a careful assessment of trends in each particular market. George Yip provides a framework for analysing 'drivers of globalisation'. In the terms of this chapter, these globalisation drivers can be thought of as 'internationalisation drivers' more generally. In this book, therefore, **Yip's globalisation framework sees international strategy potential as determined by market drivers, cost drivers, government drivers and competitive drivers** (see Figure 7.2).[3] In more detail, the four drivers are as follows:

- *Market drivers.* A critical facilitator of internationalisation is standardisation of market characteristics. There are three components underlying this driver. First, the presence of *similar customer needs and tastes*: for example, the fact that in most societies consumers have similar needs for easy credit has promoted the worldwide spread of a handful of credit card companies such as Visa. Second is the presence of *global customers*: for example, car component companies have become more international as their customers, such as Toyota or Ford, have internationalised, and required standardised components for all their factories around the world. Finally, *transferable marketing* promotes market globalisation: brands such as Coca-Cola are still successfully marketed in very similar ways across the world.

- *Cost drivers.* Costs can be reduced by operating internationally. Again, there are three main elements to cost drivers. First, increasing volume beyond what a national market might support can give *scale economies*, both on the production side and in purchasing of

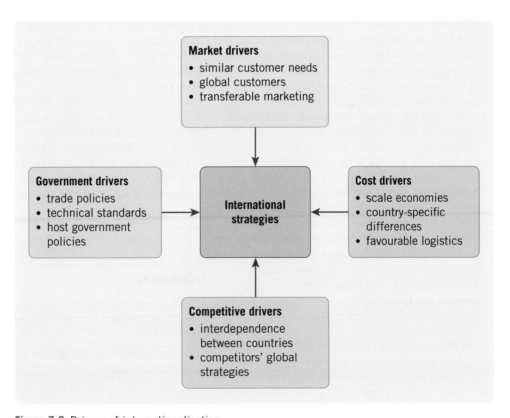

**Figure 7.2** Drivers of internationalisation

*Source*: Adapted from G. Yip, *Total Global Strategy II*, Financial Times Prentice Hall, 2003, Chapter 2.

**ILLUSTRATION 7.1**　Chinese retail: global or local?

**In China Carrefour and Walmart have found that internationalisation is not a simple process.**

China is a magnet for ambitious Western supermarket chains. With an annual growth rate of 13 per cent a year, the Chinese market is expected to grow to $1.5 (€1.2) trillion in 2015, and 520 million people are expected to join the Chinese upper middle class by 2025.

Two leading Western companies in the Chinese retail market are French supermarket chain Carrefour and the world's largest retailer, the American Walmart. The two companies have had very different strategies. French supermarket chain Carrefour was the first to enter the Chinese market in a substantial fashion, entering in 1995, after six years' experience in neighbouring Taiwan. Although Walmart and Carrefour have expanded rapidly and are among the top 10 retailers in China (Carrefour has around 200 stores and Walmart more than 370), they are far from reaching saturation and are still tiny compared to the position in their respective home countries, where they each have about 4,500 stores. Both chains have encountered challenges including problems adapting to local taste and local competition.

Carrefour is following a decentralised strategy: except in Shanghai, where it has several stores, Carrefour allows its local store managers, scattered across the many different regions of China, to make their own purchasing and supply decisions. In contrast, Walmart's initial approach had been based on its standard centralised purchasing and distribution strategy, supplying as much as it can from its new, state-of-the-art distribution centre in Shenzen. Walmart has, however, moved away from its headquarters-driven approach to give more sway to local store managers and has experimented with a smaller-scale local store format. One early discovery for Walmart was that Chinese consumers prefer frequent shopping trips in contrast to Walmart's home-based experience where customers drive to out-of-town stores and fill their cars with large multi-packs.

Another discovery for Western retailers is the amount of regional variation in this vast and multi-ethnic country and the need to give their Chinese stores a local flavour. In the north of China, soya sauces are important; in central China, chilli pepper sauces are required; in the south, it is oyster sauces that matter. For fruit, northerners must have dates; southerners want lychees. In the north, the cold means more demand for red meat and, because customers are wearing layers of clothing, wider store aisles. Northerners do not have much access to hot water, so they wash their hair less frequently, meaning that small sachets of shampoo sell better than large bottles.

The growth of companies such as Carrefour and Walmart demonstrates that there is a substantial market for the Western retail model. Carrefour, for example, was a pioneer of 'private label' goods in China, while Walmart brings logistical expertise. But progress has been slow as home-grown companies have imitated and proven they often are more flexible and experimental with new store formats. Walmart turned to profit only in 2008 and has decided to slow down its expansion in China, and Carrefour's 2–3 per cent margins are significantly below the nearly 5 per cent margins it enjoys in France. In 2011 local authorities accused Walmart of mislabelling ordinary pork as organic and closed down 13 stores for two weeks and Carrefour has repeatedly been obliged to deny that it was considering leaving China.

*Sources: Financial Times, Wall Street Journal* and *Euromonitor* (various).

---

**Questions**

1 What are the pros and cons of the different China strategies pursued by Carrefour and Walmart?

2 What might be the dangers for a large Western retailer in staying out of the Chinese market?

supplies. Companies from smaller countries such as the Netherlands, Switzerland and Taiwan tend therefore to become proportionately much more international than companies from the USA, which have a vast market at home. Scale economies are particularly important in industries with high product development costs, as in the aircraft industry, where initial costs need to be spread over the large volumes of international markets. Second, internationalisation is promoted where it is possible to take advantage of variations in *country-specific differences*. Thus it makes sense to locate the manufacture of clothing in Africa or Bangladesh where labour is still considerably cheaper, but to keep design activities in cities such as New York, Paris, Milan or London, where fashion expertise is concentrated. The third element is *favourable logistics*, or the costs of moving products or services across borders relative to their final value. From this point of view, microchips are easy to source internationally, while bulky materials such as assembled furniture are harder.

- *Government drivers*. There are three main factors here that facilitate internationalisation. First, *reduction of barriers to trade and investment* has accelerated internationalisation. During the last couple of decades national governments have reduced restrictions on both flow of goods and capital. The World Trade Organisation has been instrumental in reducing trade barriers globally.[4] Similarly, the emergence of regional economic integration partnerships like the European Union, the North American Free Trade Agreement and the Association of Southeast Asian Nations Economic Community has promoted this development. No government, however, allows complete economic openness and it typically varies widely from industry to industry, with agriculture and high-tech industries related to defence likely to be particularly sensitive. *The liberalisation and adoption of free markets* in many countries around the globe have also encouraged international trade and investments. This of course includes the collapse of the Soviet Union and liberalisation of Eastern Europe, China's free market reforms and market-based reforms in numerous Asian and South American economies. A third important government factor is *technology standardisation*. Compatible technical standards make it easier for companies to access different markets as they can enter many markets with the same product or service without adapting to local idiosyncratic standards.

- *Competitive drivers*. These relate specifically to globalisation as an integrated worldwide strategy rather than simpler international strategies. These have two elements. First, *interdependence* between country operations increases the pressure for global coordination. For example, a business with a plant in Mexico serving both the US and the Japanese markets has to coordinate carefully between the three locations: surging sales in one country, or a collapse in another, will have significant knock-on effects on the other countries. The second element relates directly to competitor strategy. The presence of *globalised competitors* increases the pressure to adopt a global strategy in response because competitors may use one country's profits to cross-subsidise their operations in another. A company with a loosely coordinated international strategy is vulnerable to globalised competitors, because it is unable to support country subsidiaries under attack from targeted, subsidised competition. The danger is of piecemeal withdrawal from countries under attack, and the gradual undermining of any overall economies of scale that the international player may have started with.[5]

The key insight from Yip's drivers framework is that the internationalisation potential of industries is variable. There are many different factors that can support it as indicated above, but others can inhibit it. For example, customer needs and tastes for many food products inhibit internationalisation of them and local governments often impose tariff barriers, ownership restrictions and local content requirements on foreign entrants. An important step in determining an internationalisation strategy is a realistic assessment of the true scope for internationalisation in the particular industry. In the Chinese retail case (Illustration 7.1), it may be that the Western entry includes both market and competitive drivers.

## 7.3 GEOGRAPHIC SOURCES OF ADVANTAGE

As for any strategy, internationalisation needs to be based on strategic capabilities providing a sustainable competitive advantage. This competitive advantage has usually to be substantial. After all, a competitor entering a market from overseas typically starts with considerable *dis*advantages relative to existing home competitors, which will usually have superior market knowledge, established relationships with local customers, strong supply chains and the like. A foreign entrant must have significant competitive advantages for it to overcome these inherent advantages of local competitors. Tesco's failure in the USA is an example of this. After seven years and investments of about £1 bn (€1.2 bn) in its US Fresh & Easy business, Tesco was forced to withdraw in 2013. Unlike in the UK, Tesco had no significant competitive advantage over the strong US domestic retailers. Internationalisation thus requires building on the sources of sustainable competitive advantage (discussed earlier in Chapters 3 and 5) including the organisation's unique strengths in resources and capabilities. While these *firm- or organisation-specific advantages* are important, competitive advantage in an international context also depends on *country-specific or geographic advantages.*[6]

As is clear from the earlier discussion of cost drivers in international strategy, the geographical location of activities is a crucial source of potential advantage and one of the distinguishing features of international strategy relative to other diversification strategies. As Bruce Kogut at Columbia University has explained, an organisation can improve the configuration of its *value chain and system*[7] by taking advantage of country-specific differences (see section 3.4.1). There are two principal opportunities available: the exploitation of particular *locational advantages*, often in the company's home country, and sourcing advantages overseas via an *international value system.*

### 7.3.1 Locational advantage: Porter's Diamond[8]

Countries and regions within them, and organisations originating in those, often benefit from competitive advantages grounded in specific local conditions. They become associated with specific types of enduring competitive advantage: for example, the Swiss in private banking, the northern Italians in leather and fur fashion goods. Michael Porter has proposed a four-pointed 'diamond' to explain why some locations tend to produce firms with sustained competitive advantages in some industries more than others (see Figure 7.3). Specifically, **Porter's Diamond** suggests that locational advantages may stem from local factor conditions; local demand conditions; local related and supporting industries; and from local firm strategy structure and rivalry. These four interacting determinants of locational advantage work as follows:

- *Factor conditions.* These refer to the 'factors of production' that go into making a product or service (i.e. raw materials, land and labour). Factor condition advantages at a national level can translate into general competitive advantages for national firms in international markets. For example, the linguistic ability of the Swiss has traditionally provided a significant advantage to their banking industry. Cheap energy has traditionally provided an advantage for the North American aluminium industry.

- *Home demand conditions.* The nature of the domestic customers can become a source of competitive advantage. Dealing with sophisticated and demanding customers at home helps train a company to be effective overseas. For example, America's long distances have led to competitive strength in very large truck engines. Sophisticated local customers in France and Italy have helped keep their local fashion industries at the leading edge for many decades.

- *Related and supporting industries.* Local 'clusters' of related and mutually supporting industries can be an important source of competitive advantage. These are often regionally based, making personal interaction easier. In northern Italy, for example, the leather footwear industry, the leatherworking machinery industry and the design services which underpin them group together in the same regional cluster to each other's mutual benefit.

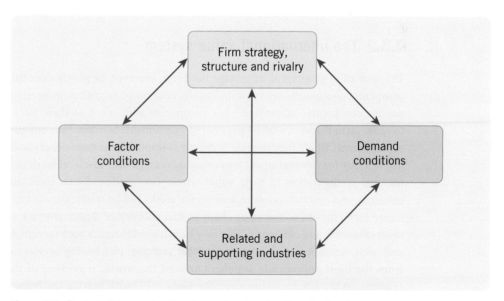

**Figure 7.3** Porter's Diamond – the determinants of national advantages

*Source*: Adapted from *The Competitive Advantage of Nations*, The Free Press (Porter, Michael E. 1990) with the permission of Simon & Schuster Publishing Group from the Free Press edition. Copyright © 1990, 1998 by Michael E. Porter. All rights reserved.

Silicon Valley forms a cluster of hardware, software, research and venture capital organisations which together create a virtuous circle of high-technology enterprise.

- *Firm strategy, industry structure and rivalry.* The characteristic strategies, industry structures and rivalries in different countries can also be bases of advantage. German companies' strategy of investing in technical excellence gives them a characteristic advantage in engineering industries and creates large pools of expertise. A competitive local industry structure is also helpful: if too dominant in their home territory, local organisations can become complacent and lose advantage overseas. Some domestic rivalry can actually be an advantage, therefore. For example, the long-run success of the Japanese car companies is partly based on government policy sustaining several national players (unlike in the United Kingdom, where they were all merged into one) and the Swiss pharmaceuticals industry became strong in part because each company had to compete with several strong local rivals.

Porter's Diamond identifies the extent to which organisations can build on home-based advantages to create competitive advantage in relation to others internationally. To compete with local actors, organisations must carefully exploit the distinct environmental conditions and structural attributes illustrated in Figure 7.3. For example, Dutch brewing companies – such as Heineken – had an advantage in early internationalisation due to the combination of sophisticated consumers and limited room to grow at home. Volvo Trucks, the Swedish truck and construction equipment manufacturer, has achieved global success by building on a local network of sophisticated engineering partners and suppliers and a local demand orientated towards reliability and safety. Before embarking on an internationalisation strategy, managers should seek out sources of general locational advantage to underpin their company's individual sources of advantage.

## 7.3.2 The international value system

The sources of geographic advantage need not, however, be purely domestic. In addition, as companies continue to internationalise, the country of origin becomes relatively less important for competitive advantage.[9] For companies with most of their sales abroad, like the telecom giant Ericsson with 95 per cent of sales outside Sweden, the configuration of the local environments where they operate is at least as important as their domestic environment. This implies that for international companies, advantage also needs to be drawn from the international configuration of their *value system* (see section 3.4.1). Here the different skills, resources and costs of countries around the world can be systematically exploited in order to locate each element of the value chain in that country or region where it can be conducted most effectively and efficiently. This may be achieved through both foreign direct investments and joint ventures but also through **global sourcing: purchasing services and components from the most appropriate suppliers around the world, regardless of their location.** For example, in the UK for many years the National Health Service has been sourcing medical personnel from overseas to offset a shortfall in domestic skills and capacity. Smaller organisations can also build on the broader system of suppliers, channels and customers as demonstrated in Illustration 7.2.

## ILLUSTRATION 7.2     The international 'Joint Effort Enterprise'

**For Blue Skies international strategy is something more than profit alone.**

Blue Skies specialises in producing fresh-cut fruit and juice products from a network of factories in Africa and South America. It supplies over 12 major European retailers, including Waitrose in the UK, Albert Heijn in the Netherlands and Monoprix in France. The company has factories in Ghana, Egypt, South Africa and Brazil. Its biggest factory is in Ghana and employs over 1,500 people and sources fruit from over 100 small to medium-sized farms. Blue Skies believes in value adding at source whereby the raw materials are processed within the country of origin rather than shipped overseas and processed elsewhere. By doing this, as much as 70 per cent of the value of the finished product stays within the country of origin, compared to as little as 15 per cent if it is processed outside.

Blue Skies works within a framework it has developed called the 'Joint Effort Enterprise' (JEE). While it is their model for a sustainable business, it is not a model which has been introduced to respond to the growing hype around 'sustainability'. Instead it is a set of principles from the foundation of the business in 1998 to ensure that the organisation would endure. The JEE is principally made up of three strands: a diverse society, a culture of respect and a drive for profit. The latter must not, however, come at the expense of all the other strands. Blue Skies believes that this model ensures that it retains the best people and conserves the resources they rely on, so that they can produce the best quality products and therefore generate the income that keeps the organisation going. Its approach is 'based on fairness in business, respect for each other and above all, trust'. In addition, Blue Skies raised over £400,000 (€480,000) in partnership with two European retailers and completed over ten projects in Ghana and South Africa including the construction of schools, latrines and community centres. The Blue Skies JEE approach has also been awarded a Queens Award for Enterprise in the Sustainable Development Category in both 2008 and 2011.

During the last few years Blue Skies has encountered several international challenges: a world recession, rising energy prices, exchange rate volatility, shortage of raw materials, etc. It realises that these are challenges that an international operation across three continents must be ready and willing to respond to. Accordingly, it has undertaken a number of initiatives:

- Developing products for local and dollar-based markets to reduce exposure to exchange rate losses and supply chain disruption.
- Expanding its supply base around the world to ensure year-round supply of fruit.
- Helping its suppliers achieve agricultural standards such as LEAF (Linking Environment and Farming) to ensure sustainability of supply.
- Growing the Blue Skies Foundation to strengthen its relationship with staff, farmers and their communities.
- Developing plans to generate renewable energy to reduce electricity costs and greenhouse gas emissions.
- Opening a European-based contingency factory to ensure consistency of supply during supply chain disruption.

*Source*: Prepared by Edwina Goodwin, Leicester Business School, De Montfort University.

### Questions

1 What internationalisation drivers (Figure 7.2) do you think were most important for Blue Skies' decision to enter its specific markets?

2 How does Blue Skies' strategy fit into a broader international value system including suppliers, channels and customers (see also Figure 3.5)?

3 To what extent is JEE key to Blue Skies' international strategy and competitive advantage or rather a social entrepreneurship effort?

Different locational advantages can be identified:

- *Cost advantages* include labour costs, transportation and communications costs and taxation and investment incentives. Labour costs are important. American and European firms, for example, have moved much of their software programming tasks to India where a computer programmer costs an American firm about one-quarter of what it would pay for a worker with comparable skills in the USA. As wages in India have risen, some IT firms have started to move work to even more low-cost locations such as Thailand and Vietnam.

- *Unique local capabilities* may allow an organisation to enhance its competitive advantage. Gradually value-creating and innovative activity becomes geographically dispersed across multiple centres of excellence within multinational organisations.[10] For example, leading European pharmaceuticals company GSK has R&D laboratories in Boston and the Research Triangle in North Carolina in order to establish research collaborations with the prominent universities and hospitals in those areas. Internationalisation, therefore, is increasingly not only about exploiting an organisation's existing capabilities in new national markets, but also about developing strategic capabilities by drawing on capabilities found elsewhere in the world.

- *National market characteristics* can enable organisations to develop differentiated product offerings aimed at different market segments. American guitar-maker Gibson, for example, complements its US-made products with often similar, lower-cost alternatives produced in South Korea under the Epiphone brand. However, because of the American music tradition, Gibson's high-end guitars benefit from the reputation of still being 'made in the USA'.

## 7.4 INTERNATIONAL STRATEGIES

Given their organisation-specific advantages and the ability to obtain sources of international competitive advantage through geographic home-based factors or international value systems, organisations still face difficult questions about what kind of international strategy to pursue. The fundamental issue in formulating an international strategy is to balance pressures for *global integration* versus those for *local responsiveness*.[11] Pressures for global integration encourage organisations to coordinate their activities across diverse countries to gain efficient operations. The internationalisation drivers discussed above (section 7.2) indicate forces that organisations can build on to achieve lower costs and higher quality in operations and activities on a global scale. However, there are conflicting pressures that also encourage organisations to become locally responsive and meet the specific needs in each individual country (see section 7.5.1 below). Values and attitudes, cultures, laws, institutions and economics differ across countries, which imply differences in customer preferences, product and service standards, regulations and human resources that all need to be addressed. These two opposing pressures – global integration vs local responsiveness – put contradictory demands on an organisation's international strategy. High pressure for global integration implies an increased need to concentrate and coordinate operations globally. In contrast, high pressure for local responsiveness implies a greater need to disperse operations and adapt to local demand.

This key problem is sometimes referred to as the **global–local dilemma**: the **extent to which products and services may be standardised across national boundaries or need to be**

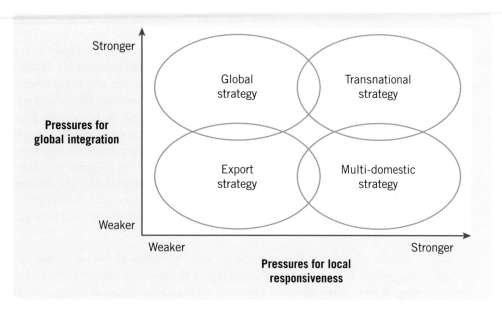

**Figure 7.4** Four international strategies

**adapted to meet the requirements of specific national markets**. For some products and services – such as televisions – markets appear similar across the world, offering huge potential scale economies if design, production and delivery can be centralised. For other products and services – such as television programming – tastes still seem highly national-specific, drawing companies to decentralise operations and control as near as possible to the local market.

This dilemma between global integration and local responsiveness suggests several possible international strategies, ranging from emphasising one of the dimensions to complex responses that try to combine both. Organisations need to assess to what degree there are potential advantages of cost and quality of global integration and balance those pressures against the need to adapt products and/or services to local conditions. This section introduces four different kinds of international strategy, based on strategic choices about this balance (see Figure 7.4). The four basic international strategies are:[12]

- *Export strategy.* This strategy leverages home country capabilities, innovations and products in different foreign countries. It is advantageous when both pressures for global integration and local responsiveness are low, as shown in Figure 7.4. Companies that have distinctive capabilities together with strong reputation and brand names often follow this strategy with success. Google, for example, centralises its R &D and the core architecture underlying its internet services at its headquarters in California in the USA and exploits it internationally with minor adaptations except for local languages and alphabets. The downside of this approach is the limits of a home country centralised view of the business with risks of skilled local competitors getting ahead. Google, for example, meets strong local rivals in Baidu in China and Naver in Korea with superior mastery of the language and understanding of consumer behaviour.

- *Multi-domestic strategy.* This is a strategy that maximises local responsiveness. It is based on different product or service offerings and operations in each country depending on local market conditions and customer preferences. Each country is treated differently, with a considerable autonomy for each country manager to best meet the needs of the local markets and customers in that particular country. As in the export strategy, this strategy is similarly loosely coordinated internationally. The organisation becomes a collection of relatively independent units with value chain activities adapted to specific local conditions. This multi-domestic approach is particularly appropriate when there are strong benefits to adapting to local needs and when there are limited efficiency gains from integration. It is common in food and consumer product industries where local idiosyncratic preferences are significant. Marketing-driven companies often pursue this type of strategy. For example, Frito-Lay, a US branded-snacks company, tailors its global products to local tastes and even creates entirely new snack products for local markets.[13] The disadvantages of a multi-domestic strategy include manufacturing inefficiencies, a proliferation of costly product and service variations and risks towards brand and reputation if national practices become too diverse.

- *Global strategy.* This is a strategy that maximises global integration. In this strategy the world is seen as one marketplace with standardised products and services that fully exploits integration and efficiency in operations. The focus is on capturing scale economies and exploiting location economies worldwide, with geographically dispersed value chain activities being coordinated and controlled centrally from headquarters. In these respects this strategy is the exact opposite of the multi-domestic strategy. A global strategy is most beneficial when there are substantial cost or quality efficiency benefits from standardisation and when customer needs are relatively homogeneous across countries. It is a common strategy for commodities or commodity-like products. Mexican Cemex, one of the largest cement companies in the world, follows a global strategy with centralised and shared services in information technology, R & D, human resources and financial services across countries and regions.[14] Non-commodity companies can also follow a global strategy, like Sweden's furniture retailer IKEA. Based on a strong home base they standardise products and marketing with limited local adaptation to gain maximum global integration efficiency. The drawback of the global strategy is reduced flexibility due to standardisation that limits possibilities to adapting activities and products to local conditions.[15] This has, for example, led IKEA to make minor modifications of some furniture offerings to suit local tastes.

- *Transnational strategy.* This is the most complex strategy that tries to maximise both responsiveness and integration. Its aim is to unite the key advantages of the multi-domestic and global strategies while minimising their disadvantages. In addition, it maximises learning and knowledge exchange between dispersed units. In this strategy products and services and operational activities are, subject to minimum efficiency standards, adapted to local conditions in each country. In contrast to the multi-domestic strategy, however, this strategy also leverages learning and innovation across units in different countries. The value chain configuration includes an intricate combination of centralised manufacturing to increase efficiency combined with distributed assembly and local adaptations. Coordination is neither centralised at home nor dispersed in foreign countries, but encourages knowledge flows from wherever ideas and innovations come from. The major advantage of this strategy is its capacity to support efficiency and effectiveness while at the same time being able to serve local needs and leverage learning across units. General

Electric has been celebrated as having a transnational strategy that emphasises seeking and exchanging ideas irrespective of where they come from. The company swaps ideas regarding efficiency, customer responsiveness and innovation across different parts of the value chain and diverse countries worldwide.[16] However, while it is argued that transnational strategies are becoming increasingly necessary, many firms find it difficult to implement, given its complexity and the fundamental trade-off between integration and responsiveness.

In practice, these four international strategies are not absolutely distinct as indicated by the overlapping ovals in Figure 7.4. They are, rather, illustrative examples of alternative international strategies. Global integration and local responsiveness are matters of degree rather than sharp distinctions. Moreover, choices between them will be influenced by changes in the internationalisation drivers introduced earlier. It is rare that companies adopt a pure form of international strategy; instead they often blend approaches and are located somewhere between the four strategies. As exemplified above, IKEA has a global strategy, but also makes some minor local adaptations, which may take it towards more of a transnational strategy.

## 7.5 MARKET SELECTION AND ENTRY

Having decided on an international strategy built on significant sources of competitive advantage and supported by strong internationalisation drivers, managers need next to decide which countries to enter. Not all countries are equally attractive. To an extent, however, countries can initially be compared using standard environmental analysis techniques, for example along the dimensions identified in the PESTEL framework (see section 2.2.1) or according to the industry five forces (section 2.3.1). However, there are specific determinants of market attractiveness that need to be considered in internationalisation strategy: the intrinsic characteristics of the market. A key point here is how initial estimates of country attractiveness can be modified by various measures of *distance*. The section concludes by considering different *entry modes* into national markets.

### 7.5.1 Market characteristics

At least four elements of the PESTEL framework are particularly important in comparing countries for entry:

- *Political*. Political environments vary widely between countries and can alter rapidly. Russia since the fall of Communism has seen frequent swings for and against private foreign enterprise. Governments can of course create significant opportunities for organisations. For example, the British government has traditionally promoted the financial services industry in the City of London by offering tax advantages to high-earning financiers from abroad and providing a 'light-touch' regulatory environment. It is important, however, to determine the level of *political risk* before entering a country. Toyota, for example, found itself the subject of an unexpected consumer boycott in China because of political tensions over a territorial dispute between China and Japan.

- *Economic.* Key comparators in deciding entry are levels of gross domestic product and disposable income which help in estimating the potential size of the market. Fast-growth economies obviously provide opportunities, and in developing economies such as China and India growth is translating into an even faster creation of a high-consumption middle class. At the same time entirely new high-growth markets are opening up in Africa including Nigeria and Ghana.

- *Social.* Social factors will clearly be important, for example the availability of a well-trained workforce or the size of demographic market segments – old or young – relevant to the strategy. Cultural variations also need to be considered, for instance in defining tastes in the marketplace.

- *Legal.* Countries vary widely in their legal regime, determining the extent to which businesses can enforce contracts, protect intellectual property or avoid corruption. Similarly, policing will be important for the security of employees, a factor that in the past has deterred business in some African countries.

A common procedure is to rank country markets against each other on criteria such as these and then to choose the countries for entry that offer the highest relative scores. However, Pankaj Ghemawat from Spain's IESE Business School has pointed out that what matters is not just the attractiveness of different countries relative to each other, but also the compatibility of the countries with the internationalising firm itself.[17] Thus Ghemawat underlines the importance of *match* between country and firm. For firms coming from any particular country, some countries are more 'distant' – or mismatched – than others. For example, a Spanish company might be 'closer' to a South American market than an East Asian market and might therefore prefer that market even if it ranked lower on standard criteria of attractiveness. As well as a relative ranking of countries, therefore, each company has to add its assessment of countries in terms of closeness of match.

Ghemawat's 'CAGE framework' measures the match between countries and companies according to four dimensions of distance, reflected by the letters of the acronym. Thus the **CAGE framework** emphasises the importance of cultural, administrative, geographical and economic distance, as follows:

- *Cultural distance.* The distance dimension here relates to differences in language, ethnicity, religion and social norms. Cultural distance is not just a matter of similarity in consumer tastes, but it also extends to important compatibilities in terms of managerial behaviours. Here, for example, US firms might be closer to Canada than to Mexico, which Spanish firms might find relatively compatible. Figure 7.5 draws on the GLOBE survey of 17,000 managers from 62 different societal cultures around the world to contrast specifically the orientations of American and Chinese managers on some key cultural dimensions. According to this GLOBE survey, American managers appear to be typically more risk-taking, while Chinese managers are more autonomous.

- *Administrative and political distance.* Here distance is in terms of incompatible administrative, political or legal traditions. Colonial ties can diminish difference, so that the shared heritage of France and its former West African colonies creates certain understandings that go beyond linguistic advantages. See also, for example, the experience of the Brazilian Vale company in Mozambique, where shared Portuguese heritage made a difference (see Illustration 7.3). Institutional weaknesses – for example, slow or corrupt administration

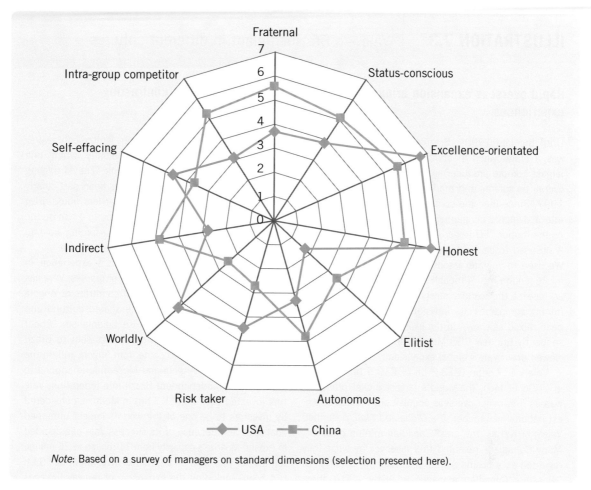

**Figure 7.5** International cross-cultural comparison

*Source*: M. Javidan, P. Dorman, M. de Luque and R. House, 'In the eye of the beholder: cross-cultural lessons in leadership from Project GLOBE', *Academy of Management Perspectives* (February 2006), pp. 67–90 (Figure 4: USA vs China, p. 82). (GLOBE stands for 'Global Leadership and Organisational Behaviour Effectiveness'.)

– can open up distance between countries. So too can political differences: Chinese companies are increasingly able to operate in parts of the world that American companies are finding harder, for example parts of the Middle East and Africa.

- *Geographical distance.* This is not just a matter of the kilometres separating one country from another, but involves other geographical characteristics of the country such as size, sea-access and the quality of communications infrastructure. Transport infrastructure can shrink or exaggerate physical distance. France is much closer to large parts of Continental Europe than to the United Kingdom, because of the barrier presented by the English Channel and the latter's relatively poor road and rail infrastructure. The possibility for individual companies to reduce geographic distances is illustrated by the development of mega-ship carriers by the Brazilian mining company Vale in Illustration 7.3.

# ILLUSTRATION 7.3 Vale – a Brazilian giant in different cultures

**Rapid overseas expansion brings this Brazilian multinational some contrasting experiences.**

Until the late 1990s, Brazil's Vale mining company was a state-owned sleeping giant. Vale, the world's largest iron-ore producer and the second-largest miner overall by volume and market value, was privatised in 1997. Since then the company has transformed itself into a dynamic conglomerate and expanded globally. As the former CEO Roger Agnelli commented in 2010: 'Vale used to be fundamentally an iron-ore company. We used to operate essentially in Brazil. Now we are in 36 countries.' Although Vale has been described as 'one of the world's most powerful and aggressive mining companies' its international experiences have been mixed as shown in the examples below and consequently the new CEO Murilo Ferreira has somewhat slowed down Vale's global expansion.

Vale's $17.6 bn (€13.2 bn or £10.5 bn) takeover in 2006 of Inco, the world's largest nickel producer, was its first major overseas acquisition. Canada's largest national newspaper, the *Globe and Mail*, described Vale's arrival as 'the great Canadian mining disaster'. Many Canadians resented this takeover by what they regarded as a business from a developing country. Of 29 senior Canadian managers in early 2007, three years later 23 had departed, mostly voluntarily. At one tense meeting a Brazilian manager riposted: 'How come, if you're so smart, you didn't take *us* over?' The clash resulted in a strike that lasted almost a year. While the conflict was finally resolved it was seen as a sign of potential confrontations when companies from emerging economies such as Brazil, China and India expand into new, unfamiliar territories.

The booming demand from China has been a gift and Vale's export of iron ore there account for about 30 per cent of revenues. Compared to main rivals Australian miners BHP and Rio Tinto, Vale, however, has a considerable disadvantage: distance. Vale's solution has been to develop giant iron-ore vessels. A fleet of 100 of the so-called 'Valemaxes' would reduce shipping costs to China by 20 per cent and carbon emission by 35 per cent. The giant ships have, however, ignited controversy among Chinese authorities, especially when one developed a crack in a ballast tank. The struggling Chinese shipbuilding community has been particularly critical as it claims that the mega-carriers would drive freight rates down. All this has resulted in a ban on the Valemaxes to dock at China's ports, forcing Vale to unload in Malaysia and the Philippines instead.

A contrast so far has been Vale's experience in Mozambique. Like many Brazilian companies, Vale has been attracted to the two African countries of Angola and Mozambique because of the shared cultural and linguistic heritage of Portuguese colonialism. About half the 3 million black African slaves sent to Brazil between 1700 and 1850 came from Angola and, in the 1820s, settlers in Angola and Mozambique applied to join the newly independent Brazil in a federation. Vale first invested $1.7 bn (€1.3 bn) in Moatize, considered by investors to be one of the world's largest untapped coal reserves. Because of its success Vale has decided to expand Moatize's capacity from 11 million to 26 million tonnes per year with an additional investment of $6 bn (€4.5 bn) including the expansion of railway linkages and infrastructure. Vale's CEO, Murilo Ferreira, confirms Africa's significance for the company's strategy: 'It's a new frontier . . . Africa is very important. We want to grow there.'

*Sources*: *Financial Times*, 25 February 2010; *Financial Times*, 9 February 2010; *Financial Times*, 11 February 2010; *Financial Times*, 12 April 2012; *Financial Times*, 1 October 2012; mining-technology.com, 24 November 2011; miningweekly.com, 18 May 2012.

## Questions

1 Suggest three reasons for Vale's different reception in Canada and Mozambique.

2 What can Vale do to mitigate the problems the company encounters when expanding globally?

- *Economic distance.* The final element of the CAGE framework refers particularly to wealth distances. There are of course huge disparities in wealth internationally: around the world, there are 4 billion people beneath the poverty income threshold of less than $2 a day.[18] Multinationals from rich countries are typically weak at serving such very poor consumers. However, these rich-country multinationals are losing out on large markets if they only concentrate on the wealthy elites overseas. University of Michigan academic C.K. Prahalad pointed out that the aggregated wealth of those at the 'base of the pyramid' in terms of income distribution is very substantial: simple mathematics means that those 4 billion below the poverty threshold represent a market of more than $2,000 bn per year. If rich-country multinationals can develop new capabilities to serve these numerically huge markets, they can bridge the economic distance, and thereby both significantly extend their presence in booming economies such as China and India and bring to these poor consumers the benefits that are claimed for Western goods. See Illustration 7.4 for examples of innovative base of the pyramid strategies.

## 7.5.2 Competitive characteristics

Assessing the relative attractiveness of markets by PESTEL and CAGE analyses is only the first step. The second element relates to competition. Here, of course, Michael Porter's Five Forces Framework can help (see section 2.3.1). For example, country markets with many existing competitors, powerful buyers (perhaps large retail chains such as in much of North America and Northern Europe) and low barriers to further new entrants from overseas would typically be unattractive. However, an additional consideration is the likelihood of retaliation from other competitors.

In the Five Forces Framework, retaliation potential relates to rivalry and entry. Here the likelihood and ferocity of potential competitor reactions are added to the simple calculation of relative country market attractiveness. As shown in Figure 7.6, country markets can be assessed according to three criteria:[19]

- *Market attractiveness* to the new entrant, based on PESTEL, CAGE and five forces analyses, for example. In Figure 7.6, countries A and B are the most attractive to the entrant.
- *Defender's reactiveness*, likely to be influenced by the market's attractiveness to the defender but also by the extent to which the defender is working with a globally integrated, rather than multi-domestic, strategy. A defender will be more reactive if the markets are important to it and it has the managerial capabilities to coordinate its response. Here, the defender is highly reactive in countries A and D.
- *Defender's clout*, which is the power that the defender is able to muster in order to fight back. Clout is typically a function of share in the particular market, but might be influenced by connections to other powerful local players, such as retailers or government. In Figure 7.6, clout is represented by the size of the bubbles, with the defender having most clout in countries A, C, D and F.

Choice of country to enter can be significantly modified by adding reactiveness and clout to calculations of attractiveness. Relying only on attractiveness, the top-ranked country to enter in Figure 7.6 is country A. Unfortunately, it is also one in which the defender is highly

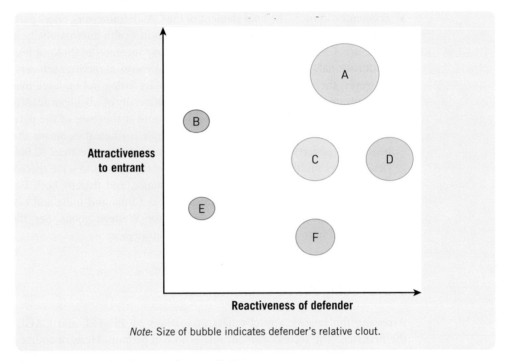

**Figure 7.6** International competitor retaliation

*Source*: Adapted from Global gamesmanship, *Harvard Business Review*, May (MacMillan, I., van Putter, S. and McGrath, R. 2003), reprinted by permission of Harvard Business Review. Copyright © 2003 by the Harvard Business School Publishing Corporation. All rights reserved.

reactive, and the one in which it has most clout. Country B becomes a better international move than A. In turn, country C is a better prospect than country D, because, even though they are equally attractive, the defender is less reactive. One surprising result of taking defender reactiveness and clout into account is the re-evaluation of country E: although ranked fifth on simple attractiveness, it might rank second overall if competitor retaliation is allowed for.

### 7.5.3 Entry modes

Once a particular national market has been selected for entry, an organisation needs to choose how to enter that market. Entry modes differ in the degree of resource commitment to a particular market and the extent to which an organisation is operationally involved in a particular location. In order of increasing resource commitment, the four key entry mode types are: *exporting*; contractual arrangement through *licensing and franchising* to local partners, as McDonald's does to restaurant operators; *joint ventures*, in other words the establishment of jointly owned businesses; and *wholly owned subsidiaries*, through either the acquisition of established companies or 'greenfield' investments, the development of facilities from scratch.

The *staged international expansion* model emphasises the role of experience in determining entry mode. Internationalisation typically brings organisations into unfamiliar territory,

## ILLUSTRATION 7.4   Base of the pyramid strategies

**Base of the pyramid strategy means more than just low prices. Base of the pyramid involves designing new products, forming partnership, reshaping distribution channels and introducing novel financing solutions.**

### Product design

A key problem in the developing world is the poor quality of piped water. Unilever Hindustan, India's largest consumer goods company, owned by Anglo-Dutch Unilever, developed a water filter that makes water as safe as boiling. It is marketed and sold through the wide Unilever distribution network. The filter has attracted over three million households, mainly in India's mega- or middle-sized cities. However, at $35 (€26) it is still unattainable for millions of Indians who live on less than a dollar a day. In an effort to reach rural customers Unilever has therefore started to market a light-version (lower capacity) of the filter. The success of the product on the Indian market has led Unilever Hindustan to introduce the water filter in other markets in Asia, Eastern Europe and South Africa.

### Partnerships

First Energy Oorja started as a partnership between the Indian Institute of Science Bangalore and British Petroleum (BP) Emerging Consumer Market (ECM) division to develop a stove using the 'power of innovation and a strong understanding of consumer energy needs'. It was later acquired by The Alchemists Ark (TAA), a privately held business consulting firm. The First Energy Oorja stoves are low-smoke, low-cost stoves, which work on pellets – an organic biofuel made of processed agricultural waste. First Energy Oorja works in close partnership with both local non-governmental organisations and dealer networks in rural markets to distribute and market the stove. This distribution model ensures that the product reaches remote Indian locations.

### Distribution channels

Bayer CropScience, a global firm that develops and manufactures crop protection products, initiated a Green World venture in Kenya. It introduced small packs of pesticides and trained a network of small, rural agrodealers to guide and educate small farmers on product handling and use. It also provided further support and marketing via radio. Bayer CropScience carefully selected dealers based on their reputation in the community and sales volumes. Today about 25 per cent of its horticultural retail revenues in Kenya now come from Green World stores.

### Financial solutions

Cemex, a global cement corporation from Mexico, has been an innovative pioneer in designing a microfinancing system, 'Patrimonio Hoy' (Property Now), for the poor in Mexico and later in the rest of Latin America. In the past, building houses for this group had often proved lengthy and risky because, without savings or access to credit, low-income families could only buy small amounts of building material at a time. Patrimonio Hoy is a solution to this. It is a combination of savings and credit schemes in which Cemex provides collateral-free financing to customers via a membership system based on small monthly fees. Customers demonstrate their savings discipline by regular monthly payments and Cemex develops trust in them by delivering building raw materials early on credit. The programme is a success and Cemex reports that it has reached 265 million families so far.

*Sources*: Swiss Agency for Development and Cooperation, 2011; Institute for Financial and Management Research, 2012; A. Karamchandani, M. Kubzansky and N. Lalwani, 'Is the bottom of the pyramid really for you?', *Harvard Business Review*, March 2011; *Business Today*, December 2011.

### Questions

1 Can you imagine any risks or dangers that Western companies might face in pursuing base of the pyramid strategies?

2 Is there anything that Western companies might learn from base of the pyramid strategies in emerging markets that might be valuable in their home markets?

requiring managers to learn new ways of doing business.[20] The **staged international expansion model proposes a sequential process whereby companies gradually increase their commitment to newly entered markets, as they build market knowledge and capabilities**. Thus firms might enter initially by licensing or exporting, thereby acquiring some local knowledge while minimising local investments. As they gain knowledge and confidence, firms can then increase their exposure, perhaps first by a joint venture and finally by creating a wholly owned subsidiary. For example, the leading Danish wind turbine manufacturer Vestas first entered the US market through exports. Subsequently Vestas established manufacturing and R&D facilities in Eastern Colorado to strengthen its competitive position versus domestic players and now supplies 90 per cent of components required for the assembly of a final turbine within the USA.

However, the gradualism of staged international expansion is now challenged by two phenomena:

- '*Born-global firms*', in other words new small firms that internationalise rapidly at early stages in their development.[21] New technologies now help small firms link up to international sources of expertise, supply and customers worldwide. For such firms, waiting till they have enough international experience is not an option: international strategy is a condition of existence. For example, companies like Twitter and Instagram internationalised quickly from being small start-ups. Other types of companies may also internationalise fast. Blue Skies in Illustration 7.2 with operations across three continents is an example of a small company that started out as a mini-multinational.

- *Emerging-country multinationals* also often move quickly through entry modes. Prominent examples are the Chinese white-goods multinational Haier, the Indian pharmaceuticals company Ranbaxy Laboratories and Mexico's Cemex cement company mentioned above.[22] Such companies typically develop *unique capabilities* in their home market that then need to be rolled out quickly worldwide before competitors catch up. For example, Haier became skilled at very efficient production of simple white goods, providing a cost advantage that is transferable outside its Chinese manufacturing base. Haier now has factories in Italy and the USA, as well as the Philippines, Malaysia, Indonesia, Egypt, Nigeria and elsewhere round the world. The rapid internationalisation made by emerging multinationals from China has largely been based on acquisitions. These are often high-profile acquisitions as illustrated by the Chinese conglomerate Wanda buying the second-biggest movie theatre chain in the USA, AMC (see the end Case example).[23]

## SUMMARY

- Internationalisation potential in any particular market is determined by Yip's four drivers of internationalisation: *market*, *cost*, *government* and *competitors' strategies*.

- *Sources of advantage* in international strategy can be drawn from both national sources of advantage, as captured in *Porter's Diamond*, and global sourcing through the *international value system*.

- There are four main types of international strategy, varying according to extent of coordination and geographical configuration: export strategy, multi-domestic strategy, global strategy and transnational strategy.

- *Market selection* for international entry or expansion should be based on *attractiveness*, multidimensional measures of *distance* and expectations of competitor *retaliation*.

- Modes of entry into new markets include export, licensing and franchising, joint ventures and overseas wholly owned subsidiaries.

- To watch an author video on the concepts discussed in this chapter please visit www.mystrategylab.com, and click on 'Author perspectives on strategic management'.

## VIDEO ASSIGNMENTS

MyStrategyLab

If you are using *MyStrategyLab* you might find it useful to watch the CISCO case study for Chapter 7.

1 Using the concepts in section 7.5, analyse and recommend the appropriate market selection and entry mode for CISCO – refer to both the markets and the mode of entry/development.

2 Using Yip's model (Figure 7.2) and insights from the video, explain and discuss the drivers of internationalisation in the IT industries.

## RECOMMENDED KEY READINGS

- A useful collection of academic articles on international business is in A. Rugman and T. Brewer (eds), *The Oxford Handbook of International Business*, Oxford University Press, 2003. An invigorating perspective on international strategy is provided by G.S. Yip and G.T. Hult, *Total Global Strategy*, Pearson, 2012.

## REFERENCES

1. For another cautious view, see M. Alexander and H. Korine, 'Why you shouldn't go global', *Harvard Business Review* (December 2008), pp. 70–7.

2. T. Friedman, *The World Is Flat: the Globalized World in the Twenty-First Century*, Penguin, 2006; and P. Rivoli, *The Travels of a T-Shirt in the Global Economy: an Economist Examines the Markets, Power and Politics of World Trade*, Wiley, 2006.

3. G.S. Yip and G.T. Hult, *Total Global Strategy*, Pearson, 2012.

4. Useful industry-specific data on trends in openness to trade and investment can be found at the World Trade Organization's site: www.wto.irg

5. G. Hamel and C.K. Prahalad, 'Do you really have a global strategy?', *Harvard Business Review*, vol. 63, no. 4 (1985), pp. 139–48.

6. For a discussion of firm-specific advantages ('FSAs') and country-specific advantages ('CSAs') see A.M. Rugman, *The Regional Multinational – MNEs and 'global' strategic management*, Cambridge University Press, 2005.

7. B. Kogut, 'Designing global strategies: comparative and competitive value added changes', *Sloan Management Review*, vol. 27 (1985), pp. 15–28.

8. M. Porter, *The Competitive Advantage of Nations*, Macmillan, 1990; and M. Porter, *On Competition*, Harvard Business Press, 2008.

9. See reference 7 above.

10. J.A. Cantwell, 'The globalization of technology: what remains of the product life cycle model?', *Cambridge Journal of Economics*, vol. 19, no. 1 (1995), pp. 155–74.

11. The integration–responsiveness framework builds on the original works by C.A. Bartlett, 'Building and managing the transnational: the new organizational challenge', in M.E. Porter (ed.), *Competition in Global Industries*, Harvard Business School Press, pp. 367–401, 1986; and C.K. Prahalad and Y. Doz, *The Multinational Mission: Balancing local demands and global vision*, Free Press, 1987.

12. The typology builds on the basic framework of C.A. Bartlett and S. Ghoshal, *Managing across Borders: the Transnational Solution*, The Harvard Business School Press, 1989 (2nd updated edn, 1998); and S. Ghoshal and N. Nohria, 'Horses for courses: organizational forms for multinational corporations', *Sloan Management Review*, vol. 34 (1993), pp. 23–35.

13. For a discussion of companies that build on the multi-domestic route see A. Rugman and R. Hodgetts, 'The end of global strategy', *European Management Journal*, vol. 19, no. 4 (2001), pp. 333–34.

14. For a detailed account of CEMEX strategy see P. Ghemawat, *Redefining Global Strategy*, Harvard Business School Press (2007).

15. For a discussion of companies that build on the multi-domestic route, see A. Rugman and R. Hodgetts (2001); endnote 13 above.

16. For a more in-depth discussion of how General Electric (GE) tries to combine a global and multi-domestic ('glocalization') strategy with innovation in emerging markets see J.R.I. Immelt, V. Govindarajan and C. Trimble, 'How GE is disrupting itself', *Harvard Business Review*, October (2009), pp. 57–65.

17. P. Ghemawat, 'Distance still matters', *Harvard Business Review*, September (2001), pp. 137–47; and P. Ghemawat, *Redefining Global Strategy*, Harvard Business School Press, 2007.

18. C.K. Prahalad and A. Hammond, 'Serving the world's poor, profitably', *Harvard Business Review*, September (2002), pp. 48–55; Economist Intelligence Unit, 'From subsistence to sustainable: a bottom-up perspective on the role of business in poverty alleviation', 24 April 2009.

19. This framework is introduced in I. MacMillan, A. van Putten and R. McGrath, 'Global gamesmanship', *Harvard Business Review*, vol. 81, no. 5 (2003), pp. 62–71.

20. For detailed discussions about the role of learning and experience in market entry see M. F. Gullén, 'Experience, imitation and the sequence of foreign entry: wholly owned and joint-venture manufacturing by South Korean firms and business groups in China 1987–1995', *Journal of International Business Studies*, vol. 83 (2003), pp. 185–98.

21. G. Knights and T. Cavusil, 'A taxonomy of born-global firms', *Management International Review*, vol. 45, no. 3 (2005), pp. 15–35.

22. For analyses of emerging-country multinationals, see T. Khanna and K. Palepu, 'Emerging giants: building world-class companies in developing countries', *Harvard Business Review* (October 2006), pp. 60–9; and the special issue on 'The internationalization of Chinese and Indian firms – trends, motivations and strategy', *Industrial and Corporate Change*, vol. 18, no. 2 (2009).

23. For a detailed analysis of the unique aspects of Chinese multinationals see M.W. Peng, 'The global strategy of emerging multinationals from China', *Global Strategy Journal*, vol. 2, no 2 (2012), pp. 97–107.

# China comes to Hollywood: Wanda's acquisition of AMC

## Introduction

Chinese acquisitions of US assets and businesses have reached record levels during the last few years, peaking at investments of about $35 bn (€26 bn or £21 bn) in 2011. Despite this, Wanda's $2.6 bn acquisition of US second-largest cinema chain AMC sent shock waves through the USA and especially Hollywood. It creates the world's largest cinema company by revenues and Wanda will control about 10 per cent of the global cinema market. It was the biggest Chinese acquisition of a US company ever and marked a new era as Chinese investment reached into the heart of US entertainment and culture. Although Chinese acquisitions in the USA have proven to be controversial before, this one may prove to be even more challenging and it was speculated that a Hollywood ending was far from certain. According to one analyst, the deal strengthens Wanda's global status as movie theatre owner:

> 'Wanda has been the largest theatre owner in the second largest film market in the world. Now the deal makes it also the owner of the second largest theatre chain in the largest film market.'

Wanda Cinema Line Corp. is China's largest operator by cinema screens with over 730 screens. Its cinema operations generated $282 m in box office revenue in 2011 at 86 movie theatres cinemas all around China. The plan is to expand to about 2,000 screens by 2015. A month before the deal Mr Wang Jianlin, the Chairman of Wanda, had said that he would announce 'a merger that surprises the world' and when the acquisition was announced he likened the deal to 'airing a huge advertisement on the international stage'. According to Mr Wang the AMC acquisition is a significant step in turning Wanda into a multinational company within ten years and a truly international business group that will last for a 'century'.

The deal means that Wanda takes a 100 per cent stake in AMC and bears all its debts and the company will also invest $500 m in AMC theatre refurbishments and advertising. AMC is the second-biggest cinema chain

**Gerry Lopez, CEO of AMC Entertainment Holdings, left, shakes hands with Zhang Lin, Vice President of Wanda during a signing ceremony in Beijing, China, Monday, 21 May 2012.**

*Source*: Ng Han Guan/Press Association Images.

operator in North America, which is the world's biggest film market with ticket sales of over $10 bn. AMC has more than 5,000 screens in 346 cinema theatres in this market and is the world's largest operator of IMAX and 3D screens including 120 and 2,170 screens respectively.

Although the announced acquisition was huge, it is relatively small compared with the rest of the Dalian Wanda real-estate conglomerate. Dalian Wanda Group Corp. Ltd includes assets of over $35 bn, annual revenue of about $17 bn and 55,000 employees. Wanda, which means 'a thousand roads lead here', consists of five-star hotels, tourist resorts, theme parks and shopping malls. The 'Wanda Plaza' complexes that combine malls with housing and hotels have been a huge success in China and can be found in more than 60 Chinese cities.

Mr Wang Jianlin, the Founder, Chairman and President of Dalian Wanda, is the sixth-richest man in China. He joined the army as a teenager and stayed in the military for 17 years. In 1988 he founded Dalian Wanda and rode the wave of China's phenomenal growth by investing in property. His military background and ties to local officials helped him as large commercial land sales are handled by local governments. As he was willing to take on whatever property the local government was ready to give, he became popular with officials. Soon Wanda was the first property company to work in several cities.

## A landmark deal

AMC was considered a 'trophy' acquisition in the American entertainment industry and it was described as a landmark deal by analysts and investors. As announced by the Chairman and President, Mr Wang:

> '**This acquisition will help make Wanda a truly global cinema owner, with theatres and technology that enhance the movie-going experience for audiences in the world's two largest movie markets.**'

Mr Wang considered the deal to be a springboard to expand Wanda's global cinema presence further with the goal to reach 20 per cent of the world movie theatre market by 2020. He also said that Wanda is considering more acquisitions abroad in entertainment, hotels and retail and said it might try to buy into a global hotel brand or hotel management company as he explained that Wanda wants to be a big company 'not just in China, but in the world'.

At the announcement of the deal AMC's Gerry Lopez, Chief Executive Officer and President, explained:

> '**As the film and exhibition business continues its global expansion, the time has never been more opportune to welcome the enthusiastic support of our new owners. Wanda and AMC are both dedicated to providing our customers with a premier entertainment experience and state-of-the-art amenities and share corporate cultures focused on strategic growth and innovation. With Wanda as its partner, AMC will continue to seek out new ways to expand and invest in the movie-going experience.**'

To further expand on its home market Wanda will benefit from the know-how of AMC, which operates on a market five times Chinese annual box office sales. AMC has an established worldwide network of cinema theatres and this will give Wanda a reputable brand. There is also a trend for more foreign movies in China and the transaction may allow Wanda to secure more Hollywood movies for distribution in China. In February 2012 China agreed to open up its cinemas to more American films, and through the acquisition Wanda gains more clout in negotiating with major Hollywood studios that are eager to expand into the rapidly growing Chinese market. Wanda is also a contestant

in the race for a licence to distribute foreign films in China, which is now in the hands of two state-owned companies. However, it is uncertain to what degree the acquisition will please the authorities and increase Wanda's chance of winning the licence. There are also opportunities for Wanda in the USA apart from the cinemas themselves, as AMC is considered to be a platform for the development of commercial property, hotels and shopping malls in the USA.

## Wanda and the Chinese entertainment industry

Wanda has a history of investing in culture and entertainment and this aligns with China's overall ambition to invest in the sector. When the deal was announced the Chairman and President of Wanda, Mr Wang, accordingly declared:

> '**Wanda has a deep commitment to investing in the entertainment business and is already the largest in this sector in China, with more than US$1.6 billion invested in cultural and entertainment activities since 2005. We share with AMC a passion for the growth of the worldwide movie industry. We look forward to partnering with AMC's management team and employees to build on the many strengths of the company.**'

Wanda's press release on the transaction continued:

> '**The Wanda Group began to massively invest in cultural industries in 2005. It has entered five industries, including central cultural district, big stage show, film production and projection, entertainment chain and Chinese calligraphy and painting collection. Wanda has invested more than $1.6 billion in cultural industries and become the nation's largest enterprise investor in cultural industries.**'

Wanda's acquisition is part of a more general effort to develop China's own home-grown culture and entertainment industry. Cinema is an increasingly popular recreational activity in China and the film market is booming. China has seen an increase of 30 per cent in box office sales during the last couple of years, reaching $2.1 bn in 2011, and passed Japan as the biggest market for Hollywood films outside the USA in 2012. The country is investing heavily in film, animation and is in the midst of a multiplex building boom to provide entertainment to the expanding middle class. It is adding an average of 8 movie screens a day to its current 9,200 screens. The goal is to build about 25,000 cinema screens nationwide in the next five years. By 2040, the government aims to have 40,000 screens (about the size in the USA in 2012). There are also efforts to build film production companies. In brief, cinema operation is a growing business as people are willing to spend on entertainment as their income increases.

## Managing the US entry

Wanda's acquisition of AMC was the largest overseas cultural investment of a Chinese private enterprise ever and raised some concerns in the USA. AMC is a US household name, 'once epitomised as the all-American movie-watching experience'. It is thus a significant expansion of Chinese influence in the American film industry and some were anxious about this effect as many American movies are censored or even banned in China. Mr Wang is after all a Communist Party member, who sits on China's top advisory council. Wanda's acquisition of AMC thus increases concerns that Chinese-style censorship of politically controversial movies may become commonplace also in the USA. As reported by *USA Today*: 'Beijing is investing heavily in projecting its "soft power", or cultural influence, by boosting Chinese state media's presence abroad, including the USA, where the Chinese government has also run advertisements in New York's Times Square.'

Chinese investments in the USA had raised concerns earlier and the US government has rejected investments in the past in the telecommunications and energy industry due to national security concerns. However, cinema is unlikely to be considered a strategic industry for the USA. The acquisition, however, requires regulatory approval in both the USA and China.

Mr Wang also assured that Wanda has 'no plans to promote Chinese films in the United States' and that AMC CEO Lopez 'will decide what movies will be shown'

in AMC theatres. It was also made clear that AMC would continue to be operated from its headquarters in Kansas City. Mr Wang said Wanda will retain AMC senior management and would not interfere with everyday operations and programming decisions, which should remain with the US management. He continued to say that the most important part of the deal was securing that more than 40 senior AMC managers would stay after the takeover and he further explained:

> **'The crucial thing is to keep the enthusiasm of the current management and the workers ... You have to put the human factors first. The only thing that changed is the boss.'**

*Sources*: *AMC* press release, 20 May 2012, Chinadaily.com, 23 May 2012, *Dalian Wanda* press release, 21 May 2012, *Financial Times*, 22 May 2012, 23 May 2012, 26 May 2012, 28 May 2012, LAtimes.com, 20 May 2012, *New York Times*, 20 May 2012, *Reuters*, 21 May 2012, *The Washington Post*, 21 May 2012, *Wall Street Journal*, 21 May 2012.

## Questions

1  Considering Yip's globalisation framework (Figure 7.2), what drivers of internationalisation do you think were most important when Wanda entered the US market through its AMC acquisition?

2  What national sources of competitive advantage might Wanda draw from its Chinese base? What disadvantages derive from its Chinese base?

3  In the light of the CAGE framework, what challenges may Wanda meet as it enters the US market?

# 8

# INNOVATION AND ENTREPRENEURSHIP

## Learning outcomes

After reading this chapter you should be able to:

- Identify key *sources of innovation*, such as technologies or markets, product or process innovations, open versus closed innovation, and the underlying business model.

- Anticipate and to some extent influence the *diffusion* (or spread) of innovations.

- Decide when being a *first-mover* or a *follower* is most appropriate in innovation, and how an incumbent organisation should respond to innovative challengers.

- Anticipate both key issues facing entrepreneurs as they go through the *stages of growth*, from start-up to exit, and the choices involved in *entrepreneurial strategies*.

## Key terms

business model p. 188

diffusion p. 190

disruptive innovation p. 195

entrepreneurial life cycle p. 198

first-mover advantage p. 193

innovation p. 184

open innovation p. 187

S-curve p. 191

tipping point p. 191

# 8.1 INTRODUCTION

This chapter is about taking new products, services and business models into the market. Sometimes such innovation comes from established organisations; sometimes innovation comes from entrepreneurial start-ups. In either form, innovation is fundamental in today's economy. But innovation also involves hard choices. For example, should an established company like Korean electronics giant Samsung strive to be a pioneer in new technologies, or rather be a fast follower, as it was traditionally? Is it better for a social media start-up like Instagram to sell out to Facebook, or rather to pursue its entrepreneurial course independently?

As Figure 8.1 shows, this chapter examines innovation under four main themes: dilemmas, diffusion, leadership or followership and entrepreneurship.

- Section 8.2 starts with four fundamental *sources of innovation*: technology push as against market pull; product innovation rather than process innovation; open versus closed innovation; and, finally, technological as opposed to broader business model innovation.

- Section 8.3 considers issues surrounding the *diffusion*, or spread, of innovations in the marketplace. Diffusion processes often follow *S-curve patterns*, raising further typical issues for decision, particularly with regard to tipping points and tripping points.

- Section 8.4 completes the discussion of innovation by considering choices with regard to timing. This includes *first-mover* advantages and disadvantages, the advantages of being '*fast second*' into a market, and the issue of how established *incumbents* should respond to innovative challengers.

- Section 8.5 addresses *entrepreneurship*. The section discusses typical choices facing entrepreneurs as their ventures progress through the uncertain stages of growth, from start-up to exit. The section also considers *entrepreneurial strategies*, influenced by the resources and visibility of the entrepreneurial business.

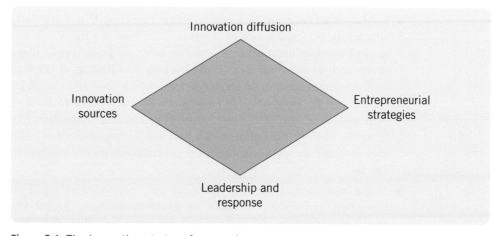

**Figure 8.1** The innovation strategy framework

## 8.2 INNOVATION SOURCES

Innovation can come from different sources. Innovation is more complex than just invention. *Invention* involves the conversion of new knowledge into a new product, process or service. The sources of invention are simply new knowledge. However, **innovation involves the conversion of new knowledge into a new product, process or service *and* the putting of this new product, process or service into actual use.**[1] Because this more extended innovation process emphasises use, the sources of innovation are more complex. Strategists have to make choices with regard to four fundamental issues: how far to follow technological opportunity as against market demand; how much to invest in product innovation rather than process innovation; how far to open themselves up to innovative ideas from outside; and finally whether to focus on technological innovation rather than extending innovation to their whole business model.

### 8.2.1 Technology push or market pull

People often see innovation as driven by technology. In the pure version of this *technology push* view, it is the new knowledge created by technologists or scientists that pushes the innovation process. Research and development laboratories produce new products, processes or services and then hand them over to the rest of the organisation to manufacture, market and distribute. According to this push perspective, managers should listen primarily to their scientists and technologists, let them follow their hunches and support them with ample resources. Generous R & D budgets are crucial to making innovation happen. The Google X research laboratory, home to the driverless car and Google Glass, leans towards technology push.

An alternative approach to innovation is *market pull*. Market pull reflects a view of innovation that goes beyond invention and sees the importance of actual use. In many sectors users, not producers, are common sources of important innovations. In designing their innovation strategies, therefore, organisations should listen in the first place to users rather than their own scientists and technologists. Two contrasting approaches to market pull are:

- *Lead users*: according to MIT professor Eric Von Hippel, in many markets it is lead users who are the principal source of innovation.[2] In medical surgery, top surgeons often adapt existing surgical instruments in order to carry out new types of operation. In extreme sports such as snowboarding or windsurfing, it is leading sportspeople who make the improvements necessary for greater performance. In this view, then, it is the pull of market experts that is responsible for innovation. Managers need to build close relationships with lead users such as the best surgeons or sporting champions. Marketing and sales functions identify the lead users of a field and then scientists and technologists translate their inventive ideas into commercial products, processes or services that the wider market can use.

- *Frugal innovation*: at the other end of the user continuum is the pull exerted by ordinary consumers, particularly the poor in emerging markets.[3] Frugal innovation involves sensitivity to poor people's real needs. Responding not only to these users' lack of money, but also to the tough conditions in which they live, frugal innovation typically emphasises low cost, simplicity, robustness and easy maintenance. The Tata Nano car is a famous example, a simple car produced for the Indian market for only $2,000. Muruganantham's cheap sanitary towels are another example, this time emphasising opportunities to create employment for the economically disadvantaged too (see Illustration 8.1).

## ILLUSTRATION 8.1 Frugal sanitary towels

### Arunachalam Muruganantham aims to transform the lives of Indian women with a fundamental innovation.

High school drop-out and welder Arunachalam Muruganantham has developed a low-cost sanitary towel the hard way. In India, only 12 per cent of women can afford to use sanitary towels for their monthly periods, the rest making do with old rags and even husks or sand. As Muruganantham's wife explained to him, if she bought the expensive sanitary towels on the market, the family would have to do without milk. But the cost for many women is infections and even cervical cancer.

Muruganantham was determined to find a cheap way of supplying Indian women with proper sanitary towels. In Indian society, however, the issue was taboo. The local hospital was unhelpful, and even Muruganantham's wife and sisters refused to talk about the problem. A survey of college girls failed. Muruganantham's prototypes were scorned by his wife. At his wits' end, Muruganantham experimented on himself, carrying a bladder inflated with goat's blood while wearing one of his own sanitary towels and women's undergarments. His tests while walking and cycling around the village created a local scandal. His wife moved out.

Muruganantham characterised the issue as a 'triple A problem – Affordability, Availability and Awareness'. But after four years of research, he finally built a machine for producing sanitary towels at less than half the price of those offered by rivals such as Procter & Gamble and Johnson & Johnson. The machines are cheap and hand-operated, enabling small-scale local production by units employing six to ten women each. Muruganantham believes that the small businesses using his machines could create up to one million jobs: 'The model of mass-production is outdated. Now it is about production by the mass of people.'

Muruganantham sells the machines to local entrepreneurs, charities and self-help groups, who produce the sanitary towels without fancy marketing. Often the women who make the towels are the best marketers, passing on the benefits by word-of-mouth. Resident women dealers are appointed for particular streets or villages, and they inform local women about the dangers of traditional methods at the same time as offering their products. Towels are often sold singly rather than in bulk packets, and are even sold through barter. Muruganantham explains the marketing: 'It's done silently and even the male members of their families don't know.'

By 2012, Muruganantham had machines operating in 23 states within India and was declaring his ambition to make India a 100 per cent sanitary towel using nation. He was also contemplating launch in Africa and spin-off projects such as nappies for babies and incontinence pads for elderly people. Muruganantham was confident about the sustainability of his model: 'We compete very comfortably with the big giants (such as Procter & Gamble). That's why they call me the corporate bomber.' His wife has moved back in with him.

*Sources*: BBC World Service, 6 August 2012; *Economic Times*, 18 January 2012; *The Hindu*, 9 February 2012.

### Questions

1 Identify the various features of Muruganantham's approach that make his sanitary towel business a typical or not so typical 'frugal innovation'.

2 Could a large company such as Procter & Gamble imitate this strategy?

Technology push and market pull are best seen as extreme views, helping to focus attention on a fundamental choice: relatively how much to rely on science and technology as sources of innovation, rather than what people are actually doing in the marketplace. The key is to manage the balance actively. Thus a stagnant technology push organisation might use more market pull; a stagnant market pull organisation might invest more in fundamental research.

## 8.2.2 Product or process innovation

Just as managers must manage the balance between technology and market pull, so must they determine the relative importance of product or process as sources of innovation. *Product innovation* relates to the final product (or service) to be sold, especially with regard to its features; *process innovation* relates to the way in which this product is produced and distributed, especially with regard to improvements in cost or reliability. Some firms specialise more in product innovation, others more in process innovation. For example, in computers, Apple has generally concentrated its efforts on designing attractive product features (for instance, the iPad tablet), while Dell has innovated in terms of efficient processes, for instance direct sales, modularity and build-to-order.

The relative importance of product innovation and process innovation typically changes as industries evolve over time.[4] Usually the first stages of an industry are dominated by product innovation based on new features. Thus the early history of the automobile was dominated by competition as to whether cars should be fuelled by steam, electricity or petrol, have their engines at the front or at the rear, and have three wheels or four.[5] Industries eventually coalesce around a *dominant design*, the standard configuration of basic features: after Henry Ford's 1908 Model T, cars generally became petrol-driven, with their engines at the front and four wheels. Once such a dominant design is established, innovation switches to process innovation, as competition shifts to producing the dominant design as efficiently as possible. Henry Ford's great process innovation was the moving assembly line, introduced in 1913.

Figure 8.2 provides a general model of the relationship between product and process innovation over time. The model has several strategic implications:

- *New developing industries* typically favour product innovation, as competition is still around defining the basic features of the product or service.

- *Maturing industries* typically favour process innovation, as competition shifts towards efficient production of a dominant design of product or service.

- *Small new entrants* typically have the greatest opportunity when dominant designs are either not yet established or beginning to collapse. Thus, in the early stages of the automobile industry, before Ford's Model T, there were more than a hundred mostly small competitors, each with its own combination of product features.

- *Large incumbent firms* typically have the advantage during periods of dominant design stability, when scale economies and the ability to roll out process innovations matter most. With the success of the Model T and the assembly line, by the 1930s there were just four large American automobile manufacturers, namely Ford, General Motors, Chrysler and American Motors, all producing very similar kinds of cars.

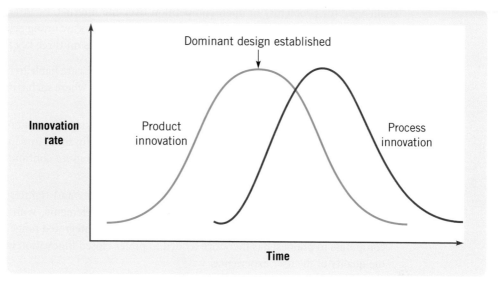

**Figure 8.2** Product and process innovation

*Source*: Adapted from J. Abernathy and W. Utterback, 'A dynamic model of process and product innovation', *Omega*, vol. 3, no. 6 (1975), pp. 142–60.

This sequence of product to process innovation is not always a neat one. However, the model does help managers confront the issue of where to focus, whether more on product features or more on process efficiency. It also points to whether competitive advantage is likely to be with small new entrants or large incumbent firms. Other things being equal, small start-ups should time their entry for periods of instability in dominant design and focus on product rather than process innovation.

### 8.2.3 Open or closed innovation

The traditional approach to innovation has been to rely on the organisation's own internal resources for generating innovations – its laboratories and marketing departments. Innovation in this approach is secretive, anxious to protect intellectual property and avoid competitors free-riding on ideas. This 'closed' model of innovation contrasts with the newer 'open model' of innovation.[6] **Open innovation involves the deliberate import and export of knowledge by an organisation in order to accelerate and enhance its innovation.** The motivating idea of open innovation is that exchanging ideas openly is likely to produce better products more quickly than the internal, closed approach. Speedier and superior products are what are needed to keep ahead of the competition, not obsessive secrecy. An example is IBM's network of ten 'collaboratories', laboratory collaborations with other companies and universities, in countries ranging from Switzerland to Saudi Arabia.

*Crowdsourcing* is an increasingly popular form of open innovation and means that a company or organisation broadcasts a specific problem to a crowd of individuals or teams often in tournaments with prizes awarded to the best solution.[7] Companies such as Procter & Gamble, Eli Lilly and Dow Chemicals use the network company InnoCentive to set innovation 'challenges' (or problems) in open competition over the internet: by 2012, a total of 1,215 challenges had been solved by a community of 260,000 'solvers', winning prizes of up to $1 m. The balance between open and closed innovation depends on three key factors:

- *Competitive rivalry.* In highly rivalrous industries, partners are liable to behave opportunistically and steal innovations. Closed innovation is better where such rivalrous behaviours can be anticipated.

- *One-shot innovation.* Opportunistic behaviour is more likely where innovation involves a major shift in technology, likely to put winners substantially ahead and losers permanently behind. Open innovation works best where innovation is more continuous, so encouraging more reciprocal behaviour over time.

- *Tight-linked innovation.* Where technologies are complex and tightly interlinked, open innovation risks introducing damagingly inconsistent elements, with knock-on effects throughout the product range. Apple, with its smoothly integrated range of products from computers to phones, has therefore tended to prefer closed innovation in order to protect the quality of the user experience.

## 8.2.4 Technological or business-model innovation

Many successful innovations do not stem simply from new science or technology, but from the reorganisation of business activities into new combinations. Here innovators are creating whole new *business models*. Innovation comes from new ways of bringing customers, producers and suppliers together, with or without new technologies.[8] A **business model describes how an organisation manages incomes and costs through the structural arrangement of its activities.** For the ultra-cheap airline Ryanair, business model innovation involved the generation of revenues via direct sales through the internet, thereby cutting out intermediary travel agents, while also using cheap secondary airports. Internet sales and cheaper airports were much more important than technological innovation. The internet technology itself was not Ryanair's creation and it had the same aeroplanes as most of its competitors. Thus it can be as effective to innovate in terms of business model as in technology.

Opportunities for business model innovation can be analysed in terms of the value chain, value net or activity systems frameworks (introduced in sections 3.4.1 and 3.4.2). These frameworks point managers and entrepreneurs to two basic areas for potential innovation:

- *The product.* A new business model may redefine what the product or service is and how it is produced. In terms of the value chain specifically, this concerns technology development, procurement, inbound logistics, operations and procurement. For example, when Nucor pioneered electric-arc mini-mill technology in the steel industry, it was able to use scrap metal as its raw material rather than pure iron, employ non-unionised labour and outsource a lot of its product development to its equipment supplier Voest Alpine.

- *The selling.* A new business model may change the way in which the organisation generates its revenues, with implications for selling and distribution. In terms of the value chain, this concerns outbound logistics, marketing, sales and service. Nucor, for example, sold its cheap but low-quality steel at standard prices on the internet, in contrast to the traditional steel producers' reliance on elaborate negotiations with individual customers on prices and specifications.

## ILLUSTRATION 8.2    Blockbuster's busted business model

**Blockbuster's store rental model is challenged by new business models for movie and game distribution.**

There are a lot of ways for people to see a movie nowadays. They can go to the cinema. They can buy a DVD from specialist retailers such as HMV or large supermarkets such as Tesco or Lidl. They can order a DVD online and receive it through the post. They can download movies via the internet. They can rent via a kiosk or vending machine. Or they can do it the old-fashioned way and rent it from a video store.

Blockbuster, of course, is famous for its stores: in 2010 it had 7,000 stores in 18 countries around the world. The first Blockbuster store opened in 1985 in Texas. Soon Blockbuster was the world's largest movie rental company, and in 1994 was bought by media conglomerate Viacom for $7.6 bn (€3 bn). Ten years later, as Blockbuster's growth stalled, Viacom spun it off as an independent company again, now valued at $7.5 bn.

Blockbuster's business model had been an attractive one. Two decades ago, in a period of limited television channels, movie rental had given customers unheard-of choice of viewing. Blockbuster used its huge buying power to obtain the latest releases from the film studios at little cost. Blockbuster would give 40 per cent of the rental income to the studios and supply them with information on usage for market research purposes. Studios typically would hold back from releasing the movie to other rental companies or to retailers for an initial period, making Blockbuster the essential outlet for the latest hits. Blockbuster was able to leverage this business model into rapid growth, using a mixture of its own stores, franchising and acquisitions. It also extended the model to the rental of video games.

However, the market is now much more complex. For a start, television channels began to proliferate. In the USA, Netflix emerged in 1997, originally using a rental-by-mail model. By 2009, Netflix had mailed its two-billionth DVD. In the United Kingdom, DVD mail-rental company Lovefilm was founded in 2002, and by 2010 had 50 per cent of the national market, as well as a strong position in Scandinavia. The mail-rental model offers customers a far greater choice (Lovefilm has 70,000 titles, against the few hundred in a typical Blockbuster store) and needs only a few centralised distribution centres, as against a labour-intensive network of retail stores. Moreover, as internet capacity has improved, both Netflix and Lovefilm have also begun to stream movies straight to customers' computers. Another rental model was pioneered by 2003 start-up Redbox, which had established a network of 22,000 DVD vending machines across the USA by the end of 2009.

Blockbuster responded in several ways. In 2004, it launched its own online rental service, with customers able to return their DVDs simply through a local store. In 2009, Blockbuster launched vending machines in the USA. The company closed more than 1,800 stores. It withdrew from some national markets altogether, for example Spain, Portugal, Ecuador and Peru. But, after continued heavy losses, Blockbuster filed for bankruptcy in 2010. The next year, the company was bought for $233 m by the satellite TV company Dish Network. Store closures continued, and the whole retail management team were dismissed.

*Sources: Financial Times, 24 February 2010; The Times, 28 December 2009; The Express on Sunday, 28 February 2010.*

### Questions

1 Compare the pros and cons of the various business models for movie consumption.

2 What potential competitive advantages did Blockbuster have as a company as the new business models emerged in the last decade or so?

The business model concept emphasises the fundamental features of how business activities are organised. In terms of business models, mature industries therefore often have a lot of standardisation. For example, most accounting firms are organised in similar ways: their business model involves earning the majority of income from audit and relying on a high ratio of junior staff to partners. Business strategy within an industry characterised by standardised business models is mostly about differentiation. Thus accounting firms might differentiate themselves within the same model by emphasising particular kinds of sectoral expertise or international networks.

However, the fundamental nature of business models means that business model innovation tends to imply radical change. Business model innovation is not just a matter of technology, but involves a wide range of the firm's activities. Thus the business model concept helps managers and entrepreneurs consider science and technology as just one part of the whole package that contributes to innovation. Innovation can be drawn from all parts of the value chain, not just technology development.

## 8.3 INNOVATION DIFFUSION

So far, this chapter has been concerned with sources and types of innovation, for example technology push or market pull. This section moves to the diffusion of innovations after they have been introduced.[9] **Diffusion is the process by which innovations spread among users.** Since innovation is typically expensive, its commercial attractiveness can hinge on the pace – extent and speed – at which the market adopts new products and services. This pace of diffusion is something managers can influence from both the supply and demand sides, and which they can also model using the S-curve.

### 8.3.1 The pace of diffusion

The pace of diffusion can vary widely according to the nature of the products concerned. It took 38 years for the television to reach 150 million units sold; it took just seven years for Apple's iPod to reach the same number. The pace of diffusion is influenced by a combination of supply-side and demand-side factors, over which managers have considerable control. On the *supply side*, pace is determined by product features such as:

- *Degree of improvement* in performance above current products (from a customer's perspective) that provides incentive to change. For example, 3G mobile phones did not provide sufficient performance improvement to prompt rapid switch in many markets. Managers need to make sure innovation benefits sufficiently exceed costs.

- *Compatibility* with other factors, for example digital TV becomes more attractive as the broadcasting networks change their programmes to that format. Managers and entrepreneurs therefore need to ensure appropriate complementary products and services are in place.

- *Complexity*, either in the product itself or in the marketing methods being used to commercialise the product: unduly complex pricing structures, as with many financial service products such as pensions, discourage consumer adoption. Simple pricing structures typically accelerate adoptions.

- *Experimentation* – the ability to test products before commitment to a final decision – either directly or through the availability of information about the experience of other customers. Free initial trial periods are often used to encourage diffusion.

- *Relationship management*, in other words how easy it is to get information, place orders and receive support. Google's 2010 launch of its first phone, the Android Nexus One, was hampered because the company was not used to providing the access to help-staff that mobile phone customers generally expect. Managers and entrepreneurs need to put in place an appropriate relationship management process to assist new users.

On the *demand side*, simple affordability is of course key. Beyond this, there are three further factors that tend to drive the pace of diffusion:

- *Market awareness.* Many potentially successful products have failed through lack of consumer awareness – particularly when the promotional effort of the innovator has been confined to 'push' promotion to its intermediaries (e.g. distributors).

- *Network effects* refer to the way that demand growth for some products accelerates as more people adopt the product or service. Once a critical mass of users have adopted, it becomes of much greater benefit, or even necessary, for others to adopt it too. With nearly one billion users, Facebook is practically the obligatory social network for many readers of this book.

- *Customer propensity to adopt*: the distribution of potential customers from early-adopter groups (keen to adopt first) through to laggards (typically indifferent to innovations). Innovations are often targeted initially at early-adopter groups – typically the young and the wealthy – in order to build the critical mass that will encourage more laggardly groups – the poorer and older – to join the bandwagon. Managers and entrepreneurs therefore need to target innovations initially at likely early-adopters.

## 8.3.2 The diffusion S-curve

The pace of diffusion is typically not steady. Successful innovations often diffuse according to a broad *S-curve* pattern.[10] The shape of the **S-curve reflects a process of initial slow adoption of innovation, followed by a rapid acceleration in diffusion, leading to a plateau representing the limit to demand** (Figure 8.3). The height of the S-curve shows the extent of diffusion; the shape of the S-curve shows the speed.

Diffusion rarely follows exactly this pattern, but none the less the S-curve can help managers and entrepreneurs anticipate forthcoming issues. In particular, the S-curve points to four likely decision points:

- *Timing of the 'tipping point'*. Demand for a new product or service may initially be slow but then reaches a tipping point when it explodes onto a rapid upwards path of growth.[11] A **tipping point is where demand for a product or service suddenly takes off, with explosive growth.** Tipping points are particularly explosive where there are strong *network effects*: in other words, where the value of a product or service is increased the more people in a network use them. Being aware of a possible tipping point ahead can help managers plan

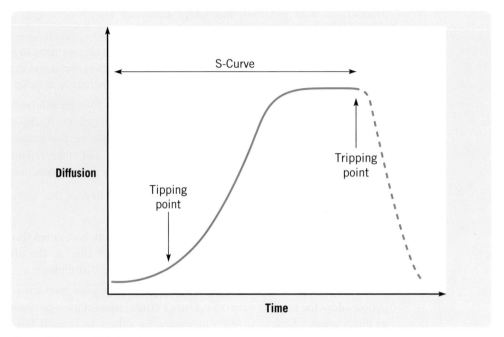

**Figure 8.3** The diffusion S-curve

investment in capacity and distribution. When Facebook reached a tipping point in 2007–2008, with users trebling to over 150 million, the company raced to ensure sufficient computer server capacity to prevent frequent denials of service. Failing to anticipate a tipping point leads to missed sales and easy opportunities for competitors.

- *Timing of the plateau.* The S-curve also alerts managers to a likely eventual slowdown in demand growth. Again, it is tempting to extrapolate existing growth rates forwards, especially when they are highly satisfactory. But heavy investment immediately before growth turns down is likely to leave firms with over-capacity and carrying extra costs in a period of industry shake-out.

- *Extent of diffusion.* The S-curve does not necessarily lead to one hundred per cent diffusion among potential users. Most innovations fail to displace previous-generation products and services altogether. For example, in music, traditional turntables and LP discs are still preferred over CD and MP3 players by many disc jockeys and music connoisseurs. A critical issue for managers then is to estimate the final ceiling on diffusion, being careful not to assume that tipping point growth will necessarily take over the whole market.

- *Timing of the 'tripping point'.* The tripping point is the opposite of the tipping point, referring to when demand suddenly collapses.[12] Of course, decline is usually more gradual. However, the presence of network effects can lead to relatively few customer defections setting off a market landslide. Such landslides are very hard to reverse. This is what happened to social networking site MySpace, as American and European users defected to Facebook. The tripping point concept warns managers all the time that a small dip in quarterly sales could presage a rapid collapse.

## 8.4 INNOVATORS AND FOLLOWERS

A key choice for managers is whether to lead or to follow in innovation. The S-curve concept seems to promote leadership in innovation. First-movers get the easy sales of early fast growth and can establish a dominant position. There are plenty of examples of first-movers who have built enduring positions on the basis of innovation leadership: Coca-Cola in drinks and Hoover in vacuum cleaners are powerful century-old examples. On the other hand, many first-movers fail. Even the powerful Microsoft failed with its tablet computer launched in 2001. Nine years later, Apple swept the market with its iPad tablet computer.

### 8.4.1 First-mover advantages and disadvantages

A **first-mover advantage exists where an organisation is better off than its competitors as a result of being first to market with a new product, process or service.** There are five potential first-mover advantages:[13]

- *Experience curve benefits* accrue to first-movers, as their rapid accumulation of experience with the innovation gives them greater expertise than late entrants still relatively unfamiliar with the new product, process or service.

- *Scale benefits* are typically enjoyed by first-movers, as they establish earlier than competitors the volumes necessary for mass production and bulk purchasing, for example.

- *Pre-emption of scarce resources* is an opportunity for first-movers, as late-movers will not have the same access to key raw materials, skilled labour or components, and will have to pay dearly for them.

- *Reputation* can be enhanced by being first, especially since consumers have little 'mind-space' to recognise new brands once a dominant brand has been established in the market.

- *Buyer switching costs* can be exploited by first-movers, by locking in their customers with privileged or sticky relationships that later challengers can only break with difficulty. Switching costs can be increased by establishing and exploiting a *technological standard*, as Microsoft did with its Office software.

But the experience of Microsoft with its tablet computer shows that first-mover advantages are not necessarily overwhelming. Late-movers have two principal potential advantages:[14]

- *Free-riding.* Late-movers can imitate technological and other innovation at less expense than originally incurred by the pioneers. Research suggests that the costs of imitation are only 65 per cent of the cost of innovation.

- *Learning.* Late-movers can observe what worked well and what did not work well for innovators. They may not make so many mistakes and be able to get it right first time.

### 8.4.2 First or second?

Given the potential advantages of late-movers, managers and entrepreneurs face a hard choice between striving to be first or coming in later. Sometimes the most appropriate response to innovation, especially radical innovation, is often not to be a first-mover, but to be a '*fast second*'.[15] A fast second (or 'fast follower') strategy involves being one of the first to imitate the original innovator. Thus fast second companies may not literally be the second company into the market, but they dominate the second generation of competitors. For example, Sony launched its eReader electronic book system in 2006, but was followed swiftly by the much more successful Amazon Kindle in 2007.

There are three contextual factors to consider in choosing between innovating and imitating:

- *Capacity for profit capture.* It is important for innovators to able to capture for themselves the profits of their innovations.[16] This depends on the ease with which followers can imitate. The likelihood of imitation depends on two primary factors. First, imitation is likely if the innovation is in itself *easy to replicate*: for example, if there is little tacit knowledge involved. Second, imitation is facilitated if *intellectual property rights* are weak, for example where patents are hard to define or defend.[17] In 2012, Apple successfully sued Samsung for breaches of its iPhone patents, leading to a \$1 bn fine on the Korean company.

- *Complementary assets.* Possession of the assets or resources necessary to scale up the production and marketing of the innovation is often critical.[18] Many small European biotech start-up companies face this constraint in the pharmaceuticals industry, where marketing and distribution channels in the USA, the world's largest market, are essential complementary assets, but are dominated by the big established pharmaceutical companies. Small European start-ups can find themselves obliged either to sell out to a larger company with the complementary marketing and distribution assets, or to license their innovation to them on disadvantageous terms.

- *Fast-moving arenas.* Where markets or technologies are moving very fast, and especially where both are highly dynamic, first-movers are unlikely to establish a durable advantage. The American electronics company Magnavox was the first to launch an electronic video game console in 1972, the Odyssey. But both the market and the technologies were evolving quickly. Magnavox only survived into the second generation of video game consoles, finally exiting in 1984. The market is now dominated by Microsoft (entered in 2001) and Sony (entered in 1994). In slower-moving markets and technologies, such as Coca-Cola's drinks arena, durable first-mover advantages are more probable.

### 8.4.3 The incumbent's response

For established companies in a market, innovation is often not so much an opportunity as a threat. Kodak's dominance of the photographic film market was made nearly worthless by the sudden rise of digital photography. Likewise, Blockbuster's network of video stores became redundant with the rise of internet film downloads (see Illustration 8.2).

As Harvard Business School's Clay Christensen has shown, the problem for incumbents can be twofold.[19] First, managers can become too attached to existing assets and skills: understandably, as these are what their careers have been built on. Second, relationships between incumbent organisations and their customers can become too close. Existing customers typically prefer incremental improvements to current technologies, and are unable to imagine completely new technologies. Incumbents are reluctant to 'cannibalise' their existing business

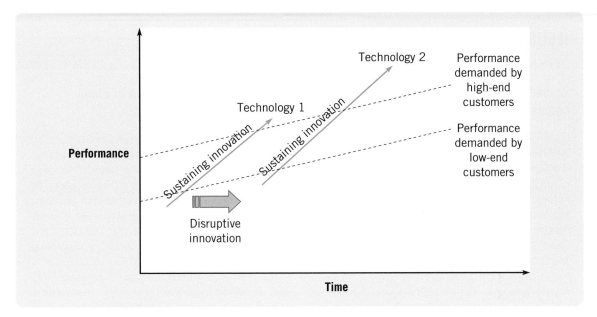

**Figure 8.4** Disruptive innovation

*Source*: From *The Innovator's Solution*, Harvard Business School Press (Christensen, C. and Raynor, M. E. 2003). Reprinted by permission of Harvard Business School Press. Copyright © 2003 by the Harvard Business School Publishing Corporation. All rights reserved.

by introducing something radically different. After all, as in Figure 8.4, incumbents usually have some scope for improving their existing technology, along the steady upwards trajectory described as Technology 1. Innovations on this trajectory are termed 'sustaining innovations', because they sustain the existing technology's ability to meet existing customer expectations, at least for a time.

The challenge for incumbents, however, is disruptive innovation. A **disruptive innovation creates substantial growth by offering a new performance trajectory that, even if initially inferior to the performance of existing technologies, has the potential to become markedly superior.** This superior performance can produce spectacular growth, either by creating new sets of customers or by undercutting the cost base of rival existing business models. Such disruptive innovation involves the shift from Technology 1 in Figure 8.4 to Technology 2. Disruptive innovations are hard for incumbents to respond to because poor performance in the early days is likely to upset existing customer relationships and because they typically involve changing their whole business model. Thus, in the music industry, the major record companies resisted the rise of online music because they preferred the quality of traditional CDs, wanted to guard their relationships with retailers, and were used to marketing through promotions and radio-plugging. The advent of cloud computing appears to be a similarly disruptive innovation (see Illustration 8.3).

Incumbents can follow two policies to help keep them responsive to potentially disruptive innovations:

- *Develop a portfolio of real options.* Companies that are most challenged by disruptive innovations tend to be those built upon a single business model and with one main

## ILLUSTRATION 8.3     The disruptive cloud

**Japanese computer giant Fujitsu plots a roadmap to navigate the transition to cloud computing.**

Fujitsu is the world's third-largest information technology services company, after IBM and Hewlett Packard. It offers a range of products and services in the areas of computing, telecommunications and microelectronics. In 2010, it launched a new cloud computing business to take advantage of the transition from the traditional model of in-house business computing. David Gentle, Director of Foresight at Fujitsu's Cloud and Strategic Service Offerings business, describes the transition as a disruptive innovation: 'It's a bit like a salmon that is swimming upstream and then has to make a leap to get to the next smooth stretch of water.'

Cloud computing relies on the internet to deliver computer services from external suppliers direct to users. Dropbox and Apple's iCloud are consumer cloud services. For business, the cloud comes in three main forms: 'Software as a Service' (SaaS), such as Microsoft Office via the internet; 'Infrastructure as a Service' (IaaS), such as Amazon's EC2 virtual computer capacity; and 'Platform as a Service' (PaaS), which provides a computing platform with operating system, web server and database, such as Google's App Engine.

Fujitsu describes the transition from the traditional model to the Cloud Computing Era in a technology 'roadmap' titled 'The Cloud Paradigm Shift'. The roadmap describes the traditional client–server model, where the computing power is supplied by in-house servers, as offering a trajectory of steadily improving *technology* efficiency. This culminates in the so-called Private Cloud, cloud services provided by the business itself. The shift to the 'Public Cloud' (with full adoption of SaaS, IaaS and PaaS) brings a leap in value. By tapping into the shared resources of external suppliers, a business gains access to huge economies of scale and the innovations possible by specialist suppliers. The new trajectory increases value by improving *business* efficiency.

The shift is disruptive, though. Purchasers in IT functions will no longer need such large investments in physical servers and staff. As traditional server products and related services decline, Fujitsu is transitioning its business to meet the demands of the new market. David Gentle explains the function of the roadmap in this context: 'This roadmap is the first slide in any conversation with customers, partners and staff internally. It shows the future, as well as anchoring on the past. It helps get everyone on the same page.'

### Questions

1 Why might some groups be apprehensive about the Cloud Computing Era?

2 What are the advantages of a visual roadmap of this kind? What are the limitations to this visual approach?

---

product or service. Often it is useful for companies to build portfolios of *real options* in order to maintain organisational dynamism.[20] Real options are limited investments that keep opportunities open for the future. Establishing an R & D team in a speculative new technology or acquiring a small start-up in a nascent market would both be examples of real options, each giving the potential to scale up fast should the opportunity turn out to be substantial. An important principle for real options is: 'Fail fast, fail cheap, try again.'

● *Develop new venture units.* New ventures, especially when undertaken from a real options perspective, may need protection from the usual systems and disciplines of a core business.

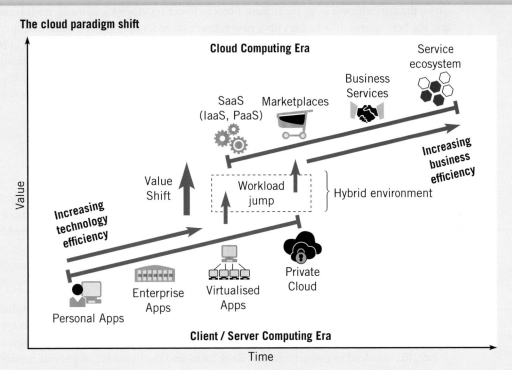

**The cloud paradigm shift**

**Fujitsu's Cloud Roadmap**

*Source*: Making the Transition to Cloud, Fujitsu Services Ltd. (Gentle, David 2011). With permission from Fujitsu Limited UK.

It would make no sense to hold the managers of a real option strictly accountable for sales growth and profit margin: their primary objective is preparation and learning. For this reason, large incumbent organisations often establish relatively autonomous 'new venture units', sometimes called new venture divisions, which can nurture new ideas or acquire fledgling businesses with a longer-term view.[21] For example, in 2011, BMW launched a new venture unit called Project i, based in New York and backed by $100 m, in order to acquire innovative new ideas from outside: one of its first investments has been in start-up company Parkatmyhouse, which links people seeking to rent a parking space or garage with those who have one to spare.

## 8.5 ENTREPRENEURIAL STRATEGY

Given the difficulties of large incumbent firms in fostering innovation, many would conclude that the best approach is to start up a new venture from scratch. Independent entrepreneurs such as the Samwer brothers, the creators of Rocket Internet, are exemplars of this entrepreneurial approach to innovation (see Case example for Chapters 3). This section introduces some key issues for entrepreneurial innovators as they develop their firms over the life cycle, including when and whether to sell out to larger firms. The section also considers typical entrepreneurial strategies.

### 8.5.1 Stages of entrepreneurial growth

Entrepreneurial ventures are often seen as going through four stages of a life cycle: see Figure 8.5. The **entrepreneurial life cycle progresses through start-up, growth, maturity and exit**.[22] Of course, most ventures do not make it through all the stages – the estimated failure rate of new businesses in their first year is more than one-fifth, with two-thirds going out of business within six years.[23] However, each of these four stages raises key questions for entrepreneurs:

- *Start-up*. There are many challenges at this stage, but one key question with implications for both survival and growth are sources of capital. Loans from family and friends are common sources of funds, but these are typically limited and, given the new-business failure rate, likely to lead to embarrassment. Bank loans and credit cards can provide funding too, and there is often government funding, especially for new technologies or economically disadvantaged social groups or geographical areas. For a very select few companies with high growth potential, specialised investors such as *venture capitalists* may be a source of funds.

- *Growth*. A key challenge for growth ventures is management. Entrepreneurs have to be ready to move from doing to managing. Typically this transition occurs as the venture grows beyond about 20 employees. The choice entrepreneurs have to make at this stage is whether to rely on their own managerial skills or to bring in professional managers. In 2010, Twitter's co-founder Evan Williams handed over as chief executive to Dick Costolo, previously a manager in technology giant Google.

- *Maturity*. The challenge for entrepreneurs at this stage is retaining their enthusiasm and commitment and generating new growth. This is a period when entrepreneurship changes to *intrapreneurship*, the generation of new ventures from inside the organisation. An important option is usually *diversification* into new business areas, a topic dealt with in Chapter 6. Amazon.com in the USA has moved from book-selling to automotive parts, groceries and clothing. When generating new ventures at this stage, it is critical to recall the odds on success. Many small high-tech firms fail to manage the transition to a second generation of technology, and it is often better at this point simply to look for exit.

- *Exit*. Exit refers to departure from the venture, either by the founding entrepreneurs or by the original investors, or both. At the point of exit, entrepreneurs and investors will seek

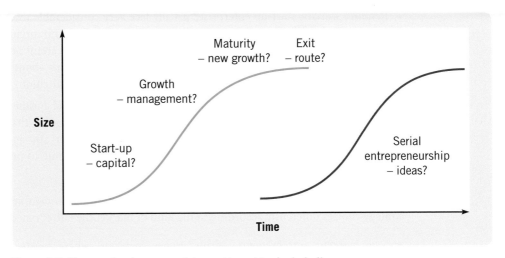

**Figure 8.5** Stages of entrepreneurial growth and typical challenges

to release capital as a reward for their input and risk-taking. Entrepreneurs may consider two prime routes to exit. A simple *trade sale* of the venture to another company is a common route. Thus in 2012 the founders of photo-sharing site Instagram sold their company to Facebook for $1 bn, just two years after starting the company. Another exit route for highly successful enterprises is an *initial public offering* (IPO), the sale of shares to the public. In 2012, Mark Zuckerberg raised $16 bn in Facebook's IPO, while retaining for himself 28 per cent ownership of the company. It is often said that good entrepreneurs plan for their exit right from start-up, and certainly venture capitalists will insist on this.

Entrepreneurs who have successfully exited a first venture often become *serial entrepreneurs*. Serial entrepreneurs are people who set up a succession of enterprises, investing the capital raised on exit from earlier ventures into new growing ventures. For example, serial entrepreneur Mark Pincus founded and sold three companies before founding the social games giant Zynga in 2007. For serial entrepreneurs, the challenge often is no longer so much funding but good ideas.

## 8.5.2 Entrepreneurial strategies

Entrepreneurs usually start with one main business, though over time they will often experiment with other ventures, and the original business itself may evolve quite radically. Given the importance of a single main business, issues of business strategy (Chapter 5) predominate over issues of corporate strategy (Chapter 6) for most entrepreneurs, at least early on. Thus entrepreneurs will typically have to choose between the generic business strategies of differentiation, cost and focus, for example (section 5.3).

For an entrepreneurial (or small) business, however, business strategy issues are not exactly the same as for more established or larger businesses.[24] There are two characteristics of entrepreneurial businesses that can be particularly influential for strategy choice:

- *Resource scarcity*: start-up enterprises usually face very considerable resource constraints, in terms of finances and managerial capacity especially. Entrepreneurial businesses therefore need to be highly selective in their strategic moves, careful not to waste scarce resources on too many initiatives. They should be extra cautious about competing head-to-head with wealthier players, where there is a risk of wars of attrition.

- *Relative invisibility*: as new and small players, entrepreneurial businesses are typically less visible to larger, established businesses. Lower visibility means that entrepreneurial businesses face less risk of prompt incumbent retaliation for any aggressive strategic moves. Entrepreneurial businesses may therefore have more time to press forward their attack before meeting any counter-attack.

This combination of resource disadvantage and invisibility advantage influences business strategy choices differently according to the kind of market the entrepreneur is operating in:

- *New markets:* entrepreneurial firms in new markets, where products and customer segments are not yet settled, generally do best by exploring potential opportunities fast. Speed of entry is important given the difficulties of competing against larger players in the same product or segment. Even if enjoying a first-mover advantage, it can be better to abandon a market position that is beginning to attract more powerful competitors, and to explore new opportunities instead. In fast-growing markets, large businesses are typically better able to assemble the resources necessary to take advantage of increasing scale. For entrepreneurial firms, therefore, timing is vital: picking the right moments to enter and then to retreat are the crucial decisions.

- *Established markets:* in more established markets, where large firms are already present, entrepreneurial firms are more successful if they can find niches that are still not occupied. These niches are often better supplied by low-cost adaptations of existing products rather than by radical innovations, which are liable to be too risky and expensive for a small-scale enterprise. The key is generally not to attack large incumbents directly and to rely on their inattention to small-scale moves to delay any competitive imitation on their part.

The above strategies are cautious ones, dictated by resource constraints and fear of large-firm retaliation or imitation. These are not the heroic entrepreneurial strategies that capture the headlines, but the strategies that are adopted by the typical new business. For every revolutionary entrepreneur that has created new markets and beaten off well-resourced challengers, there are countless forgotten failures (see Illustration 8.4 on the 'nearly billionaires'). In this respect, Google and Facebook are exceptions, not the rule.

## ILLUSTRATION 8.4     Nearly billionaires

**Adam Goldberg and Wayne Ting had the same idea as Facebook's Mark Zuckerberg – and first.**

In 2003, Golderg and Ting were engineering students at the prestigious Columbia University, New York. Goldberg was president of his class and hearing lots of complaints about a lack of community spirit. Over the summer, he designed a social network for his fellow engineers. Unlike other existing social networks such as MySpace and Friendster, this was the first network which overlaid a virtual community on a real community. Mark Zuckerberg would try the same idea at Harvard the next year.

Three-quarters of Columbia's engineering students signed up to the Columbia network over the summer. Goldberg improved the network and relaunched it as CU Community in January 2004, open to all the university's students. Most Columbia students signed up within a month. CU Community was sophisticated for its time. When Facebook launched in February 2004, it only allowed members to 'friend' and 'poke' each other. CU Community also allowed blogging, sharing and cross-profile commenting. Goldberg did not worry about Facebook: 'It was totally different. It had an emphasis on directory functionality, less emphasis on sharing. I didn't think there was much competition. We were the Columbia community, they were Harvard.'

Then in March Facebook launched in other elite American universities such as Yale, Stanford and Columbia. Goldberg, now joined by Wayne Ting, transformed CU Community into Campus Network and launched in elite American universities as well. But Facebook outpaced the new Campus Network. By summer 2004, Facebook had already overtaken Goldberg and Ting's network even at Columbia.

Goldberg and Ting now plunged into the competition full-time. They suspended their studies, and moved to Montreal, hiring three other software developers to help them. But resources were tight. Campus Network refused funds from venture capitalists and turned down some large advertisers, including MTV. The two entrepreneurs slept in the office on air mattresses, hiding them away as the three employees turned up for work so they would not know they were homeless.

Nonetheless, Campus Network developed a sophisticated product, with fully customisable pages, multiple designs and backgrounds. Facebook was simpler. The feel of Campus Network was a bit like Dungeon and Dragons, unlike the clean aesthetics of early Facebook. Ting commented on the logic behind the early development of Campus Network: 'Why would you go to a site that only had poking and a photo [like Facebook then] when you can share photos, share music and share your thoughts on a blog?' Looking back, though, he observed: 'A good website should have functionalities that 70 or 80 per cent of users want to use. We had functions that only 10 per cent wanted – nobody blogged, nobody even blogs today.'

Campus Network reached 250,000 users by 2005, but at the same point Facebook had reached one million. Goldberg and Ting decided to wind down the network and returned to Columbia as students in the autumn of 2005. The venture had cost them personally something between $100,000 and $200,000, as well as more than a year of their lives. Ting reflected in 2012, when an MBA student at Harvard Business School: 'There are still moments when you feel a deep sense of regret . . . Could we have succeeded? I think that's a really painful question . . . There are fleeting moments like that. But I'm much prouder that we took a risk and we learnt from it.'

*Sources*: Slate, 29 September 2010; BBC, 21 December 2010.

### Questions

1 What do you learn from the experience of Goldberg and Ting which could be useful to launching a new enterprise?

2 Are there any unmet needs in your community, at college or elsewhere, that could be turned into a business opportunity?

## SUMMARY

- Innovation can have several sources: *technology push* or *market pull*; *product* or *process innovation*; *open innovation* or closed innovation; and finally *business model innovation* rather than technological innovation.

- Innovations often diffuse into the marketplace according to *an S-curve model* in which slow start-up is followed by accelerating growth (the *tipping point*) and finally a flattening of demand. Managers should watch out for 'tripping points'.

- Managers have a choice between being first into the marketplace and entering later. Innovators can capture *first-mover advantages*. However, *'fast second' strategies* are often more attractive.

- Established incumbents' businesses should beware of *disruptive innovations*. Incumbents can stave off inertia by developing portfolios of *real options* and by organising autonomous *new venture units*.

- Entrepreneurs face characteristic dilemmas as their businesses go through the *entrepreneurial life cycle* of start-up, growth, maturity and exit. *Entrepreneurial strategies* are particularly influenced by *resource scarcity* and *relative invisibility*.

- To watch an author video on the concepts discussed in this chapter please visit www.mystrategylab.com, and click on 'Author perspectives on strategic management'..

## VIDEO ASSIGNMENTS

MyStrategyLab

If you are using *MyStrategyLab* you might find it useful to watch the Alyssa Smith case study for Chapter 8.

1 Using the video extracts and section 8.5.1, what can we learn about the characteristics needed to be a successful entrepreneur and the challenges that entrepreneurs typically face as they move through the 'entrepreneurial life cycle'?

2 How have the sources of Alyssa's new designs changed over time, and how typical do you think this is for small entrepreneurs such as her?

## RECOMMENDED KEY READINGS

- A. Osterwald and Y. Pigneur, *Business Model Generation*, Wiley, 2010, is an engaging, practical handbook relevant to both innovation and entrepreneurship.
- P. Trott, *Innovation Management and New Product Development*, 5th edn, Financial Times Prentice Hall, 2011, provides a comprehensive overview of innovation strategy issues. P.A. Wickham, *Strategic Entrepreneurship*, 5th edn, Pearson, 2013 covers entrepreneurial strategies.

# REFERENCES

1. This definition adapts, in order to include the public sector, the definition in P. Trott, *Innovation Management and New Product Development*, 5th edn, Financial Times Prentice Hall, 2011.

2. E. von Hippel, *Democratizing Innovation*, MIT Press, 2005; Y.M. Antorini, A. Muniz and T. Askildsen, 'Collaborating with customer communities: lessons from the Lego Group', *MIT Sloan Management Review*, vol. 53, no. 3 (2012), pp. 73–9.

3. D. Nocera, 'Can we progress from solipsistic science to frugal innovation?', *Daedalus*, vol. 143, no. 3 (2012), pp. 45–52.

4. J. Abernathy and W. Utterback, 'A dynamic model of process and product innovation', *Omega*, vol. 3, no. 6 (1975), pp. 142–60.

5. P. Anderson and M.L. Tushman, 'Technological discontinuities and dominant designs: a cyclical model of technological change', *Administrative Science Quarterly*, vol. 35 (1990), pp. 604–33.

6. H. Chesbrough and M. Appleyard, 'Open innovation and strategy', *California Management Review*, vol. 50, no. 1 (2007), pp. 57–73.

7. L.B. Jeppesen and K. Lakhani, 'Marginality and problem solving: effectiveness in broadcast search', *Organization Science*, vol. 21, no. 5 (2010), 1016–33.

8. See D.J. Teece, 'Business models, business strategy and innovation', *Long Range Planning*, vol. 43, nos 3/4 (2010), pp. 172–94 and R. Amit and C. Zott, 'Creating value through business model innovation', *MIT Sloan Management Review*, vol. 53, no. 3 (2012), pp. 41–9.

9. Innovation diffusion is discussed in C. Kim and R. Maubourgne, 'Knowing a winning idea when you see one', *Harvard Business Review*, vol. 78, no. 5 (2000), pp. 129–38; and J. Cummings and J. Doh, 'Identifying who matters: mapping key players in multiple environments', *California Management Review*, vol. 42, no. 2 (2000), pp. 83–104 (see especially pp. 91–7).

10. J. Nichols and S. Roslow, 'The S-curve: an aid to strategic marketing', *The Journal of Consumer Marketing*, vol. 3, no. 2 (1986), pp. 53–64.

11. M. Gladwell, *The Tipping Point*, Abacus, 2000.

12. S. Brown, 'The tripping point', *Marketing Research*, vol. 17, no. 1 (2005), pp. 8–13.

13. C. Markides and P. Geroski, *Fast Second: How Smart Companies Bypass Radical Innovation to Enter and Dominate New Markets*, Jossey-Bass, 2005.

14. F. Suarez and G. Lanzolla, 'The half-truth of first-mover advantage', *Harvard Business Review*, vol. 83, no. 4 (2005), pp. 121–7.

15. See B. Buisson and P. Silberzahn, 'Blue Ocean or fast-second innovation?', *International Journal of Innovation Management*, vol. 14, no. 3 (2010), pp. 359–78.

16. David Teece, the academic authority in this area, refers to the capacity to capture profits as 'the appropriability regime': see D. Teece, *Managing Intellectual Capital*, Oxford University Press, 2000.

17. A key book on intellectual property strategy is A. Poltorak and P.J. Lerner, *Essentials of Intellectual Property: Law, Economics and Strategy*, Wiley, 2009.

18. D Teece, *Managing Intellectual Capital*, Oxford University Press, 2000.

19. See J. Bower and C. Christensen, 'Disruptive technologies: catching the wave', *Harvard Business Review*, vol. 73, no. 1 (1995), pp. 43–53.

20. R.G. McGrath and I. MacMillan, *The Entrepreneurial Mindset*, Harvard Business School Press, 2000.

21. C. Christensen and M.E. Raynor, *The Innovator's Solution*, Harvard Business School Press, 2003.

22. D. Flynn and A. Forman, 'Life cycles of new venture organizations: different factors affecting performance', *Journal of Developmental Entrepreneurship*, vol. 6, no. 1 (2001), pp. 41–58.

23. D. Flynn and A. Forman, 'Life cycles of new venture organizations: different factors affecting performance', *Journal of Developmental Entrepreneurship*, vol. 6, no. 1 (2001), pp. 41–58.

24. R. Katila, E. Chen and H. Piezunka, 'All the right moves: how entrepreneurial firms compete effectively', *Strategic Entrepreneurship Journal*, vol. 6, no. 2 (2012), pp. 116–132; and M. Chen and D. Hambrick, 'Speed, stealth and selective attack: how small firms differ from large firms in competitive behavior', *Academy of Management Journal*, vol. 35, no. 3 (1995), pp. 453–82.

## Rovio Entertainment: Disney of the smart phone age?

Daryl Chapman, Metropolia Business School
Richard Whittington, Saïd Business School

### Introduction

Rovio Entertainment Ltd is most famous for its Angry Birds smart-phone game, in which colourful birds are catapulted at egg-stealing pigs. The company is based in Finland, and its management team consist of Mikael Hed, Chief Executive Officer, Niklas Hed, Head of Research and Development, and Peter Vesterbacka, Chief Marketing Officer and self-proclaimed 'Mighty Eagle'. Angry Birds became a top-selling app on Apple's App Store in 2010, the start of a stream of business ventures including broadcast media, merchandising, publishing, retail stores and playgrounds. With about 500 employees at the end of 2012, Peter Vesterbacka told *Wired* magazine that Rovio could follow the world's largest entertainment company: 'We definitely look to Disney as a model.'

### The team

Rovio was founded in 2003 by Niklas Hed and two class-mates at Helsinki University of Technology after they won a game-development competition sponsored by Nokia and Hewlett Packard. The company initially did well in work-for-hire jobs, developing games for Electronic Arts, Nokia and Real Networks. Niklas's cousin Mikael Hed, with an MBA from Tulane University in the USA, soon joined. Mikel's father, Kaj Hed, had been a successful software entrepreneur, selling an earlier business for $150 m (£100 m, €110 m). Kaj Hed invested one million euros and became company chairman: Kaj still owns 70 per cent of the equity. Peter Vesterbacka only joined full time in 2010, as Angry Birds began to take off. However, Vesterbacka, a business developer from Hewlett Packard active in the Finnish start-up scene for many years, had been encouraging Rovio and helping from the sidelines since 2003.

Although Rovio had been successful at creating games and selling them to established third-party companies, the company's ambition was to create a major game suc-cess of its own. Niklas Hed thought it would take about 15 tries to create a world-beater, but Angry Birds turned out to be Rovio's 52nd attempt. Meanwhile, there were clashes over strategy. In 2005 Mikael Hed left the com-

*Source*: Peter Parks/AFP/Getty Images.

pany after a row with his father, Kaj, whom he accused of being over-controlling. By 2008, Rovio had had to slash employment from 50 to just 12. But in 2009, Mikael came back, making peace with his father and sensing an opportunity with the new Apple iPhone and its App Store. The combination of the striking Angry Birds characters with the success of the Apple iPhone finally created a winning formula.

Rovio used Chillingo, a well-connected British games publisher, to negotiate a deal with Apple and push Angry Birds into world markets. In February 2010, Chillingo persuaded Apple to feature Angry Birds as the game of the week on the Apple App Store's front page: Angry Birds shot to No. 1 in the United Kingdom; five months later, it was top of the US charts as well. Chillingo was bought by Electronic Arts during 2010, and Rovio declared that it would no longer use any publishing intermediaries. In October, 2010, Rovio launched the free Android Angry Birds, winning two million downloads in three days. By 2011, Angry Birds and its various branded spin-offs had earned €50 m, on the back of a game which originally cost only €100,000 to develop.

In March 2011 Mikael Hed was cautiously excited, telling *Wired* magazine: 'I know how fragile the gaming industry is; I'm super-paranoid. But I feel at the moment that we are walking. We should be running.'

## The New Disney?

Like Disney with Mickey Mouse, Rovio saw the potential of transferring its powerful brand to other products. Partnering with the American toy manufacturer Commonwealth Toy & Novelty, Rovio was able to place Angry Birds soft toys and T-shirts in US shops as early as 2010. Rovio soon had more than 400 partners, including Coca-Cola, Intel and Kraft. The number of Angry Birds products reached 20,000, including board games, fridge magnets and key chains. *Fast Company* magazine estimated in 2012 that total sales of Angry Birds merchandise might approach $650 million or so. Rovio receives royalties on sales of its licensed products ranging from 5 to 20 per cent.

Rovio also partnered with Samsung to include a motion-controlled Angry Birds game on its smart televisions. Samsung was aiming to sell 25 million of these TVs in 2012. In November 2012, the company launched the Rovio Channel, letting users of the Samsung TV sets download games as well as the new Angry Birds Toons show and a comic-book series. The Rovio channel builds on the success of the Angry Birds YouTube channel, which has attracted more than 750 million viewers. The Rovio Channel is also due to launch on Mac, PC, iOS and Android devices, but Rovio prioritised TV as a medium that millions of families use together every day. An Angry Birds 3D movie is planned for release in 2016.

Meanwhile, Rovio has launched its first Angry Birds playground in Finland, in partnership with the Finnish adventure playground designer Lappset, the American entertainment designer BDR Design and the Italian roller coaster manufacturer Antonia Zamperla. In one sense, the playgrounds strategy mimics Disney's theme parks, but the playgrounds are much smaller. Rovio wants to create a more 'distributed' means of physical interaction with families and children than the occasional visit to Disneyland: the Angry Birds playgrounds are local and can be visited every day. The plan is to roll these playgrounds out internationally, with its first opening in the United Kingdom in the summer of 2012. There are already unlicensed Angry Birds playgrounds in China.

Indeed, export markets have always been important to Rovio, coming from a small northern European country as it does. The company has offices in Shanghai, Stockholm, Tokyo, Seoul, South Korea and Santa Monica, California. The USA is Rovio's largest market, followed closely by China. Rovio launched in China in 2011 and opened three retail stores in Beijing and Shanghai during 2012, with 200 more planned within the next year. Official licensed playgrounds are opening in China too. Peter Vesterbacka told *Fast Company*: 'Over time, China will be our biggest market. It's important for us to be very local. We want to be more Chinese than the Chinese companies.'

Rovio has not neglected its original core gaming business. With 63 levels when first released, Angry Birds now has more than 360. All sorts of variations have been launched, including Angry Birds Star Wars developed in conjunction with Lucasfilm. During 2012, Rovio repeated its success with the launch of Bad Piggies, featuring pigs stranded on a desert island looking for eggs: it too reached Number 1 on Apple's App Store. Amazing Alex was also launched in 2012 to create a human character for Rovio, but proved relatively less successful.

A mix of success and failure is to be expected in games. The app market is extremely dynamic, with new games and apps emerging all the time (see Table 1 for top paid apps in early 2013). Disney Mobile had five games at Number 1 on the Apple App Store during 2012. On the other hand, the one-man British developer Ndemic could score a hit with its star Plague Inc. game, at a development cost of just $5,000. Peter Parmentier, Chief Executive of Electronic Arts Mobile (responsible for Tetris, the Sims and Fifa), told the *Guardian* newspaper:

**'The marketplace in mobile is arguably the most competitive in the industry. There are more and more apps launching every day, which creates a challenging environment for developers and consumers alike. While I think we will always see that one breakaway hit that takes on a life of its own, we find that consumers seek high quality entertainment and recognisable brands in such a crowded environment.'**

**Table 1** Top paid iPhone apps, February 2013 (with developer names, countries and foundation dates)

1. Clear Vision 2 (FDG Entertainment, Germany, 2002)
2. WhatsApp Messenger (Whats App Inc., United States, 2009)
3. Minecraft – Pocket Edition (Mojang AB, Sweden, 2009)
4. Angry Birds Star Wars (Rovio, Finland, 2003)
5. Wood Camera (Bright Mango, United States, 2012)
6. Sleep Cycle alarm clock (Maciek Drejak Labs, Sweden, 2008)
7. Plague Inc (Ndemic Creations, United Kingdom, 2012)
8. Arms Cartel Global (Pixel Addicts, United States, 2001)
9. Fruit Ninja (Halfbrick Studios, Australia, 2001)
10. Bloons TD 5 (Ninja Kiwi, New Zealand, 2007)

*Source*: AppData, 2013, plus internet search.

**Table 2** Selected leading games companies

| | Key businesses | 2011 revenues | 2011 employees |
|---|---|---|---|
| Activision (US/French) | Computer, social and mobile games | $4.76 bn | 7,738 |
| Disney (US) | Film, TV, parks, merchandising, online media, etc. | $42.28 bn | 166,000 |
| Electronic Arts (US) | Computer, social and mobile games | $4.44 bn | 9,925 |
| Zynga (US) | Social and gambling games (internet and mobile) | $1.14 bn | 2,846 |

## Growth plans

Rovio's growth requires investment. In early 2011, the company raised $42 m from three venture capital funds, ceding 21 per cent of the ownership in return (Niklas Hed, Mikael Hed and Peter Vesterbacka between them were left with 8 per cent). One of the venture capitalists was Niklas Zennström, co-founder of Skype, who also joined Rovio's board. The extra capital helped Rovio make two strategic and talent acquisitions that year: first Kombo Animation Studio, then Futuremark Games Studio. During 2012, Rovio had talked of an initial public offering for 2013 with the aim of raising $1 bn for further investment. However, in early 2013, Peter Vesterbacka appeared to crush all such talk of an IPO: 'For us right now, we are running a very successful operation, we are growing very, very fast and we are insanely profitable so we can fund our own growth.'

Rovio's growth is building on a new business model for games. The original games model had involved purchasing a disc in a box for €20 or so. Rovio distributes its games over the internet either for about €1 to €4 each via Apple's App Store or, supported by advertising, for free on Android. Where Rovio differs from most other new mobile app companies is its emphasis on brand licensing for other physical products, such as soft toys, drinks and similar items. Revenues from the App Store, advertising and licensed physical products are very roughly equal, but physical products are pulling ahead. Total revenues are estimated at about €150 m for 2012. At the centre of the business are Rovio's brands, especially the Angry Birds themselves. The company believes that the brands will be valuable so long as fans are kept happy with a continuous stream of engaging new games and free upgrades. Rovio concentrates its efforts on game development and brand management: production of physical products is licensed out to partner companies. Although the early physical retail stores are being run by Rovio itself, the virtual store and logistics support are operated by partners that specialise in e-commerce and shipping.

Growth on the back of strong brands is, of course, something that Disney has long been good at (see Table 2 for a comparison with Disney and some competitors). Rovio sees itself as more than a games company, just as Disney saw itself as more than a cartoons company. The target is for more than half its revenues to come from physical products. Mikael Hed explained his ambitions for Rovio to *Fast Company* by drawing two arcs: the first a narrow curve with a pronounced fall off from its peak. the second a much broader curve triple the height of the first. A lot of our competitors have an equally myopic view. They've found this hill,' he said, drawing an arrow to the crest of the first arc, 'and say, here's the maximum amount of money you can make with a mobile game. But what we're building' – pointing to the other arc – 'is about the lifetime value of a fan. That picture is much more interesting.'

During 2012, Rovio turned down a $2 bn acquisition offer from Zynga, the US games company famous for Farmville. The Angry Birds company seems determined to aim its catapult directly at US entertainments giant Disney.

*Key sources: Wired*, 7 March 2011; *Guardian*, Media Network, 15 November 2012; *Fast Company*, 26 November 2012; *The Next Web*, 21 December 2012.

### Questions

1 What are the advantages and disadvantages of Rovio's business model?

2 How do you think innovation is different in an entrepreneurial context such as Rovio compared to a large corporate context?

# 9 MERGERS, ACQUISITIONS AND ALLIANCES

## Learning outcomes

After reading this chapter you should be able to identify:

- the potential role of *organic* (stand-alone) strategies.
- key strategic motives for *mergers and acquisitions* and *strategic alliances.*
- key issues in the successful management of *mergers and acquisitions* and
- *strategic alliances.*

## Key terms

acquisition p. 210

corporate entrepreneurship p. 209

merger p. 210

organic development p. 208

strategic alliance p. 218

## 9.1 INTRODUCTION

Mergers, acquisitions and alliances are all common methods for carrying out strategies and they are often in the news. For example, in April 2014 Facebook announced it would acquire Oculus VR the leader in virtual reality (VR) technology for US$2 bn (€1.5 bn), in anticipation of the web migrating from computers to mobiles and then to VR. Tingyi Corp. has an alliance to manufacture, sell and distribute PepsiCo's carbonated soft drinks in China, which may become the world's largest beverage market.

This chapter therefore addresses mergers, acquisitions and alliances as key methods for pursuing strategic options. It will consider them alongside the principal alternative of 'organic' development, in other words the pursuit of a strategy relying on a company's own resources. Figure 9.1 shows how the main strategic options considered in the previous three chapters – diversification, internationalisation and innovation – can all be achieved through mergers and acquisitions, alliances and organic development. Of course, these three methods can also be used for many other strategies as well, for example consolidating markets or building scale advantages.

The chapter starts with organic development. Organic development is the default option: relying on the organisation's internal resources is the natural first option to consider. The chapter then introduces the two principal external options: first mergers and acquisitions (often abbreviated as M&A) and then strategic alliances.

## 9.2 ORGANIC DEVELOPMENT

The default method for pursuing a strategy is to 'do it yourself', relying on internal capabilities. Thus **organic development is where a strategy is pursued by building on and developing**

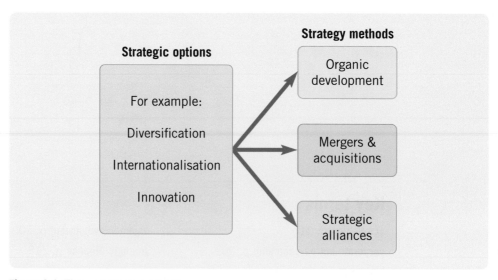

**Figure 9.1** Three strategy methods

**an organisation's own capabilities**. For example, Amazon's entry into the e-books market with its Kindle product was principally organic, relying on its own subsidiary Lab126 and drawing on its expertise in book retailing, internet retail and software. For Amazon, this do-it-yourself (DIY) diversification method was preferable to allying with an existing e-book producer such as Sony or buying a relevant hi-tech start-up such as the French pioneer Bookeen.

There are five principal advantages to relying on organic development:

- *Knowledge and learning.* Using the organisation's existing capabilities to pursue a new strategy can enhance organisational knowledge and learning. Direct involvement in a new market or technology is more likely to promote the acquisition and internalisation of deeper knowledge than a hands-off strategic alliance, for example.

- *Spreading investment over time.* Acquisitions typically require an immediate upfront payment for the target company. Organic development allows the spreading of investment over the whole time span of the strategy's development. This reduction of upfront commitment may make it easier to reverse or adjust a strategy if conditions change.

- *No availability constraints.* Organic development has the advantage of not being dependent on the availability of suitable acquisition targets or potential alliance partners. There are few acquisition opportunities for foreign companies wanting to enter the Japanese market, for example. Organic developers also do not have to wait until the perfectly matched acquisition target comes on to the market.

- *Strategic independence.* The independence provided by organic development means that an organisation does not need to make the same compromises as might be necessary if it made an alliance with a partner organisation. For example, partnership with a foreign collaborator is likely to involve constraints on marketing activity in external markets and may limit future strategic choices.

- *Culture management.* Organic development allows new activities to be created in the existing cultural environment, which reduces the risk of culture clash.

The reliance of organic development on internal capabilities can be slow, expensive and risky. It is not easy to use existing capabilities as the platform for major leaps in terms of innovation, diversification or internationalisation, for example. However, as in the example of Amazon's Kindle, organic development can be very successful and sufficiently radical to merit the term 'corporate entrepreneurship'. **Corporate entrepreneurship refers to radical change in the organisation's business, driven principally by the organisation's own capabilities.**[1] Bringing together the words 'entrepreneurship' and 'corporate' underlines the potential for significant change or novelty not only by external entrepreneurship, but also by reliance on internal capabilities from within the corporate organisation. Thus for Amazon, the Kindle was a radical entrepreneurial step, taking it from retailing into the design of innovative consumer electronic products.

The concept of corporate entrepreneurship is valuable because it encourages an entrepreneurial attitude inside the firm. There are many examples of corporate entrepreneurship, such as the creation of low-cost airline Ryanair from inside the aircraft leasing company Guinness Peat. Often, however, organisations have to go beyond their own internal capabilities and look externally for methods to pursue their strategies. The main themes of this chapter, therefore, are, first, mergers and acquisitions and, second, strategic alliances.

## 9.3 MERGERS AND ACQUISITIONS

Mergers and acquisitions (M&A) frequently grab the headlines, as they involve large sums of money and very public competitions for shareholder support. They can also provide a speedy means of achieving major strategic objectives. However, they can also lead to spectacular failures. A famous case is that of the Royal Bank of Scotland, whose 2007 takeover of the Dutch ABN AMRO ended in commercial disaster and the bank's nationalisation by the British government.

### 9.3.1 Types of mergers and acquisitions

Mergers and acquisitions are typically about the combination of two or more organisations. An **acquisition is achieved by purchasing a majority of shares in a target company.** Most acquisitions are *friendly*, where the target's management recommends accepting the acquirer's deal to its shareholders. Sometimes acquisitions are *hostile*, where target management refuses the acquirer's offer. The acquirer therefore appeals directly to the target's shareholders for ownership of their shares and the outcome is decided by which side wins the support of these shareholders. Hostile deals can be very acrimonious, with target company management obstructing efforts to obtain key information and not helping integrate the two organisations post-deal. On the other hand, **a merger is the combination of two previously separate organisations in order to form a new company.** For example, in 2012 Random House and Penguin, two big publishers, announced a merger to form Penguin Random House to reduce costs and increase their negotiating power with distributors. In practice, the terms 'merger' and 'acquisition' are often used interchangeably, hence the common shorthand M&A.

### 9.3.2 Motives for mergers and acquisitions

Motives for M&A can be strategic, financial and managerial[2] (see Illustration 9.1).

#### Strategic motives for M&A

Strategic motives for M&A involve improving the competitive advantage of the organisation. These motives are often related to the reasons for diversification in general (see section 6.3). Strategic motives can be categorised in three main ways:[3]

- *Extension.* Mergers and acquisitions can be used to extend the reach of a firm in terms of geography, products or markets. Acquisitions can be speedy ways of extending international reach. Thus in 2010 the Chinese Geely car company bought the Swedish Volvo car company in order to build its global presence. Acquisitions can also be an effective way of extending into new markets, as in diversification (see Chapter 6).

- *Consolidation.* Mergers and acquisitions can be used to consolidate the competitors in an industry. Bringing together two competitors can have at least three beneficial effects. In the first place, it increases market power by reducing competition: this might enable the newly

## ILLUSTRATION 9.1    Who bought whom?

**Movie giant Disney's acquisition of Marvel proves analysts wrong, but problems may lie ahead.**

Summer means one thing in Hollywood: big, blockbuster movies. But in 2012 a single superhero film 'ka-powed' all others with $1.5 bn (€1.12 bn, £0.9 bn) global ticket sales, becoming the third-highest grossing title of all time. *The Avengers*, from Disney's Marvel unit, stormed the box office, bringing *Iron Man*, *The Incredible Hulk* and *Thor* together. Its success largely overturned analysts' criticisms of Disney's 2009 $4 bn purchase of Marvel, as overpayment.

On paper, the acquisition looked a perfect fit. Disney was rethinking its entire approach to film making in response to a contracting home entertainment market and falling DVD sales as every studio in Hollywood was under pressure to cut costs. Ready to move to a franchise-led strategy, producing films and brands that could generate sequels and spin-offs, Disney acquired Pixar in 2006, and then Marvel, a brand that could deliver movies with stories that appealed to teenage boys – a demographic Disney found elusive.

The acquisition was not only about movies. Disney planned to use Marvel's vast library of superhero characters throughout its business, from theme parks to television shows and consumer products, adding Incredible Hulk underpants and Iron Man lunch boxes to Disney's staple inventory of Mickey Mouse merchandise. In addition the deal retained Marvel's CEO, Isaac 'Ike' Perlmutter. His hard-driving approach to gain a 'big bang for each buck' appealed to Disney: 'Marvel could make a great-looking movie for a fraction of the price of a Jerry Bruckheimer (*Pirates of the Caribbean* producer) movie.'

However, the deal also added dramatic tension to the family-orientated company based in Burbank, California – largely, it appears, because of Ike's management style. As Marvel's largest shareholder before Disney, he took much of his $1.5 bn payment in Disney shares, giving him a seat at the decision-making table. Since then he has become a force within Disney. He is a skilled cost cutter and has been described as obsessive about saving money. 'He used to do this thing in our office that people would laugh at. If there was some used paper lying around he would rip it into eight pieces and would have a new memo pad.'

But Ike's strong opinions and cost-cutting capabilities often put him at odds with colleagues. His interest in merchandising and toy licensing has shaken things up throughout Disney's consumer products division (DCP) – one of Disney's smaller divisions but accounting for 10 per cent of all group profits (2011). The head of DCP had repeated conflicts with Ike over the direction of the division and left in 2012 along with the heads of communications, publishing, HR, Disney stores, and the toys business. Three female executives hired a lawyer to seek individual financial settlements and another filed an internal complaint alleging Ike threatened her. DCP has now been reorganised around Disney's big TV and film franchises rather than individual product categories.

The box office and commercial successes Marvel has produced for Disney have won Ike admirers inside and outside the group. With sequels to *Thor*, *Captain America* and *The Avengers* in the works, analysts are speaking about the upside of the deal. But some former Disney employees warn of culture collisions ahead: 'You would think that Disney, with all its heritage and culture, would prevail, but the common question in the hallways [at DCP] was: remind me who bought who here?'

*Sources: Financial Times* 1 & 4 Sept 2009, 7 Sept 2011, 13 July and 8 Aug 2012.

### Questions

1  Why did Disney acquire Marvel?

2  Critically assess how well these companies fit together in (i) strategic and (ii) organisational terms.

consolidated company to raise prices for customers. Second, the combination of two competitors can increase efficiency through reducing surplus capacity or sharing resources, for instance head-office facilities or distribution channels. Finally, the greater scale of the combined operations may increase production efficiency or increase bargaining power with suppliers, forcing them to reduce their prices.

- *Capabilities.* The third broad strategic motive for mergers and acquisitions is to increase a company's capabilities. High-tech companies such as Cisco and Microsoft regard acquisitions of entrepreneurial technology companies as a part of their R&D effort. Instead of researching a new technology from scratch, they allow entrepreneurial start-ups to prove the idea, and then take over these companies in order to incorporate the technological capability within their own portfolio. Capabilities-driven acquisitions are often useful where industries are converging. For example, Google and Apple have made substantial acquisitions in order to gain a foothold in the new high-growth mobile advertising market where there is convergence between telephony and advertising industries.

## Financial motives for M&A

Financial motives concern the optimal use of financial resources, rather than directly improving the actual business. There are three main financial motives:

- *Financial efficiency.* It may be efficient to bring together a company with a strong balance sheet (i.e. it has plenty of cash) with another company that has a weak balance sheet (i.e. it has high debt). The company with a weak balance sheet can save on interest payments by using the stronger company's assets to pay off its debt, and it can also get investment funds from the stronger company that it could not have accessed otherwise. The company with the strong balance sheet may be able to drive a good bargain in acquiring the weaker company. Also, a company with a booming share price can purchase other companies very efficiently by offering to pay the target company's shareholders with its own shares (equity), rather than paying with cash upfront.

- *Tax efficiency.* Sometimes there may be tax advantages from bringing together different companies. For example, profits or tax losses may be transferrable within the organisation in order to benefit from different tax regimes between industries or countries. Naturally, there are legal restrictions on this strategy.

- *Asset stripping or unbundling.* Some companies are effective at spotting other companies whose underlying assets are worth more than the price of the company as a whole. This makes it possible to buy such companies and then rapidly sell off ('unbundle') different business units to various buyers for a total price substantially in excess of what was originally paid for the whole. Although this is often dismissed as merely opportunistic profiteering ('asset stripping'), if the business units find better corporate parents through this unbundling process, there can be a real gain in economic effectiveness.

## Managerial motives for M&A

Acquisitions may sometimes serve managers' interests rather than shareholders' interests. 'Managerial' motives are so called, therefore, because they are self-serving rather than efficiency-driven and may be of two types:

- *Personal ambition.* There are three ways that acquisitions can satisfy the personal ambition of senior managers, regardless of the real value being created. First, senior managers' personal financial incentives may be tied to short-term growth targets or share-price targets that are more easily achieved by large and spectacular acquisitions than the more gradualist and lower-profile alternative of organic growth. Second, large acquisitions attract media attention, with opportunities to boost personal reputations through flattering media interviews and appearances. Here there is the so-called 'managerial hubris' (vanity) effect: managers who have been successful in earlier acquisitions become over-confident and embark on more and more acquisitions, each riskier and more expensive than the one before.[4] Finally, acquisitions provide opportunities to give friends and colleagues greater responsibility, helping to cement personal loyalty by developing individuals' careers.

- *Bandwagon effects.* Acquisitions are highly cyclical, with booms in activity followed by slumps. In an upswing, there are three kinds of pressure on senior managers to join the acquisition bandwagon. First, when many other firms are making acquisitions, financial analysts and the business media may criticise more cautious managers for undue conservatism. Second, shareholders will fear that their company is being left behind, as they see opportunities for their business being snatched by rivals. Lastly, managers will worry that if their company is not acquiring, it will become the target of a hostile bid itself. For managers wanting a quiet life during a 'merger boom', the easiest strategy may be simply to join in. But the danger is making an acquisition the company does not really need and it can be one reason for paying too much.

In sum, there are bad reasons as well as good reasons for acquisitions and mergers. The average performance of acquisitions is unimpressive, with evidence suggesting that half of acquisitions fail. However, alternative growth methods also exhibit similar levels of performance. Nevertheless it is worth asking sceptical questions of any M&A strategy. The converse can be true, of course: there can be bad reasons for resisting a hostile takeover. Senior managers may resist being acquired because they fear losing their jobs, even if the price offered represents a good deal for their shareholders.

## 9.3.3 M&A processes

Acquisitions take time. First there is the search to identify an acquisition target with the best possible fit. This process may take years but under some circumstances can be completed very rapidly indeed. Then there is the process of negotiating the deal: to agree on terms and conditions and the right price. Finally managers will need to decide on the extent to which the new and old businesses will need to be integrated – and this will have significant implications for the amount of time required to create value. In other words, acquisition should be seen as a process over time. Each step in this process imposes different tasks on managers (see Figure 9.2). This section will consider three key steps: target choice, negotiation and integration.

### Target choice in M&A

There are two main criteria to apply: strategic fit and organisational fit.[5]

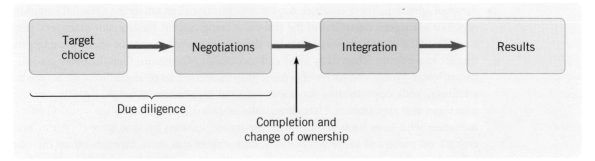

**Figure 9.2** The acquisition process

- *Strategic fit*: this refers to the extent to which the target firm strengthens or complements the acquiring firm's strategy. Strategic fit relates to the original strategic motives for the acquisition: extension, consolidation and capabilities. Managers need to assess strategic fit very carefully. The danger is that potential synergies in M&A are often exaggerated in order to justify high acquisition prices. Also, negative synergies ('contagion') between the companies involved are easily neglected.[6] An example of negative synergy was when the Bank of America bought the aggressive investment bank Merrill Lynch for $47 bn (~x33 bn) in 2008. Under its new owner, Merrill Lynch lost business because it was no longer allowed to advise on deals targeting the extensive list of corporations that were already lending clients of Bank of America. Consequently Merrill Lynch was a less valuable business with its new parent than when free to chase any deal it wanted.

- *Organisational fit*: this refers to the match between the management practices, cultural practices and staff characteristics between the target and the acquiring firms. Large mismatches between the two are likely to cause significant integration problems. The acquisition of Marvel by Disney raised many questions of organisational fit (see Illustration 9.1). International acquisitions can be particularly liable to organisational misfits, because of cultural and language differences between countries,[7] although the extent to which there is actual cultural clash will be determined by the extent of integration intended. A comparison of the two companies' cultural webs (section 4.6.5) might be helpful to highlight potential misfit.

Together, strategic and organisational fit determine the potential for the acquirer to add value (the parenting issue raised in section 6.5). Where there is bad organisational fit, attempts by the acquirer to integrate the target are likely to destroy value regardless of how well the target fits strategically.

The two criteria of strategic and organisational fit are important components of 'due diligence' – a structured investigation of target companies that generally takes place before a deal is closed. Strategic and organisational fit can be used to create a screen according to which potential acquisition targets can be ruled in or ruled out. Note that, because the set of firms that meet the criteria *and* that are actually available for purchase is likely to be small, it is very tempting for managers to relax the criteria too far in order to build a large enough pool of possible acquisitions. Strict strategic and organisational fit criteria are particularly liable to be forgotten after the failure of an initial acquisition bid. Once having committed publicly to an acquisition strategy, senior managers are susceptible to making ill-considered bids for other targets 'on the rebound'.

### Negotiation in M&A

The negotiation process in M&A is critical to the outcome of friendly deals. If top managements cannot agree because the price is not right, the terms and conditions are unacceptable, or they cannot get on with each other, the deal will not take place. In terms of price, offer the target too little, and the bid will be unsuccessful: senior managers will lose credibility and the company will have wasted a lot of management time. Pay too much, though, and the acquisition is unlikely ever to make a profit net of the original acquisition price.

Ways in which the price is established by the acquirer are through the use of various valuation methods, including financial analysis techniques such as payback period, asset valuation, discounted cash flow, asset valuation and shareholder value analysis.[8] For acquisition of publicly quoted companies, there is the additional guide of the market value of the target company's shares. However, acquirers typically do not simply pay the current market value of the target, but have to pay a so-called *premium for control*. This premium is the additional amount that the acquirer has to pay to win control compared to the ordinary valuation of the target's shares as an independent company. Depending on the state of the financial markets, this premium might involve paying at least 30 per cent more for shares in a friendly takeover than normal. Especially where the target resists the initial bid, or other potential acquirers join in with their own bids, it is very easy for bid prices to escalate well beyond the true economic value of the target.

It is therefore very important for the acquirer to be disciplined regarding the price that it will pay. Acquisitions are liable to the *winner's curse* – in order to win acceptance of the bid, the acquirer may pay so much that the original cost can never be earned back.[9] This winner's curse effect operated when the Royal Bank of Scotland's consortium competed with Barclays Bank to acquire the Dutch bank ABN AMRO: the Royal Bank of Scotland won, but the excessive price of €70 bn ($98 bn) soon drove the victor into financial collapse and government ownership. The negative effects of paying too much can be worsened if the acquirer tries to justify the price by cutting back essential investments in order to improve immediate profits. In what is called the *vicious circle of overvaluation*, over-paying firms can easily undermine the original rationale of the acquisition by imposing savings on exactly the assets (e.g. brand-marketing, product R&D or key staff) that made up the strategic value of the target company in the first place.

### Integration in M&A

The ability to extract value from an acquisition will depend critically on the approach to integrating the new business with the old. Integration is frequently challenging because of problems of organisational fit. For example, there might be strong cultural differences between the two organisations (see section 4.6) or they might have incompatible financial or information technology systems (see section 10.3). Illustration 9.2 describes some integration issues for British car company Jaguar–Land Rover after acquisition by Indian conglomerate Tata. Poor integration can cause acquisition failure so getting the right approach to integration of merged or acquired companies is crucial.

## ILLUSTRATION 9.2 — Staying power

**Hailed a triumph in 2012, Tata's acquisition of Jaguar and Land Rover (JLR) was perceived as extravagant in 2008, saying more about Indian imperial ambitions than commercial logic. How was success achieved?**

The largest privately owned Indian company, Tata group, has interests in steel, hotels, telecommunications and consulting. It has pursued internationalisation with acquisitions including Corus, the Anglo-Dutch steel company and, in 2008, JLR. At €1.7 bn (£1.4 bn, $2.2 bn), the acquisition from struggling Ford Motors gave Tata two well-known brands and enlarged its global footprint. But critics asked how could a company known for commercial vehicles and cheap cars (the Nano), do better than a gargantuan of the global auto world which had pumped billions into the brands, when there were no obvious synergies?

Unfortunately the deal coincided with the global financial crisis. Petrol prices spiked, bank collapses spooked consumers, credit markets froze and demand for luxury cars was hit hard. JLR sales plunged 32 per cent in 10 months and lost €807 m in the year. Tata's debt nearly doubled to €12.9 bn hitting its share price and credit rating. With 16,000 employees at five UK sites, there was alarm that some might close and production be sent overseas. As one banker remarked, 'if they carry on operating JLR as it is, it will fail'. Tata pleaded with the British Government for assistance, but support for JLR was refused.

Chairman Ratan Tata was quick to reassure with a personal visit to JLR. He recalled his father had bought a classic Jaguar half a century ago and talked about reviving the revered British Daimler brand and returning Jaguar to racing. A further 600 skilled staff were hired to help develop environmentally friendly cars.

JLR still faced challenges. It had relied on Ford Credit to finance its operations and sales and now needed to switch financing to other providers. All its information technology was based on Ford systems and CEO David Smith commented: 'the IT is an absolute hydra'. To improve efficiencies and save the marques, 2,200 jobs were slashed and tough cuts were made to operation costs.

However, Tata did not insist on tight integration into the group. A three-man strategy board comprised Ratan Tata, the head of Tata Automotive and David Smith, oversaw JLR. But the JLR executive committee, directly responsible for company operations, had no Tata representatives. Smith commented: 'Tata wants us to be autonomous – I've got all the executive authority I need . . . We can make decisions quickly – very different from life at Ford. Relationships with Tata are based on individual relationships.' Ratan Tata also commanded respect: 'The designers love him, because he's an architect and not only quite capable of telling them what he thinks; he can say it in the right language too' (Smith). JLR has also used Tata Motors' expertise in cost control and Tata Consultancy Division's skills in information technology.

In 2012 JLR introduced new models including the hot-selling Range Rover Evoque – an all-aluminium-bodied car originally started by Ford, boasting improved fuel consumption and better performance. Second-quarter pre-tax profits were up 77 per cent and sales were up 27 per cent on the previous year, helped by strong demand in India and China. In the UK 1,000 jobs have been added and new manufacturing capacity is being built abroad. The 'staying power' of Tata has been rewarded.

*Sources*: *Management Today*, 1 May 2009; *Financial Times*, 4 August 2008; *The Hindu*, 2 September 2012; *Financial Times*, 7 November 2012

### Questions

1 Using Haspeslagh and Jemison's matrix, assess Tata's integration approach to JLR.

2 How do you explain Tata's success at JLR?

The most suitable approach to integration depends on two key criteria:

- *The extent of strategic interdependence.* This is the need for the transfer or sharing of capabilities (for example, technology) or resources (for example, manufacturing facilities). The presumption is that significant transfer or sharing through tight integration will enable the 'creation' of value from the acquisition. Of course, some acquisitions 'capture' value purely through the ownership of assets and so there is less need for integration. These unrelated or conglomerate diversifications (see section 6.2) may only be integrated in terms of their financial systems.

- *The need for organisational autonomy.* Where an acquired firm has a very distinct culture, or is geographically distant, or is dominated by prima donna professionals or star performers, integration may be problematic. For this reason some acquisitions need high levels of organisational autonomy. But in some circumstances it is the distinctiveness of the acquired organisation that is valuable to the acquirer:[10] In this case it is best to learn gradually from the distinct culture, rather than risk spoiling it by hurried or overly tight integration.

These two criteria drive four integration approaches[11], see Figure 9.3, which have important implications for the length of integration period and choice of top management for the acquired company[12]:

- *Absorption* is preferred where there is strong strategic interdependence and little need for organisational autonomy. Absorption requires rapid adjustment of the acquired company's old strategies and structures to the needs of the new owner, and corresponding changes to the acquired company's culture and systems. In this situation a new top manager is generally appointed in order to manage the organisation differently.

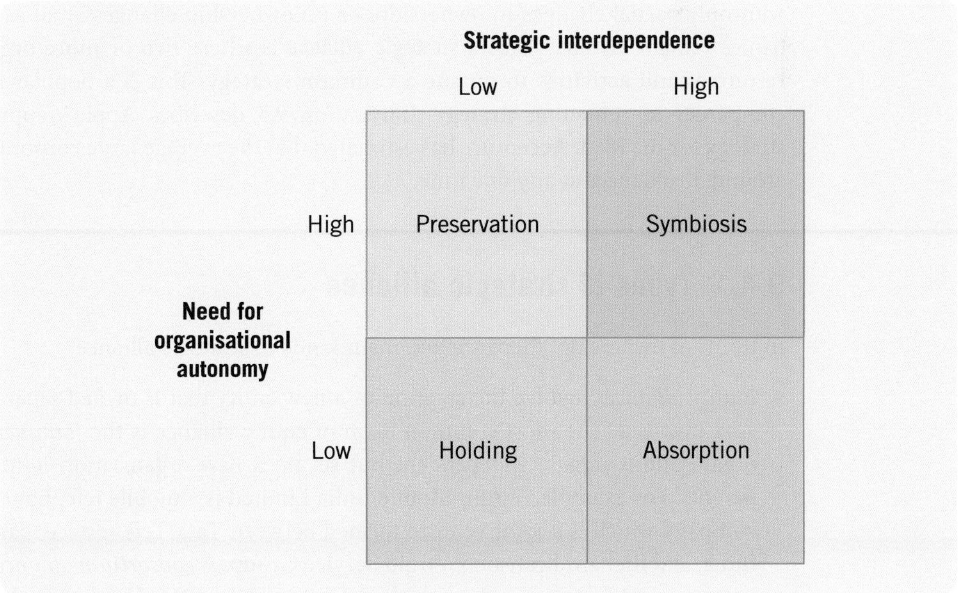

|  | **Strategic interdependence** | |
|---|---|---|
|  | Low | High |
| High | Preservation | Symbiosis |
| Low | Holding | Absorption |

(Row labels under "Need for organisational autonomy")

**Figure 9.3** Acquisition integration matrix

*Source*: P. Haspeslagh and D. Jemison, *Managing Acquisitions*, Free Press, 1991.

- *Preservation* is appropriate where the acquired company is well run but not very compatible with the acquirer. The high need for autonomy and low need for integration may be found in conglomerate deals. The preservation style depends on allowing old strategies, cultures and systems to continue in the acquired company much as before. Changes from the acquirer are generally confined to the essential minimum such as adjusting financial reporting procedures for control. In this situation the incumbent top manager is generally retained.

- *Symbiosis* is indicated where there is strong need for strategic interdependence, but also a requirement for high autonomy – perhaps in a professional services organisation dependent on the creativity of its staff. Symbiosis implies that both acquired firm and acquiring firm learn the best qualities from the other. This learning process takes time and it is often the case that it is best to retain the incumbent top manager in the early stages to stabilise the acquisition before bringing in a new top manager to make far-reaching changes.

- *Holding* is a residual category where there is little to be gained by integration and it is envisaged that the acquisition will be 'held' temporarily before being sold. Often these acquisitions are in poor financial health and rapid remedial action is required[13]. The acquirer will not integrate the company into its own business to avoid contamination. In these instances the incumbent top manager is retained as they can act more rapidly than a new appointment.

## 9.4 STRATEGIC ALLIANCES

Mergers and acquisitions bring together companies through complete changes in ownership. However, companies also often work together in strategic alliances that involve collaboration with only partial changes in ownership, or no ownership changes at all as the parent companies remain distinct. Thus **a strategic alliance is where two or more organisations share resources and activities to pursue a common strategy.** This is a popular method amongst companies for pursuing strategy. Illustration 9.3 describes Apple's approach to alliance strategy for the iPad. Accenture has estimated that the average large corporation is managing around 30 alliances at any one time.[14]

### 9.4.1 Types of strategic alliance

In terms of ownership, there are two main kinds of strategic alliance:

- *Equity alliances* involve the creation of a new entity that is owned separately by the partners involved. The most common form of equity alliance is the *joint venture*, where two organisations remain independent but set up a new organisation jointly owned by the parents. For example, Virgin Mobile India Limited is a mobile telephone service provider company which is a joint venture formed between Tata Tele service, part of Tata Group, India, and Richard Branson's Virgin Service Group. A *consortium alliance* involves several partners setting up a venture together. For example, IBM, Hewlett-Packard, Toshiba and Samsung are partners in the Sematech research consortium, working together on the latest semiconductor technologies.

**ILLUSTRATION 9.3**  Apple's iPad advantage

## Gaining competitive advantage through collaboration?

With much fanfare, a new version of Apple's iPad was launched on 16 March 2012. Apple had dominated the tablet market with its iPad for two years. The light-weight touch screen and new operating system (iOS), designed from the ground up for portable performance, had won may admirers. But amongst the first customers on 16 March were buyers who just couldn't wait to tear the gadget apart, to better understand iPad's success.

Market research firm iSuppli's 'teardown' analysis revealed the €622 (£497, $829), 4G 64GB model, cost $409 to make, just 49 per cent of its retail price. They identified Broadcom and Qualcomm as suppliers of Bluetooth and Wi-Fi chips, STMicroelectronics the gyroscope, Cirrus Logic the audio chip, three Taiwanese companies touch-screen components and Sony the camera CMOS sensor. Samsung, a rival manufacturer of its own tablet, provided a significant portion of the iPad, the expensive display, battery and processor chip.

Apple was therefore at the heart of a network. However, it had always protected its intellectual property. No hardware was licensed, ensuring control of production and maintenance of its premium pricing policy. It was impossible for any independent company to manufacture cheap iPads, in the way for instance Taiwanese manufacturers produced cheap IBM/Microsoft-compatible personal computers in the 1980s.

iPad's success attracted a swarm of companies into the accessory market, with US company Gryphon and Logitech from Switzerland supplying attractive add-ons including ultrathin keyboards, cases and touch-screen stylus. Apple licensed them the necessary technology for this and benefited from attractive complementary products and royalties. But the relationship was arm's-length, with no advanced information about new products.

Originally controlling access to iOS, Apple opened up access for the iPad, allowing third-party apps development and stimulating the new App stores industry. The attractiveness of iOS and strong consumer demand encouraged software developers to produce for Apple first.

Consumers liked the ease of use and vast ecosystem of Apple's iPad but challenges were mounting. Amazon's low-cost 'content consumption device', Kindle, offered a vast library of movies but lacked Apple's beauty and had few apps. Google's low-priced Nexus 10, manufactured by Samsung, aimed to profit from business services use rather than hardware. Its improved screen resolution and android operating system challenged iPad's technology and it shared many characteristics of other ecosystems with streaming apps and a consistent user experience. Samsung's own tablet, Galaxy Tab, had similar advantages along with compelling design and openness to non-Apple standards. Microsoft aimed to profit from its hardware, Surface, but was not particularly innovative, lacking a comparable software ecosystem and its tie to Windows could be a hindrance.

In September 2012 Apple briefly surpassed Exxon Mobile as the world's largest company by capitalisation. However, problems were surfacing, with declining growth rate in iPad sales in a growing market and Apple shares falling 30 per cent in six months. In addition, Apple was also embroiled in lawsuits against Samsung over its Galaxy Tablet design. Samsung was also counter suing. In November 2012 Apple dropped Samsung as its provider of batteries in preference for Chinese manufacturers.

*Sources*: G. Linden, K. Kraemer, and J. Dedrick, 'Who Captures Value in a Global Innovation Network?', *Communications of the ACM*, vol. 52, no. 3 (2009), pp. 140–5; Tablet Wars: *The Telegraph* 6 November 2012; F. MacMahon, 'Tablet Wars', 4 December 2012, BroadcastEngineering.com; A. Hesseldahl, 'Apple's New iPad Costs at Least $316 to Build', IHS iSuppli Teardown Shows, 16 March 2012 http://allthingsd.com .

### Questions

1  What are pros and cons of Apple's tight control of licensing?

2  What role has 'ecosystem' played in Apple's competitive advantage?

- *Non-equity alliances* are typically looser, without the commitment implied by ownership. Non-equity alliances are often based on contracts. One common form of contractual alliance is franchising, where one organisation (the franchisor) gives another organisation (the franchisee) the right to sell the franchisor's products or services in a particular location in return for a fee or royalty. Kall-Kwik printing, 7-Eleven convenience stores, McDonald's restaurants and Subway are examples of franchising. *Licensing* is a similar kind of contractual alliance, allowing partners to use intellectual property such as patents or brands in return for a fee. *Long-term subcontracting agreements* are another form of loose non-equity alliance, common in automobile supply. For example, the Canadian subcontractor Magna has long-term contracts to assemble the bodies and frames for car companies such as Ford, Honda and Mercedes.

The public and voluntary sectors often get involved in both equity and non-equity strategic alliances. Governments have increasingly encouraged the public sector to contract out the building and maintenance of capital projects such as hospitals and schools under long-term contracts. Individual public organisations often band together to form purchasing consortia as well. A good example of this is university libraries, which typically negotiate collectively for the purchase of journals and books from publishers. Voluntary organisations pool their resources in alliance too. For example, relief organisations in areas suffering from natural or man-made disasters typically have to cooperate in order to deliver the full range of services in difficult circumstances. Although public- and voluntary-sector organisations might often be seen as more naturally cooperative than private-sector organisations, many of the issues that follow apply to all three kinds of organisation.

## 9.4.2 Motives for alliances

Strategic alliances allow an organisation to rapidly extend its strategic advantage and generally require less commitment than other forms of expansion. A key motivator is sharing resources or activities although there may be less obvious reasons as well. Four broad rationales for alliances can be identified, as summarised in Figure 9.4:

- *Scale alliances*. Here organisations combine in order to achieve necessary scale. The capabilities of each partner may be quite similar (as indicated by the similarity of the A and B organisations in Figure 9.4), but together they can achieve advantages that they could not easily manage on their own. Thus combining together can provide economies of scale in the production of outputs (products or services). Combining might also provide economies of scale in terms of inputs, for example by reducing purchasing costs of raw materials or services. Thus health management organisations often combine together to negotiate better prices with pharmaceutical companies. Finally, combining allows the partners to *share risk* as well. Instead of organisations stretching themselves to find enough resources on their own, partnering can help each partner avoid committing so many resources of its own that failure would jeopardise the existence of the whole organisation.
- *Access alliances*. Organisations frequently ally in order to access the capabilities of another organisation that are required in order to produce or sell its products and services. For example, in countries such as China and India, a Western company (in Figure 9.4, organisation A) might need to partner with a local distributor (organisation B) in order to

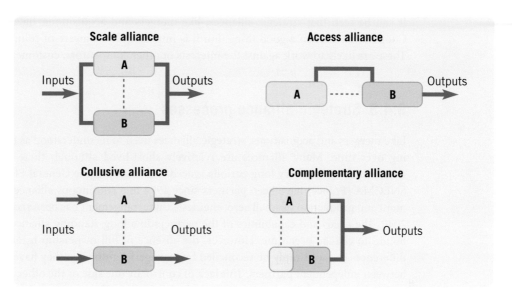

**Figure 9.4** Strategic alliance motives

access effectively the national market for its products and services. Here organisation B is critical to organisation A's ability to sell. Access alliances can work in the opposite direction. Thus organisation B might seek a licensing alliance in order to access inputs from organisation A, for example technologies or brands. Here organisation A is critical to organisation B's ability to produce or market its products and services. Access can be about tangible resources such as distribution channels or products as well as intangible resources such as knowledge.

- *Complementary alliances.* These can be seen as a form of access alliance, but involve organisations at similar points in the value network combining their distinctive resources so that they bolster each partner's particular gaps or weaknesses. Figure 9.4 shows an alliance where the strengths of organisation A (indicated by the darker shading) match the weaknesses of organisation B (indicated by the lighter shading); conversely, the strengths of organisation B match the weaknesses of organisation A. By partnering, the two organisations can bring together complementary strengths in order to overcome their individual weaknesses. An example of this is the General Motors–Toyota NUMMI alliance: here the complementarity lies in General Motors getting access to the Japanese car company's manufacturing expertise, while Toyota obtains the American car company's local marketing knowledge.

- *Collusive alliances.* Occasionally organisations secretly collude together in order to increase their market power. By combining together into cartels, they reduce competition in the marketplace, enabling them to extract higher prices from their customers or lower prices from their suppliers. Such collusive cartels amongst for-profit businesses are generally illegal, so there is no public agreement between them (hence the absence of brackets joining the two collusive organisations in Figure 9.4) and regulators will act to discourage this activity. For instance, mobile phone operators are often accused of collusive behaviour. In 2012 Thailand's three largest mobile phone operators bid 41.63 bn baht (€1.0 bn, $1.3 bn) for a 3G license, just 2.8 per cent higher than the minimum price, giving rise to criticism that they had colluded.

It can be seen that strategic alliances, like mergers and acquisitions, have mixed motives. Cooperation is often a good thing, but it is important to be aware of collusive motivations. These are likely to work against the interests of other competitors, customers and suppliers.

## 9.4.3 Strategic alliance processes

Like mergers and acquisitions, strategic alliances need to be understood as processes unfolding over time. Many alliances are relatively short-lived although there are examples of some which last for very long periods indeed. For example, the General Electric (USA) and SNECMA (France) have been partners since 1974 in a continuous alliance for the development and production of small aero-engines – this arrangement has been recently extended to 2040. The needs and capabilities of the partners in a long-standing alliance such as this are bound to change over time. However, the absence of full ownership means that emerging differences cannot simply be reconciled by managerial authority; they have to be negotiated between independent partners. This lack of control by one side or the other means the managerial processes in alliances are particularly demanding. The management challenges, moreover, will change over time.

The fact that neither partner is in control, while alliances must typically be managed over time, highlights the importance of two themes in the various stages of the alliance process:

- *Co-evolution*. Rather than thinking of strategic alliances as fixed at a particular point of time, they are better seen as co-evolutionary processes.[15] The concept of co-evolution underlines the way in which partners, strategies, capabilities and environments are constantly changing. As they change, they need realignment so that they can evolve in harmony. A co-evolutionary perspective on alliances therefore places the emphasis on flexibility and change. At completion, an alliance is unlikely to be the same as envisaged at the start.

- *Trust*. Given the probable co-evolutionary nature of alliances, and the lack of control of one partner over the other, trust becomes highly important to the success of alliances over time.[16] All future possibilities cannot be specified in the initial alliance contract. Each partner will have made investments that are vulnerable to the selfish behaviour of the other. This implies the need for partners to behave in a trustworthy fashion through the whole lifetime of the alliance. Trust in a relationship is something that has to be continuously earned. Trust is often particularly fragile in alliances between the public and private sectors, where the profit motive is suspect on one side, and sudden shifts in political agendas are feared on the other.

The themes of trust and co-evolution surface in various ways at different stages in the lifespan of a strategic alliance. Figure 9.5 provides a simple stage model of strategic alliance evolution. The amount of committed resources changes at each stage, but issues of trust and co-evolution recur throughout:

- *Courtship*. First there is the initial process of courting potential partners, where the main resource commitment is managerial time. This courtship process should not be rushed, as the willingness of both partners is required. Similar criteria apply to alliances at this stage as to acquisitions. Each partner has to see a strategic fit, according to the rationales

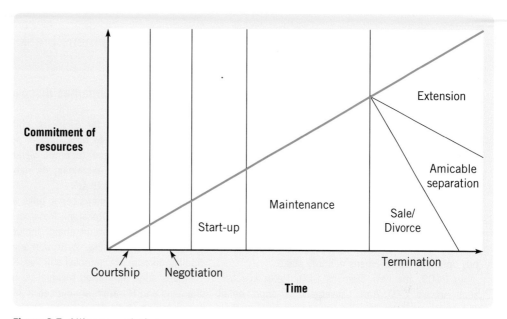

**Figure 9.5** Alliance evolution

*Source*: adapted from E. Murray and J. Mahon (1993) Strategic Alliances: Gateway to the New Europe, *Long Range Planning*, 26, p. 109.

in section 9.3.2. Equally, each partner has to see an organisational fit. Organisational fit can be considered as for acquisitions (section 9.3.3). However, because alliances do not entail the same degree of control as acquisitions, mutual trust between partners will need to be particularly strong right from the outset.

- *Negotiation.* Partners need of course to negotiate carefully their mutual roles at the outset. In equity alliances, the partners also have to negotiate the proportion of ownership each will have in the final joint venture, the profit share and managerial responsibilities. There is likely to be a significant commitment of managerial time at this stage, as it is important to get initial contracts clear and correct and it is worth spending time working out how disputes during the life of the alliance will be resolved. In the case of the Areva–Siemens joint venture (Illustration 9.4), Siemens regretted the low share that it originally agreed. Although the negotiation of ownership proportions in a joint venture is similar to the valuation process in acquisitions, strategic alliance contracts generally involve a great deal more. Key behaviours required of each partner need to be specified upfront. However, a ruthless negotiation style can also damage trust going forward. Moreover, co-evolution implies the need to anticipate change. In an acquired unit, it is possible to make adjustments simply by managerial authority. In alliances, initial contracts may be considered binding even when starting conditions have changed. It is wise to include an option for renegotiating initial terms right at the outset.

- *Start-up.* This involves considerable investment of material and human resources and trust is very important. First, the initial operation of the alliance puts the original alliance agreements to the test. Informal adjustments to working realities are likely to be required. Also, people from outside the original negotiation team are typically now obliged to work

## ILLUSTRATION 9.4    Nuclear fission: Areva and Siemens break up

**Co-evolution is not easy, as two leading French and German companies discover.**

In 2001, Siemens, the German industrial conglomerate, and Areva, the French nuclear industry giant, merged their nuclear reactor businesses into a new joint venture called Areva NP. The joint venture was 34 per cent owned by Siemens, 66 per cent owned by Areva. As the German government had promised to exit nuclear power altogether for environmental reasons, Siemens no longer saw nuclear power as central to its strategy. The joint venture agreement gave the French a right-to-buy option for the Siemens minority stake.

In 2009, the new Siemens CEO, Peter Löscher, sent Areva's CEO Ann Lauvergeon a short email announcing that the Germans would be exercising their right to sell their stake to the French. The email took Madame Lauvergeon completely by surprise: 'It made me think of those men who abandon their wives by leaving a note on the kitchen table'. What had gone wrong in the eight years? Areva NP had been a success. It was the global leader in a market for nuclear reactors that was booming again. Rising oil prices and alarm over global warming made nuclear power increasingly attractive. By 2009, after many years of minimal construction, 51 plants were being built around the world, with 171 more planned. Areva NP was active not only in Europe but also in the United States and China.

The recovery of the nuclear industry was in fact one source of the problem: with a new CEO, Siemens wanted back in. Siemens was frustrated by its lack of control as a minority shareholder, and by the slow decision-making in Areva NP generally. Moreover, it wanted to get a larger slice of the business than just the nuclear reactors – the big profits were elsewhere in the value chain, in fuel and recycling. Areva, the French parent company, already had a significant presence through the whole value chain.

During 2007, Siemens looked either to increase its stake in Areva NP to 50:50 or to take a direct stake in the French parent, Areva. But, more than 80 per cent owned by the French government, Areva was not easily for sale. Moreover, Nicolas Sarkozy, then a senior French government minister and soon French President, told German Chancellor Angela Merkel that France could not tolerate a role for Siemens while the German government refused to back nuclear power in its own country. Siemens had to enrol Merkel's support to prevent Areva from exercising its right-to-buy option and forcing Siemens to sell.

In late 2008, Siemens began talks with the Russian nuclear power giant Rosatom. Rosatom had a presence through the whole value chain, including the highly profitable fuel business. With memories of the Soviet nuclear disaster at Chernobyl still live, Rosatom needed Siemens' high reputation for quality. In March 2009, Siemens and Rosatom announced a joint venture with the ambition of displacing Areva NP as world leader.

Ending the Areva NP joint venture was not simple, however. Siemens' strength was in hardware, but Areva owned the software that made it work. Areva was obliged to buy Siemens' stake (~€4 bn; ~$5.6 bn), but lacked the funds to do so. Also, the original joint venture agreement had included an 11-year non-compete clause in case of break-down. So far as Areva was concerned, Siemens' new joint venture put it in breach of the contract, and so not entitled to the full value of its stake. And the two companies were still working together on various nuclear power stations. Indeed, Areva and Siemens were being jointly sued for €2 bn for cost and time over-runs on a project in Finland. In 2009 Areva took sole control of the joint venture but disputes continued. In 2012 the European Commission ruled the non-compete clause was excessive, anti-competitive and unduly onerous on Siemens – it had to be reduced to three years post joint venture. It was a messy divorce.

*Sources: L'Expansion,* 1 April 2009; *Financial Times,* 28 April 2009; http://www.europa.eu/rapid/press-release_IP-12–618_en.htm

### Question

1 Why did co-evolution break down in the Areva NP joint venture?

2 Why was the termination of this joint venture messy?

together on a day-to-day basis. They may not have the same understanding of the alliance as those who initiated it. Without the mutual trust to make adjustments and smooth misunderstandings, the alliance is liable to break up. This early period in an alliance's evolution is the one with the highest rate of failure.

- *Maintenance.* This refers to the ongoing operation of the strategic alliance, with increasing resources likely to be committed. The lesson of co-evolution is that alliance maintenance is not a simple matter of stability. Alliances have to be actively managed to allow for changing external circumstances. The internal dynamics of the partnership are likely to evolve as well as the partners build experience. Here again trust is extremely important. Gary Hamel has warned that alliances often become *'competitions for competence.'*[17] Because partners are interacting closely, they can begin to learn each other's particular competences. This learning can develop into a competition for competence, with the partner that learns the fastest becoming the more powerful. The more powerful partner may consequently be able to renegotiate the terms in its favour or even break up the alliance and go it alone. If on the other hand the partners wish to maintain their strategic alliance, trustworthy behaviour that does not threaten the other partner's competence is essential to maintaining the cooperative relationships necessary for the day-to-day working of the alliance.

- *Termination.* Often an alliance will have had an agreed time span or purpose right from the start, so termination is a matter of completion rather than failure. Here separation is amicable. Sometimes the alliance has been so successful that the partners will wish to extend the alliance by agreeing a new alliance between themselves, committing still more resources. Sometimes too the alliance will have been more of a success for one party than the other, with one partner wishing to buy the other's share in order to commit fully, while the other partner decides to sell out. The sale of one party's interest need not be a sign of failure as their strategic agenda may have changed since alliance formation. However, sometimes it can end in bitter divorce, as when Areva threatened to take Siemens to court (see Illustration 9.4). Termination needs to be managed carefully, therefore. Co-evolution implies that mutual trust is likely to be valuable after the completion of any particular partnership. Partners may be engaged in several different joint projects at the same time. For example, Cisco and IBM are partners on multiple simultaneous projects in wireless communications, IT security, data centres and data storage. The partners may need to come together again for new projects in the future. Thus Nokia, Ericsson and Siemens have had mobile telephone technology joint projects since the mid-1990s. Maintaining mutual trust in the termination stage is vital if partners are to co-evolve through generations of multiple projects.

## SUMMARY

- There are three broad methods for pursuing a growth strategy: *mergers and acquisitions, strategic alliances* and *organic development.*

- Organic development can be either continuous or radical. Radical organic development is termed *corporate entrepreneurship.*

- Acquisitions can be *hostile* or *friendly.* Motives for mergers and acquisitions can be *strategic, financial or managerial.*

- The acquisition process includes *target choice, negotiation* and *integration.*

- Strategic alliances can be *equity* or *non-equity.* Key motives for strategic alliances include *scale, access, complementarity and collusion.*

- The strategic alliance process relies on *co-evolution* and *trust.*

- To watch an author video on the concepts discussed in this chapter please visit www.mystrategylab.com, and click on 'Author perspectives on strategic management'..

## VIDEO ASSIGNMENTS

MyStrategyLab

If you are using *MyStrategyLab* you might find it useful to watch the *Love Da Pop* case study.

1 What are the main benefits that 'Love Da Pop' might expect to gain from working with Corn Poppers? Are there any risks for Love Da Pop?

2 What does it take for strategic alliances, such as that between Love Da Pop and Corn Poppers, to work effectively and be sustained over a long period?

## RECOMMENDED KEY READINGS

- A comprehensive book on mergers and acquisitions is: S. Sudarsanam. *Creating value from mergers and acquisitions, the challenges.* 2nd edition, FT Prentice Hall, 2010. For some alternative perspectives, see the collection by D.N. Angwin (ed.), *Mergers and Acquisitions,* Blackwell, 2007.

- A useful book on strategic alliances is J. Child, D. Faulkner and S. Tallman, *Cooperative Strategy: Managing Alliances, Networks and Joint Ventures,* 2nd edition, Oxford University Press, 2005.

## REFERENCES

1. P. Sharma and J. Chrisman, 'Towards a reconciliation of the definitional issues in the field of corporate entrepreneurship', *Entrepreneurial Theory and Practice,* Spring (1998), pp. 11–27; D. Garvin and L. Levesque, 'Meeting the challenge of corporate entrepreneurship', *Harvard Business Review,* October (2006), pp. 102–12.

2. D.N. Angwin, 'Motive archetypes in mergers and acquisitions (M&A): the implications of a configurational approach to performance', *Advances in Mergers and Acquisitions*, vol. 6 (2007), pp. 77–105. A useful conceptual model of motives and mitigating variables is J. Haleblian, C.E. Devers, G. McNamara, M.A. Carpenter, and R.B. Davison, 'Taking Stock of What We Know About Mergers and Acquisitions: A Review and Research Agenda', *Journal of Management*, vol. 35 (2009), pp. 469–502.

3. This adapts J. Bower, 'Not all M&As are alike – and that matters', *Harvard Business Review*, March (2001), pp. 93–101.

4. M. Hayward and D. Hambrick, 'Explaining the premiums paid for large acquisitions: evidence of CEO hubris', *Administrative Science Quarterly*, vol. 42 (1997), pp. 103–27. J-Y. Kim, J. Haleblian, S. Finkelstein, 'When Firms are Desperate to Grow via Acquisition: The Effect of Growth Patterns and Acquisition Experience on Acquisition Premiums', *Administrative Science Quarterly* vol. 56, no. 1 March (2011), pp. 26–60.

5. This builds on D. Jemison and S. Sitkin, 'Corporate acquisitions: a process perspective', *Academy of Management Review*, vol. 11, no. 1 (1986), pp. 145–63.

6. J.M. Shaver, 'A paradox of synergy: contagion and capacity effects in mergers and acquisitions', *Academy of Management Review*, vol. 31, no. 4 (2006), pp. 962–78.

7. See J. Child, D. Faulkner and R. Pitkethly, *The Management of International Acquisitions*, Oxford University Press, 2001.

8. A useful discussion of valuation methods in acquisitions is in Chapter 9 of D. Sadlter, D. Smith and A. Campbell, *Smarter Acquisitions*, Prentice Hall, (2008).

9. N. Varaiya and K. Ferris, 'Overpaying in corporate takeovers: the winner's curse', *Financial Analysts Journal*, vol. 43, no. 3 (1987), pp. 64–70.

10. G. Stahl and A. Voigt, 'Do cultural differences matter in mergers and acquisitions? A tentative model and examination', *Organization Science*, vol. 19, no. 1 (2008), pp. 160–78.

11. D.N. Angwin, 'Typologies in M&A research', in D. Faulkner, S. Teerikangas and R. Joseph (eds) *Oxford Handbook of Mergers and Acquisitions*, Oxford University Press, Oxford (2012), pp. 40–70.

12. D.N. Angwin, and M. Meadows 'The Choice of Insider or Outsider Top Executives in Acquired Companies', *Long Range Planning*, vol. 37, (2009), pp. 239–257.

13. D.N. Angwin and M. Meadows, 'Acquiring poorly performing companies during recession', *Journal of General Management,* vol. 38, no. 1 (2012), pp. 1–22.

14. Andersen Consulting, *Dispelling the Myths of Strategic Alliances*, (1999).

15. A. Inkpen and S. Curral, 'The coevolution of trust, control, and learning in joint ventures', *Organization Science*, vol. 15, no. 5 (2004), pp. 586–99; R. ul-Huq, *Alliances and Co-evolution in the Banking Sector*, Palgrave, (2005).

16. A. Arino and J. de la Torre, 'Relational quality: managing trust in corporate alliances', *California Management Review*, vol. 44, no. 1 (2001), pp. 109–31.

17. G. Hamel, *Alliance Advantage: the Art of Creating Value through Partnering*, Harvard Business School Press (1998).

## *'Final Fantasy'*? Acquisitions and alliances in electronic games

After several difficult years Japanese games maker Square Enix posted revenues in 2012 of ¥127.9 bn ($1.6 bn, £993 m, €1.23 bn), an increase of 2.1 per cent over the prior year, with net profits of ¥6.1 billion – a marked improvement on the previous year's loss of ¥12 billion. Famous for its role-playing games such as the *Final Fantasy* series, this turnaround in fortunes followed several years of radical strategic initiatives including strategic alliances with the strategy games developers Double Helix and Gas Powered Games in the United States and Wargaming.net in the United Kingdom. Most radically in 2009, it had also acquired the British Eidos Group, famous for the Lara Croft games. Square Enix President Yoichi Wada commented at the time:

*Source*: webphotographeer/Getty Images.

> 'Our goal is to become one of the top ten players in the world's media and entertainment industry. Since the games market is global, both our contact with our customers and our game development must become global too.'

### The Japanese games industry

Square Enix's strategic moves in 2009 came at a challenging time for the Japanese games industry. The Japanese had enjoyed two decades of domination built on the worldwide success of Japanese consoles such as the Sony PlayStation. But the growing success of Microsoft's Xbox gave an opportunity to American games developers to return to the console market. Indeed, American games developers found that their development skills were more transferable in the new cross-over markets, where games needed to be developed for PCs, consoles and mobile phones alike. Moreover, the Americans had the advantage of proximity to Hollywood, bringing in new creative talent and offering opportunities for film tie-ins. At the same time, Japan's ageing population was shrinking the market for traditional electronic games.

Square Enix's Yoichi Wada recognised the predicament of the Japanese industry vis-à-vis the Americans:

> 'In the last five to ten years, the Japanese games industry has become a closed environment, with no new people

coming in, no new ideas, almost xenophobic . . . The lag with the US is very clear. The US games industry was not good in the past but it has now attracted people from the computer industry and from Hollywood, which has led to strong growth.'

At the same time, the basic economics of the games industry are changing, with rising costs due to growing technological sophistication. A typical modern game can cost from $3,000,000 to over $20,000,000 to develop.[1] Games generally take from one to three years to develop. Yet only one in twenty games is estimated ever to make a profit. In other words, the risks are very high and the necessary scale to compete is rising.

### Square Enix's strategy

Square Enix itself was a merger in 2003 between Square (founded 1983 and famous for *Final Fantasy* role-playing game) and Enix (founded 1975 with its role-playing *Dragon Quest* series). Y4ichi Wada, President of Square, became the president of the new merged company.

Square Enix's strategy is based on 'polymorphic content'. Its various franchises (*Final Fantasy*, *Dragon Quest* and so on) are developed for all hardware or media, such as consoles, mobile phones, online, PCs rather than any single gaming platform. There are also spin-offs including

TV series, films, comics and novels. In 2005, Square Enix bought the Japanese arcade-game company Taito Corporation, famous for its *Space Invaders* game. *Space Invaders* versions have appeared on PlayStation, Xbox and Wii consoles, as well as PCs.

By 2008, Yoichi Wada was presiding over a company that was increasingly diversified, with sales of d136 bn (about €1 bn) and just over 3,000 employees. However, it was still overwhelmingly Japanese (85 per cent of sales at home) and lacked scale by comparison with competitors such as Electronic Arts and Activision. On the plus side, Square Enix reportedly had a 'war-chest' available for acquisitions of about ¥40 bn (about €300 m). During the summer of 2008, Square Enix made a friendly bid for the Japanese game developer Tecmo, whose fighting games *Ninja Garden* and *Dead or Alive* were popular in North America and Europe. Tecmo rejected the bid. Wada began to look overseas.

## Lara Croft falls

Eidos is a British games company best-known for the action-adventure games series, *Tomb Raider*, starring the extraordinary Lara Croft. However, during 2008, disappointing sales for *Tomb Raider: Underworld* drove its share-price down from £5 (~€5.5; ~$7.5) to around 30 pence. Eidos' founder and chief executive, Jane Cavanagh, was forced to resign. The company declared losses of £136 m, on sales of £119 m (down from £179 m two years earlier). In April 2009, Square Enix bought the company for £84 m, a premium of 129 per cent over Eidos' current market value. Given the declining success of the *Tomb Raider* franchise, many speculated that Square Enix had overpaid for its first overseas acquisition.

The acquisition of Eidos did offer Square Enix global reach, however. About one-third of Eidos' sales were in the United States and 40 per cent in Europe, excluding the United Kingdom. Eidos also brought Square Enix its first studios outside Japan, with studios in the United Kingdom, Denmark, Hungary, the United States, Canada and China. Yoichi Wada commented: 'It is significant that we have opened a window for creative talents worldwide.'

Wada chose to keep Phil Rogers, the new Eidos chief executive, and the rest of his management team in place. Wada described a new Group structure, in which Square Enix, the arcade business Taito and Eidos would each be stand-alone divisions: 'Our aim is to implement a hybrid management structure which avoids the extremes of being either too global or too local' He continued: 'The Group's management and administration departments will be integrated, while our product and service delivery will be established locally in each territory to maximise our business opportunities through better understanding of local customers' tastes and commercial practices.' Wada also recognised the new strength that Eidos brought in action-adventure games, by contrast with Square Enix's traditional core of role-playing games. He declared his commitment both to sharing technologies across the businesses and to sustaining particular strengths: 'While promoting shared technology and expertise amongst our studios, we will also develop products which reflect the unique identity of each studio, regardless of locality.' Wada also commented on the nature of the skilled games developers he was acquiring: 'It is always difficult to manage creatives anywhere in the world. We want to cherish the Eidos studio culture but change it where it is necessary.'[2]

One thing that Square Enix was quick to do was to end the Eidos distribution agreement with Warner Bros for its products in the United States. Square Enix regarded itself as strong enough to do that itself.

## Strategic alliances

At the same time as acquiring Eidos, Square Enix cemented three significant strategic alliances. In the United Kingdom, Square Enix tied up with the strategy game developer Wargaming.net (famous for the *Massive Assault* series) in order to produce the World War II game *Order of War*. This would enter the market at the end of 2009 as Square Enix's first global product release. In the United States, Square Enix formed partnerships with Gas Powered Games (producer of the *Supreme Commander* strategy game) and with Double Helix (producer of the *Front Mission* strategy series). Together with the Eidos acquisition, these partnerships significantly extended Square Enix's range beyond its traditional core in role-playing games. They also extended the company's geographical reach. Yoichi Wada commented:

> '**We see great opportunities in North American and European markets, both of which are expected to be maintaining sustainable growth over these coming years. Therefore it is crucial that we create alliances with proven developers such as Gas Powered Games in order to serve these significant markets better by providing products and services in tune with customer tastes.**'

All three of these new partners were relatively small (around 100 employees each), privately owned and had their origins as start-ups during the 1990s. The founders' motivations are explained by Chris Taylor at Gas Powered Games:

'I had that dream really from the day I first walked into my first full time job as a games programmer. I wanted to be the guy running the company . . . We've created our own original IPs (intellectual properties) consistently. Some are great, some are not so great, but the fact is you have to keep throwing darts at the board. You have to keep trying to make great stuff, and you can't do that if you're inside of a large megalithic corporation to the same degree . . .'

Chris Taylor described how Square Enix, traditionally a role-playing company, and Gas Powered Games, more a strategy game developer, were working together on their first venture, *Supreme Commander 2*:

'One of the things that we took as a cue from Square Enix was the way they embrace character and story. We were all into that, so that was easy. When we asked them, 'How should we develop our game to work with their philosophy?', they said, 'Don't do that because we want you to do what you do. You make games for the Western market, and we're interested in making games for the Western market.' So if we changed, we would be missing the point. Which was terrific, because that meant we could do what we loved to do, make great RTS (real-time strategy) games . . . and if we tried to change them in any way, we'd be moving away from the goal.'

## A games enthusiast's view

Through alliances and mergers, Square Enix had transformed its profile. From its base in Japanese-style role-playing games, it was developing a significant presence in strategy and action adventure. It had studios across the world. Its various games titles were big across Asia, Europe and America. Games enthusiast Randy commented:

'Square Enix publishing a western-developed game? Is the far-reaching JRPG (Japanese role-playing game) developer dumping the androgynous boy-heroes and shovel-wide swords for WWII fatigues and M1 Carbines? No, not entirely. But they *are* bringing Wargaming.net into the fold to do it for them. First, Square Enix buys out the house that Lara Croft built, and now they're into real-time strategy war games. *Nothing in this life makes sense anymore.*'[3]

## Looking forwards

Following the alliances and mergers, Square Enix's financial performance began to suffer, particularly in the increasingly competitive console market. However, in 2012 the digital division was performing well with *Final Fantasy* XIII-2, *Deus Ex: Human Revolution* and the Mobage simulation game *Sengoku Ixa* – with 2 million registered users – spurring the division to revenues of ¥71.9 billion, up 11.9 per cent year-on-year, and operating profit of ¥12.6 billion, up 11.7 per cent. Square Enix reported it had 'internal reserves' for investments that could 'enhance the company's value'. This could include 'capital investments and M&A to expand and develop new businesses'. Such deals would be a part of a broader strategy to meet the demands of an increasingly digital, networked, multi-device world market.

*Sources and references:* M. Palmer, 'Square Enix views Eidos as a jump to next level', *Financial Times*, 28 April 2009; 'Cost of making games set to soar', www.bbcnews.co.uk, 17 November 2005; 'Square Enix needs to show growth scenario to market', *Nikkei*, 9 October 2007; Joint interview with Yoichi Wada and Phil Rogers, www.square-enix.com, 26 May 2009; M. Palmer, 'Square Enix views Eidos as a jump to next level', *Financial Times*, 28 April 2009; 'Square Enix and Gas Powered Games announce strategic partnership', *Newswire Association*, 12 November 2008; P. Elliott, 'Foot on the gas', *gamesindustry.biz*, 19 August 2008; X. de Matos, 'Interview: Chris Taylor on Supreme Commander 2', *joystiq.com*, 9 June 2009; Randy, 'Square Enix tries hand at WWI RTS with Order of War', *Gaming Nexus*, 17 April 2009.

### Questions

1 Explain why Square Enix chose alliances in some cases and acquisitions in others.

2 How should Square Enix manage its Eidos acquisition in order to maximise value creation, and how might that management approach change over time?

3 What are the strengths and weaknesses of the alliance strategy, and what problems might Square Enix anticipate over time?

4 What methods of expansion would you recommend to the management of Square Enix now they appear to have the resources and intention to grow?

# 10 STRATEGY IN ACTION

## Learning outcomes

After reading this chapter you should be able to:

- Analyse the main *structural types* of organisations in terms of their strengths and weaknesses.

- Identify key issues in designing organisational *control systems* (such as planning, performance targeting and cultural systems).

- Recognise how the three strands of strategy, structure and systems should reinforce each other as *organisational configurations*.

- Identify and assess different change leadership *roles* and *styles.*

- Identify different types of *strategic change programmes*.

- Underatke a *forcefield analysis* to identify levers for strategic change.

## Key terms

balanced scorecards p. 242

configuration p. 242

cultural systems p. 239

forcefield analysis p. 252

functional structure p. 233

leadership p. 243

matrix structure p. 236

McKinsey 7-S Framework p. 242

multidivisional structure p. 235

organisational ambidexterity p. 250

performance targets p. 240

planning systems p. 238

## 10.1 INTRODUCTION

Chapter 1 explained that strategic management can be thought of as having three main elements: understanding *the strategic position* of an organisation, making *strategic choices* for the future and managing *strategy in action* (see Figure 1.3). As this book is about the fundamentals of strategy, it mainly concentrates on the first two elements, position and choice. But even the most shrewdly chosen strategy is valueless unless it can be turned into action and that is the theme of this chapter. Moreover in deciding what strategy an orgnaisation might follow, managers need to think through whether it is feasible (see the Appendix) and therefore take account of the issues raised here.

This chapter focuses on three topics fundamental to achieving strategy in action (see Figure 10.1):

- *Structures:* the formal roles, responsibilities and lines of reporting in organisations. The chapter considers the main types of structures, including functional, divisional and matrix structures.

- *Systems* supporting and controlling people within and around an organisation. These systems include direct mechanisms such as performance targeting and planning, and more indirect ones such as cultural and market systems.

- *Leading strategic change*, in particular the *styles of leadership* employed and the purposes and characteristics of different *strategic change programmes*.

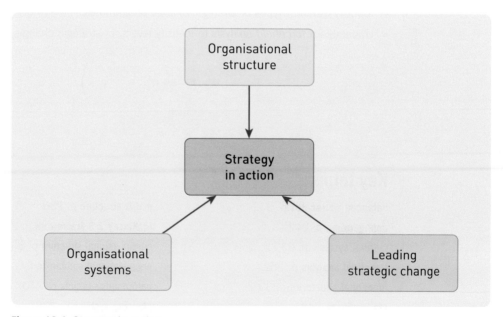

**Figure 10.1** Strategy in action

# 10.2 STRUCTURAL TYPES

Managers often describe their organisation by drawing an organisation chart, mapping out its formal structure. These charts are important to managers because they identify the 'levels' and roles in an organisation and who is responsible for what. They can also have major implications for organisational priorities and interactions in the marketplace: as at Qwikster, getting the structure wrong can be very damaging (see Illustration 10.1).

This section reviews three basic structural types: functional, multidivisional and matrix.[1] Broadly, the first two of these tend to emphasise one structural dimension over another, either functional specialisms or business units. The matrix structure mixes structural dimensions more evenly, for instance trying to give product and geographical units equal weight. The most appropriate structure depends on the characteristics (sometimes called 'contingencies') of an organisation including organisational size, extent of diversification and type of technology. This implies that the first step in organisational design is deciding what the key challenges facing the organisation are that arise from the questions considered in the previous chapters.

## 10.2.1 The functional structure

Even a small entrepreneurial start-up, once it involves more than one person, needs to divide up responsibilities between different people. The **functional structure divides responsibilities according to the organisation's primary specialist roles such as production, research and sales**. Figure 10.2 represents a typical organisation chart for such a functional organisation. This kind of structure is particularly relevant to small or start-up organisations, or larger organisations

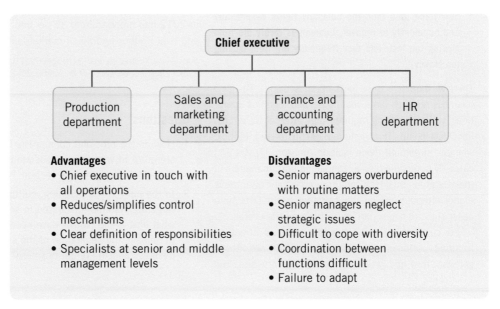

**Figure 10.2** A functional structure

## ILLUSTRATION 10.1 Structural fault: Qwikster's quick demise

**Netflix's introduction of the new Qwikster structure was a multi-billion-dollar failure.**

In 2011, Netflix, the USA's largest online DVD rental and internet streaming company, faced a dilemma. Internet streaming of movies was clearly a growth business, one which competitors such as Amazon were beginning to enter. On the other hand, DVD rental by mail was facing long-term decline. In September 2011, Reed Hastings, CEO and joint founder of the company, responded to the dilemma with a structural solution. He proposed to split his business into two separate parts: henceforth streaming would be done exclusively under the Netflix label, while DVD rental would be done exclusively in a new organisational unit called Qwikster. In a blog post, Hastings explained his motivation:

> 'For the past five years, my greatest fear at Netflix has been that we wouldn't make the leap from success in DVDs to success in streaming. Most companies that are great at something – like AOL dial-up or Borders bookstores – do not become great at new things people want (streaming for us) because they are afraid to hurt their initial business. Eventually these companies realise their error of not focusing enough on the new thing, and then the company fights desperately and hopelessly to recover. Companies rarely die from moving too fast, and they frequently die from moving too slowly.'

There were other reasons for the proposed split. The DVD business requires large warehouse and logistics operations, while streaming requires large internet resources. For DVDs, competitors include Blockbuster and Redbox, whereas streaming rivals include Amazon, iTunes and cable TV companies. As a standalone unit, managers in the streaming business could promote their alternative model without worrying about protecting the DVD business, still the larger part of Netflix's profits overall.

For customers, though, the split was less attractive. In future, customers would have to deal with two sites to get what they had previously got through one site. The DVD site offered many more movies, and tended to have more recent releases. Movie viewing recommendations for one site would not transfer to the other site. DVD renters would no longer receive the distinctive Netflix DVD envelopes which had strong brand loyalty.

The customer response was hostile. In the month following Qwikster's launch Netflix lost hundreds of thousands of subscribers. The Netflix share price fell more than 60 per cent, wiping out more than $3 bn in value. CEO Reed Hastings joked in a Facebook message that he feared poisoning by some of his investors: 'I think I might need a food taster. I can hardly blame them.'

On 10 October 2011, three weeks after the original Qwikster announcement, Hastings blogged that the new unit would not go ahead after all, and that all business would continue under the Netflix label. Hastings explained: 'There is a difference between moving quickly – which Netflix has done very well for years – and moving too fast, which is what we did in this case.' Despite his reversal of the structural change, repercussions were still being felt a year later: Netflix's market share of DVD rentals in 2012 had dropped from 35 per cent to 27 per cent, and rival Redbox had taken market leadership.

*Sources*: *Wall Street Journal*, 11 October 2011; *Strategy+Business*, 2 April 2012; *PC Magazine*, 17 September 2012.

### Questions

1 How do the pros and cons of the Qwikster structure fit with those associated with the divisional structure (see section 10.2.2)?

2 In the light of the planning, cultural and targeting systems (discussed in section 10.3), what else would Netflix have needed to do to manage the separation of the streaming business and the rental business?

that have retained narrow, rather than diverse, product ranges. Functional structures may also be used within a multidivisional structure (see below), where the divisions themselves may split themselves up according to functional departments.

Figure 10.2 also summarises the potential advantages and disadvantages of a functional structure. Advantages include giving senior managers direct hands-on involvement in operations and allowing greater operational control from the top. It also provides a clear definition of roles and tasks, increasing accountability. Functional departments also provide concentrations of expertise, thus fostering knowledge development in areas of functional specialism.

However, there are disadvantages, particularly as organisations become larger or more diverse. A major concern in a fast-moving world is that senior managers focus too much on their functional responsibilities, becoming overburdened with routine operations and too concerned with narrow functional interests. As a result, they find it hard either to take a strategic view of the organisation as a whole or to coordinate separate functions quickly. Thus functional organisations can be inflexible and poor at adapting to change. Separate functional departments tend also to be inward-looking – so-called 'functional silos' – making it difficult to integrate the knowledge of different functional specialists. Finally, because they are centralised around particular functions, functional structures are not good at coping with product or geographical diversity. For example, a central marketing department may try to impose a uniform approach to advertising regardless of the diverse needs of an organisation's various business units around the world.

## 10.2.2 The divisional structure

A **divisional structure is built up of separate divisions on the basis of products, services or geographical areas**. Divisionalisation often comes about as an attempt to overcome the problems that functional structures have in dealing with the diversity mentioned above.[2] Each division can respond to the specific requirements of its product/market strategy, using its own set of functional departments. A similar situation exists in many public services, where the organisation is structured around *service departments* such as recreation, social services and education.

Figure 10.3 summarises the potential advantages and disadvantages of a multidivisional structure. There are several potential advantages. Divisional managers have greater personal ownership for their own divisional strategies. As self-standing business units it is, however, possible to control divisions from a corporate centre by monitoring business performance. Having divisions also provides flexibility because organisations can add, close or merge divisions as circumstances change. Geographical divisions – for example, a European division or a North American division – offer a means of managing internationally. There can be benefits of specialisation within a division, allowing competences to develop with a clearer focus on a particular product group, technology or customer group. Management responsibility for a whole divisional business is also good training in taking a strategic view for managers expecting to go on to a main board position.

Divisional structures can, however, also have disadvantages. First, divisions can become so self-sufficient that they are *de facto* independent businesses, but duplicating the functions and costs of the corporate centre of the company. In such cases it may make more sense to split the company into independent businesses, and de-mergers of this type have become common.

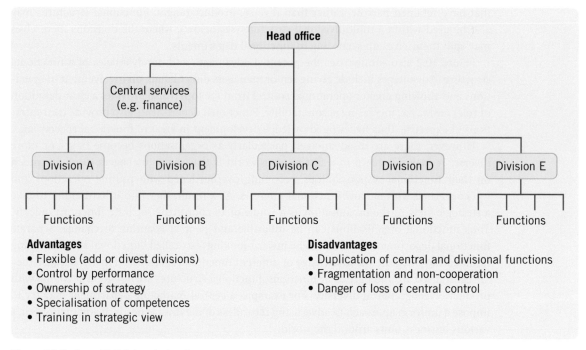

**Advantages**
- Flexible (add or divest divisions)
- Control by performance
- Ownership of strategy
- Specialisation of competences
- Training in strategic view

**Disadvantages**
- Duplication of central and divisional functions
- Fragmentation and non-cooperation
- Danger of loss of central control

**Figure 10.3** A multidivisional structure

Second, divisionalisation tends to get in the way of cooperation and knowledge-sharing between business units. Expertise is fragmented and divisional performance targets provide poor incentives to collaborate with other divisions. Finally, divisions may become too autonomous, especially where joint ventures and partnership dilute ownership. Here, divisions pursue their own strategies almost regardless of the needs of the corporate parent. In these cases, multidivisionals become *holding companies*, where the corporate centre effectively 'holds' the various businesses in a largely financial sense, exercising little control and adding little value.

### 10.2.3 The matrix structure

A **matrix structure** combines different structural dimensions simultaneously, for example product divisions and geographical territories or product divisions and functional specialisms.[3] In matrix structures, staff typically report to two managers rather than one. Figure 10.4 gives examples of such a structure.

Matrix structures have several advantages. They promote *knowledge-sharing* because they allow separate areas of knowledge to be integrated across organisational boundaries. Particularly in professional service organisations, matrix organisation can be helpful in applying particular knowledge specialisms to different market or geographical segments. For example, to serve a particular client, a consulting firm may draw on people from groups with particular knowledge specialisms (e.g. strategy or organisation design) and others grouped according to particular markets (industry sectors or geographical regions). Figure 10.4 shows how a school might combine the separate knowledge of subject specialists to create programmes

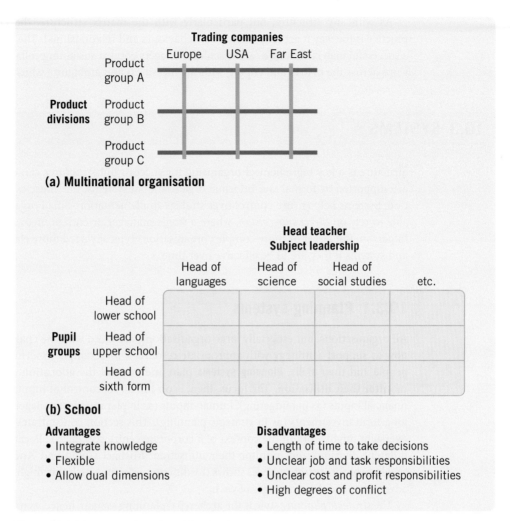

**Figure 10.4** Two examples of matrix structures

of study tailored differently to various age groups. Matrix organisations are *flexible*, because they allow different dimensions of the organisation to be mixed together. They are particularly attractive to organisations operating globally, because of the possible mix between local and global dimensions. For example, a global company may prefer geographically defined divisions as the operating units for local marketing because of their specialist local knowledge of customers. But at the same time it may still want global product units responsible for the worldwide coordination of product development and manufacturing, taking advantage of economies of scale and specialisation.

However, because a matrix structure replaces single lines of authority with multiple cross-matrix relationships, this often brings problems. In particular, it will typically take *longer to reach decisions* because of bargaining between the managers of different dimensions. There may also be *conflict* because staff find themselves responsible to managers from two structural dimensions. In short, matrix organisations are hard to control.

As with any structure, but particularly with the matrix structure, the critical issue in practice is the way it actually works (i.e. behaviours and relationships). The key ingredient in a successful matrix structure can be senior managers good at sustaining collaborative relationships across the matrix and coping with the messiness and ambiguity which that can bring.

## 10.3 SYSTEMS

Structure is a key ingredient of organising for success. But structures can only work if they are supported by formal and informal organisational systems, the 'muscles' of the organisation. Systems help ensure control over strategy implementation. Small organisations may be able to rely on *direct supervision*, where a single manager or entrepreneur monitors activity in person. But larger or more complex organisations typically need more elaborate structures and systems if they are to be effective over time.

### 10.3.1 Planning systems

All organisations, but especially large organisations, are faced with the challenge of deciding how to support a strategy with appropriate resources; for example in terms of funding and people and their skills. **Planning systems plan and control the allocation of resources and monitor their utilisation**. The focus, then, is on the direct control of inputs. These might be financial inputs (as in budgeting), human inputs (as in planning for managerial succession) or long-term investments (as in strategic planning). This section concentrates on how strategic oversight might work in the context of a corporate centre seeking to allocate resources to its different divisions and monitor their utilisation. Michael Goold and Andrew Campbell's[4] typology of three *strategy styles* shows the different ways in which this might be done and the advantages and disadvantages of each.

The *strategic planning* style is the archetypal planning system, hence its name. In the Goold and Campbell sense, the strategic planning style combines both a strong planning influence on strategic direction from the corporate centre with relatively relaxed performance accountability for the business units. The logic is that if the centre sets the strategic direction, business unit managers should not be held strictly accountable for disappointing results that might be due to an inappropriate plan in the first place. In the strategic planning style, the centre focuses on inputs in terms of allocating resources necessary to achieve the strategic plan, while exercising a high degree of direct control over how the plan is executed by the businesses.

The *financial control* style involves very little central planning. The business units each develop their own strategic plans, probably after some negotiation with the corporate centre, and are then held strictly accountable for the results against these plans. This style differs from the strategic planning style in that control is against financial outputs, similar to a performance targeting system (see section 10.3.3). If the businesses devised the plans, then they should take full responsibility for their success or failure. Business unit managers in the financial control style have a lot of autonomy and typically receive high bonus payments for success. But failure may easily lead to their dismissal. The financial planning style fits with the portfolio manager role of the corporate centre (referred to in Chapter 6).

The *strategic control* style is in the middle, with a more consensual development of the strategic plan between the corporate centre and the business units and moderate levels of business unit accountability. Under the strategic control style, the centre will typically act as coach to its business unit managers, helping them to see and seize opportunities. This style often relies on strong cultural systems to foster trust and mutual understanding (see section 10.3.2). Consequently, the strategic control style is often associated with the synergy manager or parental developer roles of the corporate centre (discussed in Chapter 6).

Thus the three strategy styles vary with regard to their reliance on, and application of, planning systems. The direct control of inputs characteristic of the strategic planning style is only appropriate in certain circumstances. In particular, it makes sense where there are large, risky and long-range investments to be allocated: for example, an oil company typically has to take the decision to invest in the ten-year development of an oilfield at the corporate centre, rather than risk delegating it to business units whose resources and time-horizons may be limited. On the other hand, the financial control style is suitable where investments are small, relatively frequent and well understood, as typically in a mature, non-capital-intensive business. The strategic control style is suitable where there are opportunities for collaborating across businesses and there is a need to nurture new ones. The strategic planning style (not the practice of strategic planning in general) has become less common in the private sector in recent years. The style is seen as too rigid to adapt to changing circumstances and too top-down to reflect real business circumstances on the ground.

## 10.3.2 Cultural systems

Organisations typically have distinctive cultures which reflect basic assumptions and beliefs held by organisation members and define taken-for-granted ways of doing things (see Chapter 4). Despite their taken-for-granted nature, organisational cultures can seem a tempting means of managerial control. Managers may therefore try to influence organisational culture in various ways to achieve the kinds of employee behaviour required by their strategy. This, then, is an *indirect* form of control rather than direct supervision: it becomes a matter of willing conformity or *self*-control by employees.

Three key cultural systems are:

- *Recruitment*. Here cultural conformity may be attempted by the selection of appropriate staff who will 'fit' with the desired strategy.
- *Socialisation*. Here employee behaviours are shaped by social processes. This often starts with the integration of new staff through training, induction and mentoring programmes. It may continue with further training throughout a career. Symbols can also play a role in socialisation, for example the symbolic example of leaders' behaviours or the influence of office décor, dress codes or language.
- *Reward*. Appropriate behaviour can be encouraged through pay, promotion or symbolic processes (for example, public praise). The desire to achieve the same rewards as successful people in the organisation will typically encourage imitative behaviour.

It is important to recognise, however, that organisations' cultures are not fully under formal management control. Sometimes aspects of organisational culture may persistently contradict managerial intentions, as with peer-group pressure not to respond to organisational strategies. Cynicism and 'going through the motions' are also common. On the other hand, some cultures can bring about desired results, even without deliberate management intervention.

### 10.3.3 Performance targeting systems

**Performance targets focus on the *outputs* of an organisation (or part of an organisation), such as product quality, revenues or profits.** These targets are often known as key performance indicators (KPIs). The performance of an organisation is judged, either internally or externally, on its ability to meet these targets. However, within specified boundaries, the organisation remains free on how targets should be achieved. This approach can be particularly appropriate in certain situations:

*Within large businesses*, corporate centres may choose performance targets to control their business units without getting involved in the details of how they achieve them (as in the financial control style in section 10.3.1). These targets are often cascaded down the organisation as specific targets for sub-units, functions and even individuals.

In *regulated markets*, such as privatised utilities, government-appointed regulators increasingly exercise control through agreed KPIs, such as service or quality levels, as a means of ensuring 'competitive' performance.

In *the public services*, where control of resource inputs was the dominant approach historically, governments are attempting to move control processes towards outputs (such as quality of service) and outcomes (for example, patient mortality rates in healthcare).

There are at least three potential problems with targets:[5]

- *Inappropriate measures* of performance are quite common. For example, managers often prefer indicators that are easily measured or choose measures based on inadequate understanding of real needs on the ground. The result is a focus on the required measures rather than the factors that might be essential to long-term success. In the private sector, focus on short-term profit measures is common, at the expense of investment in the long-run prosperity of the business. To take a public-sector case, inappropriate 'national indicators' appeared to be a problem with child protection services in Illustration 10.2.

- *Inappropriate target levels* are a common problem. Managers may give their superiors pessimistic forecasts so that targets are set at undemanding levels, which can then be easily met. On the other hand, superiors may over-compensate for their managers' pessimism, and end up setting excessively demanding targets. These may either demotivate employees, who see no hope of achieving them regardless of their effort, or encourage risky or dishonest behaviours in order to achieve the otherwise impossible.

- *Excessive internal competition* can be a result of targets focused on individual or sub-unit performance. Although an organisation by definition should be more than the sum of its parts, if individuals or sub-units are being rewarded on their performance in isolation, they will have little incentive to collaborate with the other parts of the organisation. The struggle to meet individualistic targets will reduce the exchange of information and the sharing of resources.

# ILLUSTRATION 10.2  Structure, systems and saving children's lives

**Changing structures and systems is not a quick fix in protecting children from parental abuse and neglect.**

England and Wales have a problem: the homicide of children by their own parents. In the period 1998 to 2008, an average of about 40 children were killed by their parents annually. In 2008, about 200,000 children were living in households with a known high risk of domestic abuse and violence.

The death of nine-year-old Victoria Climbié in 2000 at the hands of her great aunt and boyfriend prompted a major reform of child protection services in England and Wales. Victoria Climbié's death had come after nine months of regular warning signs to the local social, police and medical services. The lack of coordination in picking up signs of abuse between these agencies was seen as a major weakness. One result was the merger of local education and children's social services into *unified children's services departments*. Another was to create 'common assessment frameworks' (CAFs), a way for all agencies (from police to doctors) to record their dealing with a particular child on a standardised form accessible to all. A system of *national indicators* for measuring child protection was also introduced, measuring clear quantifiable variables such as numbers of case review meetings and re-registrations on the child protection register.

The homicide rate drifted down after the implementation of the reforms between 2003 and 2005, but then started to climb back towards the average, with 43 homicides in 2007–8. The 2007 death by neglect and abuse of 17-month-old 'Baby P' – in the same local authority area as Victoria Climbié and again after months of warning signs to police, medical and social work services – prompted a further review of services. The review found that under 10 per cent of local authorities had adopted the national indicators for child protection: local authorities complained that the targets were focused excessively on proper process and timescales, rather than meaningful outcomes. None the less, the review basically confirmed the new structure and systems, while urging more effective implementation through better training of social workers, revised indicators, more resources, centralised computer support and improved communications between agencies.

On the ground, however, there was considerable dissatisfaction with the post-Climbié reforms. Some 81 per cent of professionals in one poll claimed that the merger between educational and social services was not working (www.publicservice.co.uk). Most of the merged departments were headed by former directors of education, with little understanding of the social work for which they were responsible. Social workers complained about excessive form filling in order to demonstrate correct procedures. A boy told the review: 'It seems like they have to do all this form filling – their bosses' bosses make them do it – but it makes them forget about us.' An academic commentator estimated that social workers were now spending 80 per cent of their time in front of computers rather than with clients. The common assessment framework (CAF) form is eight pages long. One school head reported to the *Guardian* newspaper: 'You can no longer pick up the phone to the agencies for advice or referral without hearing "Where is the CAF?".'

Speaking to the *Guardian*, Maggie Atkinson, Director for Learning and Children in the town of Gateshead, urged patience: 'Bringing services together into one department creates a different culture, not immediately, but over a period of time. This change in culture is only really beginning to be embedded in local services and to put it into reverse would be a wasted opportunity. It doesn't matter whether the director comes from education or social services. What you need to do the job is broad shoulders, effective management and a very strong team around you.'

*Sources*: L. Lightfoot, 'A marriage on the rocks', *Guardian*, 17 March 2009; 'The Protection of Children in England: a Progress Report', *Every Child Matters*, March 2009.

## Questions

1  List the advantages and disadvantages of the new structure and systems for children's services.

2  What kinds of actions and initiatives might be appropriate in terms of the cultural systems of children's services?

These acknowledged difficulties with targets have led to the development of techniques designed to encourage a more balanced approach to target-setting. The most fundamental has been the development of the balanced scorecard approach.[6] **Balanced scorecards set performance targets according to a range of perspectives, not only financial**. They typically combine four specific perspectives: the *financial perspective*, which might include profit margins or cash flow; the *customer perspective*, which includes targets important to customers, such as delivery times or service levels; the *internal perspective*, with targets relating to operational effectiveness such as the development of IT systems or reductions in waste levels; and the future-orientated *innovation and learning perspective*, which targets activities that will be important to the long-run performance of the organisation, for example investment in training or research. Attending to targets relevant to all four perspectives seeks to ensure that managers do not focus on one set of targets (e.g. financial) at the expense of others, while also keeping an eye to the future through innovation and learning.

## 10.4 ORGANISATIONAL CONFIGURATION: THE MCKINSEY 7-S FRAMEWORK

It is important that there is compatibility between the structures and systems of organisations. One way of thinking about this is in terms of the concept of organisational configuration. A configuration is **the set of organisational design elements that interlink in order to support the intended strategy**. A well-known means of considering this is the **McKinsey 7-S framework** which highlights the importance of fit between strategy, structure, systems, staff, style, skills and superordinate goals.[7] Together these seven elements can serve as a checklist in an organisational design exercise: see Figure 10.5.

The rest of the book has been concerned with strategy and this chapter has already addressed structure and systems. This section will comment on the remaining four elements of the 7-S framework.

- *Style* here refers to the leadership style of top managers in an organisation (discussed in section 10.5.2) The important point to emphasise is that leadership style should fit other aspects of the 7-S framework: for example, a highly directive or coercive style is not likely to fit a matrix organisation structure.

- *Staff* is about the kinds of people in the organisation and how they are developed. This relates to systems of recruitment, socialisation and reward (see section 10.3.2). A key criterion for the feasibility of any strategy is: does the organisation have the people to match? A common constraint on structural change is the availability of the right people to head new departments and divisions.

- *Skills* relates to staff, but in the 7-S framework refers more broadly to capabilities in general (see Chapter 3). The concept of capabilities here raises not only staff skills but also issues to do with how these skills are embedded in and captured by the organisation as a whole. For example, how do the organisation's training schemes, information technology and reward systems transform the talents of individuals into the organisational capabilities required by the strategy?

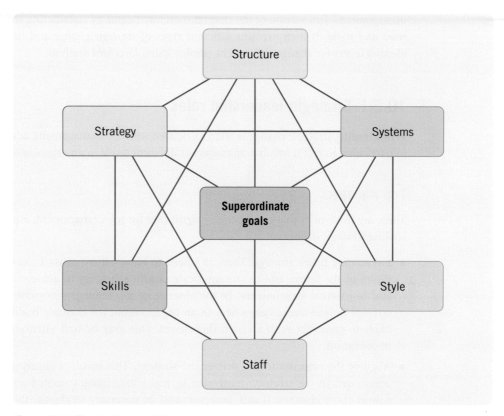

**Figure 10.5** The McKinsey 7-S

*Source*: R. Waterman, T. Peters and J. Phillips, 'Structure is not organisation', *Business Horizons*, June 1980, pp. 14–26: p. 18.

- *Superordinate goals* refers to the overarching goals or purpose of the organisation as a whole, in other words the mission, vision and objectives that form the organisational purpose (see Chapter 4). Superordinate goals are placed at the centre of the 7-S framework: all other elements should support these.

The McKinsey 7-S framework highlights at least three aspects of organising. First, organising involves a lot more than just getting the organisational structure right; there are many other elements to attend to. Second, the 7-S framework emphasises fit between all these elements: everything from structure to skills needs to be connected together. Third, if managers change one element of the 7-S, the concept of fit suggests they are likely to have to change all the other elements as well in order to keep them all appropriately aligned to each other. Changing one element in isolation is liable to make things worse until overall fit is restored.

# 10.5 LEADING STRATEGIC CHANGE

Turning an intended strategy into strategy in action invariably involves change. As Harvard's John Kotter points out, 'coping with change'[8] is what distinguishes **leadership** from the bringing of order and consistency to operational aspects of organisations that characterises 'good management.' This section of the chapter therefore begins by considering *strategic leadership roles and styles*. It then explains different *types of strategic change* and how leaders might identify levers for change they might employ using *forcefield analysis*.

## 10.5.1 Strategic leadership roles

While leading strategic change is often associated with top management, and chief executives in particular, in fact it involves managers at different levels in an organisation.

### Top managers

There are three roles that are especially significant for top management, especially a CEO, in leading strategic change:

- *Envisioning future strategy*. There is a need to ensure there exists a clear and compelling vision of the future and to communicate clearly a strategy to achieve it both internally and to external stakeholders. In the absence of top managers not doing so, those who attempt to lead change elsewhere in an organisation, for example middle managers, are likely to construct such a vision themselves. This may be well intentioned but can lead to confusion.

- *Aligning* the organisation to deliver the strategy. This involves ensuring that people are committed to the strategy, motivated to make the changes needed and empowered to deliver those changes. It can, however, also be necessary to change the management of the organisation to ensure such commitment, which is why top teams often change as a precursor to or during strategic change.

- *Embodying change*. Top managers will be seen by others, not least those within the organisation, but also other stakeholders and outside observers, as intimately associated with a future strategy and a strategic change programme. They are, then, symbolically highly significant in the change process and need to be a role model for future strategy.

### Middle managers

Middle managers are typically seen as implementers of top management strategic plans. Here their role is to ensure that resources are allocated and controlled appropriately and to monitor the performance and behaviour of staff. In the context of strategic change, however, there are four other roles to emphasise for middle managers:

- *Advisers* to top management on requirements for change, given they are often the closest to indications of market or technological changes. They are also well placed to be able to identify likely blockages to change.

- '*Sense making*' of strategy. Top management may set a strategic direction, but how it is explained and made sense of in specific contexts (e.g. a region of a multinational or a functional department) may be left to middle managers. If misinterpretation of that intended strategy is to be avoided, it is therefore vital that middle managers understand and feel an ownership of it.

- *Reinterpretation and adjustment* of strategic responses as events unfold (e.g. in terms of relationships with customers, suppliers, the workforce and so on); this is a vital role for which middle managers are uniquely qualified because they are in day-to-day contact with such aspects of the organisation and its environment.

- *Local leadership of change*: middle managers therefore have the roles of aligning and embodying change, as do top management, but at a local level.

## 10.5.2 Leadership styles

Leaders are often categorised in two ways:

- *Transformational* (or *charismatic*) *leaders*, whose emphasis is on building a vision for the organisation and energising people to achieve it. This approach to leadership has beneficial impact on people's motivation and job performance[9] and wider business performance especially in situations of uncertainty.[10]

- *Transactional leaders*, who focus more on 'hard' levers of change such as designing systems and controlling the organisation's activities. The emphasis here, then, is more likely to be on changes of structures, setting targets to be achieved, financial incentives, careful project management and the monitoring of organisational and individual performance.

Within these two generic approaches there are different styles of strategic leadership as shown in Table 10.1:

- *Persuasion* of the need for and means of strategic change. Four phases of this style of change leadership have been advocated:[11]

  - Convince employees that change is imperative and why the new direction is the right one.

  - Since change is likely to be interpreted differently throughout the organisation, frame the changes in ways relevant to the different groups and functions that have to enact the change and gather feedback on how this is understood and communicated within those groups.

  - Ensure ongoing communication of the progress of change.

  - Reinforce behavioural guidelines in line with the change and reward the achievement of change goals.

  However, the assumption that reasoned argument in a top-down fashion will overcome perhaps years of embedded assumptions about what 'really matters' may be optimistic. There may be apparent acceptance of change without its actually being delivered. Such an approach to change can also take a long time and be costly, for example in terms of training and management time.

- *Collaboration*[12] in the change process is the involvement of those affected in setting the change agenda: for example, in the identification of strategic issues, the strategic decision-making process, the setting of priorities, the planning of strategic change or the drawing up of action plans. Such involvement can foster a more positive attitude to change. People may also see the constraints the organisation faces as less significant and feel increased

**Table 10.1** Styles of leading change

| Style | Description | Advantages | Disadvantages |
|---|---|---|---|
| Persuasion | Gain support for change by generating understanding and commitment through e.g. small-group briefings and delegation of responsibility for change. | Develops support for change and a wide base of understanding. | Time consuming. Fact-based argument and logic may not convince others of need for change. Or may gain notional support without active change. |
| Collaboration | Widespread involvement of employees on decisions about both what and how to change. | Spreads not only support but also ownership of change by increasing levels of involvement. | Time consuming. Little control over decisions made. |
| Participation | Change leaders retain overall coordination and authority but delegate elements of the change process. | Spreads ownership and support of change, but within a controlled framework. Easier to shape decisions. | Can be perceived as manipulation. |
| Direction | Change leaders make most decisions about what to change and how. Use of authority to direct change. | Less time consuming. Provides a clear change direction and focus. | Potentially less support and commitment, so changes may be resisted. |

*Source*: Adapted from J. Balogun and V. Hope Hailey, *Exploring strategic change*, 3rd edn, Prentice Hall, 2008.

ownership of, and commitment to, a decision or change process. It may therefore be a way of building readiness and capability for change.

However, there are potential problems here too. People may propose change solutions that are not in line with, or do not achieve, the expectations of top management or key stakeholders. For example, there is the risk that solutions will be limited to those in line with the existing culture or that the agenda for change will be negotiated and may therefore be a compromise. A leader who takes this approach may, therefore, need to retain the ability to intervene in the process, though this runs the risk of demotivating employees who have been involved in the change process.

- *Participation* involves delegating *elements* of the change process while retaining overall responsibility for that change, monitoring its progress and ensuring it occurs. Particular stages of change, such as ideas generation, data collection, detailed planning, the development of rationales for change or the identification of critical success factors, may be delegated to project teams or task forces. Such teams may not take full responsibility for the change process, but become involved in it and see their work building towards it. An advantage is that it involves people in the *partial implementation* of solutions, helping build commitment to the change. It may also be that the retention of the agenda and means of change by the strategic leader reduces the possibility of a negotiated compromise and means that more radical change can be achieved. The potential problem is that employees may see this approach as manipulation and consequently become disenchanted and demotivated.

- *Direction* involves the use of personal authority to establish clarity on both future strategy and how change will occur. It is top-down management of strategic change where change 'solutions' and the means of change are 'sold or told' to others who are tasked with implementing them. The need here is for both clarity of strategic vision and the specifics of a change programme in terms of critical success factors and priorities. The approach may be required if there is a need for fast change or control over the change agenda (e.g. to meet the expectations of dominant external stakeholders). The danger is that it can result in explicit resistance to change or people going along with the rhetoric of change while passively resisting it. It is also worth noting that even where top management people see themselves adopting participative styles, their subordinates may perceive this as directive and, indeed, may welcome such direction if they see major change is needed. In its most extreme form direction may take the form of coercion, the imposition of future strategy by the explicit use of power, but this is unlikely to be successful unless, for example, the organisation is facing a crisis.

Styles of change leadership are not mutually exclusive. For example, change may be initiated with clear direction accompanied by the 'hard levers' of change associated with transactional leadership but be followed through with the more collaborative or participatory approaches more associated with transformational leadership. Different styles may also be needed in different parts of an organisation facing different circumstances or at different times as situations change. In short, required change leadership styles are likely to need to differ according to context.

## 10.5.3 Types of strategic change

Julia Balogun and Veronica Hope Hailey[13] identify four generic types of strategic change. The axes in Figure 10.6 are concerned with (i) the extent of change and (ii) the nature and urgency of change. In terms of the *extent* of change, the question is whether change can occur in line with the current business model and within the current culture as a *realignment* of strategy. Or is the change required more significant in terms of the current business model or culture, in effect more *transformational* change? Some of the tools of analysis in Chapters 3 and 4 can help identify the extent of change required. For example, does the change require a substantial reconfiguration of the value chain (section 3.4.1), significant changes in strategic capabilities (section 3.2) or major cultural change (section 4.6)? The other axis in Figure 10.6, the nature of change, is concerned with the speed at which change needs to happen. Arguably, it is beneficial for change in an organisation to be *incremental* since this allows time to build on the skills, routines and beliefs of those in the organisation. However, if an organisation faces crisis or needs to change direction fast, a '*big bang*' approach to change might be needed. As Figure 10.6 suggests, therefore, there are four types of strategic change.

### Adaptation

Strategies often build on rather than fundamentally change prior strategy. It is what Figure 10.6 refers to as *adaptation*. Change is gradual, building on or amending what the organisation has been doing in the past and in line with the current business model and organisational culture. This might include changes in product design or methods of production, launches of new products or related diversification. Though less common, the leadership of change is more often associated with the other more fundamental types of change identified in Figure 10.6.

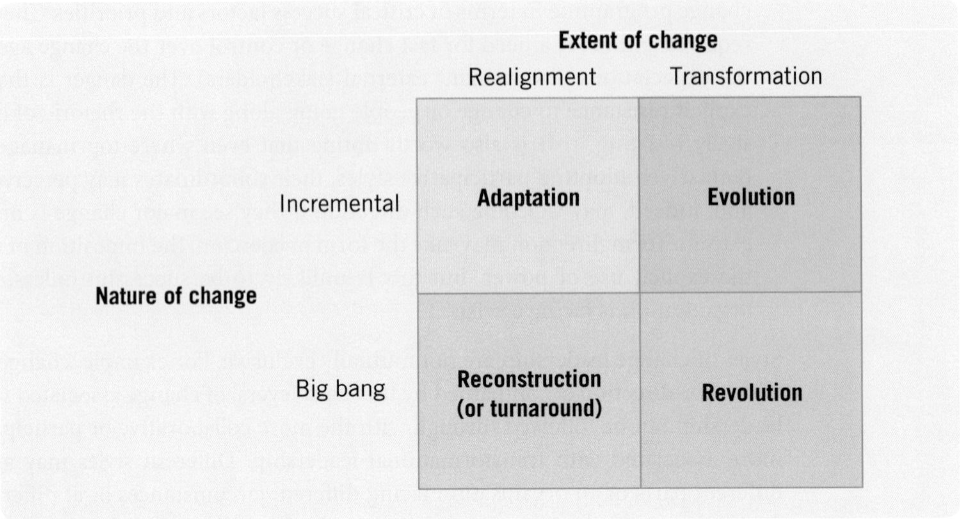

**Figure 10.6** Types of change

*Source*: Adapted from J. Balogun and V. Hope Hailey, *Exploring Strategic Change*, 3rd edn, Prentice Hall, 2008.

### Reconstruction: turnaround strategy

*Reconstruction* is change that may be rapid and involve a good deal of upheaval in an organisation, but which does not fundamentally change the culture or the business model. There could be a need for major structural changes or a major cost-cutting programme to deal with a decline in financial performance or difficult market conditions, in the absence of which a business could face closure, enter terminal decline or be taken over. This is commonly referred to as a *turnaround strategy*, where the emphasis is on speed of change and rapid cost reduction and/or revenue generation. The need is to prioritise the things that give quick and significant improvements. Typically it is a situation where a directive approach to change (see section 10.5.2) is required. Some of the main elements of turnaround strategies are as follows:[14]

- *Crisis stabilisation.* The aim is to regain control over the deteriorating position. This requires a focus on cost reduction and/or revenue increase, typically involving a reduction of labour and senior management costs, productivity improvement, the reduction of inventory, the tightening of financial control and the identification and elimination of non-profitable products or services. There is nothing novel about these steps: many of them are good management practice. The differences are the speed at which they are carried out and the focus of managerial attention on them. The most successful turnaround strategies also focus on reducing direct operational costs and on productivity gains. Less effective approaches pay less attention to these and more on the reduction of overheads.

- *Management changes.* Changes in management may be required, especially at the top. This usually includes the introduction of a new chairman or chief executive, as well as changes to the board, especially in marketing, sales and finance, for three main reasons. First, because the old management may well be the ones that were in charge when the problems developed and be seen as the cause of them by key stakeholders. Second, to bring in management with experience of turnaround management. Third because new management from outside the organisation may bring different approaches to the way the organisation has operated in the past.

- *Gaining stakeholder support.* Poor quality of information may have been provided to key stakeholders. In a turnaround situation it is vital that key stakeholders, perhaps the bank or key shareholder groups, and employees are kept clearly informed of the situation and improvements as they are being made.

- *Clarifying the target market(s) and core products.* Central to turnaround success is ensuring clarity on the target market or market segments most likely to generate cash and grow profits. A successful turnaround strategy also involves getting closer to customers and improving the flow of marketing information, especially to senior levels of management, so as to focus revenue-generating activities on key market segments. Of course, a reason for the poor performance of the organisation could be that it had this wrong in the first place. Clarifying the target market also provides the opportunity to discontinue or outsource products and services that are not targeted on those markets, eating up management time for little return or not making sufficient financial contribution.

- *Financial restructuring.* The financial structure of the organisation may need to be changed. This typically involves changing the existing capital structure, raising additional finance or renegotiating agreements with creditors, especially banks.

## Revolution

*Revolution* differs from turnaround (or reconstruction) in two ways that make managing change especially challenging. First, the need is not only for fast change but, very likely, also for cultural change. Second, it may be that the need for change is not as evident to people in the organisation as in a turnaround situation, or that they have reasons to deny the need for change. This situation may have come about as a result of many years of relative decline in a market, with people wedded to products or processes no longer valued by customers. Or it could be that the problems of the organisation are visible and understood by its members, but that people cannot see a way forward. Leading change in such circumstances is likely to involve:

- *Clear strategic direction.* The need for the articulation of a clear strategic direction and decisive action in line with that direction is critical. This is where individual CEOs who are seen to provide such direction are often credited with making a major difference.

- *Top management changes.* The replacement of the CEO, senior executives or, perhaps, changes in board membership is common. Existing top management may be embedded within the past culture and their network of colleagues, customers or suppliers. New top managers do not have these established networks, nor are they embedded in the existing culture, so they may bring a fresh perspective and initiate or be ready to adopt new ideas. The introduction of new top management also signals the significance of change internally and externally. For similar reasons consultants may also be used not only to provide an analysis of the need for change, but also to signal how meaningful the change process is.

- *Multiple styles of change management.* While a *directive style* of change management is likely to be evident, this may need to be accompanied by other styles. It may be supported by determined efforts to *persuade* people about the need for change and the use of *participation* to involve people in aspects of change in which they have specific expertise or to overcome their resistance to change.

- *Culture change.* It may be possible to work with elements of the existing culture rather than attempt wholesale culture change. This involves identifying those aspects of culture that can be built upon and developed and those that have to be changed – in effect a forcefield approach (see section 10.5.4).

- *Monitoring change.* Revolutionary change is likely to require the setting and monitoring of unambiguous targets that people have to achieve. Often these will be linked to overall financial targets and in turn to improved returns to shareholders.

### Evolution

*Evolution* is change in strategy that results in transformation, but incrementally. Here two ways in which this might be achieved are considered.

**Organisational ambidexterity means both the exploitation of existing capabilities and the search for new capabilities.** It is, of course, appropriate and necessary that an organisation should seek to *exploit* the capabilities it has built up over time in order to achieve and sustain competitive advantage. In so doing the tendency is towards *incremental* change since strategy will be built on established ways of doing things. If transformational change is to be achieved, however, there needs to be *exploration* for new capabilities and innovation. This is likely to be problematic because the different processes associated with exploitation and exploration pose contradictions such as being both focused and flexible, efficient yet innovative, looking forward and backward and operating in multiple time frames. There are, however, suggestions as to how this might be possible, some of which are shown in Illustration 10.3:

- *Structural ambidexterity.* Organisations may maintain the main core of the business devoted to exploitation with tighter control and careful planning but create separate units or temporary, perhaps project-based, teams for exploration[15]. These exploratory units will be smaller in size, less tightly controlled[16] with much more emphasis on learning and processes to encourage new ideas.

- *Diversity rather than conformity.* Contradictory behaviours may be beneficial, so there may be benefits from a diversity of managers' experience or different views on future strategy, which can give rise to useful debate.

- *The role of leadership.* Leaders therefore need to encourage and value different views and potentially contradictory behaviours rather than demanding uniformity. This may mean running with new ideas and experiments to establish what makes sense and what does not. However, they also need to have the authority, legitimacy and recognition to stop such experiments when it becomes clear that they are not worthwhile pursuing and make decisions about the direction that is to be followed, which, once taken, are followed by everyone in the organisation.

- *Tight and loose systems.* All this suggests that there needs to be a balance between 'tight' systems of strategy development that can exploit existing capabilities – perhaps employing the disciplines of strategic planning – and 'looser' systems that encourage new ideas and experimentation. This might, in turn, be linked to the idea that there needs to be some overall common 'glue', perhaps in the form of a clear *strategic intent* in terms of mission and values (see Chapter 4) such that different units in the organisation may be allowed to express how such mission is achieved in their different ways.

## ILLUSTRATION 10.3 Traditions of successful evolutionary strategic transformation

**An historical study identifies management bases of evolutionary transformational strategic change.**

Very few companies have demonstrated the ability to both make transformational strategic changes while maintaining high levels of profitability. Such change usually follows a major downturn or crisis. A research study identified and traced the management processes over four decades in three UK firms that had achieved such transformations. The researchers identified 'traditions' that gave rise to such transformation, traditions that developed over time. They were not introduced by any one executive or written into documents or plans; they became part of the 'DNA' of the businesses. One of the companies was the retailer, Tesco.

### A tradition of alternative coalitions

The companies had created parallel coalitions of senior executives. The first group, typically the more senior, focused on reinforcing current capabilities, current strengths and current successes. The second group, usually younger but still senior, actively looked to develop new strategies and new capabilities. This parallel system came to be an accepted part of how the company operated. It was encouraged and eventually institutionalised.

For instance, the original Tesco model was to 'pile it high and sell it cheap', which founder Jack Cohen perpetuated through a personal command and control management style. None the less, an alternative coalition around Ian MacLaurin and his team of operations-orientated managers developed in the 1960s that began to pursue more modern retail practices, introducing Tesco to a corporate model of management control. This alternative coalition took charge in the 1980s and 1990s and, in turn, there developed a new alternative coalition around Terry Leahy who developed the next stage of Tesco's strategy built around multiple segmented retail offerings. Leahy himself then took over in the 1990s through to 2011.

### A tradition of constructive contestation

The development of alternative coalitions frequently originated in the context of significant conflict. At Tesco such conflict could be traced to boardroom battles between family members in the Cohen era and then between the two coalitions of managers in the 1960s and 1970s. Over time, however, such conflicts became less intense and more respectful, evolving into 'constructive contestation'. This was not just a matter of senior executives advocating different points of view. Such contestation became culturally embedded; for example, if managers wanted to progress in the firm it was expected that they would 'fight their corner' in meetings with senior executives.

### The tradition of exploiting 'happy accidents'

The two traditions of alternative coalitions and constructive contestation meant that new ideas continually surfaced. In turn this meant that the companies were well positioned to turn problems into opportunities. The researchers called these 'happy accidents', unanticipated circumstances or events which the alternative coalition used to develop new strategies. For example, the economic downturn in the early 1990s hit Tesco, with its less established and younger customer portfolio. Puzzled why the business was not maintaining its recent levels of success, the CEO of that time, David Malpas, spent a day visiting competitors' stores in the company of the up-and-coming Terry Leahy. This exposed him to Leahy's views that Tesco had lost sight of its customers and needed to rethink its customer proposition. In turn this led to Leahy's elevation, the launch of multiple retail formats, a significantly reduced size of headquarters staff, streamlined management layers and international expansion.

*Sources*: M. Hensmans, G. Johnson and G. Yip, *Strategic Transformation: Changing while Winning*, Palgrave, 2013; also G. Johnson, G. Yip and M. Hensmans, 'Achieving successful strategic transformation', *MIT Sloan Management Review*, vol. 53, no. 3 (2012), pp. 25–32.

### Questions

1 How do the 'traditions' relate to the explanations of evolutionary strategic change and, in particular, the concept of organisational ambidexterity?

2 If the 'traditions' took decades to develop, is it possible for executives to manage their introduction into organisations? How?

A second way of conceiving of strategic change as evolution is in terms of *stages of strategic change* perhaps over many years. Here the principles that might guide change leaders are these:

- *Stages of transition*. Identifying interim stages in the change process is important. For example, there may be insufficient readiness or an insufficient capacity to make major changes initially. It will therefore be important to establish these conditions before other major moves are taken.

- *Irreversible changes*. It may be possible to identify changes that, while not necessarily having immediate major impact, will have long-term and irreversible impacts. For example, a law firm or accountancy firm that wishes to achieve an evolutionary approach to strategic change might change the criteria for appointment of partners. The time horizons for the effects of such changes to take effect would be many years but, once made, the effects would be difficult to reverse.

- *Sustained top management commitment* will be required. The danger is that the momentum for change falters because people do not perceive consistent commitment to it from the top.

- *Winning hearts and minds*. Culture change is likely to be required in any transformational change. This may be more problematic than for revolutionary change because people may simply not recognise that there are problems with regard to the status quo. The likely need is for multiple levers for change to be used consistently: *persuasion* and *participation* as styles of managing change to allow people to see the need for change and contribute to what that change should be; the signalling of the meaning of change in ways that people throughout the organisation understand both rationally and emotionally; and levers that signal and achieve improved economic performance.

## 10.5.4 Identifying levers for change: forcefield analysis

Leaders of change will need to identify levers for change. A **forcefield analysis provides a view of forces at work in an organisation that act to prevent or facilitate change**. It allows some key questions to be asked:

- What aspects of the current situation would block change, and how can these be overcome?

- What aspects of the current situation might aid change in the desired direction, and how might these be reinforced?

- What needs to be introduced or developed to aid change?

Illustration 10.4 shows how a forcefield analysis was used by managers considering the intention to devolve strategic decisions within the European division of a global manufacturer.

A forcefield analysis can be informed by concepts and frameworks explained in this text:

- *Mapping activity systems* (section 3.4.2) can provide insights into aspects of an organisation that have underpinned its past success. These may be a basis upon which future change might be built, or they may be ways of doing things that have ceased to be advantageous but are difficult to change.

**ILLUSTRATION 10.4**  A forcefield analysis for devolving strategy

**A forcefield analysis can be used to identify aspects of the organisation that might aid change, blockages to change and what needs to be developed to aid change.**

A Japanese multinational manufacturer had always been centralised in terms of strategic direction and, in particular, new product development. It had been hugely successful in Japan and had also developed a global footprint, largely through acquisitions of local manufacturers related to its core business. These acquired businesses operated largely independently of each other as manufacturing units reporting to Japan. Regionally based sales offices were responsible for selling the range of company products and identifying customer needs and, again, reported through to Japan.

In 2012 top management in Japan took the decision to devolve strategic decisions to geographic regional divisions. The decision was based on the desire to grow non-Japanese markets given the changing competitive landscape, especially the growing power of European customers in the world market, but also the need to understand and respond to local markets better. The view was that competitive strategy and innovation needed to originate and develop nearer to regionally based customers rather than centrally in Japan.

Managers in Europe were charged with developing a plan to implement this devolution of strategy. They undertook a forcefield analysis to identify the key issues to be addressed, a summary of which is shown here.

It was market forces and a head office decision that were the main 'pushing forces' for change. But local managers also recognised that their career prospects could be enhanced. The 'resisting forces' were not only a function of the existing organisational structure, but also the lack of any pan-European infrastructure and the lack of European managers with strategic, as distinct from operational, expertise. The forcefield underlined the importance of establishing such an infrastructure and highlighted the need for IT systems to share information and ideas. It also raised the strategic importance of management development at the strategic level.

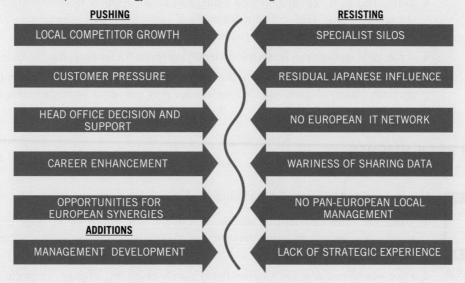

## Questions

1  What might the problems be in devolving strategy to a European division?

2  Undertake a forcefield analysis for an organisation of your choice.

- *Stakeholder mapping* (section 4.4.2) can provide insight into the power of different stakeholders to promote change or to resist change.

- *The cultural web* (section 4.6.5). Strategic change often goes hand in hand with a perceived need to change the culture of the organisation. The cultural web is a means of diagnosing organisational culture and therefore an understanding of the symbolic, routinised as well as structural and systemic factors that may be taken for granted and can act for or against change. It can also be used to envisage what the culture of an organisation would need to look like to deliver future strategy.

- *The 7-S framework* (section 10.4) can highlight aspects of the infrastructure of an organisation that may act to promote or block change.

## SUMMARY

- There are different *structural types* (e.g. functional, divisional and matrix), with their own strengths and weaknesses.

- There is a range of different organisational *systems* to facilitate and control strategy.

- The structure and systems of organisations should contribute to a coherent *organisational configuration* summarised in the *McKinsey 7-S Framework*.

- Translating intended strategy into strategy in action requires the *leadership of strategic change*. This may take different forms such as *incremental change, reconstruction (or tunaround), revolutionary and evolutuionary change*.

- A *forcefield analysis* can be useful in identifying levers for leading strategic change.

- To watch an author video on the concepts discussed in this chapter please visit www.mystrategylab.com, and click on 'Author perspectives on strategic management'..

## VIDEO ASSIGNMENTS

MyStrategyLab

If you are using *MyStrategyLab* you might find it useful to watch the *Wilmington* case study.

1 Using the video extracts and section 10.2 of the text, which of the basic organisation structural types best describes the structure of Wilmington? What are the advantages and disadvantages of this structure?

2 How would you describe Charles Brady's style of leading change (see section 10.5.2)? Why might this style be particularly suited to a company like Wilmington?

3 Charles Brady claims that there have been significant changes in the company. In terms of section 10.5.3 what type of change does he describe? What might the advantages and disadvantages of this be?

## RECOMMENDED KEY READINGS

- The best single coverage of issues relating to organisational structures and systems is in R. Daft, *Understanding the Theory and Design of Organisations*, South-Western, 2009.

- J. Balogun, V. Hope Hailey, *Exploring Strategic Change*, Prentice Hall, 3rd edition, 2008, builds on and extends the discussion of strategic change in this chapter.

## REFERENCES

1. A good review of new and old structural types can be found in G. Friesen, 'Organisation design for the 21st century', *Consulting to Management – C2M*, vol. 16, no. 3 (2005), pp. 32–51.

2. This view of divisionalisation as a response to diversity was originally put forward by A.D. Chandler, *Strategy and Structure*, MIT Press, 1962. See R. Whittington and M. Mayer, *The European Corporation: Strategy, Structure and Social Science*, Oxford University Press, 2000, for a summary of Chandler's argument and the success of divisional organisations in contemporary Europe.

3. For a review of current experience with matrix structures, see S. Thomas and L. D'Annunzio, 'Challenges and strategies of matrix organisations: top-level and mid-level managers' perspectives', *Human Resource Planning*, vol. 28, no. 1 (2005), pp. 39–48, and J. Galbraith, *Designing Matrix Structures that Actually Work*, Jossey-Bass, 2009.

4. M. Goold and A. Campbell, *Strategies and Styles*, Blackwell, 1987.

5. The value of goals and performance targets has been debated vigorously: see L. Ordonez, M. Schweitzer, A. Galinksy and M. Bazerman, 'Goals gone wild: the systematic side effects of overprescribing goal setting', *Academy of Management Perspectives*, vol. 23, no. 1 (2009), pp. 6–16 and E. Locke and G. Latham, 'Has goal setting gone wild?', *Academy of Management Perspectives*, vol. 23, no. 1 (2009), pp. 17–23.

6. See R. Kaplan and D. Norton, 'Having trouble with your strategy? Then map it', *Harvard Business Review*, vol. 78, no. 5 (2000), pp. 167–76 and R. Kaplan and D. Norton, *Alignment: How to Apply the Balanced Scorecard to Strategy*, Harvard Business School Press, 2006.

7. R. Waterman, T. Peters and J. Phillips, 'Structure is not organization', *Business Horizons*, June 1980, pp. 14–26.

8. J. Kotter, 'What leaders really do', *Harvard Business Review* (December 2001), pp. 85–96.

9. See T.A. Judge and R.F. Piccolo, 'Transformational and transactional leadership: a meta analytic test of their relative validity', *Journal of Applied Psychology*, vol. 89 (2004), pp. 755–68.

10. For this evidence see D.A. Waldman, G.G. Ramirez, R.J. House and P. Puranam, 'Does leadership matter? CEO leadership attributes and profitability under conditions of perceived environmental uncertainty', *Academy of Management Journal*, vol. 44, no. 1 (2001), pp. 134–43.

11. For example, D.A. Garvin and M.A. Roberto, 'Change through persuasion', *Harvard Business Review* (February 2005), pp. 104–12.

12. For a fuller explanation of collaboration see H. Ibarra and M.T. Hansen, 'Are you a collaborative leader?', *Harvard Business Review* (July–August 2011), pp. 69–74.

13. This part of the chapter draws on Chapter 3 of *Exploring Strategic Change* by J. Balogun and V. Hope Hailey, 3rd edn, Prentice Hall, 2008.

14. Turnaround strategy is extensively explained in D. Lovett and S. Slatter, *Corporate Turnaround*, Penguin Books, 1999; and P. Grinyer, D. Mayes and P. McKiernan, 'The sharpbenders: achieving a sustained improvement in performance', *Long Range Planning*, vol. 23, no. 1 (1990), pp. 116–25. Also see V.L. Barker and I.M. Duhaime, 'Strategic change in the turnaround process: theory and empirical evidence', *Strategic Management Journal*, vol. 18, no. 1 (1997), pp. 13–38.

15. M.L. Tushman, and C.A. O'Reilly, 'Ambidextrous organizations: managing evolutionary and revolutionary change', *California Management Review*, vol. 38, no. 4 (1996), pp. 8–30.

16. R. Duncan, 'Characteristics of organisational environments and perceived environmental uncertainty', *Administrative Science Quarterly*, vol. 17, no. 3 (1972), pp. 313–27.

# Sergio Marchionne: leading change in Fiat and Chrysler

With dual Canadian and Italian citizenship, Sergio Marchionne speaks fluent English and Italian. With a first degree in philosophy, a MBA and a law degree, he first worked in accountancy, then in management positions in the printing, entertainment and chemicals industries before being elected to the board of Fiat S.p.A. in May 2003. Though he had no direct management experience in the automobile industry, he was then appointed Fiat's CEO in 2004. Since that time he has overseen turnaround programmes at Fiat, Europe's second largest car manufacturer, then Chrysler, the third largest in the USA.

Whether in his office, on a public platform or even an award ceremony, Sergio Marchionne adopts an informal relaxed image, typically in a sweater rather than the traditional managerial suit. His relaxed manner does not, however, disguise his distinct views on his role as a business leader: 'My job as CEO is not to make decisions about the business but to set stretch objectives and help our managers work out how to reach them.

In his assessment of those he selects to lead businesses he emphasises, amongst other qualities, the need for decisiveness, creativity, but also the ability to rethink assumptions and to lead change. He also believes in giving such leaders responsibility and the latitude to explore new ideas, accepting that means there will be 'hits and misses; you have to let them miss.'

## Turnaround at Fiat

When he took over as CEO at Fiat in 2004 he was the fifth CEO since 2001. The company was unprofitable, the products had a reputation for poor quality, its most recent new car launch had been unsuccessful and relationships with the unions were poor.

He spent his first 50 days touring the business, listening to people and analysing the situation. He found that senior executives were unused to taking responsibility for decisions; everything was referred upwards to the CEO. It was also common for executives to communicate to each other via their secretaries and spend their time firefighting or avoiding problems. The company was dominated by

**Sergio Marchionne**

*Source*: Bloomberg via Getty Images.

engineers and it was engineering that provided the traditional career progression to senior management positions. The development of new models was also in their hands; they would then pass a new car to sales and marketing, complete with sales targets and price. As well as being inefficient, not surprisingly this gave rise to tensions between departments.

Following initial measures to reduce Fiat's debt level, Marchionne turned his attention to the leadership of the business. He decided that at the most senior levels, the habit of upward referral to the CEO was so ingrained it could not be changed: so, many senior executives were 'let go'. In addition, 2000 other managers and staff were retired early. On the other hand, as he toured the company, he had identified young talented managers, often in areas such as marketing that were not the traditional routes to the top, or in geographic areas such as Latin America that were less influenced by head office and where managers tended to behave more autonomously and take personal initiative. He drew on this 'talent spotting' to make 20 leadership appointments as well as other promotions.

Marchionne prioritised taking a personal interest in high potential talent and regarded his personal engagement with them as more valuable than more formal assessment. He also believed that such personal engagement helped develop a top team with strongly held common values. His expectation of this new top cadre of leaders was that they should be given the responsibility of achieving the turnaround. He recognised that this was demanding:

'As I give people more responsibility, I also hold them more accountable. A leader who fails to meet an objective should suffer some consequences, but I don't believe that failing to meet an objective is the end of the world. . . . (but) if you want to grow leaders, you can't let explanations and excuses become a way of life. That's a characteristic of the old Fiat we've left far behind.'

Marchionne brought this team together to come up with a business plan around a stretch target, announced in July 2004, to make 2 billion euros in 2007. He recognised that this imposed target was highly ambitious – indeed some thought it unrealistic – but believed its virtue was that it forced managers to think differently and challenge old ways of doing things. To achieve greater integration and speed things up, Marchionne also took out several layers of management, eliminated a proliferation of committees and replaced them with a Group Executive Council that brought together executives from disparate operations such as tractors and trucks. To run Fiat Auto he also established a 24-person team with the aim of getting all parts of the company to talk to one another. To further encourage the sharing of ideas, he also began to move executives from one part of the business to another and required his top managers to accept multiple responsibilities for different parts of the business.

Marchionne saw one of his own major roles as the challenging of assumptions. He cites the example of questions he asked about why it took Fiat four years to develop a new model. The questions helped identify processes that could be removed which meant that the new Cinquecento was developed and launched in just 18 months in 2006. 'You start removing a few bottlenecks in this way, and pretty soon people catch on and begin ripping their own processes apart.' Such challenging of assumptions and processes was also aided by recruiting managers from outside the car industry and by benchmarking, not just against other car makers but also companies like Apple.

Not all of the moves were at top-management level. Attention was also paid to the workforce, many of whom worked in the manufacturing units that Marchionne had seen to be inefficient and dispiriting.

'The easy thing for me to do would have been to shut down two plants and start reaggregating assets elsewhere. But had I done that, we would have had a very disgruntled workforce . . . We've opened kindergartens and grocery stores next to the plant to make it easier for people to balance their work and domestic obligations. We've redecorated all the dressing rooms and bathrooms . . . We're doing it because we recognise that the commitment we make as leaders to our workforce goes beyond what's negotiated in our labour contracts.'

By 2006 Fiat was profitable.

## Turnaround at Chrysler

By 2009 Chrysler was near to bankruptcy, it had no market value, investment had been slashed and potentially 300,000 jobs were on the line. With the support of the US and Canadian governments and trade unions, the Fiat Group formed a strategic alliance with Chrysler with a 20 per cent stake. Marchionne was appointed CEO. His vision was that Fiat and Chrysler together could create a leading global player in the automobile sector, given potential synergies in terms of purchasing power, distribution capabilities and product portfolios – Chrysler's jeeps, mini vans and light trucks and Fiat's small cars and fuel efficient engines.

When Marchionne took over at Chrysler in 2009, not only did he inherit a $6 billion high interest government loan, he also found a fearful workforce and, like most of Detroit's car manufacturers, a company riddled with bureaucracy. One of his first acts was to point out in a memo to Chrysler employees, the parallels with Fiat:

'Five years ago, I stepped into a very similar situation at Fiat. It was perceived by many as a failing, lethargic automaker that produced low-quality cars and was stymied by endless bureaucracies.'

Like Fiat, Chrysler was highly hierarchical with managers reluctant to take decisions:

'This place was run by a chairman's office . . . on the top floor (known as the Tower). It's empty now. . . . Nothing happens there. I'm on the floor here with all the engineers.'

Again Marchionne changed the management. He identified 26 young leaders from two or three levels below top management who had hitherto been stifled by the hierarchy. These reported directly to him in a flattened out organisation. The re-organisation also involved managers leaving who failed to match up to Marchionne's expectations.

Again Marchionne emphasised cost-control; for example the 2009 plan identified savings of $2.9 billion by 2014 by sharing parts and engines with Fiat. But there was also an emphasis on product development. Here he drew on the experience of his new executive team to focus on improvements to the product range: Ralph Gilles, in charge of product design:

> 'Everyone knew what was wrong with the cars. You ask any employee in the company, they could list ten things that they would do better. And when you're given the chance to do those ten things better, you end up with a product that exceeds the sum of its parts.'

Another key component of the recovery was to deal with the product quality problem. Chrysler had been organised such that each brand had its own quality department. These separate departments were merged and new ways to measure quality introduced to provide greater oversight over all the brands. This attention to product and quality improvement went hand in hand with plant modernisation. The result was an upgrading of 16 models in 18 months.

When the Jefferson North assembly plant in Detroit was revamped the workforce was kept occupied with its most thorough cleaning since it opened in 1991. They welcomed Marchionne when he visited to review progress, but were even more delighted when President Obama later toured the plant and called it 'this magnificent factory'. Industrial relations were not, however, always so positive. The efforts to reduce costs meant cutting jobs, closing plants, holding down wages and terminating established union agreements. Union activists staged protests at presentations made by Marchionne.

By 2011 Chrysler announced an operating profit of $2 billion (compared with a net loss of $652 million in 2010) and repaid all government loans.

## New challenges

In July 2011, Fiat's stake in Chrysler was increased to 53.5 per cent and in September 2011, Marchionne became Chairman of Chrysler. However, he faced new challenges.

By 2012 Chrysler was prospering. Capital spending was planned to rise to $4 billion from $3.1 billion in 2011 and profits were holding up. Fiat, however, was struggling to cope with five years of industry-wide decline in recessionary Europe, with Italy performing particularly

badly. Fiat's cars were still ranked second-worst in terms of product quality in the US, it was making losses, sales forecasts and investment in Europe were being reduced and Italian plants were operating at 50 per cent capacity.

Marchionne was trying to promote European industry-wide efforts to cut production capacity and, after one closure in 2011, was threatening to close a second Italian factory. He was also calling for government intervention to make it easier to close unprofitable factories and lay off workers. There seemed little support for industry-wide rationalisation from Volkswagen, BMW and Daimler whose profits, whilst also suffering, did not have Fiat's level of excess factory capacity in Europe. One industry observer suggested that, under Sergio Marchionne, the next few years at Fiat and Chrysler would be a 'white knuckle ride'.

*Sources and references:* Sergio Marchionne, 'Fiat's extreme makeover', *Harvard Business Review*, December 2008 p. 46; Sergio Marchionne, 'Leading From Hell and Back', Lecture at Ross School of Business, Michigan University, 13 January 2012; *Harvard Business Review*, December 2008, p. 46; *Harvard Business Review*, December 2008, p. 47; *Harvard Business Review*, December 2008, p. 48; Peter Gumbel, 'Chrysler's Sergio Marchionne: The Turnaround Artista', *Time Magazine*, 18 June 2009; 'Resurrecting Chrysler', 60 minutes, CBS; interview with Steve Kroft, 25 March 2012, http://www.youtube.com/watch?v=h3ppoyWNN7s; 'Resurrecting Chrysler', 60 minutes, CBS; interview with Steve Kroft 25 March 2012; J.D. Power and Associates, 2012 US Initial Quality Study; Tommaso Ebhardt, 'Marchionne Seen Missing Fiat Sales Target by $19 Billion', *Business Week*, 29 October 2012; Tommaso Ebhardt, 'Marchionne Seen Missing Fiat Sales Target by $19 Billion', *Business Week*, 29 October 2012.

### Questions

1 In relation to section 10.5, what was the type of change pursued at Fiat and Chrysler? Was this appropriate to the change context?

2 How would you describe the change style of Sergio Marchionne? Was this appropriate to the change context?

3 What levers for change were employed by Sergio Marchionne? What others might have been used and why?

4 Assess the effectiveness of the change programmes.

# APPENDIX
## EVALUATING STRATEGIES

### Learning outcomes

After reading this Appendix you should be able to:

- Assess the *performance* of existing strategies
- Determine the need for new strategies using *gap analysis*.
- Employ the three *success criteria (SAFe)* for evaluating strategic options:
  - *Suitability*: whether a strategy addresses the key issues relating to the *opportunities and constraints* an organisation faces.
  - *Acceptability*: whether a strategy meets the *expectations* of stakeholders.
  - *Feasibility*: whether a strategy could *work in practice*.

## INTRODUCTION

Evaluation is fundamental to strategy. First it's important to evaluate the performance of existing strategies; second, it is important to evaluate new strategic options. This Appendix starts by describing various approaches to assessing the performance of existing strategies. Here *gap analysis* is used to determine any possible shortfall between existing performance and strategic objectives. The Appendix concludes with the three *SAFe* (Suitable, Acceptable and Feasible) criteria for evaluating strategic options that might help fill any identified shortfall.

## ORGANISATIONAL PERFORMANCE

This section introduces performance measures, performance comparisons and gap analysis.

### Performance measures

Strategic performance is typically measured in terms of various direct economic outcomes. These economic outcomes have three main dimensions:

- *Product markets*: for example, sales growth or market share. In the public sector, this could be user numbers, for example.
- Accounting measures of *profitability*: for example, profit margin or return on capital employed (see discussion of Acceptability below). In the public sector, an equivalent might be cost per user.
- *Financial market* measures: i.e. movements in share price, available for companies quoted on public stock-exchanges. Share price movements are more future orientated: a rise in price can be an indicator of investor confidence about future performance.

These economic measures may seem objective, but they can be conflicting and need careful interpretation. For example, sales growth may be achieved by cutting prices, but at the cost of lower profit margins. Short-term rises in share prices may reflect speculation, for example about a possible take-over bid. The complexity of economic performance measures suggests that economic performance is best evaluated by more than one measure. It is also why many organisations now look to more comprehensive measures of performance as well. Here the *balanced scorecard* is valuable: it simultaneously considers the perspectives of the customer, internal business operations, innovation and learning, and financial performance (see Chapter 10.3.3).

## Performance comparisons

When considering performance, it is important to be clear about what you are measuring *against*: in other words, performance relative to what? There are three main comparisons to consider:

- *Organisational targets*: a key set of performance criteria are management's own targets, whether expressed in terms of overall vision and mission or more specific objectives, for instance economic outcomes such as sales growth or profitability.
- *Trends over time*: investors and other stakeholders are clearly concerned about whether performance is improving or declining over time. Improvement may suggest good strategy and increasing momentum into the future. Decline may suggest poor strategy and the need for change. It is typically useful to examine trends over several years in order to smooth out short-run cyclical effects, for example.
- *Comparator organisations*: the final comparison is performance relative to other comparable organisations. Comparators are typically competitors, but in the public sector comparison might be against similar units in different regions, for example. Again, the trend over an extended time period is generally useful. For quoted companies, it is possible to compare share price performance against that of specific competitors, or against an index of competitors in the same industry, or against the overall index for the stock market in which they are quoted.

## Gap analysis

Gap analysis compares achieved or projected performance with desired performance. It is particularly useful for identifying performance shortfalls ('gaps') and, when involving

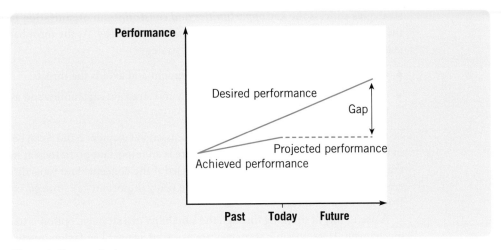

**Figure 1** Gap analysis

projections, can help in anticipating future problems. The size of the gap provides a guide to how far the strategy needs to be changed. Figure 1 shows a gap analysis where the vertical axis is some measure of performance (e.g. sales growth or profitability) and the horizontal axis shows time, both up to 'today' and into the future. The upper line represents the organisation's desired performance, in terms of strategic objectives or perhaps the standard set by competitor organisations. The lower line represents both achieved performance to today and projected performance based on a continuation of the existing strategy into the future (this is necessarily an estimate). In Figure 1, there is already a gap between achieved and desired performance: performance is clearly unsatisfactory.

However, the gap in Figure 1 is projected to become even bigger on the basis of the existing strategy. Assuming ongoing commitment to the desired level of performance, the organisation clearly needs to find ways of adjusting its existing strategy in order to close the gap. We turn now to the evaluation of strategic options.

# EVALUATION CRITERIA

If performance analysis has established the need for new strategies, then strategic options need evaluating. The rest of this Appendix discusses the three SAFe evaluation criteria: Suitability, Acceptability and Feasibility.

## S: Suitability

Early chapters explained how the strategic position of an organisation can be understood in terms of key drivers and expected changes in its *environment* (Chapter 2) and its *strategic capabilities* (Chapter 3). These factors provide opportunities but also place constraints on the future direction of an organisation. **Suitability is concerned with assessing which proposed** strategies address the *key opportunities and constraints* an organisation faces. Suitability is therefore concerned with the overall *rationale* of a strategy. At the most basic level, the need is to assess the extent to which a proposed strategy:

- exploits the opportunities in the environment and avoids the threats;
- capitalises on the organisation's strength and strategic capabilities and avoids or remedies the weaknesses.

So the concepts and frameworks already discussed in Chapters 2 and 3 can be especially helpful in understanding suitability. However, there is an important point to bear in mind. It is likely that a great many issues will have been raised if the concepts and tools discussed have been employed. It is therefore important that the really important *key strategic issues* are identified from amongst all these.

A useful way of thinking through the suitability of a strategic option is to employ a *ranking* mechanism. Here possible strategies are assessed against key factors relating to the strategic position of the organisation and a score (or ranking) established for each option. The Illustration on the next page gives an example. One of the advantages of this approach is that it forces a debate about the implications and impacts of specific key factors on specific strategic proposals. It therefore helps overcome a potential danger in strategy evaluation: namely that managers are likely to interpret the impact of particular factors, or have preferences for proposed strategies, in terms of their own subjectivity.

More sophisticated approaches to ranking can assign weightings to factors in recognition that some will be of more importance in the evaluation than others. It should, however, be remembered that assigning numbers, of itself, is not a basis of evaluation; any scoring or weighting is only a reflection of the quality of the analysis and debate that goes into the scoring.

## A: Acceptability

**Acceptability is concerned with whether the expected performance outcomes of a proposed strategy meet the expectations of stakeholders.** The issue of stakeholder expectations was introduced in Chapter 4. There are three ways of assessing Acceptability, represented by the '3Rs': *risk*, *return* and *stakeholder reactions*.

**Risk concerns the extent to which the outcomes of a strategy can be predicted.** For example, risk can be high for organisations with major long-term programmes of innovation, where high levels of uncertainty exist about key issues in the environment, or about market behaviour, or where there are high levels of public concern about new developments. Formal risk assessments are often incorporated into business plans as well as the investment appraisals of major projects. Developing a good understanding of an organisation's strategic position (Chapters 2–4) is at the core of good risk assessment. However, it is also useful to consider how sensitive a proposed strategy is to deviations in the assumptions underpinning it. Sensitivity analysis can help here. It allows each of the important assumptions underlying a particular strategy to be questioned and challenged. In particular, it tests how sensitive the predicted performance or outcome (e.g. profit) is to each of these assumptions. For example, if the central assumption of market growth was 5 per cent per annum, a sensitivity analysis would ask about the knock-on effects of market growth at just 2 per cent or 10 per cent.

# ILLUSTRATION Ranking options for SRR Consulting

**Ranking can usefully provide an initial view of the suitability of strategic options by comparing strategic options against the key strategic factors from the SWOT analysis.**

Simon and Ruth were both IT specialists who returned to their companies after completing their MBAs. Raj, a friend of theirs, had been an IT consultant who did the same MBA course a year later. His MBA project looked at the feasibility of setting up an IT consultancy partnership with Simon and Ruth. SRR was established in 2008. Their strategy was initially to build on 'outsourcing' the IT needs of the organisations they worked for. Raj had worked on IT assignments for business start-ups for a consultancy: 'It was not big business for them and they were delighted to have me operate as an associate; in effect outsourcing that work.' Simon worked for a medium-sized local engineering business and Ruth for a retailer with a small chain of local shops. As Simon explained: 'Neither of our employers really needed IT specialists full-time: an outsourced facility made good economic sense.'

Ruth continues:

'Our first year went well. We provided a good service to our previous employers together with developing business with some other contacts. We are both the owners and the consultants of SRR and our overheads are pretty low so we have made a reasonable living. Our problem now is, where from here? We are keen to grow the business, not just because we would like a higher income, but because with our rather limited client base we are vulnerable. We have built on our IT expertise and the sectors we know, but we have reached something of a ceiling with regard to our personal contacts. We can see a number of possible options. There is an opportunity on the management development aspects of IT; how can IT be used to aid better management? Most of our clients don't understand this. Our problem is that we are not trainers so we would need to develop those skills or hire someone who has them. Another option is to actively go out and develop new contacts. The problems here are that it means branching out into sectors unfamiliar to us and that will take our time – which won't be fee earning – so it would reduce our income at least in the short term. Linked to this is the possibility of going for much bigger clients. This might get us bigger fees, perhaps, but it would quite possibly mean competition with some big competitors. In the last year our business has also been very local. We could stick with the same sectors we know but broaden the geographic area. The problem there, of course, is we are not known. Finally we have been approached by another IT consultancy about the possibility of a merger. They operate in complementary sectors and do have training capabilities, but it is bigger than us and I don't know if we are ready to lose our own identity yet.'

Simon, Ruth and Raj had begun a ranking exercise to look at these options as shown below.

## Questions

1 Are there other options or factors that you think Simon, Ruth and Raj should consider?

2 How could you improve the ranking analysis?

3 Consider the most favoured options in terms of acceptability and feasibility criteria.

## Ranking exercise

| Strategic options | Key strategic factors | | | | | | | | Ranking |
|---|---|---|---|---|---|---|---|---|---|
| | Fit with technical competences | Fit with sector know-how | Builds on our known reputation | Increases non-fee-earning management time | Reached our 'contact ceiling' | Builds on client need | Higher fee income | Increased competition | |
| 1. Develop new contacts | ✓ | X | ✓ | X | ✓ | ? | ? | ? | 3–1 (B) |
| 2. Develop bigger clients | ✓ | ? | X | X | ✓ | X | ✓ | X | 3–3 (C) |
| 3. Geographic market development | ✓ | ✓ | ✓ | X | ✓ | ✓ | X | X | 5–3 (B) |
| 4. Develop IT training | X | ✓ | ✓ | X | ✓ | ✓ | ✓ | ✓ | 6–2 (A) |
| 5. Merger | ✓ | ✓ | ? | ✓ | ✓ | ? | ? | ✓ | 5–0 (A) |

✓ = favourable; X = unfavourable; ? = uncertain or irrelevant.
A = most suitable; B = possible; C = unsuitable.

The second R is **returns**. These are **the financial benefits which stakeholders are expected to receive from a strategy**. In the private sector typically these are shareholders and lenders; in the public sector the equivalent is funders, typically government departments. Measures of return are a common way of assessing proposed new ventures or major projects within businesses. So an assessment of financial and non-financial returns likely to accrue from specific strategic options could be a key criterion of acceptability of a strategy – at least to some stakeholders.

Three commonly used bases of financial analysis are:

- Forecasting the *return on capital employed (ROCE)* for a specific time period after a new strategy is in place. The ROCE (typically profit before interest and tax, divided by capital employed) is a measure of the earning power of the resources used in implementing a particular strategic option.

- Estimating the *payback period* is a cash flow measure. This is the length of time it takes before the cumulative cash flows for a strategic option become positive. This measure has the virtue of simplicity and is most often used where the difficulty of forecasting is high and therefore risk is high. In such circumstances this measure can be used to select projects or strategies that have the quickest payback.

- Calculating *discounted cash flows (DCF)*. This is a widely used investment appraisal technique using common cash flow forecasting techniques with the purpose of identifying which proposed projects are likely to achieve the best cumulative cash flow. The resulting measure is the net present value (or NPV) of the project, one of the most widely used criteria for assessing the financial viability of a project. On the face of it, the project with the best NPV should be selected. However, given that a DCF is only as valid as the assumptions built into it, (a) sensitivity testing of assumptions is important and (b) it may be more prudent to regard any project with a positive NPV as worthy of further consideration and evaluation.

Readers may wish to consult one or more standard texts on finance and accounting. For example: G. Arnold, *Corporate Financial Management*, 5th edn, Financial Times Prentice Hall, 2012; P. Atrill, *Financial Management for Decision Makers*, 6th edn, Financial Times Prentice Hall, 2011.

Whichever approach is used, it is important to remember:

- There are no absolute standards as to what constitutes good or poor return. It will differ between industries, countries and different stakeholders. So it is important to establish what return is seen as acceptable by which stakeholders. Views also differ as to which measures give the best assessment of return.

- Be wary of the apparent thoroughness of the various approaches to financial analysis. Most were developed for the purposes of investment appraisal. Therefore, they focus on discrete projects where the additional cash inflows and outflows can be predicted with relative certainty: for example, a retail chain opening a new store has a good idea about likely turnover based on previous experience of similar stores in similar areas. Such assumptions are not necessarily valid in many strategic contexts because the costs and outcomes are much less certain.

- Financial appraisals tend to focus on direct *tangible* costs and benefits rather than the strategy more broadly. However, it is often not easy to identify such costs and benefits, or the cash flows specific to a proposed strategy, since it may not be possible to isolate them from other ongoing business activities. Moreover such costs and benefits may have spill-over effects. For example, a new product may look unprofitable as a single project. But it may make strategic sense by enhancing the market acceptability of other products in a company's portfolio or by opening up options in the future.

- Financial analysis is only as good as the assumptions built into the analysis. If assumptions about sales levels or costs are misguided, for example, then the value of the analysis is reduced, even misleading. This is one reason why sensitivity testing based on variations of assumptions is important.

The third R is the likely *reaction* of stakeholders to a proposed strategy. Section 4.4 showed how *stakeholder mapping* can be used to understand the political context and consider the political agenda in an organisation. Stakeholder mapping can also be used to consider the likely reactions of stakeholders to new strategies and thus evaluate the acceptability of a strategy.

## F: Feasibility

Feasibility is concerned is concerned with whether a strategy could *work in practice*: in other words, whether an organisation has the capabilities to deliver a strategy. An assessment of feasibility is likely to require two key questions to be addressed: (a) do the resources and competences currently exist to implement a strategy effectively? And (b) if not, can they be obtained? These questions can be applied to any resource area that has a bearing on the viability of a proposed strategy. However, typically there are three key issues.

### Financial feasibility

A central issue in considering a proposed strategy is the funding required for it so *cash flow analysis and forecasting* required for evaluating the acceptability of possible strategies is relevant here. The need is to identify the cash required for a strategy, the cash generated by following the strategy and the timing of any new funding requirements. This then informs consideration of the likely sources for obtaining funds.

### People and skills

Chapter 3 showed how organisations that achieve sustainable competitive advantage may do so on the basis of competences that are embedded in the skills, knowledge and experience of people in that organisation. Indeed, ultimately the success of a strategy will likely depend on how it is delivered by people in the organisation. Three questions arise: do people in the organisation currently have the competences to deliver a proposed strategy? As explained in Chapter 10, are the structures and systems to support those people fit for the strategy? If not, can the competences be obtained or developed?

### Strategic change

As Chapter 10 also explains, a strategy's success will also depend on what the implications are for the nature and extent of strategic change and whether management can put into place an effective programme of change to achieve this.

# GLOSSARY

**Acceptability** expected performance outcomes of a proposed strategy to meet the expectation of the stakeholders (p. 262)

**Acquisition** when one firm takes over the ownership ('equity') of another; hence the alternative term 'takeover' (p. 210)

**Backward integration** develop activities that involve the inputs into a company's current business (p. 138)

**Balanced scorecards** performance targets set according to a range of perspectives, not only financial (p. 242)

**Barriers to entry** factors that need to be overcome by new entrants if they are to compete in an industry (p. 31)

**Blue Oceans** new market spaces where competition is minimised (p. 41)

**(Boston Consulting Group) matrix** uses market share and market growth criteria to determine the attractiveness and balance of a business portfolio (p. 146)

**Business-level strategy** the plan of how an individual business should compete in its particular market(s) (p. 6)

**Business model** describes how an organisation manages incomes and costs through the structural arrangement of its activities (p. 188)

**Buyers** the organisation's immediate customers, not necessarily the ultimate consumers (p. 32)

**CAGE framework** emphasises the importance of cultural, administrative, geographical and economic distance (p. 170)

**Competences** the ways in which an organisation may deploy its assets effectively (p. 50)

**Competitive advantage** how a strategic business unit creates value for its users which is both greater than the costs of supplying them and superior to that of rival SBUs (p. 107)

**Competitive strategy** how a strategic business unit achieves competitive advantage in its domain of activity (p. 107)

**Complementor** an organisation that enhances your business attractiveness to customers or suppliers (p. 33)

**Configuration** the set of organisational design elements that interlink together in order to support the intended strategy (p. 242)

**Conglomerate (unrelated) diversification** diversifying into products or services that are not related to the existing business (p. 132)

**Corporate entrepreneurship** refers to radical change in an organisation's business, driven principally by the organisation's own capabilities (p. 209)

**Corporate governance** concerned with the structures and systems of control by which managers are held accountable to those who have a legitimate stake in an organisation (p. 84)

**Corporate-level strategy** concerned with the overall scope of an organisation and how value is added to the constituent businesses of the organisation as a whole (p. 6)

**Corporate social responsibility (CSR)** the commitment by organisations to behave ethically and contribute to economic development while improving the quality of life of the workforce and their families as well as the local community and society at large (p. 92)

**Corporate values** are the underlying and enduring core 'principles' that guide an organisation's strategy and define the way that the organisation should operate (p. 80)

**Cost-leadership strategy** this involves becoming the lowest-cost organisation in a domain of activity (p. 108)

**Critical success factors (CSF)** those factors that are either particularly valued by customers or which provide a significant advantage in terms of costs. [Sometimes called key success factors (KSF)] (p. 40)

**Cultural systems** these aim to standardise norms of behaviour within an organisation in line with particular objectives (p. 239)

**Cultural web** shows the behavioural, physical and symbolic manifestations of a culture (p. 96)

**Differentiation** involves uniqueness in some dimension that is sufficiently valued by customers to allow a price premium (p. 112)

**Diffusion** the process by which innovations spread amongst users (p. 190)

**Disruptive innovation** this creates substantial growth by offering a new performance trajectory that, even if initially inferior to the performance of existing technologies, has the potential to become markedly superior (p. 195)

**Diversification** increasing the range of products or markets served by an organisation (p. 132)

**Dominant logic** the set of corporate-level managerial competences applied across the portfolio of businesses (p. 136)

**Dynamic capabilities** an organisation's ability to renew and re-create its strategic capabilities to meet the needs of changing environments (p. 51)

**Economies of scope** efficiency gains made through applying the organisation's existing resources or competences to new markets or services (p. 136)

**Entrepreneurial life cycle** this progresses through start-up, growth, maturity and exit (p. 198)

*Exploring Strategy* **Model** this includes understanding *the strategic position* of an organisation (context); assessing *strategic choices* for the future (content); and managing *strategy in action* (process) (p. 9)

**Feasibility** whether a strategy can work in practice (p. 265)

**First-mover advantage** where an organisation is better off than its competitors as a result of being first to market with a new product, process or service (p. 193)

**Focus strategy** this targets a narrow segment of domain of activity and tailors its products or services to the needs of that specific segment to the exclusion of others (p. 113)

**Forcefield analysis** provides a view of forces at work in an organisation that act to prevent or facilitate change (p. 252)

**Forward integration** developing activities concerned with the output of a company's current business (p. 138)

**Functional structure** this divides responsibilities according to the organisation's primary specialist roles such as production, research and sales (p. 233)

**Global–local dilemma** the extent to which products and services may be standardised across national boundaries or need to be adapted to meet the requirements of specific national markets (p. 166)

**Global sourcing** purchasing services and components from the most appropriate suppliers around the world, regardless of their location (p. 164)

**Global strategy** this involves high coordination of extensive activities dispersed geographically in many countries around the world (p. 157)

**Governance chain** this shows the roles and relationships of different groups involved in the governance of an organisation (p. 84)

**Industry** a group of firms producing products and services that are essentially the same (p. 27)

**Inimitable capabilities** those capabilities that competitors find difficult to imitate or obtain (p. 56)

**Innovation** the conversion of new knowledge into a new product, process or service *and* the putting of this new product, process or service into actual use (p. 184)

**International strategy** a range of options for operating outside an organisation's country of origin (p. 157)

**Key drivers for change** the environmental factors likely to have a high impact on the success or failure of strategy (p. 25)

**Leadership** the process of influencing an organisation (or group within an organisation) in its efforts towards achieving an aim or goal (p. 243)

**Market** a group of customers for specific products or services that are essentially the same (for example, a particular geographical market) (p. 28)

**Market development** this offers existing products to new markets (p. 134)

**Market penetration** this implies increasing share of the current markets with the current product range (p. 132)

**Market segment** a group of customers who have similar needs that are different from customer needs in other parts of the market (p. 39)

**Matrix structure** this combines different structural dimensions simultaneously, for example product divisions and geographical territories or product divisions and functional specialisms (p. 236)

**McKinsey 7-S Framework** this highlights the importance of fit between strategy, structure, systems, staff, style, skills and superordinate goals (p. 242)

**Merger** the combination of two previously separate organisations, typically as more or less equal partners (p. 210)

**Mission statement** this aims to provide the employees and stakeholders with clarity about the overriding purpose of the organisation (p. 79)

**Multidivisional structure** this is built up of separate divisions on the basis of products, services or geographical areas (p. 235)

**Objectives** statements of specific outcomes that are to be achieved (often expressed in financial terms) (p. 80)

**Open innovation** this involves the deliberate import and export of knowledge by an organisation in order to accelerate and enhance its innovation (p. 187)

**Operational strategies** these are concerned with how the components of an organisation effectively deliver the corporate- and business-level strategies in terms of resources, processes and people (p. 7)

**Organic development** this is where a strategy is pursued by building on and developing an organisation's own capabilities (p. 208)

**Organisational culture** the taken-for-granted assumptions and behaviours that make sense of people's organisational context (p. 94)

**Outsourcing** activities that were previously carried out internally are subcontracted to external suppliers (p. 139)

**Paradigm** the set of assumptions held in common and taken for granted in an organisation (p. 95)

**Parental developer** an organisation that seeks to use its own central capabilities to add value to its businesses (p. 144)

**Parenting advantage** in this 'market for corporate control', corporate parents must show that they have parenting advantage, on the same principle that business units must demonstrate competitive advantage (p. 141)

**Performance targets** these focus on the *outputs* of an organisation (or part of an organisation), such as product quality, revenues or profits (p. 240)

**PESTEL framework** this categorises environmental influences into six main types: political, economic, social, technological, environmental and legal (p. 22)

**Planning systems** these plan and control the allocation of resources and monitor their utilisation (p. 238)

**Porter's Diamond** this suggests that locational advantages may stem from local factor conditions; local demand conditions; local related and supporting industries; and from local firm strategy structure and rivalry (p. 163)

**Porter's Five Forces Framework** this helps identify the attractiveness of an industry in terms of five competitive forces: the threat of entry; the threat of substitutes; the power of buyers; the power of suppliers; and the extent of rivalry between competitors (p. 28)

**Portfolio manager** he or she operates as an active investor in a way that shareholders in the stock market are either too dispersed or too inexpert to be able to do so (p. 143)

**Product development** organisations deliver modified or new products, or services, to existing markets (p. 134)

**Rare capabilities** those capabilities that are possessed uniquely by one organisation or by a few (p. 56)

**Related diversification** diversifying into products or services that are related to the existing business (p. 132)

**Resource-based view (RBV) of strategy** this states that the competitive advantage and superior performance of an organisation is explained by the distinctiveness of its capabilities (p. 49)

**Resources** assets possessed by an organisation, or that it can call upon (e.g. from partners or suppliers) (p. 50)

**Returns** the financial benefits that stakeholders are expected to receive from a strategy (p. 264)

**Risk** the extent to which the outcomes of a strategy can be predicted (p. 262)

**Rivals** organisations with similar products and services aimed at the same customer group (NB not the same as substitutes) (p. 28)

**Scope** indicates how far an organisation should be diversified in terms of products and markets (p. 130)

**S-curve** the shape of the curve reflects a process of initial slow adoption of an innovation, followed by a rapid acceleration in diffusion, leading to a plateau representing the limit to demand (p. 191)

**Shareholder model** prioritises shareholder interests and is dominant in public companies, especially in the USA and UK (p. 85)

**Staged international expansion model** this proposes a sequential process whereby companies gradually increase their commitment to newly entered markets as they build market knowledge and capabilities (p. 176)

**Stakeholder mapping** this identifies stakeholder expectations and power, and helps in the understanding of political priorities (p. 89)

**Stakeholder model** recognises the wider set of interests that have a stake in an organisation's success such as employees, local communities, local governments, major suppliers and customers and banks. (p. 87)

**Stakeholders** those individuals or groups that depend on an organisation to fulfil their own goals and on whom, in turn, the organisation depends (p. 78)

**Statements of corporate values** these communicate the underlying and enduring core 'principles' that guide an organisation's strategy and define the way that the organisation should operate (p. 80)

**Strategic alliance** where two or more organisations share resources and activities to pursue a strategy (p. 218)

**Strategic business unit (SBU)** this supplies goods or services for a distinct domain of activity (p. 106)

**Strategic capabilities** the capabilities of an organisation that contribute to its long-term survival or competitive advantage (p. 50)

**Strategic choices** these involve the options for strategy in terms of both the *directions* in which strategy might move and the *methods* by which strategy might be pursued (p. 11)

**Strategic groups** organisations within an industry or sector with similar strategic characteristics, following similar strategies or competing on similar bases (p. 37)

**Strategic position** this is concerned with the impact on strategy of the external environment, the organisation's strategic capability (resources and ompetences), the organisation's goals and the organisation's culture (p. 10)

**Strategy** the long-term direction of an organisation (p. 2)

**Strategy canvas** this compares competitors according to their performance on key success factors in order to develop strategies based on creating new market spaces (p. 39)

**Strategy statements** these should have three main themes: the fundamental *goals* that the organisation seeks, which typically draw on the organisation's stated mission, vision and objectives; the *scope* or domain of the organisation's activities; and the particular *advantages* or capabilities it has to deliver all of these (p. 7)

**Substitutes** products or services that offer a similar benefit to an industry's products or services but by a different process (p. 32)

**Suitability** assessing which proposed strategies address the *key opportunities and restraints* an organisation faces (p. 261)

**Suppliers** those who supply the organisation with what it needs to produce the product or service (p. 33)

**SWOT** the strengths, weaknesses, opportunities and threats likely to impact on strategy development (p. 68)

**Synergy** the benefits gained where activities or assets complement each other so that their combined effect is greater than the sum of parts (p. 136)

**Synergy manager** a corporate parent seeking to enhance value for business units by managing synergies across business units (p. 144)

**Three horizons framework** this suggests that every organisation should think of itself as comprising three types of business or activity, defined by their 'horizons' in terms of years (p. 3)

**Threshold capabilities** those capabilities that are needed for an organisation to meet the necessary requirements to compete in a given market and achieve parity with competitors in that market (p. 53)

**Tipping point** this is where demand for a product or service suddenly takes off, with explosive growth (p. 191)

**Value** strategic capabilities are of value when they provide potential competitive advantage in a market at a cost that allows an organisation to realise acceptable levels of return (p. 55)

**Value chain** the categories of activities within an organisation which, together, create a product or a service (p. 60)

**Value curves** a graphic depiction of how customers perceive competitors' relative performance across the critical success factors (p. 40)

**Value innovation** the creation of new market space by excelling on established critical success factors on which competitors are performing badly and/or by creating new critical success factors representing previously unrecognised customer wants (p. 40)

**Value system** most organisations are also part of a wider value system, the set of inter-organisational links and relationships that are necessary to create a product or service (p. 60)

**Vertical integration** entering into activities where the organisation is its own supplier or customer (p. 137)

**Vision statement** concerned with the desired future state of the organisation (p. 80)

**VRIO** the four key criteria by which capabilities can be assessed in terms of their providing a basis for achieving such competitive advantage: value, rarity, inimitability and organisational support (p. 54)

**Yip's globalisation framework** this sees international strategy potential as determined by market drivers, cost drivers, government drivers and competitive drivers (p. 159)

# INDEX OF NAMES

# GENERAL INDEX

Note: Page numbers in **bold** refer to definitions in the Glossary

# PUBLISHER'S ACKNOWLEDGEMENTS

We are grateful to the following for permission to reproduce copyright material:

## Figures

Figure 1.2 from *The Alchemy of Growth: Practical Insights for Building the Enduring Enterprise* Texere Publishers (Baghai, M., Coley, S. and White, D. 2000) Fig. 1.1, p. 5, reproduced with permission of PERSEUS PUBLISHING via Copyright Clearance Center; Figures 2.3 and 5.8 adapted from *Competitive Strategy: Techniques for Analysing Industries and Competitors* The Free Press (Porter, Michael E. 1998), adapted with the permission of Simon & Schuster Publishing Group from The Free Press edition. Copyright © 1980, 1998 by The Free Press. All rights reserved; Figure 2.4 adapted from The Right Game, *Harvard Business Review*, July–August, pp. 57–64 (Brandenburger, A. and Nalebuff, B. 1996), reprinted by permission of Harvard Business Review. Copyright © 1996 by the Harvard Business School Publishing Corporation. All rights reserved; Figure on page 63 from Ian Sayers, Senior Adviser for the Private Sector, Division of Trade Support Services, International Trade Centre, Geneva. E-mail: sayers@intracen.org; Figures 3.3, 3.4 and 5.2 adapted from *Competitive Advantage: Creating and Sustaining Superior Performance* The Free Press (Porter, Michael E. 1998), adapted with the permission of Simon & Schuster Publishing Group from The Free Press edition. Copyright © 1985, 1998 by Michael E. Porter. All rights reserved; Figure 4.3 adapted from David Pitt-Watson, Hermes Fund Management, reproduced with permission; Figure 5.5 adapted from The US airlines relative positioning, *Tourism Management*, 26 (1), Fig. 1, p. 62 (Gursoy, D., Chen, M. and Kim, H. 2005), Copyright ©2005, with permission from Elsevier; Figure 5.6 adapted from *The Essence of Competitive Strategy* Prentice Hall (Faulkner, D. and Bowman, C. 1995), reproduced with permission from Pearson Education Ltd.; Figure 5.7 adapted from *Hypercompetition: Managing the Dynamics of Strategic Manoeuvring* The Free Press (D'Aveni, Richard with Robert Gunther 1994), adapted with the permission of Simon & Schuster Publishing Group from The Free Press edition. Copyright © 1994 by Richard D'Aveni. All rights reserved; Figure on page 150 adapted from *The New Corporate Strategy* John Wiley & Sons, Inc. (Ansoff, H. 1988) Copyright © 1988 (and owner). Reprinted by permission of John Wiley & Sons, Inc., and the Ansoff Family Trust; Figure 6.2 adapted from *Corporate Strategy* Penguin (Ansoff, H. I. 1988) Ch. 6, with permission of The Ansoff Family Trust; Figure 6.4 adapted from *Corporate Level Strategy* Wiley (Goold, M., Campbell, A. and Alexander, M. 1994) Copyright © 1994 John Wiley & Sons,

Inc. Reproduced with permission of John Wiley & Sons Inc.; Figure 7.3 adapted from *The Competitive Advantage of Nations* The Free Press (Porter, Michael E. 1990), adapted with the permission of Simon & Schuster Publishing Group from the Free Press edition. Copyright © 1990, 1998 by Michael E. Porter. All rights reserved; Figure 7.5 from In the eye of the beholder: cross-cultural lessons in leadership from Project GLOBE (GLOBE stands for 'Global Leadership and Organizational Behavior Effectiveness') *Academy of Management Perspectives*, February, pp. 67–90 (Javidan, M., Dorman, P., de Luque, M. and House, R. 2006); Figure 7.6 adapted from Global gamesmanship, *Harvard Business Review*, May (MacMillan, I., van Putter, S. and McGrath, R. 2003), reprinted by permission of Harvard Business Review. Copyright © 2003 by the Harvard Business School Publishing Corporation. All rights reserved; Figure on page 197 from *Making the Transition to Cloud*, Fujitsu Services Ltd. (Gentle, David 2011) with permission from Fujitsu Limited UK; Figure 8.2 from A dynamic model of process and product innovation, *Omega*, 3 (6), pp. 639–656 (Abernathy, J. and Utterback, W. 1975), Copyright © 1975, with permission from Elsevier; Figure 8.4 from *The Innovator's Solution* Harvard Business School Press (Christensen, C. and Raynor, M. E. 2003) Reprinted by permission of Harvard Business School Press. Copyright © 2003 by the Harvard Business School Publishing Corporation. All rights reserved; Figure 9.3 from *Managing Acquisitions* The Free Press (Haspeslagh, P. and Jemison, D. 1991), reproduced with permission from the authors; Figure 9.5 from Strategic alliances: gateway to the new Europe *Long Range Planning*, 26 (4), August, p. 109 (Murray, E. and Mahon, J. 1993), Copyright © 1993, with permission from Elsevier; Figure 10.5 from Structure is not organization, *Business Horizons*, 23, pp. 14–26 (Waterman, R., Peters, T. J. and Phillips, J. R. 1980), McKinsey & Company, reproduced with permission; Figure 10.6 adapted from *Exploring Strategic Change*, 3rd ed., Prentice Hall (Balogun, J. and Hope Hailey, V. 2008) Reproduced with permission from Pearson Education Ltd.

## Tables

Tables on pages 45 and 46 from ZenithOptimedia, September 2012, reproduced with permission; Table 10.1 adapted from *Exploring Strategic Change*, 3rd ed., Prentice Hall (Balogun, J. and Hope Hailey, V. 2008) Reproduced with permission from Pearson Education Ltd.

## Text

Illustration 1.2 adapted from www.samsung.com, reproduced with permission; and adapted from University of Utrecht Strategic Plan, 2012–16, www.uu.nl, reproduced with permission; Extract on page 104 from 'Barclays emails reveal a climate of fear and fierce tribal bonding among traders', *The Guardian*, 28/06/2012 (Luyendijk, Joris) © Guardian News & Media Ltd.; Illustration 5.2 adapted from 'Volvo takes a lead in India', *Financial Times*, 31/08/2009 (Leahy, J.), © The Financial Times Limited. All Rights Reserved; Illustration 6.3 from Berkshire Hathaway, extracts from Annual Reports. The material is copyrighted and used with permission of the author.

PUBLISHER'S ACKNOWLEDGEMENTS

## Photographs

16 Getty Images: Matt Cardy / Stringer, 44 Getty Images: Balint Porneczi / Bloomberg via Getty Images, 74 Dieter Mayr Photography, 102 Rex Features, 125 Getty Images: The Asahi Shimbun, 151 Rex Features: Steve Bell, 179 Press Association Images, 204 Getty Images: Peter Parks / AFP, 228 Getty Images: webphotographeer, 256 Getty Images: Bloomberg via Getty Images.

Cover image: Getty Images

In some instances we have been unable to trace the owners of copyright material, and we would appreciate any information that would enable us to do so.